SOUTHEAST ASIA

The Long Road Ahead
Third Edition

SOUTHEAST ASIA
The Long Road Ahead

Third Edition

LIM Chong Yah
Nanyang Technological University, Singapore

Assisted by

SNG Hui Ying & Sarah S.F. CHAN

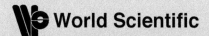
World Scientific

NEW JERSEY · LONDON · SINGAPORE · BEIJING · SHANGHAI · HONG KONG · TAIPEI · CHENNAI

Published by

World Scientific Publishing Co. Pte. Ltd.

5 Toh Tuck Link, Singapore 596224

USA office: 27 Warren Street, Suite 401-402, Hackensack, NJ 07601

UK office: 57 Shelton Street, Covent Garden, London WC2H 9HE

British Library Cataloguing-in-Publication Data
A catalogue record for this book is available from the British Library.

SOUTHEAST ASIA: THE LONG ROAD AHEAD (Third Edition)

ISBN-13 978-981-4280-80-8
ISBN-13 978-981-4280-81-5 (pbk)

For My Loved Ones

NANA

FERN & YANG, WUN & CHRIS, LYNN, RON & CLAIR

SHENGWU, HUANWU, SHIMEI, SHIQUAN, SHAOWU, SHIWEI, SHIXUAN

About the Author

Born in the British Straits Settlement of Malacca in 1932, he was awarded a Malacca Settlement Scholarship to study Economics at the University of Malaya, then located in Singapore. Later, he won a British Commonwealth Scholarship to read Economics at the University of Oxford, where he obtained his doctorate degree. He taught Economics at the University of Malaya (in Kuala Lumpur), where he became the first Head of the Division of Applied Economics. Subsequently, he was Reader and later Professor and Senior Professor of Economics at the University of Singapore (later renamed the National University of Singapore), where he was also Head of the Department. He is currently Professor of Economics at the Nanyang Technological University and Emeritus Professor at the National University of Singapore.

For nearly three decades (1972–2001), he served as the Founder Chairman of the National Wages Council, Singapore. He also served as the Founder Chairman of the Skills Development Fund Advisory Council. He was officially appointed as Consultant to the Mauritian Government on wage reforms. He was the Founder of the Federation of Asean Economic Associations (FAEA), and became its President on three separate occasions. He once served as Senior Economic Advisor to ECAFE and Economic Consultant to the World Bank Lester Pearson Commission on World Development and UNESCO-IAU Commission on Higher Education and Economic Development in Southeast Asia. He was the Founder Chairman of the Singapore National Committee for Pacific Economic Co-operation (SINCPEC).

Professor Lim publishes widely. His impressive research and publication record includes more than 160 refereed journal articles, monographs and books. His book publications, as a single author, include the *Economic Development of Modern Malaya* (1967), *Economic Development in Southeast Asia (1981), Economic Restructuring in Singapore* (1984),

Development and Underdevelopment (1991), *Economic Essays by Lim Chong Yah* (2001) and *Southeast Asia: The Long Road Ahead* (2001, 2004). His publications have been translated into Chinese, Malay and Japanese. One has gone into Braille.

For his eminent scholarship and outstanding public service, he received many distinguished awards, including *The Distinguished Service Award* by the National Trades Union Congress in 1999, and in 2000, *The Distinguished Service Order* (*Darjah Utama Bakti Cemerlang*) by the Singapore Government. There is also a Professorship under his name established by the National University of Singapore. He was conferred the *Doctor Honoris Causa* by Soka University in Japan, awarded an *Honorary Professorship* by Hainan University and Honorary Chairman of the Hainan University Council by the Provincial Government of Hainan. The Indiana University conferred on him the John W. Ryan Alumni Award for "Distinguished Contribution to International Education".

He is married with four grown-up children and seven grandchildren. His hobbies are mountain trekking, travelling, gardening and golfing.

Other Books by the Author

* **1967.** *Economic Development of Modern Malaya*, Kuala Lumpur: Oxford University Press. Reprinted in 1969.

* **1971.** *Elements of Economic Theory*, with Lee Sheng-Yi and Chia Siow Yue, Kuala Lumpur: Oxford University Press. Translated into Chinese and Malay. Adapted for use in Pakistan. Second Edition, 1975. Third Edition, 1984.

* **1973.** *Economic Structure and Organisation*, with Chia Siow Yue, Bhanoji Rao and Ow Chwee Huay, Kuala Lumpur: Oxford University Press. Translated into Chinese and Malay. Revised Edition, 1977. Went into Braille.

* **1981.** *Economic Development in Southeast Asia*, Singapore: Federal Publications.

* **1984.** *Economic Restructuring in Singapore*, Singapore: Federal Publications.

* **1986.** *Report of the Central Provident Fund Study Group*, Chairman of Group, *Singapore Economic Review*, Special Issue, Vol. XXXI, No. 1.

* **1988.** *Policy Options for the Singapore Economy*, with Associates, Singapore: McGraw-Hill. Translated into Japanese, 1995.

* **1991.** *Development and Underdevelopment*, Singapore: Longman.

* **1998.** *Wages and Wages Policies: Tripartism in Singapore*, Co-Editor and Contributor, Singapore: World Scientific.

* **2001.** *Economic Essays by Lim Chong Yah*, Singapore: World Scientific.

* **2001.** *Southeast Asia: The Long Road Ahead* (1st Edition), Singapore: World Scientific.

* **2004.** *Southeast Asia: The Long Road Ahead* (2nd Edition), Singapore: World Scientific.

Preface to the Third Edition

The Third Edition has to be done for two reasons. 1) The facts and figures and even some important assessments and evaluations, though completed only in July 2003, have gone very much out of date by December 2008, when this revision was completed. 2) The Second Edition, to our most pleasant surprise, had gone out of stock. The Publisher had to reprint it to fulfil orders.

This Third Edition would not have been undertaken by me but for the willingness and commitment to assist in the revision by Dr SNG Hui Ying, Lecturer in Economics and Ms Sarah CHAN, my Research Associate, both of the Nanyang Technological University. Whilst grateful for their invaluable help, I am solely responsible for whatever remaining inadequacies and imperfections, particularly in the assessment and evaluation aspects of the book.

Hopefully, the book which covers different important facets of the 10 Southeast Asian economies taken singly and taken together will continue to serve a useful purpose for those interested in Southeast Asian economic development and under development. Important economic facets from the rice, rubber and oil palm industries to industrialization, from monetary and fiscal policy to Asean economic co-operation, from international trade and market-orientation to the 1997/98 exchange rate and the current global financial crises are analyzed. Issues arising from population explosion are also discussed. For a comparative study on various topics, such as in this book, the subject index is particularly useful for each specific country and for specific topics and issues.

The book, hopefully, will promote Southeast Asian consciousness, and Southeast Asians' interest in and concern for one another in the process of facing common economic problems on the long road to become a more integrated developed region.

LIM Chong Yah
January 2009

Preface to the Second Edition

My first debt of gratitude must go to Ms SNG Hui Ying and Ms HO Woon Yee. Both are young Lecturers in Economics in the School of Humanities and Social Sciences, Nanyang Technological University. They volunteered to help me to update the book, particularly the statistics, when the First Edition went out of print. We had to comb through every chapter. We tried also to remove whatever awkward expressions or opaqueness we found on the way. The whole exercise turned out to be much more time-consuming than we first thought. All remaining inelegances and inadequacies, however, remain my responsibility. Without their undertaking to help, I would have left this book un-updated and un-revised.

I would also like to express my appreciation to my beloved professorial colleagues in the Division of Applied Economics in NTU, each commenting on one or two chapters of the revised draft. My benefactors are: Joseph ALBA, LEU Gwo-Jiun Mike, LIU Yunhua, NG Beoy Kui, PARK Donghyun, Shubhasree SESHANNA, SOON Lee Ying, TAN Kim Heng and YIP Sau Leung, Paul.

Outside my Division, my gratitude for useful and helpful comments goes to Dr TAN Khee Giap, an Associate Professor in the Division of Banking and Finance, NTU and Professor Mukul ASHER, Professor of Public Policy Programme, National University of Singapore. The usual disclaimer remains. Only the author is responsible for the book with whatever blemishes that still remain.

In the Second Edition, a few discussion topics at the back of each chapter have been added. Hopefully, these will be useful to professors and students using the book in seminar and tutorial discussion.

LIM Chong Yah
Professor of Economics
Nanyang Technological University
SINGAPORE
July 2003

Preface to the First Edition

This is a book on the economics of Southeast Asia. It deals with cross-country and inter-temporal analyses of the macroeconomic problems, issues, policies and trends in all the ten countries that form ASEAN (Association of Southeast Asian Nations). Hopefully, the book is of use to all graduate students on Southeast Asia, not just economics graduate students. Hopefully too, the book is also of interest and use to policy makers in the region and to others interested in the policy options in these ten countries.

As the Table of Contents of the book shows, this book discusses and evaluates population policies, trade policies, industrialisation policies, agricultural policies, monetary policies, fiscal policies, regional co-operation, the 1997/98 financial crisis and prospects for further development. Some basic facts and key dates on each of the ten countries are also separately given for ease of reference. Readers familiar with Southeast Asia can ignore the basic information. Similarly, the book need not be read in the sequence that is being presented. As Southeast Asia is still essentially an agricultural region, several chapters have been devoted to agricultural development.

The book is entitled *The Long Road Ahead*. It is intended, *inter alia*, to focus attention on the distance between Southeast Asia and the developed countries. It also discusses some of the wrong roads taken, because of special circumstances, by these countries.

Let us hope that the vision for Southeast Asia to become a developed region economically can be realised sooner than later, but hopefully, not indefinitely. I also hope that this book can be of some use or help in supplying ideas and concepts to transform the region from underdevelopment to development.

The book is written by an "insider", looking at his own region, Southeast Asia; not by an "outsider" evaluating the Southeast Asian region.

Lastly, the analysis in the book shows that the road ahead to achieve developed country status is long for the Southeast Asian region as a whole. It must, however, be added that although the attainment of affluence is a worthy objective, of importance too is how that affluence is to be achieved, as Ursula K. LeGuin beautifully puts it "It is good to have an end to journey toward; but it is the journey that matters, in the end."

LIM Chong Yah
Nanyang Business School
Nanyang Technological University
SINGAPORE
December 2000

Acknowledgements to the First Edition

This book *Southeast Asia: The Long Road Ahead* cannot be completed without the help, at varying times, of four persons. They are:

(1) Associate Professor Bhanoji RAO, who for more than two decades was a colleague of mine at the Department of Economics of the National University of Singapore.

(2) Mr Aidi Abdul RAHIM, *M. Soc. Sci.* (*Economics*) from the NUS who worked as my Research Associate.

(3) Mr LEE Chee Tong, *M. Business* from the Nanyang Technological University who helped me as a Research Associate after Mr RAHIM.

(4) Ms SNG Hui Ying, *M. Soc. Sci.* in Applied Economics from the National University of Singapore and who is a Lecturer at NTU since August 2000.

I could not have the invaluable help from Mr Aidi RAHIM and later Mr LEE Chee Tong as my Research Associates but for the research grants given to me by the NTU, for which I would like to acknowledge with thanks and gratefulness.

I am also grateful to Associate Professor Ernest Chew, a distinguished Southeast Asian historian at the National University of Singapore (NUS) and Associate Professor Teofilo C. Daquila of the Southeast Asian Studies Programme also at the NUS for their useful comments on an earlier draft on the Basic Facts and Key Dates of Southeast Asia.

Lastly, I would also like to acknowledge the help and insights that I have received from all the authors and publications cited at various places in this book. However, the remaining mistakes and weaknesses in presentation, in facts and in judgement remain my own and sole responsibility.

LIM Chong Yah
Nanyang Business School
Nanyang Technological University
SINGAPORE
December 2000

Contents

List of Tables

List of Diagrams

Southeast Asia: Overall Picture, 2007

Country	Population ('000)	Land Area (sq km)	GDP (US$ mil)	GDP, PPP (International $ mil)	GDP Per Capita (US$)	GDP Per Capita, PPP (International $)
Brunei	389	5,270	11,562	19,059	29,702	49,898
Cambodia	14,446	176,520	8,628	26,032	597	1,802
Indonesia	225,630	1,811,570	432,817	841,140	1,918	3,728
Lao PDR	5,860	230,800	4,008	12,538	684	2,140
Malaysia	26,550	328,550	180,714	355,225	6,807	13,380
Myanmar	48,783	657,550	16,300	40,970	334	854
Philippines	87,892	298,170	144,129	299,678	1,640	3,410
Singapore	4,589	689	161,347	230,824	35,163	50,304
Thailand	63,832	510,890	245,818	519,439	3,851	8,138
Vietnam	85,140	310,070	71,216	221,346	836	2,600
Total SEA	**563,111**	**4,330,079**	**1,276,539**	**2,566,251**	**2,267**	**4,557**

Source: World Bank, *WDI Online*, 11 Nov. 2008, http://publications.worldbank.org/WDI/ and EIU, *Myanmar Country Profile* 2008.
Note: Myanmar's GDP (PPP) and GDP per capita (PPP) figures refer to year 2006.

Southeast Asia: Overall Picture, 2007

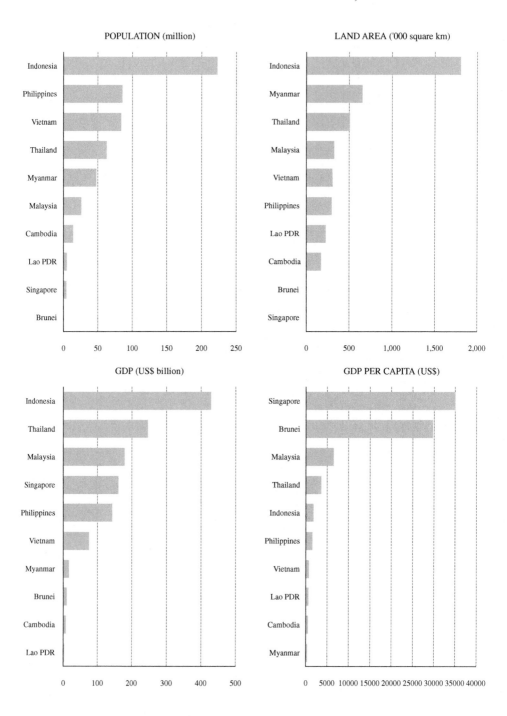

Southeast Asia and Other Regions, 2007

Region/Country	Population ('000)	Land Area (sq km)	GDP (US$ bil)	GDP, PPP (International $ bil)	GDP Per Capita (US$)	GDP Per Capita, PPP (International $)
Southeast Asia	**563,111**	**4,330,079**	**1,277**	**2,566**	**2,267**	**4,557**
Northeast Asia	1,529,260	11,394,476	9,235	13,557	6,039	8,865
China	1,327,389	9,328,558	3,501	7,369	2,637	5,552
Japan	127,771	364,500	4,377	4,284	34,254	33,525
Euro Area	318,702	2,464,900	12,179	10,371	38,215	32,543
India	1,123,319	2,973,190	1,171	3,092	1,042	2,753
United States	301,621	9,161,920	13,811	13,811	45,790	45,790
World	6,612,040	129,644,587	54,347	65,435	8,219	9,896

Source: World Bank, *WDI Online*, 11 Nov. 2008, http://publications.worldbank.org/WDI/ and International Monetary Fund, *World Economic Outlook Database (October 2008 Edition)*, 7 Dec. 2008, http://www.imf.org/external/pubs/ft/weo/2008/02/weodata/index.aspx.

Notes: China includes Hong Kong and Macao.

Northeast Asia includes China, Japan, South Korea, Taiwan and Mongolia.

Macao's GDP, GDP (PPP), GDP per capita and GDP per capita (PPP) figures refer to year 2006.

Southeast Asia and Other Regions, 2007

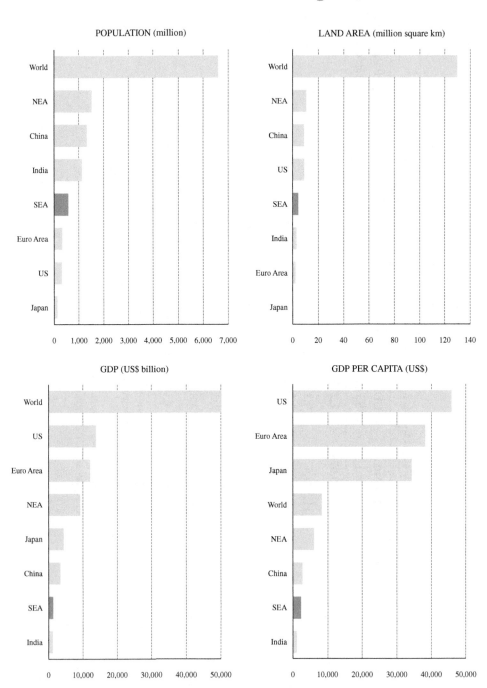

Basic Facts and Key Dates of Each Southeast Asian Country

Negara Brunei Darussalam

Basic Information	
Geographical Co-ordinates:	4 30 N, 114 40 E
Total Area:	5,770 sq. km
Coastline:	161 km
Population:	381,950
Nationality:	Bruneian
Capital:	Bandar Seri Begawan
Climate:	Tropical, hot, humid, rainy
Natural Resources:	Petroleum, natural gas, timber
Ethnic Groups:	66% Malay, 11% Chinese, 3% Indigenous, 19% Others
Languages:	Malay (official), English and Chinese
Religions:	67% Muslim (official), 13% Buddhist, 10% Christian, 10% Others (includes indigenous beliefs)
Head of State:	HM Paduka Seri Baginda Sultan Haji Hassanal Bolkiah Mu'izzaddin Waddaulah

Independence: 1 January 1984 (from UK)

Type of Government: Constitutional Sultanate

Currency: Brunei dollar

Key Dates

1950	Sultan Haji Omar Ali Saifuddien became 28th Sultan of Brunei.
1959	Regained control over internal affairs. British retained responsibility for State's defence and foreign affairs.
1962	Brunei People's Party (BPP) won election. Prevented from forming Government. BPP revolted but was put down.
1967	Sultan Haji Omar Ali Saifuddien abdicated. Sultan Haji Hassanal Bolkiah became Sultan. Issued own currency.
1970	Brunei Town, the State capital, renamed Bandar Seri Begawan.
1979	Treaty of Friendship and Co-operation with Britain.
1 January 1984	Regained full political sovereignty. Joined ASEAN as sixth member.
1992	Joined Non Aligned Movements (NAM).
1998	Prince Haji Al-Muhtadee Billah proclaimed Crown Prince.
2000	Prince Jefri, the Sultan's brother, was charged with misappropriating US$14.8 billion in state funds to subsidise his lavish lifestyle.
2004	The Legistrative Council (Legco), suspended since 1984, was reconvened as a wholly appointed chamber.

2005	A new Legco, with five indirectly elected members, was convened. Plans have been announced to introduce a legislature of 45 members, 15 of whom would be elected by popular vote, but no timetable for an election has been announced.
2007	40th anniversary of the Currency Interchange-ability Agreement (CIA) between Brunei and Singapore.
2008	Signed free trade agreement (FTA) with Japan.

Kingdom of Cambodia

Basic Information

Geographical Co-ordinates:	13 00 N, 105 00 E
Total Area:	181,040 sq. km
Coastline:	443 km
Population:	14,196,610
Nationality:	Cambodian
Capital:	Phnom Penh
Climate:	Tropical; rainy, monsoon season from May to November, dry season from December to April, little seasonal temperature variation
Natural Resources:	Oil and gas, timber, gemstones, iron ore, manganese, phosphates, hydropower potential
Ethnic Groups:	90% Khmer, 5% Vietnamese, 1% Chinese, 4% Others
Languages:	Khmer (official), French and English
Religions:	95% Theravada Buddhist, 5% Others
Head of State:	King Norodom Sihamoni
Prime Minister:	Hun Sen
Independence:	9 November 1953 (from France)
Type of Government:	Constitutional Monarchy
Currency:	Riel

Key Dates

9 November 1953	King Norodom Sihanouk proclaimed Independence from France.
1955	Sihanouk abdicated in favour of his father, Norodom Suramarit, so that he could pursue politics.
1970	Premier Lon Nol ousted Sihanouk.
	Sihanouk formed National United Front of Kampuchea with Khmer Rouge to fight Lon Nol Government.
1975	Lon Nol Regime overthrown by Pol Pot.
	Start of Khmer Rouge Regime.
1978	Invaded by Vietnam.
1979	Pol Pot ousted by Vietnamese forces.
	People's Republic of Kampuchea set up. Hun Sen as Foreign Minister.
1991	Peace Treaty in Paris.
	Sihanouk returned to Phnom Penh.
1993	UN-run election held. Prince Ranariddh's FUNCINPEC party won the election. Prince Ranariddh served as the first Prime Minister in a coalition government with Hun Sen as Second Prime Minister.
	Constitutional Monarchy restored. Sihanouk reinstated King.
1997	Hun Sen ousted Prince Ranariddh in a coup.
1998	Pol Pot died.
	General Election held. New coalition led by Hun Sen formed with Hun Sen as prime minister and Prince Ranariddh as chairman of the National Assembly.
1999	Joined ASEAN as tenth member.
2002	Commune (local government) elections were held for the first time. Hun Sen's Cambodian People's Party

	(CPP) won the most votes. The elections, however, were marred by violence and intimidation.
2003	Reached an agreement with the UN on holding a Khmer Rouge tribunal.
	Third General Election held.
2004	Norodom Sihamoni was named by a nine-member throne council to become the next king following the abdication of his father Norodom Sihanouk.
2006	Prince Ranariddh stepped down as National Assembly chairman in March, and was ousted from FUNCINPEC in October. Subsequently he established the Norodom Ranariddh Party (NRP).
2007	Prince Ranariddh was found guilty of breach of trust in an embezzlement lawsuit, and sentenced in *absentia* to a prison term of 18 months.
	Commune elections took place in relative calm, and the CPP recorded a solid victory.
	UN-sponsored Khmer Rouge tribunal got underway.
2008	US opened an office of the Federal Bureau of Investigation (FBI) in Cambodia.

Republic of Indonesia

Basic Information	
Geographical Co-ordinates:	5 00 S, 120 00 E
Total Area:	1,919,440 sq. km
Coastline:	54,416 km
Population:	223,041,630
Nationality:	Indonesian
Capital:	Jakarta
Climate:	Tropical, hot, humid
Natural Resources:	Petroleum, tin, natural gas, nickel, timber, bauxite, copper, fertile soils, coal, gold, silver
Ethnic Groups:	41% Javanese, 15% Sundanese, 3% Madurese, 3% Minangkabau, 2% Betawi, 2% Bugis, 2% Banten, 2% Banjar, 30% Others or unspecified
Languages:	Bahasa Indonesia (official), English, Dutch and local dialects
Religions:	86% Muslim, 6% Protestant, 3% Roman Catholic, 2% Hindu, 3% Others or unspecified
Head of State:	President Susilo Bambang Yudhoyono
Independence:	17 August 1945 (proclaimed Independence)
Type of Government:	Republic
Currency:	Indonesian Rupiah

Key Dates

17 August 1945	Sukarno and Hatta declared Independence. Became President and Vice-President respectively.
1949	After a bitter nationalist struggle, won Independence from the Dutch.
1955	Sukarno's party, two Moslem parties and the Communist Party won the election.
1957	Sukarno turned Government over to national advisory council.
1959	Sukarno set aside the Parliamentary Constitution with military support, restored the 1945 Constitution, and imposed "Guided Democracy".
1960	Sukarno dissolved Parliament.
1963	Formed Malphilindo with Malaysia and Philippines.
1964	Sukarno launched "Confrontation" Campaign against Malaysia.
1965	Six senior army generals killed in an abortive Communist coup.
	General Suharto took over command of military and crushed coup attempt.
1966	Sukarno transferred power to Suharto.
	Suharto banned Communist Party of Indonesia.
1967	Suharto confirmed as President by People's Consultative Assembly (MPR).
	Became a founding member of ASEAN.
1971	National election was held for first time in 16 years.
1973	Nine opposition parties were streamlined into two parties: Unity Development Party (PPP) and Indonesia Democratic Party (PDI).
1975	Invaded former Portuguese Colony of East Timor.

1976	East Timor was integrated into Indonesian Republic.
1983	MPR adopted a resolution making Pancasila the sole official ideology.
	MPR bestowed Suharto with the title of "Father of Development".
1996	Megawati Sukarnoputri ousted from PDI leadership by Government-backed faction.
1997	Asian financial crisis spread to Indonesia.
	Indonesia approached IMF for help.
1998	Asian financial crisis deepened.
	Suharto resigned. Succeeded by Vice-President B. J. Habibie.
1999	East Timor voted for Independence from Indonesia.
	Abdurrahman Wahid and Megawati Sukarnoputri were elected Indonesia's President and Vice-President respectively.
2001	Megawati Sukarnoputri became President after the impeachment of Abdurrahman Wahid.
2002	A bomb explosion occurred in Bali killing at least 190 people from around the world, mainly Australians.
	Tommy Suharto, the son of former President Suharto, was sentenced to 18 months of imprisonment for corruption charges.
2003	Indonesian military had a major clash with rebels in Aceh.
2004	Parliamentary elections were held. Golkar, the former ruling party of the Suharto era, won the largest number of seats, defeating former President Megawati Sukarnoputri's Indonesian Democratic Party-Struggle (PDI-P).

	The first direct Presidential Election was held. Susilo Bambang Yudhoyono of Democratic Party was elected as President.
2005	President Yudhoyono visited Beijing, China, and signed a strategic partnership agreement with the Chinese president, Hu Jintao.
2006	Elected to the UN Security Council, securing the non-permanent seat reserved for Asian countries for 2007–08.
	Elections were held in Aceh to appoint a provincial governor and 21 district heads.
2007	Police captured the Indonesia's leader of the Jemaah Islamiyah (JI) terrorist organisation and the head of its military wing.
	Russian president, Vladimir Putin, visited Indonesia.

Lao People's Democratic Republic

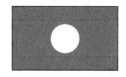

Basic Information

Geographical Co-ordinates:	18 00 N, 105 00 E
Total Area:	236,800 sq. km
Coastline:	0 km (landlocked)
Population:	5,759,400
Nationality:	Laotian
Capital:	Vientiane
Climate:	Tropical monsoon; rainy season from May to September, dry season from October to April
Natural Resources:	Timber, hydropower, gypsum, tin, gold, gemstones
Ethnic Groups:	55% Lao, 11% Khmou, 8% Hmong, 26% Others (over 100 minor ethnic groups)
Languages:	Lao (official), French, English, and various ethnic languages
Religions:	67% Buddhist, 2% Christian, 32% Others and unspecified
Head of State:	President Lt. Gen. Choummaly Sayasone
Prime Minister:	Bouasone Bouphavanh
Independence:	19 July 1949 (from France)
Type of Government:	Communist State
Currency:	Kip

Key Dates

1945	Prince Phetsarath proclaimed reunification of country, but claim subsequently negated by King.
1946	France re-established control after Second World War.
19 July 1949	Independence from France.
1957	Formed Government of National Union.
1960	Kong Le's coup.
1975	Communist Pathet Lao seized complete power.
	Lao People's Democratic Republic established.
	Monarchy abolished. King Sisavang Vatthana abdicated. Prince Souphanouvong became President and Kaysone Phomvihan Prime Minister.
1986	Prince Souphanouvong retired.
	New Economic Mechanism launched.
1989	First elections held since 1975. Communists retained power.
1991	Khamtay Siphandone became Prime Minister.
	Adopted the new and present Constitution.
1994	"Friendship bridge" over the Mekong linking Laos and Thailand opened.
1995	US lifted its 20-year aid embargo.
1997	Joined ASEAN as member.
1998	President Nouhak Phomsavan retired and was replaced by General Khamtay Siphandone.
2000	Government embarked on decentralization process, granting more autonomy and budgetary responsibilities to provinces.
2002	Parliamentary elections held. All but one of the 166 candidates were from the governing Lao People's Revolutionary Party.

2004	The US government granted Laos Normal Trade Relations (NTR) status.
2006	The National Assembly election held.
	Choummaly Sayasone succeeded Khamtay Siphandone as president.
2008	Hosted the Greater Mekong Subregion Summit.

Basic Information

Geographical Co-ordinates:	2 30 N, 112 30 E
Total Area:	329,750 sq. km
Coastline:	4,675 km
Population:	26,113,700
Nationality:	Malaysian
Capital:	Kuala Lumpur
Climate:	Tropical; south-west monsoon from April to October and north-east monsoon from October to February
Natural Resources:	Tin, petroleum, timber, copper, iron ore, natural gas, bauxite
Ethnic Groups:	61% Malay and other indigenous, 24% Chinese, 7% Indian, 8% Others
Languages:	Bahasa Melayu (official), English, Chinese, Tamil, and several indigenous languages (East Malaysia)
Religions:	60% Muslim, 19% Buddhist, 9% Christian, 6% Hindu, 3% Confucianism, Taoism, other traditional Chinese religions, 2% Others or unknown, 1% None
Head of State:	Paramount Ruler Sultan Mizan Zainal Abidin
Prime Minister:	Abdullah bin Ahmad Badawi
Independence:	31 August 1957 (from UK)

Type of Government: Constitutional Monarchy

Currency: Ringgit

Key Dates

1946	The Straits Settlements of Penang and Malacca joined the other Malay States to form the Malayan Union.
1948	The British declared a State of Emergency to deal with Communist insurgency and subversion.
	Federation of Malaya formed.
31 August 1957	Gained independence from the British.
	Tunku Abdul Rahman became first Prime Minister of Federation of Malaya.
1960	The Communist Emergency, first declared in 1948, ended.
1963	Formed Malphilindo with Indonesia and Philippines.
	Formed Federation of Malaysia with Singapore, Sabah and Sarawak.
1967	Became a founding member of ASEAN.
1968	Government implemented National Economic Policy.
	British announced withdrawal of troops by 1971.
1969	May 13 racial riots.
1970	Tunku Abdul Rahman resigned. Succeeded by Abdul Razak, his Deputy.
1971	Formed Five Power Defence Arrangement (FPDA) with Australia, Britain, New Zealand and Singapore.
1974	Normalised relations with China.
1976	Hussein Onn succeeded Abdul Razak as Prime Minister.

1977	Agreed with Philippines to end dispute over Sabah in exchange for Malaysia's implicit agreement not to help the Moro Muslim rebels with arms.
1981	Dr Mahathir Mohamad became Prime Minister.
1987	Dr Mahathir narrowly defeated challenge from Tengku Razaleigh, Trade and Industry Minister, for the Presidency of UMNO.
1997	Asian financial crisis spread to Malaysia.
1998	Asian financial crisis deepened.
	Introduced capital controls.
	Dr Mahathir sacked his Deputy, Anwar Ibrahim, who was subsequently jailed for corruption and sodomy.
2001	Daim Zainuddin, who was partly responsible for Malaysia's recovery from the Asian Financial Crisis, resigned as Finance Minister.
2002	Abdullah Ahmad Badawi, the Deputy Prime Minister was named to succeed Dr Mahathir as Prime Minister.
2003	Mahathir Mohamad retired after 22 years of strong leadership and was succeeded by his deputy, Abdullah Badawi.
2004	Barisan Nasional (BN) won its largest-ever election victory.
	The High Court overturned the conviction for sodomy of Anwar Ibrahim, who was set free after serving nearly six years for corruption.
2005	Removed the currency peg against US dollar. Adopted crawling peg managed float system against a basket of currencies.
2006	Dr Mahathir called on UMNO to replace Mr Abdullah as party leader.
2007	Anwar Ibrahim returned to national politics.

2008	General Election held. BN won, but was denied a two-thirds supermajority in Malaysian Parliament. In addition, 5 of 13 state legislatures were won by the opposition, compared with only one in the last election.
	Anwar Ibrahim won a by-election to return him to Parliament. He vowed to oust the Federal Government.
	Abdullah Badawi brought forward the date he would step down from 2010 to March 2009, paving the way for Deputy Prime Minister Najib Razak to succeed him.

Union of Myanmar

Basic Information	
Geographical Co-ordinates:	21 00 N, 98 00 E
Total Area:	678,500 sq. km
Coastline:	1,930 km
Population:	48,379,200
Nationality:	Myanmar
Capital:	Yangon
Climate:	Tropical monsoon; cloudy, rainy, hot humid summers south-west monsoon, from June to September; less cloudy, scant rainfall, mild temperatures, lower humidity during winter north-east monsoon, from December to April
Natural Resources:	Petroleum, timber, tin, antimony, zinc, copper, tungsten, lead, coal, marble, limestone, precious stones, natural gas, hydropower
Ethnic Groups:	68% Burman, 9% Shan, 7% Karen, 4% Rakhine, 3% Chinese, 2% Mon, 2% Indian, 5% Others
Languages:	Burmese (official), minority ethnic groups have their own languages
Religions:	89% Buddhist, 4% Muslim, 3% Baptist, 1% Roman Catholic, 1% Animist, 2% Others
Head of State:	Chairman of the State Peace and Development Council (SPDC) Senior General Than Shwe

Prime Minister:	Lt. General Thein Sein
Independence:	4 January 1948 (from UK)
Type of Government:	Military junta
Currency:	Kyat

Key Dates

1947	General Aung San and six of his top governmental associates were assassinated.
4 January 1948	Gained Independence from British.
	Communist insurrection led by Than Tun.
1948	Karen National Defence Organisation rebelled.
1952	Premier U Nu launched four-year economic plan.
1953	Government officially banned Burma Communist Party.
1960	Signed Sino-Burmese border agreement.
1962	General Ne Win seized Government, imprisoned U Nu, and imposed military rule.
1964	Shut itself off from the rest of the world.
1969	U Nu went into self-exile.
1988	National League for Democracy (NLD) formed.
	General Saw Maung formed new Government and established the State Law and Order Restoration Council (SLORC).
1989	Aung San Suu Kyi was put under house arrest.
1990	SLORC declared martial law.
	National election held. NLD led by Aung San Suu Kyi won 392 out of 485 parliamentary seats.
1992	General Than Shwe was appointed Chairman of SLORC.

1995	Aung San Suu Kyi was released after six years of house arrest.
1997	Joined ASEAN as member.
	SLORC was renamed State Peace and Development Council (SPDC) with no changes made to its policy stance.
	US imposed sanctions.
2000	Aung San Suu Kyi and other senior leaders of the NLD were placed on house arrest again.
2002	A series of talks between the NLD and the SPDC resulted in the release of Aung San Suu Kyi.
2003	Further anti-democracy crackdown.
	Aung San Suu Kyi was attacked while touring northern Myanmar and was detained together with some members of the NLD.
	General Khin Nyunt took over as prime minister. He announced a road map for political reform.
2004	The National Convention on the new constitution reopened.
	General Khin Nyunt was sacked.
2006	The 88 Generation launched a petition for the release of political prisoners.
2007	The military junta detained leaders of the 88 Generation group.
	Protests against the regime escalated. Further crackdown.
	Ibrahim Gambari, the UN special envoy to Myanmar, finally was allowed to visit the country.

Republic of the Philippines

Basic Information	
Geographical Co-ordinates:	13 00 N, 122 00 E
Total Area:	300,000 sq. km
Coastline:	36,289 km
Population:	86,263,710
Nationality:	Filipino
Capital:	Manila
Climate:	Tropical marine; north-east monsoon from November to April, south-west monsoon from May to October
Natural Resources:	Timber, petroleum, nickel, cobalt, silver, gold, salt, copper
Ethnic Groups:	28% Tagalog, 13% Cebuano, 9% Ilocano, 8% Bisaya/Binisaya, 8% Hiligaynon Ilonggo, 6% Bikol, 3% Waray, 25% Others
Languages:	Filipino (official, based on Tagalog), English (official)
Religions:	81% Roman Catholic, 5% Muslim, 3% Evangelical, 2% Iglesia ni Kristo, 2% Aglipayan, 4% Other Christian
Head of State:	President Gloria Macapagal Arroya
Independence:	12 June 1898 (from Spain) 4 July 1946 (from US)
Type of Government:	Republic
Currency:	Philippine Peso

Key Dates

1942	Hukbalahap Rebellion.
4 July 1946	Gained Independence from USA.
1949	President Elpidio Quirino introduced land reform and new plans for industrialisation.
1953	Ramon Magsaysay, who had as Defence Secretary crushed the Huk Rebellion, became President.
1954	Joined Southeast Asia Treaty Organisation (SEATO).
1957	Magsaysay died in an air crash, and was succeeded by Carlos Garcia.
1961	Diosdado Macapagal was elected President.
1963	Formed Maphilindo with Malaysia and Indonesia.
1965	Ferdinand Marcos was elected President.
1967	Became a founding member of ASEAN.
1972	Ferdinand Marcos proclaimed martial law.
1975	Imelda Marcos was appointed Governor of Manila.
1976	Signed Tripoli Agreement with Moros National Liberation Front and promised autonomy to 13 provinces in Southern Philippines.
1981	Martial law lifted.
1983	Benigno Aquino was assassinated.
1986	Corazon Aquino became President through People Power Movement.
	Ferdinand Marcos fled to Hawaii.
1987	Honasan launched coup against Corazon Aquino.
1989	Ferdinand Marcos died.
1992	USA handed back Subic Naval base.
	Fidel Ramos succeeded Aquino as President.

1996	Signed a peace agreement with the Moro National Liberation Front (MNLF), the main Muslim secessionist movement in Mindanao.
1998	Joseph Estrada became President.
2000	Launched a campaign that drove the Moro Islamic Liberation Front (MILF) out of its bases in Mindanao.
2001	Joseph Estrada was removed from presidency after mass street demonstrations demanding his resignation. He was replaced by his vice president, Gloria Macapagal Arroyo. Signed a ceasefire agreement with the MILF.
2002	Launched a military campaign against Abu Sayyaf, a small extremist Muslim rebel group, with assistance from US forces.
2003	Coup attempt against Ms Macapagal Arroyo was quelled.
2004	Presidential election held. Ms Macapagal Arroyo won with a slim margin.
2006	President Macapagal Arroyo declared a week-long state of emergency after a failed coup attempt.
2007	Mid-term congressional elections held. Pro-Arroyo parties retained its massive majority in the House of Representatives, but lost its majority in the Senate. A third attempt to impeach the President failed, leaving her immune to another charge for the next 12 months.

Republic of Singapore

Basic Information	
Geographical Co-ordinates:	1 22 N, 103 48 E
Total Area:	693 sq. km
Coastline:	193 km
Population:	4,483,900
Nationality:	Singaporean
Capital:	Singapore
Climate:	Tropical monsoon; hot, humid; no pronounced rainy or dry seasons; thunderstorms are common
Natural Resources	Fish, deepwater ports
Ethnic Groups:	77% Chinese, 14% Malay, 8% Indian, 1% Others
Languages:	English (official), Chinese (official), Malay (official and national), Tamil (official)
Religions:	43% Buddhist, 15% Muslim, 9% Taoist, 4% Hindu, 5% Catholic, 10% Other Christian
Head of State:	President S. R. Nathan
Prime Minister:	Lee Hsien Loong
Independence:	9 August 1965 (from Malaysia)
Type of Government:	Republic
Currency:	Singapore dollar

Key Dates

1945	Return of British rule after Japanese Occupation.
1946	Became separate Crown Colony from pre-war British Malaya.
1948	The British declared a State of Emergency to deal with Communist insurgency and subversion.
1950	Maria Hertogh riots.
1953	Sir George Rendel was appointed to review country's Constitutional position and make recommendations. The proposals were accepted and became basis of new Constitution.
1955	David Marshall became Singapore's first Chief Minister.
1958	Constitutional Agreement was signed in London.
1959	Attained Self-Government. State of Singapore established.
	The People's Action Party (PAP) won the General Election, and Lee Kuan Yew became the first Prime Minister.
	Yusof bin Ishak became the first local Head of State.
1963	Joined Federation of Malaya, Sabah and Sarawak to form the Federation of Malaysia.
1964	During the outbreak of two racial riots, curfews were imposed.
9 August 1965	Attained Independence after being separated from the Federation of Malaysia. State of Singapore became Republic of Singapore.
	Yusof bin Ishak became Republic's first President.
	Admitted to the United Nations.
	Became a Member of Commonwealth of Nations.
1967	Became founding member of ASEAN.
1971	After the death of Yusof Ishak, Dr Benjamin Sheares became the Republic's second President.

1981	C. V. Devan Nair became the third President, serving until his resignation in 1985.
1985	Wee Kim Wee became the Republic's fourth President.
1990	Goh Chok Tong became Singapore's second Prime Minister.
1993	Ong Teng Cheong, a former Deputy Prime Minister, became the first elected President.
1998	Hit by Asian financial crisis.
1999	S. R. Nathan became Singapore's second elected President.
2000	Bilateral Free Trade Agreement with New Zealand concluded.
2001	General Election held. PAP won 82 out of 84 seats, including 55 walkovers.
	Bilateral Free Trade Agreement with Japan concluded.
2002	Bilateral Free Trade Agreement with Australia concluded.
2003	Concluded Free Trade Agreement with the U.S.
	Outbreak of SARS (Severe Acute Respiratory Syndrome) between March and May which severely affected the economy.
2004	Lee Hsien Loong, with Goh Chok Tong as Senior Minister, became Prime Minister.
2005	Concluded Comprehensive Economic Co-operation Agreement with India.
2006	General Election held. PAP won 82 out of 84 seats and 67% of the vote.
	Hosted IMF and World Bank meetings.
2008	International Court of Justice at The Hague awarded sovereignty over Pedra Branca, a small islet, to Singapore.

Hosted FIA Formula One World Championship. The race, held on a street circuit, was the first night-time event in Formula One history.

Signed Free Trade Agreement with China (PRC).

Kingdom of Thailand

Basic Information

Geographical Co-ordinates:	15 00 N, 100 00 E
Total Area:	514,000 sq. km
Coastline:	3,219 km
Population:	63,443,900
Nationality:	Thai
Capital:	Bangkok
Climate:	Tropical; rainy, warm, cloudy south-west monsoon from mid-May to September; dry cool north-east monsoon from November to mid-March
Natural Resources:	Tin, rubber, natural gas, tungsten, tantalum, timber, lead, fish, gypsum, lignite, fluorite, arable land
Ethnic Groups:	75% Thai, 14% Chinese, 11% Others
Languages:	Thai (official), English and ethnic and regional dialects
Religions:	95% Buddhist, 5% Muslim, 1% Christian
Head of State:	King Bhumibol Adulyadej
Prime Minister:	Abhisit Vejjajiva
Independence:	1238 (founding date, never colonised by the West)
Type of Government:	Constitutional monarchy
Currency:	Thai Baht

Key Dates

1946 Pridi Government formed.

1948 Phibun Songkhram staged coup and became Prime Minister.

1952 Thai Communist Party banned.

1954 Joined Southeast Asia Treaty Organisation (SEATO).

1957 Phibun Songkhram was overthrown by Sarit Thanarat in a bloodless coup d'etat.

Phibun Songkhram went into exile.

1962 Rusk-Thanat Assistance Agreement with the USA.

1963 Sarit Thanarat died and was succeeded by Thanom Kittikachorn.

1967 Became founding member of ASEAN.

1973 Demonstration by university students.

Thanom Kittikachorn and his deputy were ordered out of the country by King.

Sanya Thammasak became Prime Minister.

1977 General Kriangsak Chomanan became Prime Minister.

1980 Prem Tinsulanond became Prime Minister.

1983 Pridi Phanomyong died.

1988 Chatichai Choonhavan became Prime Minister.

1991 General Suchinda Kraprayoon staged a coup d'etat and appointed Anand Punyarachun as Prime Minister.

1992 Pro-democracy parties demanded Suchinda's resignation and resulted in the largest protest ever.

Chuan Leekpai was elected Prime Minister.

1995 Banharn Silapa-Archa became Prime Minister.

1996 Chavalit Yongchaiyudh became Prime Minister.

1997 Asian financial crisis erupted.

Chuan Leekpai re-elected Thailand's Prime Minister.

Thailand turned to IMF for help. IMF lent a total of US$14.3 billion to Thailand between 1997 and 2000.

2001   Thaksin Shinawatra, the leader of the Thai Rak Thai (TRT) party, became Prime Minister.

2003   Loan from IMF fully repaid.

2005   TRT won 377 seats in the House of Representatives, enabling it to form a single-party government, the first in modern Thailand.

2006   The tax-free sale of Thaksin's family members' controlling stake in Shin Corp to Temasek Holdings of Singapore triggered anti-Thaksin demonstrations.

Thaksin dissolved parliament. The opposition parties boycotted the poll. The election result was later annulled.

The military took power in a bloodless coup. A retired general, Surayud Chulanont, was appointed prime minister.

2007   The TRT was dissolved. The 111 members of the party' executive committee, including Thaksin, were banned from politics for five years.

The pro-Thaksin People Power Party (PPP) was returned to power in a fresh election.

2008   Samak Sundaravej, head of PPP, became prime minister.

Samak Sundaravej was ousted for hosting a television cookery programme.

Somchai Wongsawat, also of PPP, succeeded as Prime Minister.

Thailand's Constitutional Court dissolved the ruling PPP and two coalition partners, forcing Prime Minister Somchai Wongsawat and dozens of leaders to step down and banning them from politics for five years.

Abhisit Vejjajiva, leader of Democrat Party, became prime minister.

Socialist Republic of Vietnam

Basic Information	
Geographical Co-ordinates:	16 00 N, 106 00 E
Total Area:	329,560 sq. km
Coastline:	3,444 km (excluding islands)
Population:	84,108,100
Nationality:	Vietnamese
Capital:	Hanoi
Climate:	Hot, rainy season from mid-May to mid-September and warm, dry season from mid-October to mid-March
Natural Resources:	Phosphates, coal, manganese, bauxite, chromate, offshore oil and gas deposits, forests, hydropower
Ethnic Groups:	86% Kink (Viet), 2% Yaynese, 7% Others (Muong, Tai, Meo, Khmer Man, Cham)
	86% Kinh (Viet), 2% Tay, 2% Thai, 10% Others (Muong, Khome, Hoa, Nun, Hmong)
Languages:	Vietnamese (official), Chinese, English, French, Khmer and tribal languages
Religions:	Buddhism, Taoism, Roman Catholicism, Islam, Protestantism, Cao Dai, Hoa Hao
	9% Buddhist, 7% Catholic, 2% Hoa Hao, 1% Cao Dai, 81% None
Head of State:	President Nguyen Minh Triet

Prime Minister:	Nguyen Tan Dung
Independence:	2 September 1945 (from France)
Type of Government:	Communist state
Currency:	Dong

Key Dates

1930	Ho Chi Minh founded Communist Party of Indochina.
1941	Ho Chi Minh formed League of Independence of Vietnam, better known as Viet Minh.
2 September 1945	Monarchy abolished. Ho Chi Minh proclaimed Independence and established Democratic Republic of Vietnam.
1954	French defeated at Dien Bien Phu. Vietnam was divided into North and South Vietnam.
1955	Ngo Dinh Diem proclaimed himself as President of Republic of Vietnam (South Vietnam).
1960	National Liberation Front (NLF) established in Saigon.
1961	People's Liberation Army (Viet Cong) formed under NLF.
1963	Ngo Dinh Diem assassinated.
1964	After the Tonkin Gulf incident, American military involvement in South Vietnam escalated.
1968	Tet Offensive.
1969	Ho Chi Minh died, and was succeeded by Le Duan.
1973	US-Vietnam Peace Agreement signed in Paris.
1975	Communists captured Saigon, and occupied the whole of South Vietnam.

1976	Vietnam reunified as Socialist Republic of Vietnam. Saigon renamed Ho Chi Minh City.
1978	Invaded Cambodia.
1979	Sino-Vietnam border war.
1986	Le Duan died, and was succeeded by Truong Chinh and then Nguyen Van Linh, a reformist General Secretary.
	Sixth Communist Party Congress launched limited economic liberalisation, known as "Doi Moi".
1991	Vietnam-China relations normalised.
1994	US lifted trade embargo.
1995	Vietnam-US relations were normalised.
	Joined ASEAN as seventh member.
1997	The National Assembly selected Phan Van Khai as Prime Minister and Tran Duc Luong as President.
1998	Joined Asia-Pacific Economic Co-operation (APEC) forum.
2000	Signed a treaty with China delineating their common land border.
2001	The moderate Nong Duc Manh was chosen as General Secretary of the Communist Party.
	A Bilateral Trade Agreement with the US came into effect.
2004	Outbreak of avian influenza (bird flu).
2005	Prime minister Phan Van Khai made a historic trip to the US.
	The National Assembly passed the country's first anti-corruption law.
2006	Nguyen Tan Dung succeeded Mr Khai as prime minister and Nguyen Minh Triet became the new president.
	Hosted the annual meeting of the APEC group.

2007	Became a member of the WTO and was accorded permanent normal trade relations status by the US.
	A general election produced a new 493-member National Assembly, of which Vietnam's communist party won more than 91% of seats.

Chapter 1

The Land and Its History

For forms of Government let fools contest;
Whatever is best administered is best.
Alexander Pope, *An Essay on Man: Epistle III*

Objectives

✓ Point out the similarities and differences among Southeast Asian countries.
✓ Describe the geographical attributes of the region.
✓ Highlight the common colonial past.
✓ Explain the formation and evolution of ASEAN.
✓ Identify some potential challenges to the region.

Introduction

Scholarly interests in Southeast Asia increased after World War II. This is reflected in the proliferation of published works on the area. Several factors contributed to the lack of interest before the Second World War. The minimal role Southeast Asia played in world affairs in the past is one explanation. Another reason was the lack of economic development in the region. The colonisation by the Western powers is probably the most important *raison d'être*. Interests in individual countries were confined to the colonising powers, as other countries had no incentive to contribute to the knowledge of these colonies. However, all these are fast changing. Brunei, the last colony in Southeast Asia, achieved Independence from the British in 1984. Most economies in Southeast Asia were turning in spectacular economic performances. Absolute poverty level has been on the declining trend in all countries. All went through a successful industrialisation process. For decades, economic growth rates of these economies have been much higher than those achieved by developed nations. Furthermore, some countries in the region are taking on more and more international responsibilities. Besides, during the Cold War era, Southeast Asia was a hot-bed of struggle for supremacy and dominance between anti-communist and non-communist forces on the one hand, and communist forces on the other, with the Western powers deeply involved against the spread of communism. Today, after the 2001 September 11 terrorist attack in the United States and the Bali attack exactly one year, one month and one day later; and the pre-emptive detention of terrorist members in Malaysia and Singapore and the arrest and sentencing of terrorist members in Indonesia, Southeast Asia, especially maritime Southeast Asia, has become a hot-bed of conflict between the majority of Muslims of good standing and the small minority of militant Muslims.

Southeast Asia, which is located south of China and east of India, can be divided into two main sub-regions, mainland Southeast Asia, which comprises Cambodia, Laos, Myanmar, Thailand and Vietnam, and maritime Southeast Asia, which comprises Brunei, Indonesia, Malaysia, the Philippines and Singapore. Such a categorisation, although simple, is at times useful. The classification can be used as a dividing line to separate Southeast Asia physically and culturally, if not also economically. While mainland Southeast Asia is contiguous, maritime Southeast Asia is fragmented. Indonesia, for example, is made up of more than 13,000 islands, while the Philippines has over 7,000 islands. Most of the world's great religions are found in Southeast Asia. Mainland Southeast Asia is dominated by Buddhism. On the other hand, Islam found its way to some of the countries in maritime Southeast Asia, namely Brunei, Indonesia and Malaysia, as early as the 13th century. In the Philippines, Catholicism was introduced to the Filipinos by their colonial master, the Spaniards, in the 16th century. Notwithstanding the presence of a dominant religion, small pockets of followers of other religions exist. For example, in the southern islands of the Philippines, there is a very large Muslim community. Similarly, in Western New Guinea and Bali, two of the many islands in the Indonesian Archipelago, Christianity and Hinduism are the principal religions respectively. Economically, in 2007, mainland Southeast Asia had a weighted-average GDP per capita of US$1,590 while countries in maritime Southeast Asia had a weighted-average GDP per capita of US$2,700, a higher level. The three countries that have the highest levels of per capita income in Southeast Asia, namely Singapore, Brunei and Malaysia, are located in maritime Southeast Asia, but the per capita income weightage for maritime Southeast Asia as a whole is largely determined by Indonesia, a far larger entity. If the canal at the Isthmas of Kra in Southern Thailand is cut, the separation between mainland and maritime Southeast Asia would become more distinct.

Other significant differences among Southeast Asian nations include population sizes and the political systems. Southeast Asia contains one of the most populous countries in the world. With a population of 226 million in 2007, Indonesia is just after China, India and the United States of America in terms of population size. Interestingly, one of the smallest countries in the world can also be found in Southeast Asia. With a population of only 389,000 in 2007, Brunei is considered relatively small.

The political system differs greatly among the Southeast Asian countries. For example, Indonesia, the Philippines and Singapore are republics, while Laos and Vietnam are communist states, and Brunei, Cambodia, Malaysia and Thailand are constitutional monarchies. In Myanmar, a military regime is running the country.

Diversity juxtaposes with commonality. Anthropologists segregate the human race into three distinct groups, namely Caucasoid, Mongoloid and Negroid. Under this system of classification, all the people in Southeast Asia fall under the category of Mongoloid, which in anthropological jargon, refers to the group of people native to Central and Eastern Asia. However, such a classification is now outdated and has condescending connotations. The term Mongoloid has come to mean demented physical and mental developments, features similar to the Asiatic race. A more appropriately neutral, modern term would thus be the East Asian race, from Mongolians, Koreans, Chinese and Japanese in the North to Burmese, Laotians, Cambodians, Vietnamese, Thais, Malaysians, Singaporeans, Filipinos and Indonesians in the South.

Southeast Asia, because of its geographical proximity, has fairly homogeneous climatic conditions. All the countries, partially or wholly, lie in the path of the monsoons. Southeast Asian countries are mainly agricultural-based (except for the city-state of Singapore), and the cultivation of wet rice is a common sight when travelling in the region. Countries in Southeast Asia also have a part of their history in common. All the countries except Thailand were not too long ago colonies of Western powers. Brunei, Malaysia, Myanmar and Singapore were colonised by the British, Indonesia by the Dutch, the Philippines by the Spaniards and later by the Americans. Cambodia, Laos and Vietnam were colonised by the French. Although Thailand was not colonised, it lost some of its territories to the Europeans. In the Anglo-Siamese Treaty of 1909, or Bangkok Treaty of 1909, Thailand relinquished its claims to sovereignty over the present states of Kedah, Kelantan, Perlis and Terengganu in Peninsular Malaysia, while the area around modern Pattani, Narathiwat, Songkhla, Satun and Yala remained under Thai control. During WWII, these states were returned to Thailand by the victorious Japanese Imperial Army. When WWII ended, these states were taken back as a part of British Malaya.

Another commonality observed in Southeast Asia is the emancipation of women in the region after WWII. Over the years, the status of women has improved, most noticeably in Malaysia, the Philippines, Singapore and Thailand. Progress in women's education has been substantial. The closing of the adult illiteracy gap between the sexes in most Southeast Asian countries signifies equal educational opportunities. The employment prospects for women have also become better and more numerous. This is evident in the increased female participation rate in the labour force. However, there have been some fears in recent years that Muslim women might be forced back to the old traditional role in some Muslim societies in Southeast Asia.

A milestone achieved in the history of Southeast Asia is the formation of the Association of Southeast Asian Nations (ASEAN) in 1967. The original motive was political. However, over the years, ASEAN has evolved into a more economic-oriented organisation. In 1999, ASEAN admitted its tenth and final member, Cambodia; thus fulfilling a long-standing wish of its founding fathers. Southeast Asia has indeed come a long way. However, a more meaningful exercise would involve finding the answer to the question of what lies ahead. What are some of the challenges facing

Southeast Asia and the problems that each country must overcome to achieve greater prosperity and at the same time greater cohesion within each country and with one another. The road for Southeast Asia to catch up with the developed economies is still a very long one, and some might say, a very winding one. However, opportunities arise in the midst of adversities. With increasing challenges, a vast horizon also awaits. Much remains for Southeast Asia to rise to the occasion.

Geographical Attributes

Southeast Asia, which spans from 29°N to 11°S latitudes and from 92°E to 141°E longitudes, covers a total land area of 4,330,000 square kilometres. Lying within the Tropics of Cancer and Capricorn (except for a small portion of Myanmar), the region has climatic conditions similar to those in tropical countries. Temperatures vary slightly, both across the region and throughout the year, although differences in altitude can result in great climatic disparity.

Southeast Asia experiences two periods of monsoon each year. From November to March, the North-East monsoon prevails. High atmospheric pressure caused by the winter season in the northern hemisphere forces cold, dry air to flow towards the Equator, which in that season has a lower atmospheric pressure. As the cold, dry wind blows across the South China Sea, it absorbs moisture along the way. When it reaches maritime Southeast Asia, the moisture-laden air will result in heavy rainfall. On crossing the Equator, the wind is deflected to the left as a result of the Earth's rotation. So, the wind arrives as the North-West monsoon in the southern hemisphere. Thus, during the season of the North-East monsoon, mainland Southeast Asia (except for some coastal areas in Vietnam and parts of Southern Thailand) experiences very little rainfall. On the other hand, there is a wet season for most countries in maritime Southeast Asia.

The South-West monsoon reigns from the months of May to September. During this period, the atmospheric pressure in the southern hemisphere is higher due to the winter season and this causes the air to move towards the Equator in a south-easterly direction, carrying a lot of moisture with it. This wind brings plenty of rain to the Indonesian Archipelago. On crossing the Equator, the wind is deflected to the right due to the rotation of the Earth.

The wind, which now moves in a south-westerly direction ultimately, brings plenty of rainfall to countries in mainland Southeast Asia after blowing across the Indian Ocean.

The periods from April to May and from October to November are transitional periods for the North-East and South-West monsoons. Although rainfall in mainland Southeast Asia is determined largely by the South-West monsoon, relief rain also plays a role in determining the local climatic conditions. In maritime Southeast Asia, evergreen rainforests thrive. Conversely, due to an uneven rainfall and a longer dry season, tropical rainforests are more common in mainland Southeast Asia.

Agricultural systems in Southeast Asia can be divided into three main types, namely shifting cultivation, wet rice cultivation and plantation crops agriculture. Shifting cultivation (also known as slash-and-burn agriculture or swidden agriculture) is found in the forested highlands in all countries in Southeast Asia, except for the city-state of Singapore. In East Malaysia, for example, shifting cultivation is commonly practised by the Dayaks (hill tribes) of Sarawak. Currently, the Dayaks make up about 50% of Sarawak's population. The main crop cultivated is dry paddy. The land is first cleared by burning, and the ash is used to fertilise the soil. This is followed by short periods of cultivation. Once the soil becomes exhausted, the shifting cultivators abandon the land so as to allow secondary forest to regenerate. After an interval of five to twenty or more years, the land goes through a new cultivation cycle. There are two types of shifting cultivators. The first type is settled shifting cultivators. Once the land loses its fertility, these shifting cultivators will move on to cultivate a new piece of land without relocating their settlement. On the other hand, migratory shifting cultivators will relocate their settlement once the land becomes exhausted.

Another form of agricultural system that can be found in Southeast Asia is the cultivation of wet rice (sawah agriculture). Wet rice cultivation in most Southeast Asian countries is for own consumption. Only Thailand, Vietnam and to a lesser extent, Myanmar grow rice for the export markets. In mainland Southeast Asia, the deltas that were formed by nutrient-rich alluvial deposits brought by the rivers in the region, such as Irrawaddy, Chao Phraya and Mekong, provide excellent ground for wet rice cultivation. Similarly, in Central Java of Indonesia and Luzon in the Philippines, the rich volcanic soil is very suitable for the planting of rice. However, the uneven rainfall in mainland Southeast Asia restricts the cultivation of rice to one crop per year. To overcome this problem, sophisticated irrigation systems have been constructed to ensure a stable supply of water. In some countries, the presence of an irrigation system allows farmers to practise double cropping, thus greatly enhancing the productivity of these rice farmers. Another significant development in the cultivation of wet rice in Southeast Asia was the introduction of HYVs (high yielding varieties of rice. The use of higher yielding rice strains and chemical fertilisers, coupled with better irrigation systems, has been termed the "Green Revolution".

The cultivation of cash crops in plantations was only introduced to Southeast Asia during the period of colonial rule. It was a lucrative source of income for the colonial powers. The cash crops, which are grown mainly for export markets, can be divided into food crops such as coffee and sugar cane, and agricultural raw materials such as rubber. Some cash crops fall under both categories. For example, oil palm can be further processed into edible cooking oil, or it can be used to manufacture non-food products such as soaps and diesel substitutes. For decades, Malaysia had been the main producer of natural rubber in the world. However, the law of comparative advantage has since enabled Malaysia to move into oil palm cultivation instead. In recent years, the same law of comparative advantage has also resulted in Thailand succeeding Malaysia in becoming the world's most important producer and exporter of natural rubber, followed by Indonesia. Compared to wet rice cultivation, planting of cash crops has certain advantages. The perennial nature of these crops allows continuous harvest, thus providing income and employment throughout the year. In Southeast Asia, cash crops are also cultivated by smallholders. Smallholdings are family businesses that cultivate cash crops but on a smaller scale.

It was said that before the post-Independence industrialisation of Southeast Asia, much of Southeast Asian life was dominated by the three Rs: Religion, Rice and Rubber. The importance of rice for subsistence farmers and the importance of rubber as an export crop have necessitated the need for a full separate chapter on rice and another chapter on rubber in this book. Please see Chapter 3: Agriculture: Rice; and Chapter 4: Agriculture: Rubber, Oil Palm and Other Crops.

A Common Past — Colonisation and Its Legacy

A similarity shared by Southeast Asian countries is their colonial past. Documentation on Western colonisation of the region dates back to as early as the 16th century. The rationales for colonisation were mainly economic. The Industrial Revolution in Europe had given rise to the need for raw materials. Given its richness in natural resources, Southeast Asia was a good target for colonisation. The colonies also provided ready markets for manufactured goods of the colonising powers. The desire to protect and secure the trade route between India and China through the strategic Straits of Malacca was another reason.

Colonisation brought about significant changes to Southeast Asia. Whether these changes benefited countries involved remains controversial. The most conspicuous impact was the introduction of a money economy by the colonial rulers. Farmers in the region began to sell their produce for money; either from a surplus production of subsistence crops such as rice or from the cultivation of cash crops such as rubber. Furthermore, the "new economic environment" also encouraged farmers to increase their production by clearing more land for cultivation. With modern way of life, local population increased, often by leaps and bounds, mainly as a consequence of falling mortality rates.

To facilitate the movement of goods and resources, the colonial powers built ports, railways, and roads. The development of inland infrastructure, however, also benefited the locals. People from remote villages could now easily communicate with those in the cities, thus allowing expansion of social and economic activities. But, as the purpose of the network of roads and railways was to link up the various areas of export commodity production and distribution, a characteristic pattern emerged. This pattern of selective transport development in the region meant that some areas were incorporated into the modern global capitalist economy while other areas not affected by the production for exports remained relatively undeveloped. Hospitals and schools were also established by the colonial powers but investment in human capital was very low compared with post-Independence achievements. All over the world, including Southeast Asia, the colonising powers followed the divide-and-rule policy. A great deal of colonial legacy has yet to be satisfactorily resolved in the post-Independence states.

Colonisation also changed the social fabric and racial composition of the colonised countries. This was especially striking in some parts of Southeast Asia. The new mines and plantations required large numbers of skilled and unskilled labourers. Troubled by labour shortages, the colonial powers had no alternative but to import labour from neighbouring over-populated countries, India and China, to work in the tin mines and rubber plantations. However, in the process of development, Thailand, not under colonial rule, also had an influx of immigrants who were escaping from the extreme poverty and political turmoil in China. Nonetheless, most of the unstable parts of Southeast Asia today, such as Aceh in Indonesia, Pattani in Thailand and Mindanao in the Philippines have nothing to do with the new immigrants to Southeast Asia. Indeed, it is said that in Southeast Asia the higher the proportion of these newer immigrants and their descendents, the higher the level of economic development in the country.

Colonialism also brought in the modern public service structure, the modern legal system and the rule of law other than the colonial export-oriented primary producing economic system. The economic system was based essentially on the utilisation of extensive tropical land and cheap labour other than markets for manufactured goods from the metropolitan powers. The increase in affluence in the opened up areas plus much improved general public health and public order also resulted in population explosion. If colonialism in Southeast Asia were to be judged in terms of exponential increases in native populations, it would be considered a great success.

Nevertheless, in the march towards Independence by the subject peoples, it was natural that colonial legacies and systems received particular condemnation. Each Southeast Asian group wanted to govern itself, not to be governed by European colonial rulers from London, Paris, Amsterdam or Washington, D.C. The basic issue was political, was human dignity, not economic, although economic issues also featured in the disparagement of colonial rule. Even today, 46 years after Malayan and later Malaysian Independence, former Prime Minister of Malaysia, Dr Mahathir Mohamad, still speaks of neo-colonialism when he perceives that Malaysia is badly treated by Western powers.

The development of colonisation, not surprisingly, gave rise to nationalism. The paradox, however, was that the nationalist movements were led mainly by local intellectuals that were trained in the West or in schools established by the colonial powers and were inculcated with Western values. Furthermore, the nationalist movement, in most cases, was not due to oppressive rule but was because of exposure to the more open and liberalised political system in the West. The Japanese interregnum accelerated the nationalist movement in Southeast Asia by shattering the myth of Western supremacy. Except for Thailand, each Southeast Asian nation had to cope with attempts by the colonial powers to regain their lost colonies. The struggle for Independence from the colonial powers ranged from peaceful negotiation to bloody warfare. For example, Indonesia and Myanmar were fighting for Independence immediately after the Second World War. Indonesia proclaimed Independence in 1945, but it was only in 1949, after four long years of fighting the Dutch, that the country became a sovereign nation. The struggle for Independence was even longer for Myanmar and Vietnam. The French only withdrew its troops from Vietnam in 1954. In contrast, except for the armed revolt of the Malayan Communist Party, Malaysia and Singapore did not engage in a war for Independence. Instead, the two countries negotiated with the British over a period of more than a decade.

There were residual effects from Independence. For example, in Indonesia, the Dutch did not put in place an effective group of Indonesian officials to run the public sector. On the other hand, in the Philippines, the system of taxation and tributes that was established by the Spaniards served as a model for the landlord system which eventually became an important element in the political and economic life of the Filipinos. Notwithstanding this, the public sector became a handicap rather than a blessing in the subsequent economic development of the Philippines, and also of Indonesia. Malaysia, Singapore and Brunei inherited from the British a respectable civil service structure. In Singapore, in particular, this civil service structure has been further improved since Independence as a vehicle for national economic development. Malaysia allowed it to deteriorate, particularly in the administration of law and order. Malaysia racialism and Malay interests took precedence over other national considerations. All standards, particularly in the public sector, were compromised to promote this special interest, especially during the time when Dr Mahathir was the Prime Minister.

Of all the Southeast Asian nations, Myanmar is still unable to leave the colonial legacy of divide and rule and still has a military regime.

Before Independence, as part of the divide-and-rule policy, the British Government did not allow the majority ethnic group, the Burmans, to join the army and the Civil Service, which had to be staffed by Burmese ethnic minorities and Indians. After Independence, the majority Burmans re-exerted their rights, expelled the economically and educationally very important group of Indians and went to war to seek unity with other ethnic minorities.

Malaysia, however, appears to have a much more encouraging story to tell. Affirmative action by the Malay majority with enough freedom given to ethnic Chinese and ethnic Indians has enabled the country to develop national unity with ethnic diversity. Much of this success in this Malay-dominated multi-racial society must be attributed to the statesmanship of several generations of Malaysian Prime Ministers, from the great Founding Father, Tunku Abdul Rahman, to Tun Abdul Razak, and to Tun Hussein Onn.

Myanmar has not been that fortunate. Many of its first echelon of leaders headed by Aung San Suu Kyi's father as Prime Minister were assassinated. This great tragedy appears to have had a long-term crippling effect, particularly in terms of national unity. Obviously, post-Independence history has unfolded differently in each country in Southeast Asia, much like the historical diversity in European colonisation history in the region.

The Formation and Evolution of ASEAN

One of the most significant events in the history of Southeast Asia after Independence has been the formation of ASEAN in 1967. The objective of the formation was two-fold. First, it was a means to promote peace and stability in the region. At that time, Southeast Asia was divided by ideological conflict and war. Coupled with territorial disputes and racial tensions between neighbours, there was a possibility that the differences could degenerate into a full-blown armed conflict, leading to a prolonged fragmentation of Southeast Asia. Another motivation for the formation was to contain the spread of communism to Southeast Asian countries. China at that time had openly adopted a policy to export revolutions to Southeast Asia and had supported a number of local insurgency movements led by the communist parties in Indonesia, Malaysia, the Philippines, Singapore and Thailand.

ASEAN was not the first regional grouping created to act as a forum for dialogues between leaders of the various countries. The Association of Southeast Asia (ASA), comprising the former Federation of Malaya, the Philippines and Thailand, was formed in 1961. However, the organisation became defunct one year later, after the Sabah dispute between the Federation of Malaya and the Philippines. Diplomatic ties between Kuala Lumpur and Manila were severed during 1962–1966. The confrontation launched by Indonesia's late President Sukarno also led to the demise of Malphilindo, which included Indonesia, the Federation of Malaya and the Philippines. The concept of Malphilindo was mooted by former Philippines President Macapagal.

The political stability of Malaya (then a collective name for Singapore and the Federation of Malaya) was threatened by the militancy of the Communists. In the former Federation of Malaya, the Communists carried out insurgent activities purportedly to free the country from British rule. Singapore was also in danger of being taken over by a Communist-backed faction of the ruling party. A series of leftist-inspired strikes and a wave of student demonstrations rocked the Singapore economy in the late 1950s and early 1960s. The fear instilled by a Communist-controlled Singapore contributed to the proposition of forming an alliance comprising Brunei, the Federation of Malaya, Sabah, Sarawak and Singapore. However, an important minority of people were against the alliance. Some minorities were uneasy over the political dominance of the Malay people in the new Federation. In 1962, referendums conducted by the Cobbold Commission in Sabah, Sarawak and Singapore showed that a majority of people were in favour of joining the new Federation of Malaysia. Brunei, on the other hand, had rejected the idea of joining the Federation, as it was feared that the country would lose control of its vast oil reserves after joining the new Federation. Thus, in 1963, the Federation of Malaysia, which consisted of only Singapore, Sabah, Sarawak and the Federation of Malaya, was formed.

The formation of the Federation of Malaysia was not viewed positively by some surrounding countries. In 1963, President Sukarno ordered the Indonesian paratroopers to launch a military attack on Malaysia and to initiate acts of sabotage in Singapore. His intention was to direct attention away from the severe internal discontent that had arisen due to Sukarno's mismanagement of the economy and the implementation of guided democracy. However, Sukarno's pretext was that the new Federation of Malaysia was a neo-colonial plot to surround the Republic of Indonesia. The confrontation ceased in 1965, after an abortive coup that led to the overthrow of President Sukarno and the subsequent reaching of an agreement between Malaysia and Indonesia under the new Indonesia's President, President Suharto. The Philippines also refused to recognise the new Federation, because of its dispute with Malaysia over the claim of Sabah.

Shortly after forming the Federation of Malaysia, the ruling party in Singapore, People's Action Party (PAP) began to expand its activities into Peninsular Malaysia. The leaders were aggressively pushing for the concept of a "Malaysian Malaysia". Under this concept, national interests would precede communal interests. This greatly alarmed the Malay-dominated ruling party in Malaysia (United Malays National Organisation, UMNO) and it retaliated with similar activities amongst the Malays in Singapore. The atmosphere in the two countries was tense and the eruption of massive racial riots seemed imminent. It was under these circumstances that Singapore was asked to leave the Federation of Malaysia in 1965.

All these disruptive developments and particularly the common fear of communism led to the formation of ASEAN. Although all the countries in Southeast Asia were invited to join the organisation, Brunei, Cambodia, Laos, Myanmar and Vietnam declined. In 1984, Brunei joined ASEAN as its sixth member. This was followed by Vietnam in 1995, and Myanmar and Laos in 1997. Cambodia was not admitted until 1999 because of unresolved internal political issues.

Although the main impetus for the formation of ASEAN was political in nature, economic co-operation was also high on the agenda of the organisation. The fall of the Berlin Wall in 1989 marked the end of the Cold War. This dramatic change in political environment rendered insignificant one of the two major reasons for forming ASEAN. ASEAN has since evolved into a more economic-oriented organisation. When ASEAN was established in 1967, intra-regional trade was a mere 12% to 15%. By 2006, the amount of intra-regional trade had increased to approximately 25%. Examples of earlier economic co-operation included the ASEAN Industrial Project (AIP) scheme and ASEAN Industrial Complementation (AIC) scheme. Under the AIP scheme, each member country was allocated an industrial project.

Indonesia and Malaysia were each to have a urea plant; phosphate fertiliser was to go to the Philippines, soda ash to Thailand and diesel engine to Singapore. The AIC scheme was launched in 1981. The first project under the scheme was the production of the 'ASEAN car'. However, these earlier projects failed to take off successfully. Notwithstanding earlier disappointments, prospects for the later projects look more promising. These include the SIJORI growth triangle which covers Singapore, the Riau Islands of Indonesia and the Johor state of Malaysia. The ASEAN Free Trade Area (AFTA), whose objective is to increase the region's competitive advantage as a single production unit, was mooted in 1992 at the Fourth ASEAN Summit in Bangkok. The plan of AFTA was to remove all existing tariffs by means of the Common Effective Preferential Tariff (CEPT) scheme. In terms of trade in goods, the AFTA has been effectively realised in the ASEAN-6. The successful implementation of AFTA would mean that a much bigger ASEAN-wide market will emerge. This may act as a partial counter-weight to the much bigger market in China, located just north of Southeast Asia. As of January 2005, 98.98% of commodities traded within the region by Brunei, Indonesia, Malaysia, Philippines, Singapore and Thailand under the CEPT Agreement were in the tariff range of 0–5%. The target date for Vietnam to reduce tariff rates to 0–5% range is 2006, for Laos and Myanmar 2008 and for Cambodia 2010. Further elaboration on Southeast Asian cooperation and ASEAN are discussed as a separate chapter: Chapter 8: Economic Regionalism.

Future Challenges

In spite of the excellent economic performances of the original ASEAN-5 countries, Southeast Asia's progress is still hindered by several unresolved issues. One major obstacle Southeast Asia must overcome in order to improve the quality of life of its people is to abolish abject poverty and to lessen lopsided development within individual countries. Another challenge faced by Southeast Asia concerns the productivity improvement of the agricultural sector. This is of paramount importance, as most Southeast Asian countries are still primarily agricultural economies. The quagmire faced by shifting cultivators also warrants special attention. There is also the pressing need for Southeast Asian countries to address the issue of proper utilisation of the region's natural resources. Proper exploitation of natural resources can be and has been used to jump start the process of economic development. However, any economic progress must not be achieved at the expense of environmental degradation. To take on the intense competition posed by an increasingly globalised economy, Southeast Asian countries must develop their human resources to the fullest. This involves not only the provision of education and training especially in the field of science and technology, but also the proper management of the country's population size and growth, and the all important employment opportunities. A country's economic development must also not be hampered by internal political and social instability. Finally, the spectacular economic growth of China provides both opportunities and challenges.

Poverty and Inequality

The essence of poverty is captured by the World Bank (2000), which states that "Poverty is pronounced deprivation in well being... To be poor is to be hungry, to lack of shelter and clothing, to be sick and not cared for, to be illiterate and not schooled... Poor people are particularly vulnerable to adverse events outside their control. They are often treated badly by the institutions of states and society and excluded from voice and power in those institutions." Such a description shows that poverty is a multi-faceted concept. However, in practice, poverty is often viewed from a purely economic perspective. A commonly used tool to measure absolute poverty in a country is the proportion of population living under the poverty line, which is generally computed based on a basket of minimum needed consumption goods per person. According to the World Bank, 1.4 billion people in the developing world (one in four) were living on less than $1.25 a day[1] in 2005, down from 1.9 billion (one in two) in 1981 (Chen and Ravallion, 2008). Poverty in East Asia, the world's poorest region in 1981, has fallen from nearly 80 percent of the population living on less than $1.25 a day in 1981 to 18 percent in 2005 (about 340 million), largely owing to dramatic progress in poverty reduction in China (Chen and Ravallion, 2008). If national

---

[1]The new international poverty line of $1.25 a day at 2005 prices is the mean of the national poverty lines for the 10–20 poorest countries of the world.

Table 1.1

Percentage of Population Living Below National Poverty Line

	Survey year	National (%)	Urban (%)	Rural (%)
Thailand	1998	14	n.a.	n.a.
Indonesia	1999	27	16	34
Vietnam	2002	29	7	36
Cambodia	2004	35	18	38
Philippines	1997	37	22	51
Lao PDR	1997–98	39	27	41

Source: World Bank (2007).
Note: National Poverty Line is the minimum level of income deemed necessary to achieve
an adequate standard of living in a given country.

poverty line is used, 27% to 39% of the total population in Indonesia, Vietnam, Cambodia, Philippines and Laos lived below the national poverty line (see Table 1.1). In the more developed economies of Thailand, the percentage was 14%.

The national absolute poverty line used has often masked the severity of the absolute poverty problem in rural areas. Table 1.1 shows the percentage of population living below the national absolute poverty line in Southeast Asia. In all the countries shown, the rural population has a higher percentage of people living in absolute poverty compared to its urban counterpart. There is a close link between poverty and unemployment as well as underemployment. Without employment and consequently the absence of a regular stream of income, the incidence of poverty rises. If this phenomenon of unemployment or underemployment persists, the gap between the haves and have-nots widens, contributing to growing income inequality.

Although economic growth is a necessary condition for reducing absolute poverty, it is not a sufficient condition. If the incomes of the rich are rising faster than those of the poor, then the rich will become richer and the poor will become poorer, in a relative sense. One key to the eradication of poverty is thus the creation of enough job opportunities to eliminate as much unemployment and underemployment as possible. This indirectly implies that for many low-income economies population growth must be moderated to help to ensure that jobs created are sufficient to absorb past surplus labour and new labour seeking employment.

Diagram 1.1
Lorenz Curve

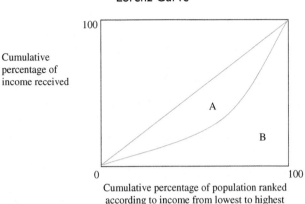

When dealing with relative poverty, a common measure of income distribution is to divide the incomes received by the bottom 20% by the incomes received by the top 20%. This figure indicates the degree of inequality between the two extremes of the very rich and the very poor in a country.

Another way to measure income inequality is to draw the Lorenz curve. The curve shows the relation between the cumulative population proportion and the cumulative proportion of income received (see Diagram 1.1). The diagonal line is the line of equality. The area between the line of equality and the Lorenz curve is marked as A while the area outside the Lorenz curve is marked as B. When the distribution of income becomes less equal, the Lorenz curve diverges from the diagonal line. In other words, the area denoted by A increases. The more the Lorenz curve diverges, the greater the degree of inequality.

To facilitate comparison, a number derived from the Lorenz curve, known as the Gini coefficient, is used. A Gini coefficient of zero represents perfect equality while an index of 100 implies perfect inequality.

$$\text{Gini coefficient} = \frac{A}{A + B}$$

Table 1.2 shows the income distribution of countries in Southeast Asia. Laos has the lowest Gini coefficient of 34.6 while Malaysia has the highest. Dividing the incomes received by the lowest 20% by the incomes

Table 1.2

Measures of Income Distribution

	Survey Year	Gini coefficient	Lowest 20% over highest 20%
Lao PDR	2002	34.6	0.19
Vietnam	2004	37.0	0.16
Indonesia	2005	39.4	0.15
Cambodia	2004	41.7	0.14
Thailand	2002	42.0	0.13
Singapore	1998	42.5	0.10
Philippines	2003	44.5	0.11
Malaysia	1997	49.2	0.08

Source: World Bank, WDI Online, 28 Nov. 2008, http://publications.worldbank.org/WDI/.

received by the highest 20% yields a similar conclusion. However, one must take into account the time differences in between different surveys conducted and the different concepts used in estimating incomes in different countries.

Simon Kuznets (1955) postulated that at the initial stages of economic development, income distribution is relatively equal. However, as the economy grows, the distribution of income will become more unequal. But it will reach a point where any further economic growth will result in a decrease in income inequality. This is known as the Kuznets' Inverted U hypothesis and is depicted graphically in Diagram 1.2. The hypothesis, however, was not supported by empirical studies of Singapore and Taiwan. Rao (1996) showed that Singapore's Gini coefficient decreased from a high of 46 in 1973 to a low of 42 in 1978 before it increased to a high of 47 in 1993. This is a typical U curve, albeit a relatively mild one. Similarly, in Taiwan, Lim, C. Y. (1991) showed that the Gini coefficient decreased from 36.2 in 1968 to 30.3 in 1980 before it increased to 31.7 in 1985, producing yet another U curve. On the other hand, empirical study of Malaysia supports the Kuznets inverted U-curve hypothesis; income inequality worsened in the 1960s and improved in the 1980s (Hashim, 1998). Nevertheless, the challenge faced by Southeast Asian countries must be, first of all, the eradication of absolute poverty in their respective countries. There must, however, be countries where Kuznet's Inverted U curve holds.

Diagram 1.2
Kuznets' Inverted U Hypothesis

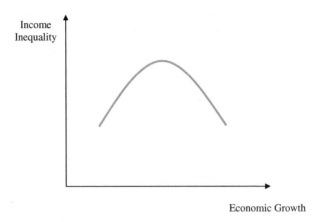

Agricultural Issues

With the exception of Singapore and Brunei, all the other economies in Southeast Asia are agricultural-based. For example, countries in mainland Southeast Asia have more than half of their economically active population employed in the agricultural sector. As mentioned earlier, there are three types of agricultural systems in Southeast Asia. The problems faced by the shifting cultivators are the most worthy of attention. It boils down largely to the question of how hill tribes and isolated families can be integrated into the modern, market-oriented, cash economy. The commercialisation and modernisation of the subsistence agricultural sector should thus be urgently looked into with a view to raise the standards of living and to enhance the quality of farmers' lives. Many have viewed the primitive nature of shifting cultivation not only as a waste of land but also as a threat to the surrounding environment. Dry paddy, which is the main crop cultivated by these tribal people, has very low productivity. Although the amount of labour and manure applied are greater than those on wet paddy, the output is lower. Furthermore, dry paddy consumes much more nutrients from the soil than wet paddy. For that reason, land used to grow dry paddy has to be left fallow for a longer period of time before it can be used for cultivation again. Because of such low productivity, the standard of living of these tribal people never rises above the subsistence level.

Shifting cultivation has also been identified as the one of the many causes of forest loss and soil erosion. The clearing of forest by burning is a major source of air pollution. Moreover, it adds to the greenhouse gases and thus contributes to global warming. The biodiversity of the country is also reduced as the clearing of land for cultivation destroys the natural habitat of wildlife. Shifting cultivators of some Southeast Asian countries are already under pressure from their Governments to cease this practice and switch to sedentary farming.

The tension between shifting cultivators and Governments over the use of land is expected to worsen especially when the countries require more land to develop their economies. For example in Sarawak, 1.5 million hectares of land were designated by the Malaysian Government as Native Customary Land (NCL). Under the concept of NCL, the land adjoining the dwellings of the Dayaks, marked by natural boundaries such as rivers, streams and mountain ranges belonged to the community. Furthermore, the Dayaks' rights to the land were recognised and protected by the Sarawak Land Code (SLC) of 1958. However, as the oil palm industry is expected to be Sarawak's next main engine of economic growth, the amount of land to be earmarked as oil palm plantations will also increase. Most of the land in Sarawak is found to be suitable for planting oil palm. Currently, the State Government refuses to recognise any land not continuously cultivated by the Dayaks as NCL.

The "Green Revolution" in Southeast Asia has increased the yield of wet rice cultivation. But compared to some developed and developing countries, the yield is still relatively low. This can be attributed to several reasons. For example, in some countries such as Thailand and Myanmar, the rice farmers are reluctant to cultivate HYVs. In some other countries, the lower economic status of the farmers impairs their ability to grow HYVs, which require more expensive imported chemical fertilisers and pesticides. Another problem faced by the rice farmers is the difficulty in pledging their land as collateral to secure loans. This problem has its roots in the way land ownership in some Southeast Asian countries has been structured. The lack of credit thus inhibits the rice farmers from making the necessary productive investments. Although the rice farmers have the option of turning to infor-mal sources for the required financial resources, the exorbitant interest rates charged greatly reduce the return of the undertaking. Most rice farmers run the risk of losing their land to money lenders. Many have already become landless farmers.

Small rubber estates also suffer from low productivity. In addition, they are not able to compete with the larger rubber plantations in terms of resources and manpower. These larger rubber estates are able to enjoy economies of scale because of their size; they also have professional personnel to oversee the daily operations of the plantations. In some Southeast Asian countries, the difficulties have caught the attention of the Governments. For example in Malaysia, agencies have been set up to improve the standard of living of these smallholders. One of these agencies is RISDA (Rubber Industry Smallholders Development Authority). Established in the 1970s, RISDA's primary objective is to help the smallholders by giving out grants to cover a significant portion of the replanting costs. Other agencies include FELDA (Federal Land Development Authority) and FELCRA (Federal Land Consolidation and Rehabilitation Agency), although the latter two agencies do not restrict themselves to helping only those smallholders in the rubber industry.

Natural Resource Development

Southeast Asia is one of the richest regions in the world in terms of natural resources. The resources can be broadly classified into three main groups, namely, minerals, oil, natural gas, and timber. Malaysia was, for many decades, once a leading producer of tin, both in Southeast Asia and in the world. However, the position of being the largest tin producer in Southeast Asia has been overtaken by Indonesia. Indonesia is now the world's biggest exporter of tin and the world's second largest producer of tin. The country, which is expected to produce about 90,000 tonnes of tin in 2008, was estimated to have proven tin reserves of about 800,000 tonnes. Other countries that are found to have tin deposits include Malaysia, Thailand, Laos and Myanmar. Besides tin, countries in Southeast Asia are also well endowed with other mineral resources. For example, copper can be mined in Indonesia, Malaysia, Myanmar and the Philippines, gold and silver in Indonesia, Myanmar and the Philippines, phosphates and manganese in Vietnam and Cambodia, and tungsten in Myanmar and Thailand. Lowervalue minerals are also found in some Southeast Asia countries.

Indonesia, Malaysia and Vietnam have known reserves of bauxite, a clay-like substance from which aluminium is obtained.

It has been estimated that Southeast Asia possesses around 5% of the world's proven oil and gas reserves. The important energy developers in the region are Indonesia, Malaysia, Brunei and Myanmar. For example, Brunei in 2006 produced on average 198,000 barrels of crude oil per day and extracted 22,000 barrels of natural gas per day. Myanmar has also been found to possess small quantities of oil and significant amount of natural gas. Since the completion of two offshore gas fields, Yadana and Yetagun, gas has become Myanmar's largest export in 2001. From 59 billion cubic feet of natural gas produced in 1996, the volume increased almost eight-fold to 460 billion cubic feet in 2006–07. One burning issue facing Brunei is that in less than 10 years, the country's oil reserves will be fully exploited. Its gas reserves are estimated to last longer, about 35 years. As an economy that has depended totally on earnings from the sale of petroleum, what are the options available to Brunei to sustain the growth of its economy? This illustrates the importance of proper natural and human resources management to achieve sustainable long-term economic development.

Similar arguments can be made about forest resources. About half of Southeast Asia is covered with forest. Thus, it is not surprising to note that all Southeast Asian countries except Singapore are producers of timber. Unlike non-renewable resources such as minerals and oil, forests can be replaced if given sufficient time to regenerate. However, this has not been the case. The timber export boom that began in the 1960s has resulted in an alarming rate of deforestation. But it would be unfair to blame commercial logging for all the deforestation. Other parties that are equally guilty include shifting cultivators, plantation owners and collectors of wood for fuel. For example, Indonesian forests are shrinking at an average rate of 1.87 million hectares per year between 2000 and 2005. Six main causes for the deforestation in Indonesia have been identified. Subsistence farmers are clearing the forest to cultivate subsistence and cash crops. There is also widespread illegal logging organised by local civilian and military officials and influential businessman. Natural forests are being converted to large-scale commercial agriculture and timber plantations. In addition, forests have been cleared for transmigration settlements. Lastly, the expansion of mining, oil exploration and production and other forms of industrial development have reduced the size of forests significantly.

While there is over-utilisation of several natural resources, there are also incidences of under-utilisation. Because of its active volcanic activities, Indonesia has many hot springs and these hot springs are ideal resources for developing the tourism industry and earning foreign exchange for the country. However, so far, few such projects have been undertaken.

Environmental Degradation

Some observers have pointed out that Southeast Asia's economic success has been achieved at the expense of its environment. Air and water pollution are the two most serious environmental problems cited. The increase in consumption of fossil fuel due to industrialisation, population explosion accompanied by increase in real income, and rapid urbanisation, are the main culprits for the worsening of air quality. Automobiles and industrial emissions are the two major contributors of air pollution. In major Southeast Asian cities such as Bangkok, Jakarta and Manila, the large motorcycle population produces tonnes of obnoxious fumes each day. The phenomenal economic growth over the past few decades has increased the number of people in the middle class, which has in turn increased the demand for private transportation, thus compounding the already severe problem of air pollution. The combustion of fuel releases toxic air pollutants such as sulphur dioxide, nitrogen oxide, and carbon monoxide. Thus, it is very common to see motorcyclists putting on masks to filter the air when they are on the road and to hear about traffic police developing serious respiratory problems. The fast industrialising economies of Southeast Asia also hasten the burning of fossil fuel to generate sufficient electricity for offices and factories. Factories such as those in the petrochemical industry can also contribute to air pollution by discharging harmful gases into the stratosphere.

There is also a type of air pollution that is specific to Southeast Asia. Commonly known as the haze problem, the pollution is caused by deliberately-set fires to clear land for plantations to grow cash crops such as oil palm, rubber, timber and cocoa. Take Indonesia, for instance, where plantation owners see the burning of forests as a faster and cheaper way to prepare the land for cultivation. The problem is compounded by shifting cultivators who engage in slash-and-burn agriculture. To remedy the problem, the Indonesian Government has imposed fine and jail terms on the law-breakers. Thus far, the measures have not been very effective in curbing the fire and preventing the haze from recurring. The haze problem has severe economic repercussions not only on the country involved but also on the surrounding countries. Businesses in the tourism industry are the worst hit, as tourists stayed away from the region. The health of the people is also affected. High incidence of absenteeism results in lower productivity. It has also been reported that the haze reduces visibility and sunlight hours. The latter has led to a decline in crop yields and fish landing.

Water pollution is also rampant in Southeast Asia. The most common water pollutant is sewage, which consists mainly of human excreta and domestic waste. As many parts of Southeast Asia have no proper sewage systems, rivers and streams are often used as toilets. Waste created by industrial production is another contributor to water pollution. Similar to air pollution, water pollution affects the health of the people. The effluent discharged by the factories is also detrimental to marine life and the marine ecosystem.

Another serious environmental problem faced by Southeast Asia is deforestation. The rapid rate of forest destruction as expounded earlier has had serious repercussions on the people. To ecologists, forests are nature's "lungs" responsible for recycling waste and purifying the air. They also help to prevent soil erosion that leads to landslides and flooding.

Human Resource Development

The development of human resources in Southeast Asia is another important issue that needs to be addressed. Three distinct but related areas, namely population growth, education and employment are identified. The population explosion observed in the region will compromise the increase in the quality of life, particularly in human capital formation. First of all, there is pressure on the land to produce more food to feed the people. In addition, more children born to a family also means each child will be allocated a smaller portion of the family's resources of money, energy and time. Children will have less opportunity to receive a proper education. Similarly, when population growth rate does not commensurate with growth of labour demand, unemployment and underemployment will result. The type of education affects employment too. A country may also train people not demanded by the labour market, thus contributing to unemployment and underemployment.

Between 1975 and 2007, Southeast Asia's population grew at 1.8% per year. This was faster than the world's average of 1.5% per year. One of the most serious problems associated with population explosion is overcrowding, especially in the bigger urban areas. The movement of people to the cities, especially to the primate cities, has resulted in severe congestion and the mushrooming of slums. Thus, a challenge to Southeast Asia is to have small, high quality families. The challenge is to mobilise resources, particularly in education and health care, to enhance the quality of life.

During colonial days, the literacy rate was very low in Southeast Asia. In 1960, all the countries had less than one-third of their secondary-school-going children enrolled in secondary schools. The colonial powers had very little incentive to build up the human capital of their colonies. They only wanted the population to be "hewers of wood and carriers of water". However, since Independence, the educational situation has improved over the years. Among the various fields of knowledge, science and technology must be emphasised. Technology has been a major driving force behind industrial and economic progress. Countries are known to be able to expand their output due to higher productivity. Thus, their competitiveness is enhanced through the application of technology. However, although the educational level of the population in Southeast Asia since Independence has increased significantly, it is still much lower compared to other nations. For instance, in 2005, only Singapore (87%) and the Philippines (81%) had relatively high combined primary, secondary and tertiary gross enrolment ratios among Southeast Asian countries (see Table 2.9). The ratios are marginally comparable to Japan (86%) and United States (93%). The rest of the Southeast Asian countries have ratios ranging from 50% in Myanmar to 78% in Brunei.

The attainment of full employment is another challenge for the Southeast Asia countries. Unemployment is common in the urban centres, while underemployment is prevalent, especially in the rural areas. These "spare" human resources can be better utilised to eradicate poverty and to achieve higher standards of living. Many of the themes addressed in this chapter are further elaborated and discussed in subsequent chapters.

National Unity

Another serious challenge faced by some Southeast Asian countries is how to achieve greater national cohesion among their people in a polyglot nation. Notably in Myanmar, Indonesia, the Philippines and Thailand, separatist groups are asking for greater autonomy if not total Independence. The two major fault lines that have been dividing the people are ethnicity and religion. That these people also live in separate parts of the country compounds a separate identity problem.

For the past 50 years, Myanmar has been plagued by insurgency activities by the various ethnic minorities in the country demanding greater autonomy or complete Independence. The problem dates back to the colonial days when the British followed the divide-and-rule policy. They did not allow the majority Burmese to be in the Army or Civil Service. After Independence, the position took a different turn. The ethnic minorities of Chin, Kachin, Karen, Karenni, Mon and Shan were marginalised politically and economically. Throughout the 1960s, Government troops were fighting the ethnic separatist movements. In 1989, following the break-up of the Communist Party of Burma, the Government negotiated a series of cease-fire agreements with the ethnic minorities. In all, 15 cease-fire agreements and three "surrender in exchange for immunity from prosecution"-type deals were officially made across the country. The only minority group that had not signed a cease-fire agreement with the State Law and Order Restoration Council (SLORC) was the Karens. However, the cease-fire agreements, which were observed initially, started to unravel in 1996. Following the defection in part of his Mong Tai Army in 1994 and an ongoing battle for control over key areas of the Myanmar-Thai border, Khun Sa signed a surrender deal with Yangon in January 1996. But one of Khun Sa's commanders refused to accept the deal and resurrected the long-defunct Shan United Revolution Army to fight the Government. The cease-fire agreement with the Karenni Nationalities Progressive Party (KNPP) also started to fall apart. Arguments over profit-sharing of logging deals on the Thai border with local Myanmar Government military commanders spilled over into full-scale fighting between the Karenni force and the Myanmar Army. Although ceasefire talks continue sporadically, there have been no further developments and the fighting continues.

Emboldened by Timor-Leste's success in 1999, the other restive provinces re-intensified their calls for Independence from Indonesia. Two of the main hot spots are Aceh and Western New Guinea. Aceh, a province in the northern tip of Sumatra Island, is rich in natural resources. The Dutch took more than three decades of war to subjugate Aceh in the early 20th century. To reward the Acehnese's effort in supporting Indonesia's struggle against the Dutch, Indonesia's late President Sukarno agreed to grant autonomy to the province. But the promise was not fulfilled. Aceh first rebelled against Jakarta in 1953. When Suharto took over as Indonesia's President, he promised to raise living standards and increase religious freedom. Instead, Suharto took control of Aceh's resources and sent his army to crush the rebels. In 1976, the Free Aceh Movement (Gerakan Aceh Merdeka, GAM) declared the province Independent. But by the early 1980s, the Indonesian army had recaptured the province and forced most of GAM's leaders into exile. In 1989, GAM re-emerged but was swiftly suppressed the following year. Ever since, the Acehnese have constantly demanded an Independence Referendum from Jakarta. Aceh's disdain for the Jakarta Government has been aggravated by two factors. First, the atrocities committed by the armed forces earned the wrath of the local people. Homes and even villages suspected of helping the separatist movement were set on fire, and individuals thought to be supporters of GAM were subject to arbitrary arrest, torture and execution. Second, the Central Government exploited the province's natural resources without benefiting the Acehnese. For example, most of the proceeds generated by the Arun natural gas fields in northern Aceh went to the Central Government. After Abdurrahman Wahid became President, he attempted to make amendments by establishing a civilian-military tribunal to prosecute soldiers accused of human rights violations. Other goodwill gestures included appointing an Acehnese as deputy military commander, building a $60-million railway and allowing Aceh to keep 75% of its forestry, agriculture, oil and gas earnings. Despite efforts at maintaining peace, in May 2003, a major clash erupted between the Indonesian army and rebels in the Aceh province as a result of a failed negotiation held in Tokyo. Issues of autonomy and independence remain points of contention. However in 2004, Aceh took a direct hit from a massive tsunami. Large number of people in Aceh was killed or missing or made homeless. This event helped trigger the peace agreement between the government of Indonesia and the GAM, mediated by former Finnish President Martti Ahtisaari, with the signing of an MOU on August 2005.

The conflict in Western New Guinea (formerly known as Irian Jaya) dated back to 1945. The province still belonged to the Dutch when Indonesia became independent. In 1962, the Dutch ceded the territory to the United Nations, which in 1963 transferred the rights to the territory to Indonesia on a provisional basis. Indonesia was to hold a territorial referendum within five years. The referendum did not take place. In 1969, tribal leaders were brought together to agree to the integration with Indonesia. During the same period, the separatist group, Free Papua Movement (Organisasi Papua Merdeka, OPM) was born. In 1971, OPM announced the formation of an Independent Government of West Papua and stepped up the guerrilla resistance against the Central Government. However, repression under former President Suharto hounded the separatist movement to near extinction. The bombing of suspected rebel zones in 1984 caused nearly 20,000 Irians to flee to neighbouring Papua New Guinea. Charges of violence and exploitation were also made against the Indonesian Government. It has been estimated that during the 30 years of Indonesian rule, tens of thousands to hundreds of thousands of Irians were exterminated. Western New Guinea has been estimated to possess one-quarter of Indonesia's natural resources. During the Abdurrahman Wahid administration in 2000, Papua gained a "Special Autonomy" status, an attempted political compromise between separatists and the central government.

How successful will calls for Independence be, especially for Aceh? Unlikely say most observers. The rich endowment of natural resources makes it costly for Indonesia to give up the sovereignty of the two provinces. Besides, unlike Timor-Leste, the international community has been silent on the issue. Several reasons have been put forward for this impassivity. The breakaway of Aceh would further encourage Independence movements in other provinces such as Western New Guinea and Riau, leading to a "Balkanisation" of Indonesia, which in turn would destabilise Southeast Asia politically and economically. Another reason Aceh has not captured the world's sympathy is that the rebels have been equally guilty of many misdeeds. It has been reported that the rebels burnt uncooperative villages, turned villagers into refugees and moved them to camps in mosques in a bid to control the civilian population. Rebels also went from door to door to demand donations of money and supplies.

The existence of a Muslim community in the Mindanao region in the Philippines can be traced as far back as the 13th century. Although the Spaniards colonised the country in 1565, they failed to occupy the southern Philippine islands of Mindanao and the Sulu Archipelago. Nevertheless, the colonial power was successful in converting the local people in other parts of the Philippines to Catholicism. A policy of direct rule was imposed shortly after the Americans took over the country from the Spaniards in 1898. It was at this time that the Moro province was formed and brought under the jurisdiction of the colonial Government in Manila. Several policies implemented by the Americans created widespread resentment among the Muslim community. The introduction of a secular education system and the appointment of non-Muslim teachers to the Moro schools were seen as a challenge to the authority of the religious teachers. As a result, the Moro people refused to send their children to the schools, leading to a high level of illiteracy. To further aggravate the frustration, the Americans encouraged non-Muslims to transmigrate to the Moro province by providing loans and increasing the amount of land given to these settlers. The Public Lands Act of 1919 allowed Catholic Filipinos to apply for land up to 24 hectares, while non-Catholics could only apply for no more than 10 hectares. Consequently, the Moro people lost much of their ancestral lands.

After WWII, the Muslim community started their struggle for Independence. The Philippines Government continued the discriminatory policy of its colonial master and encouraged a further influx of a Catholic population into Mindanao, making the Moro people a minority. Clashes between the Catholics and local Muslims were very common. The Jabaidah massacre led to the formation of the Muslim Independence Movement (MIM) in 1968. The Government's reconciliation effort of giving top MIM leaders high positions in the administration led to the defection of younger MIM cadres and the subsequent formation of the Moro National Liberation Front (MNLF). Bangso Moro Army, the armed wing of the MNLF, frequently engaged in guerrilla warfare against the Philippine Army. In 1976, the Marcos Government and the separatists signed the Tripoli Agreement. The agreement provided the creation of an autonomous region in Mindanao consisting of 13 provinces and nine cities. In return, the MNLF had to reduce its demand for complete Independence. However, the Tripoli Agreement collapsed subsequently due to the denial of certain technicalities by the

Marcos Government. Fighting resumed in late 1977. An internal discord in MNLF led to the establishment of the Moro Islamic Liberation Front (MILF). When Corazon Aquino became President, she granted autonomy to four provinces in Mindanao. The MNLF was still not satisfied, as it wanted autonomy in all the 13 provinces. The relationship between the separatists and the Government improved when Fidel Ramos allowed the MNLF to oversee economic development projects in all provinces in Mindanao for three years. The establishment of the Southern Philippines Council for Peace and Development with the leader of MNLF as the head also helped to restore peace and order in the southern islands. A cease-fire agreement was signed between the Philippine Government and the MNLF in January 1994. Despite these positive developments, sporadic fighting continues. In 2007, the Philippine government offered to recognize the right of self-determination for the Moros which it had never done in over three decades of conflict and intermittent negotiations.

Like all Islamic countries in Southeast Asia, Islam was spread to Pattani, a southern state in Thailand, by the Arab merchants. When Siam (the former name for Thailand) captured Pattani in the 18th century, the Siamese Government divided the state into seven provinces both for administrative purposes and to weaken Muslim power. Although there were intermittent rebellions, the Siamese Government was too strong to be overcome. To integrate the Muslims and to further weaken the Islamic identity, the Siamese Government introduced several measures. The measures, which caused great frustration to the Muslim community, included the replacement of the Islamic Shariah and adat laws with Siamese laws. Furthermore, education was made secular with the Thai language as the medium of instruction. In addition, local rulers were replaced with Thai Governors. The locals were also not allowed to wear sarongs, use Muslim names or the Malay language. After WWII, Pattani came under the direct jurisdiction of the Bangkok Government.

In 1959, an underground separatist movement, Pattani National Liberation Front (Barisan Nasional Pembebasan Pattani, BNPP) was formed with the objectives of gaining complete Independence and establishing an Islamic state. Throughout the 1960s armed guerrilla warfare and sporadic clashes occurred between the Government and BNPP separatists. Subsequent separatist movements can be divided into those carried out by Islamists and those by secularists. The Islamists founded the organisation, National Revolutionary Front (Barisan Revolusi Nasional, BRN) with the aim of forming an independence Islamic country, while the secularists formed the Pattani United Liberation Organisation (PULO). Both organisations viewed the Thai Government as an internal colonial power. Compromise was impossible. The only option was to achieve independence through armed struggle. However, the two groups did not co-ordinate their activities, choosing to pursue their guerrilla actions independently. In response to the Pattani separatist movement, the Thai Government launched a series of military operations against the guerrillas while adopting a policy of accommodating certain demands. In 1961, the Government repealed the Thai Customs Decree and allowed pondok schools to continue, provided they offered both secular and Islamic education. The Pattani Muslims were also allowed to keep Muslim names. In the 1970s, the Government offered some special privileges to Muslims. These included quotas for admissions of Muslims to the universities and government bureaucracy, the establishment of National and Provincial Councils for Islamic Affairs, study tours to Bangkok for Muslims at government expenses, and the creation of the position of state council for Islamic Affairs. Finally, the Government initiated massive economic projects to construct roads, schools, colleges and universities in the Muslim majority provinces. With respect to agriculture, the rubber plantation owners were given incentives to replace old trees with high-yielding varieties. Irrigation systems and flood control projects were introduced to the region. The Muslims did not adopt an optimistic view of these programmes. Instead, many perceived such measures as tricks by the Thai Government to penetrate Pattani culture, economy, and society. Guerrilla activities continued. In 1997, activists across the political spectrum united to form an underground organisation called the Council of the Muslim People of Pattani (MPRMP). Taking inspiration from the Moros' success, they sought to pressure the Thai Government to come to an agreement with the Pattani Muslims.

These separatist political problems in Southeast Asia are very difficult to solve, and yet they are there, and overall economic development has to take place with these problems as a part of the backdrop. A point to note is their confinement to particular regions in these countries.

Economic Growth of China

As of 2007, Southeast Asia, with a population of 0.56 billion, is considerably smaller than China, with its population of 1.33 billion. Moreover, China has just one market while Southeast Asia has ten. Southeast Asia appears fragmented in relation to China. The growing importance of China as an economic power presents many opportunities as well as challenges for ASEAN.

With expectations of China's continued growth over the coming decades, Southeast Asia can look forward to increased export opportunities into China. Since the 1990s, ASEAN countries' export share to China has shown steady increase. China's import share from ASEAN has increased from 6% to 9% over the 15 years. In the chapter on rubber, China consumed 6% of the world natural rubber supply in 1960. By 2003–05, this had increased to 20%. Much of the imports came from Southeast Asia. Southeast Asia's exports of other primary commodities such as palm oil, rice and cane sugar from Thailand and Vietnam, food and feed grain products from Malaysia and the Philippines will also benefit from the reduction of non-tariff barriers in China, a result of China's accession to the World Trade Organisation (WTO). This will help fuel growth in the Southeast Asian region. However, some ASEAN industries, such as the textile and garment industries that export to the United States and Japan started facing stiff competition from China especially when quotas on textiles and apparel from China to Europe and North America were lifted in 2005.

Overall, the collective growth of Southeast Asian vis-à-vis the rise of China hinges on the ability of ASEAN countries to tap the huge and growing market in China. Southeast Asia can also benefit from investment inflow and the inflow of cheaper goods and services from China. Even increased tourism from China can provide an additional fillip to the Southeast Asian economies. However, in the face of increasing competition from China, hollowing out of some manufacturing industries, particularly of the foot-loose varieties and the diversion of new FDI and tourism to China, is inevitable. This makes the challenge for ASEAN to have a single market a much more pressing issue than would otherwise be the case. The rest of this book deals in more detail with a comparative study of the problems of economic growth and development of Southeast Asia, focusing on and evaluating some economic sectors and economic issues and policy options facing the ten Southeast Asian nations.

Key Points

1. Southeast Asia can be divided into mainland Southeast Asia and maritime Southeast Asia. The two sub-regions are different physically, culturally, if not also economically. Notwithstanding the differences, strong similarities exist. The countries have similar climatic conditions and shared a common colonial past, and much of economic backwardness.

2. There are three types of agricultural systems in Southeast Asia, namely, shifting cultivation, wet rice cultivation and plantation agriculture. Shifting cultivation is commonly practised by the hill tribes in the forested highlands in all countries in the region except the city-state of Singapore. Wet rice cultivation is mainly for self-sufficiency but countries such as Thailand and Vietnam export part of their produce. Plantation agriculture was introduced by the colonial powers.

3. Western colonisation had significantly changed Southeast Asia, not only economically, socially but also politically. The retreat of the Western colonial powers from Southeast Asia was followed by the emergence of ten separate independent nations in Southeast Asia, each seeking its own dream of the future and each inherited a different colonial economic, social and political past.

4. The original motive for the establishment of ASEAN was political in nature. However, with the dramatic changes in the world political environment, ASEAN has evolved into a more economic-oriented organisation. ASEAN Free Trade Area is an option ASEAN as a group has agreed to pursue and implement. This will help to enlarge the ASEAN fragmented markets into a larger single entity.

5. To achieve a higher standard living for its people, Southeast Asia must overcome several challenges. One major challenge is the eradication of abject poverty and the lessening of lopsided development within the countries. With an economy that is largely agricultural, Southeast Asia must also tackle a host of agricultural-related problems. In addition, the issue of proper natural resources management without suffering from environmental degradation must also be addressed. How to develop

human resources to the fullest and how to achieve greater cohesion among people of a polyglot nation are the other two challenges facing Southeast Asia. These problems have been further compounded by population explosion in much of Southeast Asia.

Suggested Discussion Topics

1.1 "Although economic growth is a necessary condition for eradicating poverty, it is not a sufficient condition." Discuss this statement in relation to poverty in Southeast Asia. Besides poverty, discuss other challenging economic issues in Southeast Asia such as the modernisation of agriculture.

1.2 It is said that Southeast Asian nations do not have a common history except being colonised by the Western powers. Are all the major problems faced by Southeast Asia today the direct result of separate Western colonisations? Does post-Independence management have a lot to do with the well-being, especially material well-being of these nations? Discuss.

References

CHEN, Shaohua and Martin RAVALLION, 2008, "The developing world is poorer than we thought, but no less successful in the fight against poverty", *Policy Research Working Papers 4703,* The World Bank.

HASHIM, Shireen Mardziah, 1998, *Income Inequality and Poverty in Malaysia*, Lanham (Maryland): Rowman & Littlefield Publishers.

KUZNETS, Simon, 1955, "Economic growth and income inequality", *American Economic Review*, Vol. 45(1), 1–28.

LIM, Chong Yah, 1991, *Development and Underdevelopment*, Singapore: Longman.

RAO, V. V. Bhanoji, 1996, "Income inequality in Singapore: Facts and policies", in LIM Chong Yah (ed.), *Economic Policy Management in Singapore*, Singapore: Addison-Wesley.

World Bank, 2000, *World Development Report 2000/01: Attacking Poverty*, New York: Oxford University Press.

World Bank, 2007, *World Development Report 2008: Agriculture for Development*, Washington, D.C.: The World Bank.

Further Readings

ACHARYA, Amitav and Richard STUBBS, 1995, *New Challenges for ASEAN: Emerging Policy Issues*, Canada: UBC Press.

KRUMM, Kathie and Homi KHARAS (eds.), 2003, *East Asia Integrates: A Trade Policy Agenda for Shared Growth*, Advance Edition, Washington, D.C.: World Bank.

LEE, Kuan Yew, 2000, *From Third World to First: The Singapore Story: 1965–2000, Memoirs of Lee Kuan Yew*, Singapore: Singapore Press Holdings.

LEWIS, W. Arthur (ed.), 1970, *Tropical Development, 1880–1913: Studies in Economic Progress*, London: Allen & Unwin.

TEOFILO, C. Daquila, 2005, *The Economies of Southeast Asia: Indonesia, Malaysia, Philippines, Singapore and Thailand*, New York: Nova Science Publishers.

World Bank, 1997, *World Development Report 1997: The State in a Changing World*, New York: Oxford University Press.

Chapter 2

Economic Diversity

The Squirrel told the Mountain,
"If I cannot carry forests on my back,
Neither can you crack a nut."
Ralph Waldo Emerson, *FABLE*

Objectives

✓ Identify the differences in per capita income.
✓ Point out the differences in growth rates.
✓ Describe the composition of GDP.
✓ Describe the composition of labour force.
✓ Show the differences in investment rates.
✓ Highlight the differences in the degree of trade orientation.
✓ Provide explanations for the economic diversity.

Introduction

The diversity in Southeast Asia is reflected by the ten separate independent nations. The legacies from different colonial pasts, different languages used, different religious orientations and different ethnicities in demographic composition constitute the human landscape of Southeast Asia. However, the ten Southeast Asian countries are in close geographical proximity to each other, and are all contiguously sandwiched between the Indian Ocean in the West and the Pacific Ocean in the East, with the

South-China Sea sharing a common border with all of them, except Laos and Myanmar. This chapter deals with some economic aspects of the diversity among the ten Southeast Asian nations.

Economic development refers to sustained increases in per capita production of a country, normally measured by trend rates of growth in per capita Gross National Income (GNI). It is also likely to involve shifts in the composition of domestic demand and production, and changes in the composition of labour force and of foreign trade and finance. Since people all over the world share common patterns in wants, tastes and consumer demand, a universal pattern of development for countries over time can be expected. A country's development pattern is also affected by its resource endowment, market size, trade and economic policies, human resource development and the external economic environment. In addition, a country's history, its political and social objectives and the particular policies it has followed, can also influence its development pattern.

When universal forces interact with country-specific factors such as natural endowment or government policies, one expects to find different historical development patterns. This leads to a state of economic diversity among countries. There are many indicators one can use to illustrate the economic differences. However, we are going to highlight the more crucial ones, some of which have far-reaching implications for economic development.

Economic Diversity

There are approximately 563 million people in Southeast Asia in 2007. Together, the ten nations, namely Brunei, Cambodia, Indonesia, Laos, Malaysia, Myanmar, the Philippines, Singapore, Thailand and Vietnam, form the Association of Southeast Asian Nations (ASEAN). Unlike economic groupings such as the European Union, the different countries within ASEAN have different levels of economic development. Southeast Asia is dotted with internet-savvy professionals, competent managers, and surgeons and engineers who can manage sophisticated instruments and machinery. But, at the same time, in almost every country in Southeast Asia, it also has a large number of shifting cultivators and subsistence farmers. Such occupational disparity is not found in Europe and is a concern Southeast Asian leaders cannot ignore. It is the duty and responsibility of the better-endowed

Table 2.1

Size of GNI, 2007

	GNI, Atlas Method[a] (Current US$ Bn)	% of World's GNI, Atlas Method	GNI, PPP (Current Int'l $ Bn)	% of World's GNI, PPP
Lao PDR	3.4	0.01	11.4	0.02
Cambodia	7.9	0.01	24.5	0.04
Brunei[b]	10.3	0.02	19.1	0.03
Vietnam	67.2	0.13	216.9	0.33
Philippines	142.6	0.27	327.8	0.50
Singapore	149.0	0.28	222.7	0.34
Malaysia	173.7	0.33	360.2	0.55
Thailand	217.3	0.41	503.1	0.77
Indonesia	373.1	0.71	807.9	1.24
Southeast Asia[c]	1,144.6	2.18	2,493.4	3.83
China	3,120.9	5.93	7,083.5	10.87
Japan	4,813.3	9.15	4,420.6	6.79
World	52,621.4	100.00	65,144.4	100.00

Source: World Bank, WDI Online, 11 Nov. 2008, http://publications.worldbank.org/WDI/.

a: The Atlas Method is the World Bank's official estimate of the size of economies. The GNI data are in current U.S. dollars, converted from countries' respective national currencies using the Atlas method, which uses a three-year average of exchange rates to smooth effects of transitory exchange rate.

b: Data for Brunei refer to year 2006.

c: Not including Myanmar as data for Myanmar are not available.

individuals to help the lesser-endowed, not only within a nation, but also across the nations in Southeast Asia. Table 2.1 compares the size of Southeast Asian economies with other countries.

Using Lim C.Y.'s (1996) S Curve Hypothesis, we can classify the ASEAN economies into three groups. The first group consists of countries with low levels of income and low growth rates. They are called the turtle economies. The second group, which is characterised by middle income levels and high growth rates, is called the horse economies. The third group, called the elephant economies, has characteristics of high income levels but low growth rates. Using per capita GDP and per capita GDP growth rates as yardsticks (see Tables 13.1 and 13.2), the Philippines is considered a turtle economy. Singapore and Brunei can be categorised as the elephant economies; Singapore being an incipient elephant economy. The other seven economies — Indonesia, Malaysia, Thailand, Vietnam, Cambodia, Laos and Myanmar — are horse economies or in the transition of becoming horse economies. In Western Europe, however, all the economies are elephant economies.

According to the S Curve Hypothesis, turtle economies are caught in a low-level equilibrium trap. They have low income to begin with. This leads to low savings and low investment, which in turn results in lower growth. Diagram 2.1 illustrates the vicious cycle of the low-level equilibrium trap.

Turtle economies can break away from this poverty trap by raising domestic savings rate and thereafter investment rate. In the absence of

Diagram 2.1
The Low-level Equilibrium Trap

Low Investment

Low Growth

Low Savings

Low Income

Diagram 2.2
The Neo-Malthusian Trap

Higher Investment / Higher Savings

$$(\text{Higher } \frac{\Delta I}{\Delta Y} \text{ / Higher } \frac{\Delta S}{\Delta Y})$$

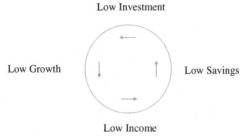

Higher Growth Rate

$(\text{Higher } \frac{\Delta Y}{Y})$

Low Income

$(\frac{Y}{N})$

Higher Population Growth Rate

$(\text{Higher } \frac{\Delta N}{N})$

an increase in domestic savings rate, investment rate could still be raised via foreign investment, foreign aid, and/or foreign borrowings. Higher investment rate would result in a higher income growth rate. However, if consequent on a higher income growth rate, population growth rate also increase, then, there may not be any improvement in the per capita income. Diagram 2.2 illustrates the vicious cycle of the Neo-Malthusian Trap.

Conversely, horse economies have the following characteristics.

1. Control explosive rate of population growth.
2. High savings function.
3. Export oriented industrialisation.
4. Conducive investment climate.
5. High investment in physical capital.
6. High investment in human capital.
7. Priority on economic achievements.
8. Emphasis on market forces as an engine of growth.
9. Good public and corporate governance.

Like the turtle economies, the elephant economies also suffer from low growth rates. However, the reasons for low growth rates are different in the elephant economies. The economic success over long periods of time has dampened these elephant economies' desire for greater economic success. This reduces the marginal utility of money and increases the propensity of leisure, thus leading to lower savings and lower investment, and ultimately lower growth rates. The ageing of the population also contributes to this phenomenon. However, none of the nascent ASEAN elephant economies are typical elephant economies, like Japan, Denmark, New Zealand or Great Britain. However, in Southeast Asia, one sees the existence of three different types of economies, turtles, horses and elephants, unlike Western Europe, where one has only elephants and Africa, where nearly all are turtles. Nevertheless, the turtles in Southeast Asia show positive signs of emerging as horses and some of the horses also show positive signs of taking a pause in development rates. Chapter 13 contains a more thorough discussion of Southeast Asian countries in relation to the S Curve analysis as well as against the other two facets of the Trinity Growth Theory, namely, the EGOIN Theory and the Triple C Theory.

Differences in Per Capita Income

The differences in per capita income reflect, to a large extent, the differences in standards of living. They also reflect differences in the productive capacity of the countries. Table 2.2 shows the divergence in per capita income levels among the countries in Southeast Asia. In 2007, for example, the level of per capita GNI for Singapore (US$32,470) was close to 60 times higher than that for Cambodia (US$540). Even if 20% to 30% discount were to be given to an urban economy like Singapore, the difference in economic diversity would still be vast. According to the World Bank classification, Malaysia belongs to the upper-middle-income category, while Thailand, the Philippines and Indonesia are in the lower-middle-income category. Singapore and Brunei are the only two high-income countries within Southeast Asia.

Even if all the ten economies were to be integrated into a single economy, there will still be vast differences in per capita income because of

Table 2.2

GNI Per Capita, Atlas Method and PPP-Adjusted, 2007

Income Level	Countries	GNI Per Capita, Atlas Method (Current US$)	GNI Per Capita, PPP (Current Int'l $)
High	Singapore	32,470	48,520
	Brunei[a]	26,930	49,900
Upper-middle	Malaysia	6,540	13,570
Lower-middle	Thailand	3,400	7,880
	Indonesia	1,650	3,580
	Philippines	1,620	3,730
Low	Vietnam	790	2,550
	Lao PDR	580	1,940
	Cambodia	540	1,690
Southeast Asia (Weighted Avg.)[b]		2,225	4,848
United States		46,040	45,850
World		7,958	9,852

Source: World Bank, WDI Online, 11 Nov. 2008, http://publications.worldbank.org/WDI/.
  a: Data for Brunei refer to year 2007.
  b: Data for SEA do not include Myanmar as data for Myanmar are not available.

Diagram 2.3
2007 Per Capita GNI, PPP (Current International $)

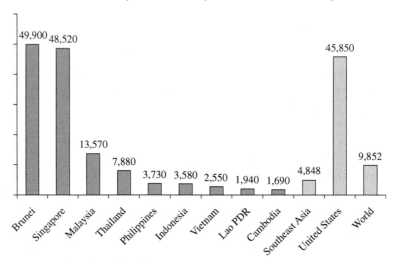

Source: Table 2.2.
Note: Data for Brunei refer to year 2006.

differences in factor endowment. Malaysia is one economy, but the capital Kuala Lumpur is much more developed than Kangar, the state capital of Perlis, one of the Malaysian states, or Kuching, the state capital of Sarawak. Similarly, in China, Shanghai and Beijing are much more developed economically than Guizhou and Shanxi. In Australia, Sydney is much better developed than Alice Springs and Albany, and yet they all belong to the same country. The reduction of differences within the country and across countries must include, *inter alia*, the removal of man-made obstacles to the flow of factors from the wealthier regions to the under-developed regions. However, within the same country, active measures can also be taken purposely to develop the less developed regions, but the forces of economic growth in favour of the more developed regions must be recognised. To spread poverty is easier done than to spread wealth or development.

Per capita income converted to US dollars using exchange rates tends to understate the relative income positions of the less developed countries in the world vis-à-vis the relatively more developed countries. This is because the bulk of the goods and services in these countries are not internationally traded and thus they have no direct impact on the balance of payments and the exchange rate (Lim C.Y., 1991). Table 2.2 illustrates the difference in per capita GNI when (3-year average) exchange rates and Purchasing Power Parity (PPP) are used.

In 2007, Malaysia's per capita GNI was 14% of the USA's per capita GNI when the official exchange rate was used. However, it was 30% of the USA's per capita GNI when the PPP was used. Among Southeast Asian countries, per capita GNI differs depending on whether the official exchange rate or the PPP is used. These differences between the official exchange rate and the PPP-adjusted per capita GNI are most obvious in Vietnam, Laos and Cambodia. Laos' per capita GNI was 9% of the Malaysia's per capita GNI when official exchange rates were used. It rose to 14% of Malaysia's per capita GNI when the figure was converted using PPP. Thus, one should bear in mind the limitations of the official exchange rates for deriving comparable per capita income estimates.

Differences in Growth Rates

Per capita income deals with levels of development. The rates of growth deal with the rates of change in such levels. Post-war economic growth rates (that is, average GDP growth rates) differed among the various countries in Southeast Asia, as illustrated in Table 2.3. The Philippines and Myanmar registered annual growth rates of over 6% in GDP in the 1950s (not shown in table), while the others lagged behind. Singapore, Thailand and Malaysia

Table 2.3
Average Annual Growth Rates of GDP (%), 1961–2007

	1961–1970	1971–1980	1981–1990	1991–2000	2001–2007	1961–2007
Indonesia	4.2	7.9	6.4	4.4	5.1	5.6
Malaysia	6.5	7.9	6.0	7.2	4.8	6.6
Myanmar[a]	3.2	4.7	1.4	6.8	9.0	4.6
Philippines	4.9	5.9	1.8	3.1	5.0	4.1
Singapore	9.9	8.8	7.5	7.6	5.3	8.0
Thailand	8.2	6.9	7.9	4.6	5.1	6.6

Source: Computed using data from World Bank, WDI Online, 6 Dec. 2008, http://publications. worldbank.org/WDI/.
a: Data for Myanmar are up to year 2005.

took over the leadership position in the 1960s. In the 1970s, Indonesia joined in with relatively high growth rates. Singapore, Malaysia, and Indonesia each registered an average annual GDP growth of over 7% in the 1970s. In the 1980s, these nations were still growing very rapidly.

Over the last 47 years, as can be seen from the last column of Table 2.3, Singapore has topped the list with an average growth rate of 8.0% per annum, followed by Thailand 6.6%, Malaysia 6.6% and Indonesia 5.6%. This is depicted graphically in Diagram 2.4.

In Simon Kuznets' seminal studies of the national incomes of the developed countries, developed countries displayed growth rates of only 2% to 3% when they were developing. After examining the dramatic economic growth, improved human welfare, and more equitable income distribution in Indonesia, Malaysia, Singapore, and Thailand from 1965 to 1990, the World Bank (1993) described these countries the "East Asian Miracle". Sound government policies promote rapid capital accumulation by making banks more reliable and encouraging high levels of domestic savings. They also increased the skilled labour force by providing universal primary schooling and better primary and secondary education. The World Bank concluded that macroeconomic stability and human and

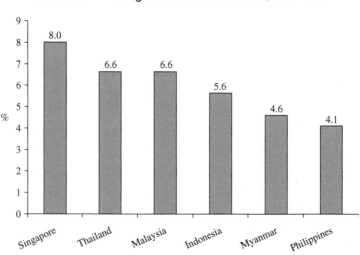

Diagram 2.4
Differences in Average Annual Growth Rates, 1961–2007

Source: Table 2.3.
Note: Data for Myanmar are for 1961–2005.

physical capital development are the foundations for their dramatic and sustainable expansion.

The last two decades were a period of very volatile economic environment for the world as a whole. For the Southeast Asian countries, the benefits and costs of expanding world trade and investment flows as well as financial and economic shocks were felt though in varying degrees. As such, the economic growth of the countries in the last decade of this century has been very uneven. Table 2.4 highlights the major economic events that affected Southeast Asia since 1990.

As mentioned in the earlier section, rapid economic growth accompanied by population explosion may not result in higher standards of living for the populace. Table 2.5 summarises the GDP per capita levels in 1960 and 2007. All member countries of the ASEAN-5 have made significant advancement in GDP per capita over the last 47 years. Of note is Thailand

Table 2.4

Major Economic Events Affecting Southeast Asia

Year	Event
1990	Burst of the Japanese economic bubble
Aug. 1990–Mar. 1991	Gulf War
1990–1992	Economic slowdown in the developed countries
Jul. 1992	European Exchange Rate mechanism crisis
Dec. 1994	Mexican Peso crisis
Feb. 1995	Japanese Yen appreciation and US dollar depreciation
Jul. 1997–Jun. 1999	Asian Financial Crisis
11 Sep. 2001	Terrorists' attack in New York city led to the tumble of the World Trade Centre
Jan. 2002	Financial Fraud: Collapse of Enron
Jul. 2002	Financial Fraud: Collapse of WorldCom
12 Oct. 2002	Bali Bomb Blast
Feb. 2003–Apr. 2003	War on Iraq
Mar. 2003–May. 2003	Outbreak of Severe Acute Respiratory Syndrome (SARS)
26 Dec. 2004	Asian Tsunami
2007–2008	Subprime mortgage crisis in the US led to worldwide financial and economic crisis

Table 2.5
GDP Per Capita (Constant 2000 US$), 1960 and 2007

Country	1960	2007	Compound Annual Growth Rate (%)
Indonesia	196	1034	3.6
Thailand	317	2713	4.7
Philippines	612	1216	1.5
Malaysia	784	4715	3.9
Singapore	2251	28,964	5.6

Source: World Bank, WDI Online, 6 Dec. 2008,
http://publications.worldbank.org/WDI/.

in 1960 which had only half the level of per capita GDP as the Philippines. However, with the rapid economic growth over the years, Thailand by 2007 was well ahead of the Philippines. The advance Singapore has made appears even more striking. Singapore has registered a compound annual growth rate of 5.6% over the last 47 years.

The Indo-Chinese countries and Myanmar compared to Thailand and Malaysia can be said to be some four decades behind in overall economic development. Myanmar and the Indo-Chinese states may not be lacking in the potential for rapid growth; however political stability and growth-oriented economic and social policies over long periods are required to raise the per capita income to significant levels. In the recent years, Indonesia, Malaysia, Thailand and the Philippines have encountered problems of political stability of varying degrees. These problems, if persisted, would have serious detrimental effects on their growth rates.

Composition of GDP

Table 2.6 shows the changes in the composition of GDP across Southeast Asia from 1970 onwards. Agriculture's share of the GDP has been declining for the past thirty over years in all countries except Myanmar. Conversely, industry's share of the GDP has been increasing in most of the countries. In other words, Southeast Asia has been going through a rapid industrialisation process in the last four decades. During this process, the agricultural sector has shrunk proportionately.

Table 2.6

Sectoral Value-Added as Percentage of GDP (%), 1970, 1990 and 2007

Country	Agriculture			Industry			Service		
	1970	1990	2007	1970	1990	2007	1970	1990	2007
Brunei[a]	n.a.	1	1	n.a.	62	73	n.a.	37	26
Cambodia[a]	n.a.	n.a.	30	n.a.	n.a.	26	n.a.	n.a.	44
Indonesia	45	19	14	19	39	47	36	41	39
Lao PDR[a]	n.a.	61	42	n.a.	15	32	n.a.	24	26
Malaysia	29	15	9	27	42	51	43	43	41
Myanmar[b]	38	57	57	14	11	10	48	32	33
Philippines	30	22	14	32	34	31	39	44	55
Singapore	2	0	0	36	35	31	61	65	69
Thailand	26	12	11	25	37	44	49	50	45
Vietnam[a]	n.a.	39	20	n.a.	23	42	n.a.	39	38

Source: World Bank, WDI Online, 6 Dec. 2008, http://publications.worldbank.org/WDI/. Asian Development Bank, *Asian Development Outlook 1996 and 1997* (for Singapore's 1970 figures).
a: Data for the third period refer to year 2006.
b: Data for the third period refer to year 2000.

Until 1970, excluding the city-state of Singapore and the oil-rich state of Brunei, agriculture made up at least a quarter of the GDP in the Southeast Asian countries. However, the trend reversed itself in the 1980s. The share of agriculture in the ASEAN-6 declined to less than a quarter. In Myanmar, the share of agriculture in GDP rose from about 38% in 1970 to 57% in 2000, largely because of the relatively sluggish growth of the non-agricultural sectors resulting from socialist economic policies. Such an autarkic policy has generally tended to prevent the inflow of capital and technology, the factors that have helped the growth of some of the other countries, notably Malaysia, Singapore, Thailand and Indonesia. In the case of Indonesia, agriculture's share in the GDP declined from 45% in 1970 to 14% in 2007. The rather heavy decline of the late 1970s and early 1980s in Indonesia was mostly due to the increase in importance of petroleum that significantly boosted the GDP share of mining and construction.

The Philippines was an early starter in manufacturing growth, but lost its lead in the subsequent decades. The manufacturing share in GDP was more

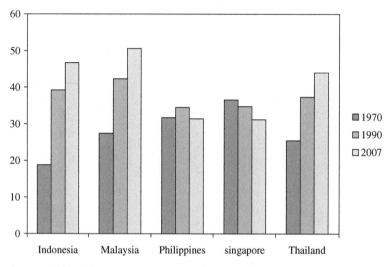

Diagram 2.5
Industry's Share of GDP, 1970, 1990 and 2007

Source: Table 2.6.

than 28% in 1960 (not shown in Diagram 2.5), the highest in Southeast Asia. Even Singapore in 1960 had only an 18% share in manufacturing. Indonesia, Malaysia and Thailand underwent rapid industrialization in the last 4 decades, with the industry sector becoming the most important pillar of their economies (see Diagram 2.5). On the other hand, Singapore's and the Philippines' economies are dominated by the service industry.

Labour Force Composition

Fisher (1935, 1939) introduced the classification of economic activities into primary, secondary, and tertiary activities. He observed that countries could be categorised in terms of the proportions of their total labour force engaged in these sectors. Fisher's insights were subsequently supported by the wide-ranging and imaginative research of a pioneer social statistician, Colin Clark. Clark (1940) calculated the sectoral labour inputs and values of output. The Fisher-Clark hypothesis specified a sequence in labour force use. At relatively low levels of economic development, the proportion of labour force employed in the primary (agriculture, forestry and fishing) sector would be quite high. This high proportion would diminish as development proceeds, and would be replaced by rising proportions first in unsophisticated and then in modern industry. This is because of the relatively high-income elasticity of demand for industrial output. As incomes continue to rise, income elasticity of demand for services of many types will gradually predominate. Labour force allocation in services will rise, as a proportion of the total, owing to improvements in productivity in industry unmatched by similar advances in the service sector. The lowest-income countries, therefore, would be characterised by the highest concentration of workers in agriculture and other primary activities; middle-income countries would feature high proportions in industry; while the highest proportions in services would be found in the high-income countries.

Some economists even propound the theory that economic development in developing countries means the transformation of the economy with 80% of the total population in the primary sector and 20% in the industrial and modern service sector to 20% in the primary sector and 80% in the secondary and tertiary sector (Singer, 1952). However, the productivity in each sector is also of paramount importance.

We can see from Table 2.7 that the labour share in agriculture has declined in almost all of the Southeast Asian countries, with the greatest fall seen in Malaysia, Thailand and Indonesia. Industry's labour share has increased,

Table 2.7
Percentage of Labour Force in Various Sectors (%), 1965 and 2005

Country	Agriculture		Industry		Services	
	1965	2005	1965	2005	1965	2005
Cambodia[a]	80.0	70.2	4.0	10.5	16.0	19.1
Vietnam[b]	79.0	57.9	6.0	17.4	15.0	24.7
Thailand	82.0	42.6	5.0	20.2	13.0	37.1
Indonesia	71.0	44.0	9.0	18.0	20.0	38.0
Philippines	57.0	37.0	16.0	14.9	27.0	48.1
Malaysia[b]	60.0	14.8	13.0	30.1	27.0	55.1
Singapore	6.0	0.0	26.0	29.5	68.0	69.6

Source: World Bank, *World Development Report*, various issues. World Bank, WDI
   Online, 6 Dec. 2008, http://publications.worldbank.org/WDI/.
   a: Data for the second period are for year 2000.
   b: Data for the second period are for year 2004.

although it has continued to remain small with the share being less than 20% in at least four of the Southeast Asian countries. Services labour share has increased in most Southeast Asian countries. From Table 2.7, the transitional economies of Laos, Cambodia, Myanmar, and Vietnam, and, to a lesser extent Thailand, can all be said to be predominantly agricultural economies, while Singapore and Malaysia are more industrialised than their neighbouring countries.

One of the key features of labour absorption needs emphasis. In Cambodia and Vietnam, the percentage of labour force in agriculture even in the 2000s remains above 50%. This is very high indeed. Malaysia provides a counter example where labour absorption in the agricultural sector is declining, falling to 15% in 2004 with the possibility of further decline. Thus, in spite of about four decades of exposure to industrialisation of one type or the other, agricultural activities continue to provide the means of livelihood for the majority of the Southeast Asians. Closely related to the dependence on agriculture is the degree of urbanisation. Malaysia and the Philippines have relatively high proportions (over 60% in 2006) of urban dwellers in the total population, as against the smaller proportions in other countries. The city-state of Singapore, of course, has a 100% urban population and more than two-thirds of the labour force in the service sector. The service sector activities in Singapore, however, are increasingly of the higher-value added activities, such as banking and finance, international transportation and communication and international trade in the more expensive products and services.

Talent Pyramid

As mentioned earlier, there exists a visible diversity of human resources in Southeast Asia in the forms of occupational and income disparity, both within countries and across countries in Southeast Asia. The diversity of human resources in Southeast Asia partly embodies the differences in the educational levels of the people.

Table 2.8 shows that while the net primary enrolment ratios of the ASEAN nations are generally high, the net secondary enrolment ratios and the gross tertiary enrolment ratios fall significantly behind those of Australia, Japan and the United States. If primary, secondary and tertiary

Table 2.8

Enrolment Ratios, 2006

Country	Net Primary Enrolment Rate (%)	Net Secondary Enrolment Rate (%)	Gross Tertiary Enrolment Ratio (%)
Cambodia	90	31	5
Myanmar	100	46	n.a.
Lao PDR	84	35	9
Indonesia	96	59	17
Philippines	91	60	28
Thailand	94	71	46
Vietnam[a]	88	69	32
Malaysia[a]	100	69	29
Brunei	94	90	15
Singapore	97	95	56
Australia	96	87	73
United States	92	88	82
Japan	100	99	57

Source: UNESCO Institute for Statistics, http://www.uis.unesco.org. United Nations, *Human Development Report 2007/2008*, http://hdrstats.undp.org/indicators/. Data on Singapore are from Singapore's Ministry of Education.

    a: Data are for 2005.

Note: The Net Primary/Secondary Enrolment rate is the number of children of official primary/secondary school age who are enrolled in primary/secondary education as a percentage of the total children of the official primary/secondary school age population. The Gross Enrolment Ratio, on the other hand, is calculated by expressing the number of students enrolled in primary/secondary levels of education, regardless of age, as a percentage of the population of official school age for the levels. Data on Net Tertiary Enrolment Rate is not available.

education enrolment ratios of a country are represented by a talent pyramid, the talent pyramid of many of the Southeast Asia countries would be similar to that depicted in Diagram 2.6, where the top of pyramid is narrow. A country with a high degree of human resource development would have a much broader top as depicted in Diagram 2.7. A highly developed country with highly developed human resources, for example the United States, will have a talent pyramid that looks more like a rectangle. Among the ten ASEAN nations, Singapore's talent pyramid is most similar to those of the developed countries.

Diagram 2.6
Talent Pyramid of a Country with Low Human Resource Development

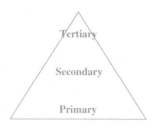

Diagram 2.7
Talent Pyramid of a Country with High Human Resource Development

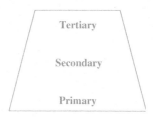

Table 2.9 shows that the combined primary, secondary and tertiary gross enrolment ratio in Australia is as high as 113% and points to the fact that the enrolment of students at certain levels of education could include those from much older age groups. Among the Southeast Asian countries, Singapore and the Philippines have the highest combined gross enrolment ratio of 87% and 81% respectively, while Myanmar and Cambodia have the lowest ratio of 50% and 60% respectively.

Most of the Southeast Asian countries have invested significantly in education over the past few decades after attaining Independence and have greatly built up their level of capital stock. The stock of human capital in each country in Southeast Asia and in Southeast Asia as a whole is still very thin at the top of the talent pyramid. The education index, calculated based on the combined primary, secondary and tertiary gross enrolment ratio as well as the adult literacy rate, constitutes a summary measure of the skills and orientation of the people. An education index of 0.66 in Laos in comparison to an index value of 0.95 in Japan reflects a wide gap in the productivity of these two countries' work force which inevitably points to the diverse GNI levels in both countries (see Table 2.1).

Table 2.9

Human Development Index, Adult Literacy Rate, Combined Gross Enrolment Ratio, and Education Index

Country	Human Development Index 2005	Education Index 2005	Adult Literacy Rate (% Aged 15 and Older) 2005	Combined Gross Enrolment Ratio for Primary, Secondary and Tertiary Education (%) 1995–2005
Myanmar	0.58	0.76	89.9	50
Cambodia	0.60	0.69	73.6	60
Lao PDR	0.60	0.66	68.7	62
Indonesia	0.73	0.83	90.4	68
Vietnam	0.73	0.82	90.3	64
Philippines	0.77	0.89	92.6	81
Thailand	0.78	0.86	92.6	71
Malaysia	0.81	0.84	88.7	74
Brunei	0.89	0.88	92.7	78
Singapore	0.92	0.91	92.5	87
United States	0.95	0.97	99.0[a]	93
Japan	0.95	0.95	99.0[a]	86
Australia	0.96	0.99	99.0[a]	113

Source: United Nations, Human Development Report 2007/2008.
   a: For purposes of calculating the HDI, a value of 99.0% was applied.

Another measurement of human capital development is the Human Development Index (HDI). The HDI measures the average achievements in a country in three basic dimensions of human development: a long and healthy life, knowledge, and a decent standard of living. Human developments vary widely among the ten ASEAN nations. Singapore, Brunei and Malaysia are ranked as countries with high human development while the other six countries are ranked as countries with medium human development. Connected with the problem of small talent pool is the problem of low literacy rate in Southeast Asia. The adult literacy rates in Southeast Asia range from 68.7% in Laos to 92.6% in Thailand and the Philippines. These rates are much lower than the 99% literacy rate achieved in countries such as Japan, the US and Australia.

Small talent pool and high adult illiteracy rates are pressing concerns since it is the talents at the top of the pyramid that are most needed in the new economies of the 21st century. In addition, it is critical to have a well-educated population in order for a country to progress together as a whole. Thus, broadening the top of the talent pyramid, especially in the fields of technology and sciences, and eliminating illiteracy are two major challenges facing the Southeast Asian Governments. It should also be emphasised that education and training should focus on areas of economic endeavour where the Southeast Asian countries have a comparative advantage, instead of areas where they lack this advantage, for example, the building of jet planes. In addition, university curriculum has to be tied closely with industry requirements to avoid the costly and socially undesirable problems of graduate unemployment.

Investment

Southeast Asia is rich in natural and human resources. Land and labour could be brought into higher productive use through investment. As can be seen from Table 2.10, Indonesia, Malaysia, the Philippines, Thailand and Singapore significantly improved their investment rates (defined as gross capital formation as a percentage of GDP) from around 10% to 16% in 1960 to around 24% to 41% in 1990. However, since the occurrence of the Asian Financial Crisis in the late 1990s, investment rates in these countries slowed down considerably from their peak in the 1980s and early 1990s. On the other hand, the emerging economies such as Vietnam, Cambodia and Laos continued to experience a growth investment rate, albeit from a lower base.

Openness and Trade Orientation

While investment in productive capacity augments the total supply in an economy, the demand side is equally important, if output is to be sold and incomes to factors are to accumulate. Several Southeast Asian countries have significant historical links with world markets and global demand for Southeast Asian products may well have been an important factor in the development of these countries. Policies towards export orientation

Table 2.10

Gross Capital Formation (% of GDP), 1960–2007

	1960	1970	1980	1990	2000	2007[a]
Brunei	n.a.	n.a.	n.a.	18.7	13.1	10.4
Cambodia	20.2	12.5	n.a.	8.2	17.5	21.5
Indonesia	9.2	15.8	24.1	30.7	22.2	24.9
Lao PDR	n.a.	n.a.	n.a.	n.a.	20.9	32.5
Malaysia	13.8	20.2	27.4	32.4	27.3	23.1
Myanmar	12.0	14.2	21.5	13.4	12.4	n.a.
Philippines	16.0	21.3	29.1	24.2	21.2	15.0
Singapore	9.7	38.7	46.4	37.1	33.3	22.6
Thailand	15.4	25.6	29.1	41.4	22.8	29.9
Vietnam	n.a.	n.a.	n.a.	12.6	29.6	35.3

Source: World Bank, WDI Online, 6 Dec. 2008, http://publications.worldbank.org/WDI/.
   a: Data for Brunei, Cambodia, Laos and Vietnam refer to year 2006.

enhance economic progress more than policies that promote import substitution. The pivotal role of the Government in the process of economic development is discussed in the EGOIN theory addressed in Chapter 13: Trinity Development Model and Southeast Asian Development. The theory encompasses a comprehensive set of ideas used to explain a country's economic growth and development.

The degree of export orientation has increased significantly in many Southeast Asian countries as indicated in Table 2.11. In the last two decades, the rapid increase in export orientation was particularly impressive in the newly emerging economies such as Cambodia, Vietnam, and to a smaller extent, Laos. Among the Southeast Asian countries, Singapore and Malaysia are most open to trade, while Myanmar can be described as a closed economy. In fact, Myanmar's relatively high export orientation (around 20% of GDP) in the 1950s greatly contributed to its relatively high economic growth rate of that period. In the decades that followed, Myanmar's trade orientation declined as the country adopted closed economy policies which adversely affected its economic development (Kohama, 1982).

Exports of primary commodities comprised some 70% to 80% of total exports of Indonesia in the 1980s. Indonesia's main primary export commodity then was crude petroleum. In Malaysia, in the 1980s, two-thirds of

Table 2.11

Export as a Percentage of GDP, 1960–2007

	1960	1970	1980	1990	2000	2007[a]
Brunei	n.a.	n.a.	93.4	61.8	67.4	71.2
Cambodia	13.9	5.8	n.a.	6.1	49.8	68.8
Indonesia	15.0	13.5	34.2	25.3	41.0	29.4
Lao PDR	n.a.	n.a.	n.a.	11.3	30.1	36.0
Malaysia	50.6	41.4	56.7	74.5	124.4	112.0
Myanmar	19.7	5.2	9.1	2.6	n.a.	..
Philippines	10.6	21.6	23.6	27.5	55.4	39.4
Singapore[b]	n.a.	132.9	208.8	182.9	195.6	230.9
Thailand	15.7	15.0	24.1	34.1	66.8	68.1
Vietnam	n.a.	n.a.	n.a.	36.0	55.0	75.7

Source: World Bank, WDI Online, 6 Dec. 2008, http://publications.worldbank.org/WDI/.
    a: Data for Brunei, Cambodia, Laos and Vietnam refer to year 2006.
    b: Singapore's figures for years 1970, 1980, 1990 and 2000 are from *UNdata*,
       United Nation Statistical Division, http://data.un.org/.

total exports were primary products, mainly rubber, palm oil, timber and iron ore. The primary export proportions in the Philippines and Thailand were around 50% to 60% in the 1980s. The Philippines' principal primary exports were sugar, coconut oil and copper, whereas the key primary export commodity from Thailand was rice. Singapore dealt with both primary and manufacturing exports. Historically, the entrepot activity for primary products has been most significant for Singapore, but manufacturing exports have become increasingly more important since the 1970s.

In 2006, the value of primary commodity exports as a percentage of total merchandise exports was 55.3% for Indonesia and 24.8% for Malaysia. Malaysia remains to this day the world's major oil palm exporter. She is also a net exporter of petroleum and natural gas. But exports of machines, transport equipment and miscellaneous manufactured goods have been growing rapidly in several Southeast Asian nations since the early 1990s. Other than rice and rubber, Thailand has been a major exporter of basic manufactures since 1980, but from 1985 onwards there has been a tremendous acceleration in the exports of machines, transport equipment and miscellaneous manufactured goods.

Explanation of Economic Diversity

Earlier, various aspects of economic diversity were identified among the Southeast Asian countries. Among them were the differences in per capita income levels and rates, differences in the sectoral composition of GDP and the extent of structural change, differences in the changes of labour force composition, differences in trade composition and orientation, differences in population size, differences in geographical size, and differences in languages used. In this section, the focus will be on the effects of natural resource endowments, country size and trade policies on the pattern of development.

The division between a large country and a small one may be somewhat arbitrary. Myanmar, Indonesia, the Philippines, Thailand and Vietnam, each have a population size exceeding 48 million people, and may be regarded in Southeast Asia as relatively large countries. The most important effect of large country size in Southeast Asia seems to have been the adoption of inward-looking development policies. In countries where primary exports and production are important — Brunei, Indonesia, Malaysia, and to some extent, Thailand — the pattern of development is affected by natural resource endowments.

One of the effects of largeness in size is the early industrialisation of an economy (Chenery and Syrquin, 1975). In particular, the most pronounced scale effects are concentrated in certain industries: basic metals, printing, rubber products, chemicals, textiles and non-metallic minerals (Chenery and Taylor, 1968). Accordingly, one expects that in large countries these industries will account for a larger share in GNI compared to small countries during the early stage of industrialisation. The textiles industry, for instance, grew rapidly in the early stage of industrialisation in the relatively larger countries of Indonesia, the Philippines and Thailand. In comparison, non-metallic products and rubber products have been important in the early industrialisation of Malaysia. In this country, the scale effect per se has been relatively small, since the population size was only around 26 million people in 2006. Resource effects, however, are important in these industries, and hence have affected the pattern of industrialisation in Malaysia. It is well known that Malaysia has been a very important producer and exporter of palm oil since the late 1980s.

As pointed out in development theories, capital formation is a requisite for economic growth. Capital formation is represented in the 'I' of the EGOIN theory, with specific reference to the economy's accumulated economic infrastructure such as transportation and communication facilities, commercial and industrial buildings and plant, machinery and equipment. In its early years of development, Singapore invested extensively in infrastructure. As shown in Table 2.10, her gross capital formation as a percentage of GDP increased more than 4-fold from less than 10% in 1960 to 46% in 1980. Indonesia, Malaysia and Thailand have seen much increase in physical capital formation in the 1980s and 1990s. While some may start early, a country such as Vietnam, whose economic development is a couple of decades later than the other old ASEAN countries, has in recent years begun to build up her infrastructure with a gross capital formation reaching 36% of GDP in 2006. As noted in Chapter 13: Trinity Development Model and Southeast Asian Development, Vietnam is progressing rapidly towards a horse economy.

Of critical importance to a country like Singapore which is poor in natural resources, the stock of human capital serves as a significant determinant of economic progress. In addition to the quantity, the quality of human capital that provides the necessary skills will also eventually set the pace of economic development. Knowledge accumulation and the creation of ideas for invention and innovation are considerations which are not to be overlooked in the growth of an economy.

While an effective Government can mobilize physical and human capital to facilitate progress, rapid economic growth ultimately also hinges on a market-oriented economic system. Market-determined prices provide the right signals in allocating resources to their best uses. In turn these prices reward the most productive resources. In order to sustain continuous economic progress, it is also necessary to produce for the global market. An export-led economic strategy complements a free market economy and the policies of a competent Government.

The industrialisation process in the Philippines, Thailand, and Indonesia generally involved the adoption of largely protectionist measures to promote industries producing for the domestic market. In a large economy, there is scope for obtaining the benefits of scale economies and domestic competition. Furthermore, transport costs provide "natural protection" to industries that are set up within the country. Also, there are conditions in large countries that favour the production of simple mass-consumption goods such as clothing, shoes, and household goods that can replace imports. Such commodities are labour-intensive (especially in unskilled labour), and these production and distribution does not involve sophisticated technology and networks of suppliers of parts, components, and accessories. With such an advantage, it can be argued that there is no need for high levels of protection during this phase of industrialisation. Despite these observations, the relatively large countries in Southeast Asia have adopted rather high levels of protection, and consequently, the import-substituting industries are not always competitive and seldom become export oriented.

Recent development literature suggests that countries, which have adopted outward-oriented strategies, have enjoyed higher growth rates (Belassa, 1980). The choice of export oriented industrialisation strategies also affects the pattern of structural change that occurs within the country. For instance, export oriented industrialising countries like Singapore tend to have a higher proportion of its labour force engaged in industry. This experience is common among other developed countries. A country's trade orientation can be driven by government policies.

Southeast Asia also provides examples of the close relationship between natural resource endowments and development patterns. Historically, in the early 19th century, tin dominated the economic life of Malaysia. Crude petroleum exports now dictate the economic upswings and downswings of Malaysia and Brunei, and until recently also of Indonesia. On the one hand, the availability of natural resources may benefit industrial development by providing domestic markets and investible funds for manufacturing industries as well as materials for further transformation. It may, on the other hand, have adverse effects on industrialisation due to the postponement of domestic policy change toward industrial development. High wages in natural resource industries tend to raise wages and hence production costs in the manufacturing industries and natural resource exports give rise to an unfavourable exchange rate for industrial activities. These are plausible factors that might delay the structural transformation of countries like Indonesia and Brunei. Sometimes, the strong exchange rate during the period of an oil-export boom is referred to as the Dutch disease.

Finally, the geographical location of a country — particularly, a favourable location — can affect its development pattern. This is clearly illustrated in the case of Singapore, which, with a favourable geographical location at the hub of Southeast Asia began its development as a centre for entrepot trade. In the course of time, Singapore has shifted its pattern of trade and production, while capitalising on the external trade expertise gained over the decades. She is now, for example, exporting 75% of the oil-rigs in the world, other than having one of the world's busiest container ports.

Key Points

1. There are enormous differences in per capita income among Southeast Asian countries, with Singapore and Brunei showing the highest and Cambodia and Laos the lowest.

2. Over a period of almost 5 decades since 1960, Singapore followed closely by Thailand, Malaysia and Indonesia displayed phenomenal growth rates, earning the World Bank's accolade as "East Asian Miracle".

3. Agriculture's share of GDP has been declining in Southeast Asia, except Myanmar, over the past four decades as a result of the rapid industrialisation process. Notwithstanding this development, by labour input, Southeast Asia is still largely an agricultural economy, with Myanmar, Cambodia, Vietnam, Indonesia and Thailand having most of their working population still in the agriculture sector.

4. The Philippines spearheaded in the industrialisation process in Southeast Asia. The momentum, however, declined, and it was superseded by Singapore, Malaysia, Thailand and Indonesia.

5. Gross investment increased by leaps and bounds in the last four decades in all the market-driven, export oriented countries of the region, namely Singapore, Indonesia, Malaysia, the Philippines and Thailand.

6. Similarly, all the rapidly growing Southeast Asian countries became increasing export oriented during the four decades or so. This is because of the export oriented strategies adopted by them, with varying degrees of success as reflected in the diversity in income growth rates.

7. Growth rates and growth levels differ widely in Southeast Asia because the aptitude and attitude of the people, particularly the leaders, differ. Their macroeconomic policies and the policy options they have pursued also differ. Different policies and different priorities have given rise to different rates and different levels of development.

Suggested Discussion Topics

2.1 Why do growth levels differ in Southeast Asia? Do differences in natural resources endowment adequately explain these differences?

2.2 Why have average growth rate in Myanmar (4.6% p.a.) in the last 47 years been much lower than Malaysia (6.6% p.a.), Thailand (6.6% p.a.) and Singapore (8.0% p.a.)? Why has the World Bank term "economic miracle" not taken place in Myanmar but in Malaysia, Thailand and particularly in Singapore? Discuss.

References

BELASSA, B., 1980, "The process of industrial development and alternative development strategies", *World Bank Staff Working Paper, No. 438*, Washington, D.C.: World Bank.

CHENERY, Hollis B. and Lance TAYLOR, 1968, "Development patterns: Among countries and over time", *The Review of Economics and Statistics*, 50(4), 391–416.

CHENERY, Hollis B. and Moshe SYRQUIN, 1975, *Patterns of Development: 1950–1970*, London: Oxford University Press.

CLARK, Colin, 1940, *The Conditions of Economic Progress*, New York: St. Martin's Press.

FISHER, A. B. G., 1935, "Economic implications of material progress", *International Labour Review*, 32.

FISHER, A. B. G., 1939, "Production: Primary, secondary and tertiary", *Economic Record*, 15.

KOHAMA, Hiroshia, 1982, *Development Strategy and Growth Performance: A Comparison of Burma and Malaysia*, Tokyo: International Development Centre of Japan.

LIM, Chong Yah, 1991, *Development and Underdevelopment*, Singapore: Longman.

LIM, Chong Yah, 1996, "The trinity growth theory: The ascendency of Asia and the decline of the west", *Accounting and Business Review*, 3(2), 175–199. Also appeared in HOOI, Den Huan and KOH Ai Tee (eds.), 2001, *Economic Essays by Lim Chong Yah*, Singapore: World Scientific, 125–146.

SINGER, H. W., 1952, "The mechanics of economic development", *The Indian Economic Review*, 1(2).

World Bank, 1993, *The East Asian Miracle: Economic Growth and Public Policy*, New York: Oxford University Press.

Further Readings

DIXON, Chris and David DRAKAKIS-SMITH (eds.), 1997, *Uneven Development in South East Asia*, Aldershot, Hants: Ashgate.

DONER, Richard F., 1991, "Approaches to the politics of economic growth in Southeast Asia", *The Journal of Asian Studies,* 50(4), 818–849.

HILL, Hal, 1997, "The challenges of subnational diversity", *Journal of the Asia Pacific Economy,* 2(3), 261–302.

LIM, Chong Yah, 1997, "The low-income trap: Theory and evidence", *Accounting and Business Review*, 4(1), 1–19. Also appeared in HOOI and KOH (eds.), *op. cit.*, 147–166.

MYINT, Hla, 1972, *Southeast Asia's Economy: Development Policies in the 1970s*, New York: Praeger.

MYRDAL, Gunnar, 1970, *The Challenge of World Poverty: A World Anti-Poverty Programme in Outline*, New York: Pantheon Books.

World Bank, 2003, *World Development Report 2003*, New York: Oxford University Press.

Chapter 3

Agriculture: Rice

Every grain of rice is the product of sweat and labour.

Chinese saying

Objectives

✓ Show that rice self-sufficiency is an objective of most Southeast Asian countries.
✓ Highlight the problem of low rice productivity.
✓ Discuss credit issues pertaining to rice farming.
✓ Examine the policies implemented by the Government.
✓ Point out the prevalence of Green Revolution.
✓ Identify the technological and organisational requirements of Green Revolution.
✓ Show the importance of Government's role in the Green Revolution.
✓ Provide some suggestions for future agricultural development.

Introduction

Agriculture provides livelihood to a very large number of people in Southeast Asia. A new impetus was given for agricultural development with the Green Revolution, which started in Southeast Asia during the latter part of the 1960s. The expression "Green Revolution" normally refers to the development of high-yielding varieties (HYVs) of rice and wheat. In Southeast Asia, however, we should also include rubber and oil palm.

In Southeast Asia, we must make a distinction between subsistence farming like rice farming and plantation crops like rubber and oil palm. Rice farming has a very long history in Southeast Asia, long long before plantation crops came in. It is a way of life that is being devastatingly challenged in the global development process. Unlike USA or Australia, rice farming in Southeast Asia is still a highly labour intensive industry. It is a way of life of the peasantry in Southeast Asia.

World Bank economists estimated that three of every four people in developing countries live in rural areas, of which 2.1 billion living on less than US$2 a day and 880 million on less than US$1 a day (World Bank, 2007). This is also true for Southeast Asia. The majority of the Southeast Asian countries are still largely dependent on the agricultural sector to provide employment for their population. This is illustrated in Diagram 3.1. Among the traditionally agricultural countries, the only exception is Malaysia, where the agricultural sector as a source of employment has steadily declined over the last 35 years to 15% of the total economically active population.

Diagram 3.1

Percentage of Economically Active Population in Agriculture, 1970 and 2005

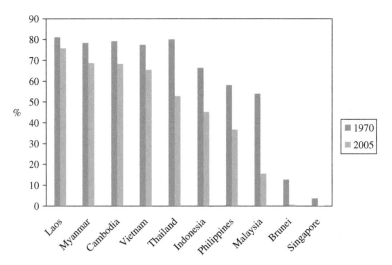

Source: Food and Agriculture Organization of the United Nations, FAOSTAT, 20 Aug. 2008, http://faostat.fao.org/.

In most of Southeast Asia, the agricultural sector has 40% or more of the economically active population. In Indonesia, by far the largest country in Southeast Asia, the proportion is 45%. In Vietnam, Cambodia, Myanmar and Laos, the proportion of economically active population in the agricultural sector is between 65% and 76%.

Value-added per worker in the agricultural sector in Southeast Asia tends to be low, so are therefore incomes and living standards. Table 3.1 shows the value-added per agricultural worker in Southeast Asian countries compared to Japan. In general, Japan's agricultural productivity is more than 30 times that of Southeast Asia. Labour productivity is generally still low in Vietnam, Cambodia, Laos, Indonesia and Thailand, notwithstanding the fact that the countries of Southeast Asia achieved considerable productivity growth in recent decades. There are disparities in the levels of agricultural labour productivity within the Southeast Asian countries, with Malaysia's value-added per worker exceeding that of Indonesia by more than 9 times. This disparity is partly due to the difference in the crops planted in the various Southeast Asian countries, (i.e. the predominance of plantation crops in some countries, such as Malaysia) and partly due to diverse degrees of under-utilisation (underemployment) of labour.

Table 3.1
Value-Added Per Worker in Agriculture, 1970–2005

Country	Value-Added Per Worker (Constant 2000 US$)				
	1970	1980	1990	2000	2005
Malaysia	1,674	2,462	3,675	4,316	5,378
Philippines	762	926	909	963	1,098
Thailand	308	375	470	533	607
Indonesia	313	425	480	523	596
Lao PDR	n.a.	n.a.	363	450	456
Cambodia	n.a.	n.a.	n.a.	286	329
Vietnam	n.a.	n.a.	210	277	313
Japan	8,541	13,971	20,839	29,801	37,389

Source: World Bank, WDI Online, 3 Sep. 2008, http://publications.worldbank.org/WDI/.
Note: Exchange rate relativity changed over the years. This imposes a limitation over cross-country and over-time comparisons of productivity.

However, it is not well known that agriculture has made an important contribution to the industrialisation process in Southeast Asia by supplying raw materials for industrial output. For instance, food, beverages and tobacco industries contribute a significant share in total manufacturing value-added in the Southeast Asian economies in 2003: 23% in the Philippines, 23% in Indonesia, and 8% in Malaysia (World Bank, WDI Online, 6 Oct. 2008).

Another important contribution of agriculture is the foreign exchange earnings accruing from the expansion of agricultural exports. The major crops produced in Southeast Asia for exports include rice, rubber, palm oil, coffee, timber and pepper. Malaysia and Indonesia are the world's top two exporters of palm oil. The world's top four exporters of natural rubber are also found in Southeast Asia, they are, in descending order, Thailand, Indonesia, Malaysia and Vietnam. Rice, an important food crop in Asia, is exported by Thailand, Vietnam and Myanmar. Coffee is another cash crop that Southeast Asian countries have established a dominant position in, with Vietnam ranking the world's second largest exporter and Indonesia ranking the world's fourth largest exporter.

Rice in Southeast Asia

Among the major crops produced in Southeast Asia, rice is the most important within the subsistence sector, as it provides not only the bulk of the peasants' incomes but is also a major source of their daily calories intake. Rice forms one of the major crops in the agricultural sector of many Southeast Asian countries, with the exception of Malaysia, Brunei and, of course, the city-state of Singapore.

The cultivation of rice can be broadly classified into dry paddy and wet paddy. Dry paddy is grown on dry ground very much the same as other cereals, whilst wet paddy is grown on standing water. While dry paddy was at one time the only form of paddy cultivated in several parts of Southeast Asia, the cultivation of wet paddy has now exceedingly overtaken that of dry paddy. There are several advantages of wet paddy over dry paddy. Firstly, output per hectare of wet paddy has been usually very much higher than that of dry paddy, although labour and the manure input of dry paddy have been normally much greater. Secondly, dry paddy consumes much more nutrients from the soil than wet paddy, and often the land has to be fallowed for one or two seasons after one or two seasons of cropping. Thirdly, the "Green Revolution" in Southeast Asia has significantly increased the yield of wet rice cultivation, rendering the productivity differences between wet and dry paddy even greater. Today, dry paddy cultivation is very much associated with the "slash-and-burn" agriculture carried out by the tribal people in the less developed regions.

As shown in Chapter 1, rural poverty continues to be a concern in Southeast Asia. The percentage of rural population living below national poverty line is more than 30% in the Philippines, Laos, Cambodia, Vietnam and Indonesia. Land fragmentation, credit indebtedness and population explosion are causes of poverty among the rural population. Unlike countries such as Australia and US, where rice cultivation generally takes place on a mega scale, rice farming in Southeast Asia is characterised by smallholdings, often subsistence smallholdings. Upon the death of the proprietor, his property is often divided among his heirs, resulting in fragmentation of farmland. A smaller plot of land is less efficient in terms of utilisation of machinery, and even the time and effort of the farmer. At times, the farmland is so small in size that profitable farming is not at all possible. Another important cause of poverty among paddy farmers is credit indebtedness. The root cause of indebtedness is capital shortage, which in turn could arise from a variety of causes, including extravagant wedding ceremonies, illness of farmers and poor harvests. Given that poor rural farmers have low average propensity to save, these farmers often have to resort to borrowing from the informal market in times of need, paying exorbitant interest rate in the process. As the consumption levels of the majority of paddy farmers are already around subsistence level, some misfortune in one or two years on one or two occasions would render the farmer indebted. Once seriously indebted they may forever remain so. Woes never come single. Last but not least, population explosion in the rural sector also plays a part in rural poverty. This is especially so when the population growth outstrips the technological progress in the farm or agriculture sector.

Apart from being an important crop, rice development in Southeast Asia also has a number of common characteristics.

1. Rice self-sufficiency is an objective of most Southeast Asian economies;
2. Yields are low compared to the Northeast Asian countries;

3. Serious problems persist in some aspects of institutional development, notably in the area of agricultural credit; and
4. Government policies, especially price policies, play an important role in the growth of the rice sector.

Production and Export

As shown in Table 3.2, Thailand, Vietnam, Myanmar and Indonesia are exporters of rice, although Indonesia was a net importer in 2005. Table 3.2 also

Table 3.2

Rice Production and Export ('000 Tons), 1970–2005

		1970	1980	1990	2000	2005
World	Production	316,346	396,871	518,556	598,894	631,868
	Export	8,255	12,566	12,367	23,821	29,747
Thailand	Production	13,850	17,368	17,193	25,844	30,292
	Export	1,064	2,800	4,017	6,141	7,537
Vietnam	Production	10,173	11,647	19,225	32,530	35,791
	Export	18	33	1,624	3,477	5,250
Myanmar	Production	8,162	13,317	13,972	21,324	25,364
	Export	641	653	214	251	58
Indonesia	Production	19,331	29,652	45,179	51,898	54,151
	Export	-	10	2	1	42
USA	Production	3,801	6,629	7,080	8,658	10,125
	Export	1,743	3,065	2,542	3,150	4,433
India	Production	63,338	80,312	111,517	127,400	137,690
	Export	27	483	505	1,534	4,025
Pakistan	Production	3,298	4,685	4,891	7,204	8,321
	Export	230	1,087	744	2,016	2,891
PRC	Production	113,102	142,877	191,615	189,814	182,059
	Export	1,695	1,377	405	3,072	672

Source: Food and Agriculture Organization of the United Nations, FAOSTAT, 20 Aug. 2008, http://faostat.fao.org/.

shows that the increase in rice exports from Vietnam between 1970 and 2005 is particularly impressive, while rice of exports from Myanmar is dwindling.

Of note from the table is that only two Southeast Asian countries, namely Thailand and Vietnam, are significant exporters of rice. The other important exporters include USA, India, Pakistan and People's Republic of China (PRC). The Southeast Asian rice exporters have to compete with them for markets, particularly outside Southeast Asia.

Rice Self-Sufficiency

Except Brunei, Malaysia and Singapore, Southeast Asian countries are self-sufficient or nearly so in rice. As Table 3.3 shows, Thailand, Vietnam, Laos and Myanmar experienced significant increase in production versus consumption over the period 1970 and 2003, thus enlarging their export capacity. Also noteworthy from Table 3.3 is that rice production in Brunei has fallen dramatically over the last three decades. In 1970, Brunei produced 35% of its rice consumption; in 2003, domestic production provided

Table 3.3

Domestic Production in Consumption of Rice (%), 1970 and 2003

	1970	2003
Thailand	170	275
Vietnam	101	168
Laos	118	166
Myanmar	128	158
Cambodia	223	149
Indonesia	108	112
Philippines	123	102
Malaysia	85	87
Brunei	35	2
Singapore	0	0

Source: Derived from Food and Agriculture Organization of the United Nations, FAOSTAT, 20 Aug. 2008, http://faostat.fao.org/.

Note: Food consumption quantity was converted back into primary equivalents, i.e. paddy, by FAO.

only 2% of Brunei's rice consumption. The high standard of living of this petroleum-producing country in part explains the decline of its rice-farming sector. Rice farming simply cannot yield that level of income and comfort in Brunei. Within the region, Brunei and Singapore thus provide important markets for rice in the Southeast Asian region. In this sense, the Brunei and Singapore economies are complementary to the rice exporting economies of Southeast Asia.

Insofar as the relationship between population growth and food supplies is of importance, it is useful to compare the growth rates of rice production and of population in the Southeast Asian economies. Table 3.4 shows that over the period 1961–2007, aggregate rice production rate has increased more rapidly than population growth in many Southeast Asian countries, including Laos, Myanmar, Indonesia, the Philippines, Vietnam, and Thailand. Brunei is the only country in Southeast Asia where population growth (3.3% per annum) far exceeds rice production (−3.0% per annum). Increases in land area devoted to rice as well as yield increases over the period explain the growth of rice production, with the latter yield factor becoming increasingly more important. We have to take note that the comparison done in Table 3.4 is highly important in a closed economy,

Table 3.4
Compound Annual Growth Rate of Rice Production and Population (%), 1961–2007

	Rice Production	Population
Laos	3.7	2.3
Myanmar	3.5	1.8
Indonesia	3.4	1.8
Philippines	3.1	2.5
Vietnam	3.0	1.9
Thailand	2.2	1.7
Cambodia	2.0	2.1
Malaysia	1.6	2.5
Brunei	−3.0	3.3

Source: Food and Agriculture Organization of the United Nations, FAOSTAT, 20 Aug. 2008, http://faostat.fao.org/.

as it indicates the ability of a nation to feed its people. However, in an open economy, where trade can take place, a country can always import its food requirements and the comparison is irrelevant.

The issue of rice self-sufficiency took on considerable urgency in 2008 due to a sudden spike in rice prices. As we can see from Diagram 3.2, rice prices were on a general downward trend from 1981 to 2001. Rice prices embarked on a steady upward climb since 2001, but spiked suddenly in early 2008. Comparing to the previous month, rice price increased by 22% in February 2008, 40% in March 2008, and by another 51% in April 2008. By April 2008, rice price was 158% higher than in January 2008.

The price spike was partly due to a global rice shortage, which was in turn partly due to droughts in Australia and China. In their effort to secure sufficient stock for their domestic consumption, rice-exporting nations such as China, India, Egypt, Vietnam and Cambodia imposed export bans or export tariff. This further aggravated the price increase. The sharp increase in rice prices had set off violent protests in many countries including

Diagram 3.2
Rice Price (US$ Per Metric Tonne), 1980 Jan.–2008 Sep.

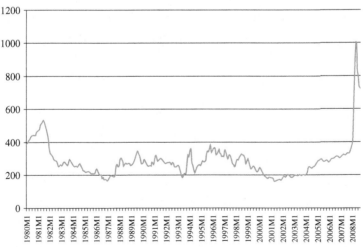

Source: IMF Primary Commodities Prices, 15 Oct 2008, http://www.imf.org/
external/np/res/commod/index.asp.
Note: Prices used refer to the white milled, 5 percent broken, Thailand
nominal price quotes, FOB Bangkok.

Cameroon, Egypt, Ethiopia, Haiti, Indonesia, Italy, Ivory Coast, Mauritania, the Philippines, Thailand, Uzbekistan and Yemen.

Although rice prices had eased since middle of 2008, the potential social unrest as a result of high food prices and the "beggar-thy-neighbour" actions by the rice-exporting nations to ban exports in time of crisis have serious ramification on food self-sufficiency policy of many nations. For example, the Malaysian government announced plan in April 2008 to achieve more self-sufficiency in rice by growing large amounts of rice in Sarawak. The Malaysian government has also urged private corporations to take up large-scale food-production ventures. In response, palm oil giant Sime Darby announced plans to diversify into rice production with an initial area of 7,000 ha in Sarawak, and integrated timber corporation Ta Ann Holdings also revealed plans of diversification into rice cultivation.

While it is an impressive technical and administrative achievement for a rice deficit country to produce all its rice requirements domestically, it is nevertheless, an issue as to whether it is economically worthwhile even though it may be justified from a strategic point of view (Fitzpatrick, 1991). Man does not live on rice alone. The higher the percentage of expenditure on rice consumption in a household, the poorer is the household. This is at times referred to as a variant of Engel's Law. In rice production, economic efficiency must be judged not by whether the country can export rice or is self-sufficient in rice, but by the productivity of rice per farmer and the relative productivity of other sectors. This issue of self-sufficiency will be further dealt with in Chapter 5.

Low Yields Compared to East Asian Countries

There exists a considerable productivity gap in rice production between Southeast Asia and other major rice exporters. This can be seen from Table 3.5. Although Vietnam and Indonesia had the highest rice yield among the Southeast Asian countries, it was only about half of that achieved in Egypt, which was producing 9.9 tonnes per hectare. Rice yields in Southeast Asia are also low when compared to USA and China. There is, *a priori*, still great scope for rice yields in Southeast Asia to improve. If productivity is

Table 3.5

Average Rice Yields (Tons/Ha), 1971–1975 and 2003–2007

	1971–1975	2003–2007
Vietnam	2.2	4.8
Indonesia	2.5	4.6
Myanmar	1.7	3.7
Philippines	1.5	3.6
Laos	1.3	3.4
Malaysia	2.6	3.3
Thailand	1.9	2.8
Cambodia	1.3	2.3
Brunei	2.3	1.0
Egypt	5.3	9.9
USA	5.1	7.7
China	3.4	6.2
India	1.7	3.1
Pakistan	2.3	3.1
World	2.4	4.1

Source: Derived from Food and Agriculture Organization of the
United Nations, FAOSTAT, 20 Aug. 2008,
http://faostat.fao.org/.

relatively low, income will also be relatively low, and then the standards of living will be relatively low too.

Notwithstanding the productivity gap, rice yields improved across most of the Southeast Asian countries. The highest average yield achieved by a Southeast Asian country during the period 2003–2007 was Vietnam with 4.8 tonnes per hectare; this was more than double the yield of the period 1971–1975. The rice yield improvements were equally impressive for Laos, the Philippines, Vietnam and Myanmar. On the other hand, the yield improvement made by Malaysia and Thailand were just mediocre. The slow improvement in rice yield in Thailand can be attributed to the predominance of the rain-fed rice ecosystem and the farmers' preference to grow high-quality, low-yielding traditional

Diagram 3.3
Average Rice Yields (Tons/Ha) 1971–1975 and 2003–2007

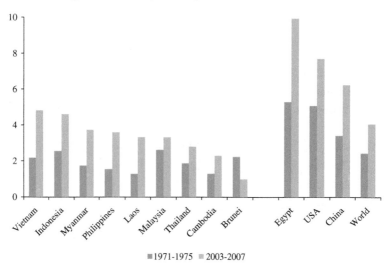

■ 1971-1975   ■ 2003-2007

Source: Table 3.5

aromatic Thai rice varieties that fetch a premium price in the domestic and the world market.

Productivity in rice growing, however, is not just a function of the skills and practices of the rice farmers per se, it is also a function of the essential capital input of fertilizer, irrigation facilities, better seeds, pest control, sale prices, planting and harvesting traditions, storage and transportation methods, and credit supply, many of which are outside their control.

System of Credit

Traditionally, credit institutions in Southeast Asian countries consider lending without tangible collateral (mainly land) to be an unsound practice. This requirement of collateral tends to discriminate against small and landless tenant farmers, who consequently may not have much access to institutional credit. Instead, they may have to turn to the informal market — the village moneylender, a local shopkeeper or a large landowner, for their funding needs. Rates of interest in the informal markets tend to be high due in part to monopoly elements, but more importantly because of the large overhead costs of small loans and the high risk of default due to a lack of collateral. The lenders may consider them as sub-prime loans. The large farms may become the main beneficiaries of institutional credit. Thus, the capital market may be fragmented with the large farms paying less than the social opportunity cost of capital, while small peasants often paying substantially more.

However, by the 1970s, credit institutions in most of the Southeast Asian countries had changed their practice on collateral for lending (Asian Development Bank, 1978). Agriculture was designated by most Governments in Southeast Asia as one of the priority sectors and banks generally had to provide some minimum lending to agriculture. Collateral was not required for lending while status as a cultivator was sufficient to give eligibility for short-term institutional credit. Moreover, institutions could provide credit to the farmer, which would cover his total requirements. Loans were also extended for long-term farm projects. Often, Governments compensated the banks for the costs of lending to agriculture. Such a development of credit programmes reflects, firstly, the concern of most Southeast Asian countries to increase agricultural output, and secondly, the recognition of the growth potential of the HYVs. The credit programs typically had the following features: heavy fiscal and administrative costs, high degree of loan default, bias toward larger and well-to-do farmers, and negative real interest rates (Herath and Jayasuriya, 1996).

Two of the most widely publicised agricultural development programmes illustrating the change in attitude regarding the expansion of credit extended to farmers have been the BIMAS/INMAS (crop intensification) programmes in Indonesia and the Masagana 99 programme in the Philippines. A basic objective of both programmes was to increase rice production by providing credit and modern inputs to farmers. The BIMAS programme was launched in 1967 and reorganised in 1971 following substantial problems with loan defaults. The volume of credit was greatly increased by 1971 but provisions were inadequate for ensuring a high rate of repayment, and default rates tended to be high. A new BIMAS programme commenced in 1973–74, but loan default was again very high. However, helped by the availability of new HYVs better suited to Indonesian irrigated rice environment, adoption accelerated and rice self-sufficiency was achieved in 1984 (Herath and Jayasuriya, 1996). The Masagana 99 programme in the Philippines was a subsidized credit and fertilizer programme introduced in 1973. Although the default rate was high, the programme played a positive role in stimulating early adoption of HYVs (Herath and Jayasuriya, 1996).

Another aspect of the credit system in the Southeast Asian countries is the adoption of a low interest-rate policy to encourage the purchase of agricultural inputs by small farmers. There was not enough evidence, however, to suggest that this policy had been successful (Asian Development Bank, 1978). Instead, given a shortage of credit, low interest rates have often encouraged large farmers to pre-empt the scarce institutional credit. What little credit that is available through organised institutions has probably tended to be rationed among those with secure titles to land and supplied at a relatively low rate of interest.

Government Pricing Policies

An important component of government policies aimed at rice production growth is the policies on rice price. Until the mid-1960s, the general orientation of policy-makers in the Southeast Asian countries was to keep food prices depressed. Government intervention to suppress economic incentives by pricing food products below competitive equilibrium levels is based on: (1) an under-emphasis on agriculture's contribution to economic development and (2) the assumption that the market mechanism permits middlemen to exploit the poor urban consumers. Policies that depress food prices relative to manufacturing prices have also been adopted in the belief that manufacturing provides the only means of rapid economic growth. The policy of depressed food prices, however, has generally been reversed after the mid-1960s.

As food-deficit countries in the region aspired to achieve self-sufficiency, and emphasised domestic production of food grains, raising food grain prices was considered to be an incentive for increased production. In Indonesia, the Government's recognition of the need for the farmer to receive an adequate price incentive if he were to expand his purchases of yield-increasing inputs that might bring rapid production growth, led to the establishment of BULOG, a food stock authority directly responsible to the President. BULOG generally succeeded over the 1970's in increasing nominal and real prices for the paddy farmers by periodically raising the floor price, with real price of rice rising by 47% during the period 1971–80 (Mears, 1981). Policies aimed at raising agricultural prices are, however, not without costs. Higher food-grain prices are likely to result eventually in higher industrial wages, leading to an increase in industrial product prices after a time lag. With food and industrial product prices both higher, a rise in the general price level, that is, inflation, is virtually inevitable in LDCs where a high proportion of income is spent on food. Though other macroeconomic factors are also important in explaining inflation, the contribution of food price increases cannot be understated.

Green Revolution in Rice

The large rice productivity differentials existing between the Southeast and Northeast Asian countries provided the impetus to narrow such gaps such as by the introduction of high yields varieties or HYVs.

The first semi-dwarf indica variety of rice was developed by plant breeders in Taiwan in 1956. The variety is known as Taichung Native I, and it is on this plant material that most of the subsequent research has been based. This is especially true of the important work done at the International Rice Research Institute (IRRI) at Los Banos, the Philippines.

IRRI was established by the Ford and Rockefeller Foundations.[1] Research on the Institute's 80-hectare farm started in 1962 and by 1965 many genetic lines had been developed. The best of these lines had doubled the yield potential of traditional rice varieties. The high-yielding varieties have short, upright leaves, which enable sunlight to penetrate. They are only mildly sensitive to length of day, and, therefore can be planted at any time of the year. Furthermore, they have a grain to straw ratio of 1.0 as compared to 0.6 or 0.7 of the indigenous varieties. Under ideal (experimental) conditions, the maximum yield of the HYVs is over 10 metric tons per hectare, and even in the cloudy, monsoon season yield can exceed 5 tons per hectare. In comparison, the average yield of rice in most LDCs, using local varieties, was less than 2 tons per hectare (Griffin, 1979).

In November 1966, the first of the IRRI varieties, IR-8, was introduced for general use. It was hailed as "Miracle Rice". Since then, the global rice

---

[1]*En passant*, the National University of Singapore conferred an honorary doctorate upon the Director General of IRRI for its outstanding achievement in kicking off the Green Revolution in Asia.

harvest has more than doubled, a pace that is slightly faster than population growth. IR-8 was followed by other new varieties of rice. Efforts were made to develop varieties that would suit local conditions. The rate of adoption of HYVs, however, differed among countries, with the Philippines being the most responsive and Thailand the least. Accordingly, one expects that, *a priori*, the spread and hence the impact of the Green Revolution differed among countries.

The magnitude and spread of the Green Revolution hinges heavily on institutional transformation, since productivity increases in agriculture depend not only upon the strength of technological innovations but also upon the favourable interaction of the technological change with the institutional environment. Wherever the necessary institutional support has not been forthcoming, this has prevented the diffusion of productivity gains from occurring more widely to provide a more viable base for the ultimate agricultural transformation.

Technological Possibilities

While the Green Revolution has not led to a dramatic increase in the trend rate of growth of rice production in some countries of the region, the introduction of HYVs has nevertheless brought about improvements in average yields. Rice yield per hectare has more than doubled over the period 1971–2007 in Laos, the Philippines, Vietnam and Myanmar (Table 3.5). The increase has been relatively rapid in Indonesia (increased by 81%) and Cambodia (increased by 76%), and relatively moderate in Thailand (increased by 50%) and Malaysia (increased by 21%) over the same period.

While the introduction of HYVs can lead to very substantial yield increases, their introduction has some technical demands. The successful adoption of HYVs requires not only large quantities of fertilisers and pesticides but also a well-developed system of irrigation capable of proper control over water supply to the individual fields. The problem of supplying these modern inputs on an adequate scale is very considerable — the most formidable problem being the provision of irrigation facilities. In many Southeast Asian countries, however, the share of irrigated land to total arable land and permanent cropland has not shown any significant increase.

Investment in irrigation and drainage systems is a priority in order for the technological innovation to have its full effect. This is due to the fact that within the region, a significant factor affecting rice production is the damage caused by natural disasters — drought or flood — in much of the planted rice area. For example, according to available data in Thailand for a 58-year period (1907–1965), there were natural disasters in 24 years, each affecting more than 10% of the cropped area. In some years, more than 30–40% of the rice area was damaged, with production dropping by more than 30% (Asian Development Bank, 1969).

A new technological possibility arising from the Green Revolution is the shorter harvesting time required. It, therefore, offers a real opportunity for a more intensive use of available land by growing at least two crops a year instead of the single crop that characterises the extensive agriculture of much of Southeast Asia. Large scale double cropping of rice in the traditionally single-cropping areas, however, involves comprehensive preparation and well-coordinated operation by the farmers, workers and all others concerned. Precise timing must be followed for practically every step of the operation because of the limited time available for each crop. It is the time element that generally creates difficulties with most double-cropping programmes in rice in their initial stages, and subsequently causes some reduction in the production targets.

The time element also necessitates finding future technological solutions to many problems that are not crucial in single cropping. A system of double cropping also requires a change, not only in cropping patterns, but also in harvesting methods. In addition, mechanical drying and increased storage facilities will be required for harvesting rice during the wet season.

Continuous research, not only by international research centres but also by individual countries, is necessary if the technological innovation is to have greater long-term impact in individual Southeast Asian economies. Apart from the longer-term research on plant protection and diversified breeding to reduce the risks of large-scale crop failures through disease and infestation, there are at least three fields of research that are of immediate economic importance (Myint, 1972). Firstly, research is needed to adapt the new high yielding varieties to the divergent local conditions of different Southeast Asian countries. Secondly, research is needed to make the new varieties of rice more appealing to consumers' tastes. Otherwise, the domestic market for them will remain limited. Alternatively, attempts will have to be made to change the consumers' taste, which can be a Herculean task, certainly a long-term rather than a short-term measure. Thirdly, in order to obtain the full benefits from the Green Revolution, a more intensive use of land and the full exploitation of multiple cropping are necessary. This is also required to enable the farmers to earn adequate incomes, especially if they have to pay for irrigation, modern inputs and credit. Research to widen the range of the Green Revolution to other crops is also an important new research direction closely related to multiple cropping.

Organisational Issues

An important organisational requirement to ensure the spread of the potential benefits of the technological innovation is the framework for the distribution of credit, seeds, fertilisers and pesticides to farmers. The basic issue that arises here is whether the function is best performed by the market network of traders and middlemen or a Government sponsored centralised agency. Purely in terms of organisational efficiency, it is recognised that the task of distributing inputs to a large number of farmers all over the country is generally more efficiently performed by the former. For, it is costly for the central agency to open a sufficiently large number of local branches to deal directly with the farmers. The overhead costs of the local traders and money-lenders are relatively low. Co-ordination of the traders at various levels (wholesale or retail) is efficiently performed by the market, while bureaucracy may or may not be able to perform this function.

Another set of problems requiring the attention of policy-makers is in milling, grading, storing, transporting and marketing of output. With increased output, there is a need to market the agricultural surplus. Inadequate milling, storage and transport facilities can create bottlenecks in marketing these surpluses. In some of the Southeast Asian countries, the purely physical problems of marketing have also been exacerbated by social factors where specific ethnic or racial groups have traditionally controlled most of the commerce. Governments, in order to eliminate some middlemen for political reasons, tend to promote public marketing agencies, which may not be efficient. Often, such agencies create bottlenecks in the smooth flow of production and distribution. Another way out is to break the monopolies through the introduction of competitors, to remove institutional rigidities and to free the markets so to speak. More competition by granting licences to more middlemen should be considered.

Price Support and Other Policies

To launch the Green Revolution, Governments have typically raised the price of rice to farmers by price supports or by import restrictions, which raise the domestic price above the world market price. In addition, input prices are subsidised. Moreover, it is generally argued that the factor markets in rural areas are distorted and that factor prices fail to reflect social opportunity costs. One effect of the distorted factor prices is that they tend to be biased in favour of large landowners who can adopt innovations more quickly than smallholder peasants.

The fact that factor market distortions need corrective policies can be illustrated with reference to rural credit markets where the interest rate charged on loans by the organised segment tends to be much lower than the rate charged by the unorganised segment. The majority of the rural people seeks credit in the unorganised capital market and pays the high interest rate. On grounds of equity and efficiency, this situation should be corrected. Suppliers of credit should not be restricted. Their number should be encouraged to increase in order to have more competitors in credit supply. The Government should also adopt policies to ensure that small peasants have access to the organised market on terms, which are not inferior to those enjoyed by large landlords.

In principle, similar policies should be advocated to ensure that small owner-operators have equal or preferential access to technological assistance, irrigation, and other inputs, which are vital to the success of the Green Revolution. Such policies are important because small farmers tend to be discriminated against in virtually all factor markets — either in terms of price, the way scarce resources are allocated by rationing, or because of restricted access to the bureaucracy.

The use of price supports by Governments has not been aimed towards turning the terms of trade in favour of agriculture as a whole, but towards raising the prices of particular items whose production needed to be encouraged. It may be argued that since the introduction of high yielding seeds reduces total costs of grain production — and therefore raises farm profits and leads to increased output — it should not be necessary for Governments to support the Green Revolution by maintaining the domestic price of any particular commodity above that prevailing in the world at large. On the contrary, a sensible objective of government policy would be to ensure that lower costs are passed on to the community in the form of lower food prices. Already, large farms often benefit from what are in effect subsidised material inputs. If the same farms now receive a subsidy on output as well, the consequences for resource allocation will be serious. Undoubtedly, the price supports and input subsidisation would have induced farmers to expand their output rapidly through the private profit motive. The question, however, is whether the economic incentives given to the farmers are appropriate for the efficient allocation of the resources between rice production and other crops, and more generally, between agriculture and the rest of the economy. A country that has no real comparative advantage in rice should be encouraged to reallocate resources to other crops in which price and demand prospects are more attractive. This is an important economic efficiency issue often overlooked by the authorities.

There is also the serious problem of fragmentation of land, which has come about for a variety of reasons. Included in these is the inheritance law and practice, resulting in small lots not economically viable for cultivation. In Malaya in 1958, the Payne Land Administration Commission once stated (Lim C. Y., 1967: 170–171), "Without attempting to find fantastic cases, but merely looking through records at random, we came across nine persons having shares in a smallholding in the following proportions:

$$\frac{12522}{57024}, \frac{12522}{57024}, \frac{6276}{57024}, \frac{3080}{57024}, \frac{1540}{57024}, \frac{1464}{57024}, \frac{732}{57024}, \frac{1569}{57024}, \frac{10893}{57024}.$$

"In another holding of two acres, one rood, the shares held by eight people respectively were:

$$\frac{1}{2}, \frac{1}{14}, \frac{1}{14}, \frac{1}{14}, \frac{1}{14}, \frac{331737}{2286144}, \frac{27909}{2286144}, \frac{130242}{2286144}.$$

"Numerous similar illustrations could be given. In one instance we were informed that the share of rural land inherited by one beneficiary amounted to three square feet, and he insisted on having it!"

According to the World Bank (2007), panel data that followed household heads and their offspring in the Philippines and Thailand over roughly 20-year period show declines in average farm sizes and increases in landlessness. More discussion on land reform will be done in Chapter 5.

A similar issue of economic efficiency arises in the allocation of resources in the public sector, since the Green Revolution requires heavy government investments, particularly in irrigation, transport and storage facilities. Thus, policy-makers have to face the question of how much of the available resources should be allocated to promoting the Green Revolution and how much of it should be allocated to public investment in other sectors of the economy. In the rice-growing sector, obviously, without the help of important many-faceted extension services provided by the state, it would be difficult to raise productivity, and most farmers would have to resign to their fate of subsistence living and poverty. Public policy makers should also bear in mind that in developed economies, agricultural subsidy is the vogue, whereas in much of Southeast Asia, dependence on taxes on farmers, including export taxes, are still not out of fashion.

Lessons for the Future

The picture that emerges from the earlier analysis of the impact of the Green Revolution can be summarised as follows: a technology that has vast potential to increase yield has been introduced into environments in which institutional factors have sometimes been adverse. Evidence from the last few decades suggests that, if it is to be successful, an agricultural strategy must be based on the recognition and understanding of the inter-relationship between technology and institutions. The nature of this inter-relationship is seen, for instance, in the inaccessibility of credit by small farmers. In many areas, small farmers did not adopt improved food grain technologies or only adopted them after a considerable time lag. A major reason for this is the higher cash outlay usually involved and the limited access that small farmers have to formal credit institutions. There is also the problem of land tenure and fragmentation of land to be solved. Where rice farming is carried out by tenant farmers, the problem becomes more serious. The problem is compounded with rapid population increase.

The above discussion, of course, assumes that profitable technologies are in fact available which are appropriate for a wide range of environments found in Southeast Asia. However, to date, the research efforts to generate better technology have favoured the cultivation of rice under conditions of good water management. Hence, the available technology is not easily transferable from one area to another. The technology development in agriculture in the future will have to address the more stringent environmental conditions imposed in most Southeast Asia by poor soils, lack of easy access to adequate water, and sometimes, social and cultural resistance to rapid change. An examination of the directional and content of agricultural research is an essential pre-requisite for evolving an appropriate strategy.

Finally, in view of the high incidence of poverty within the rural sector in most of the Southeast Asian countries, policies to raise the welfare level of the rural population require not only technological and institutional developments in agriculture, but more appropriately, more broad-based basic needs strategies affecting family size, education, health, sanitation and the allied social sectors. A multi-faceted big-push approach will have to be adopted. In some cases, where the comparatively disadvantages in rice growing are obvious, a deliberate movement away from rice farming to other more profitable cash crops might have to be encouraged and policy adjustment to ensure rice supply for consumption will have to be appropriately carried out. The aim must be a higher standard of living and a higher quality of life for the farmers.

Key Points

1. Agriculture plays an important role in most Southeast Asian countries. It can be separated into subsistence farming and plantation crops. Among subsistence farming, the growing of rice is the most common and has a long history in Southeast Asia.
2. Most Southeast Asian countries are self-sufficient or nearly so in rice. Thailand, Vietnam and Myanmar are net exporters of rice. Man, however, does not live on rice alone. Thus, for some countries, such as Brunei

and Malaysia, it may not be economically rational to be self-sufficient in rice. Comparative advantages in rice growing cannot and should not be ignored and the price of rice will have to be factored into the self-sufficiency equation.

3. Rice farming in Southeast Asia suffers from low productivity. Rice farmers are still using outdated technologies and inputs to grow their rice.
4. Credit systems in place were either biased or poorly managed.
5. The response to the introduction of HYVs is mixed. Indonesia and the Philippines are the most receptive to the new strain of rice. On the other hand, Thailand is the least receptive.
6. The Green Revolution has increased rice production in Southeast Asia but the benefits were not fully reaped. This could be attributed partially to the inability to have adequate modern inputs, such as irrigation facilities, fertilisers and pesticides as well as shortcomings with the system of credit and the land tenure and ownership systems.
7. To raise productivity in the rice sector, a concerted action by the Government covering different facets of the rice industry is necessary, not just through the adoption of higher-yielding rice seeds only.

Suggested Discussion Topics

3.1 Evaluate the "Green Revolution" in relation to rice farming in Southeast Asia. Discuss the obstacles that have to be overcome before the Green Revolution can be successfully implemented in the region.
3.2 Explain the low productivity in rice production in Southeast Asia. What could be done to help increase the productivity (and income) of the rice farmers?

References

Asian Development Bank, 1969, *Asian Agricultural Survey*, Tokyo: University of Tokyo Press.

Asian Development Bank, 1978, *Rural Asia: Challenge and Opportunity*, New York: Praeger Publishers.

FITZPATRICK, Ellen, 1991, "Agricultural self-sufficiency in Southeast Asia: Malaysia and Thailand," in RUPPEL, J. Fred and Earl D. KELLOG, (eds.),

National and Regional Self-Sufficiency Goals: Implications for International Agriculture, Boulder and London: LynneRiener.

GRIFFIN, Keith, 1979, *Political Economy of Agrarian Change: An Essay on the Green Revolution*, London: MacMillan.

HERATH, Gamini and Sisira JAYASURIYA, 1996, "Adoption of HYV technology in Asian countries: The role of concessionary credit revisited", *Asian Survey*, 36(12), 1184–1200.

LIM, Chong Yah, 1967, *Economic Development of Modern Malaya*, Kuala Lumpur: Oxford University Press.

MEARS, Leon, 1981, *The New Rice Economy of Indonesia*, Indonesia: Gadjah Mada University Press.

MYINT, Hla, 1972, *Southeast Asia's Economy: Development Policies in the 1970s*, New York: Praeger Publishers.

World Bank, 2007, *World Development Report 2008: Agriculture for Development*, Washington, D.C.: The World Bank.

Further Reading

GHATAK, S. and K. INGERSENT, 1984, *Agriculture and Economic Development*, Brighton, Sussex: Wheatsheaf Books.

Chapter 4

Agriculture: Rubber, Oil Palm and Other Crops

*Earth is here so kind, that just tickle her with a hoe
and she laughs with a harvest.*

Douglas Jerrold, *A Land of Plenty*

Objectives

✓ Outline the formation and development of the rubber industry in Southeast Asia.

✓ Highlight the changes in the consumption market of natural rubber.

✓ Discuss the competition posed by synthetic rubber to natural rubber.

✓ Evaluate the various rubber export price stabilisation schemes.

✓ Highlight the dynamism of the changing comparative advantages of the Southeast Asian countries in the production of various plantation crops.

✓ Outline the development of the palm oil industry in Southeast Asia.

✓ Evocate a more rapid development of the palm oil industry for domestic consumption and exports.

✓ Identify the major producers and exporters of other plantation crops, such as maize, sugar cane, coffee beans, cocoa beans, pepper, bananas and cassava.

Introduction

A part from rice, Southeast Asian countries are also major producers of raw materials. However, unlike their subsistence-crop counterpart, plantation crops (sometimes they are also known as cash crops) such as rubber and oil palm, are grown mainly for export. To numerous families, notably those in Thailand, Indonesia and Malaysia, the cultivation of rubber trees is a basic source of income. However, due to their low productivity, they are meagrely compensated, which also means a lower standard of living for them. Their livelihood as rubber farmers are further jeopardised by the competition from the synthetic rubber industry both internally and externally. Coupled with a dramatic shift in the demand away from natural rubber among various major consumers in the developed countries, it is no wonder that some called the natural rubber industry a sunset industry. Is it?

On the other hand, there is great potential for the oil palm industry. More and more resources are devoted to the development of this industry. The transition is especially conspicuous in Malaysia and Indonesia. More and more land is planted with oil palm. Government institutions such as Palm Oil Research Institution of Malaysia (PORIM) and Malaysian Palm Oil Promotion Council (MPOPC) are set up to help in the development of the country's oil palm industry. Other cash crops planted in Southeast Asia include coffee, cocoa beans, pepper and sugar cane. However, their scale of cultivation pales into insignificance besides those of oil palm and rubber.

There is also another group of crops that is cultivated by farmers in Southeast Asia. Unlike cash crops, this group that includes maize and cassava are grown mainly for own consumption. They are in fact the main source of carbohydrates for some people in many developing countries.

Rubber

The cultivation of rubber trees in Southeast Asia dates back to the late 19th century. Some 2,000 rubber seedlings were transplanted from the Kew Gardens in England to Ceylon (Sri Lanka) and Malaya (Singapore and Peninsula Malaysia) in 1877. As rubber trees (*Hevea Brasiliensis*) grow best in tropical climate, this makes Southeast Asia a very suitable region for rubber tree cultivation. However, it is not uncommon to see rubber farms further up north. Vietnam, Myanmar and Cambodia have also become producers of rubber. Vietnam is in fact fast catching up to be a major producer of rubber in Southeast Asia.

Once a rubber tree matures, which generally takes 5 to 8 years, it is ready to be tapped. Its productivity increases with age, but as the trees grow older, normally after the teens, productivity declines progressively. Productivity of the rubber trees, like rice, is also very much a function of the seedlings used. Tapping involves the excision of the bark of the rubber tree to obtain latex. Besides encouraging the widespread cultivation of rubber trees in Malaya, H. N. Ridley, who was the Head of the Botanical Gardens in Singapore, was also the first person to introduce a better way of tapping the rubber trees, known as "ibidem" tapping (Lim, 1967).

Two important innovations in the 19th century increased the demand for natural rubber. They were the discovery of vulcanisation and the invention of pneumatic tyres. Unvulcanised rubber suffers from several shortcomings. It softens and becomes sticky at high temperatures and hardens and cracks easily when too cold. In 1839, Charles Goodyear discovered that rubber coated with sulphur remains stable under extreme temperatures. This was the first known case of vulcanisation. The pneumatic tyres were invented by John Dunlop in 1888. Pneumatic tyres improve the speed and comfort of transportation that was impossible with other types of tyres. Its creation led to new demand for rubber. However, it was the advances made in the motoring industry that sparked off a dramatic increase in the demand for rubber for making rubber tyres. Other important uses of rubber today include the making of rubber gloves, condoms, aeroplane tyres, bicycle tyres, pillows, balloons and floats.

Production and Export

As shown in Table 4.1, the four most important world rubber exporters currently are Thailand, Indonesia, Malaysia and Vietnam. However, in 1970, Malaysia alone produced nearly half of the world's rubber. The amount was 1.6 times as much as that produced by Indonesia and 4.4 times as much as that produced by Thailand. During the period 1970–2005, output in Indonesia increased by about 180% and in Thailand, it was more than ninefold. However, during the same period, Malaysia's output fell

Table 4.1
Natural Rubber Production and Export ('000 Metric Tons), 1970–2005

		1970	1980	1990	2000	2005
World	Production	2986	3748	5225	7040	9346
	Export	2853	3325	4064	5574	7133
Thailand	Production	287	465	1418	2378	2977
	Export	276	455	1133	2327	2952
Indonesia	Production	802	1020	1275	1501	2271
	Export	770	981	1084	1380	2025
Malaysia	Production	1269	1530	1292	928	1126
	Export	1346	1526	1322	978	1147
Vietnam	Production	33	41	58	291	482
	Export	24	33	76	273	249
Philippines	Production	6	22	61	71	316
	Export	1	7	18	31	40
Myanmar	Production	13	16	15	27	40
	Export	7	11	1	20	34
Cambodia	Production	13	6	32	42	20
	Export	14	1	24	13	7

Source: Food and Agriculture Organization of the United Nations, FAOSTAT, 12 Oct. 2008,
        http://faostat.fao.org/.

by 11%. In fact, Malaysia's output hit a low of around 800,000 tonnes in late 1990s and early 2000s on the back of low rubber prices. The rubber output recovered somewhat in the recent years due to an increase in rubber prices. The percentage decline in Malaysia's rubber output is, nevertheless, not unexpected. Since the late 1970s, production of natural rubber in Malaysia has gradually declined. In 2005, Malaysia's share of world's rubber output dropped to 12%. Thailand and Indonesia have well surpassed Malaysia as global rubber producers. Obviously, comparative and competitive advantages in rubber growing in Southeast Asia have greatly shifted away from Malaysia to Thailand, Indonesia and Vietnam.

Looking at the rest of Southeast Asia, also of significant interest is the increasing role of Vietnam, and to a lesser extent, the Philippines, Myanmar,

Table 4.2
Natural Rubber Harvested Area ('000 Hectares), 1970–2007

	1970	1980	1990	2000	2007
World	4,621	5,412	6,656	7,565	8,944
Indonesia	1,391	1,612	1,866	2,400	3,175
Thailand	812	1,240	1,400	1,524	1,763
Malaysia	1,500	1,615	1,614	1,300	1,400
Vietnam	106	88	222	412	512
Philippines	22	54	86	81	95
Myanmar	49	48	40	52	73
Cambodia	15	10	35	34	21

Source: Food and Agriculture Organization of the United Nations, FAOSTAT, 12 Oct. 2008, http://faostat.fao.org/.

and Cambodia in the export of rubber. Vietnam in particular has captured about 3.5% of the world's export market for rubber in 2005. Southeast Asia is expected to remain as the world's main producer and exporter of rubber in the foreseeable future.

Table 4.2 shows the harvest area of natural rubber in the rubber-producing countries in Southeast Asia. With the exception of Malaysia which saw her harvested area of natural rubber decreasing by 7% between 1970 and 2007, all other countries were devoting more land to the rubber crop. The expansion was particularly significant for Vietnam and the Philippines, whose harvested area increased by more than 300% between 1970 and 2007. In Malaysia, harvested area of natural rubber peaked in 1980.

A major structural change in the natural rubber industry has been the steady decline in estate involvement and the increasing importance of the smallholder area (UNCTAD, *INFOCOMM*, http://www.unctad.org/infocomm). According to data from the International Rubber Study Group (IRSG), smallholdings accounted for over 80% of world natural rubber production in 2005. The ratios are even higher in Thailand, Indonesia and Malaysia. One important driving force behind the decline of estate involvement is the switch by the estates to less labour-intensive crops such as oil palm. While productions in Thailand, Indonesia and Malaysia are predominantly smallholder based, estates still predominate in the former centrally planned economies such as China, Vietnam and Cambodia.

Table 4.3
Average Rubber Yields (Hg/Ha), 1971–1975 and 2003–2007

	1971–1975	2003–2007
Thailand	3,629	17,788
Cambodia	7,919	10,409
Vietnam	2,719	9,785
Malaysia	8,392	8,800
Indonesia	5,215	7,790
Myanmar	3,016	6,025
Philippines	3,000	n.a.
World	6,273	11,080

Source: Food and Agriculture Organization of the United Nations, FAOSTAT, 12 Oct. 2008, http://faostat.fao.org/.

Note: The rubber yield for the Philippines jumped from 11,000 Hg/Ha in 2003 to around 38,000 Hg/Ha from 2004 onwards. The very high yields from 2004 onwards are more likely to be an error. The yield in the Philippines is more likely to be around 11,000 Ha/Ha, which is also the world average yield.

The average rubber yields for the various Southeast Asian rubber-producing countries are highlighted in Table 4.3. Not surprisingly, Malaysia was the most productive country in the early 1970s, producing 0.84 tonne of rubber per hectare. However, Thailand has since caught up with Malaysia and during 2003–2007, Thailand produced 1.78 tonnes of rubber per hectare, compared to 0.88 tonnes for Malaysia.

In Southeast Asia, as stated earlier, the rubber farms are mostly small and are mainly family businesses. They lose out to the estates, whose plantation size range from a few hundred to thousands of hectares, in several ways. Not only do rubber estates get to enjoy the economies of scale due to their large sizes, the plantations are also run by a team of professional managers who have the luxury of employing experts to advise them on issues ranging from planting to processing to marketing of their rubber (Barlow, Jayasuriya and Tan, 1994). However, with increasing competition from synthetic rubber, the rubber estates have increasingly shifted to other crops like oil palm in Malaysia. The smallholders find it more difficult to shift. Their land size is too small to become viable for oil palm cultivation. Moreover, more people have become rubber smallholders in most parts of Southeast Asia.

Smallholders continue to suffer from low productivity. This is true not just in Thailand, but also in Malaysia and Indonesia. This could be attributed to their outdated farming techniques and inadequate factor inputs, such as fertiliser. Because of their low productivity, they have extremely low incomes. Some smallholders even have to resort to tapping their rubber trees several times a day in order to earn enough for them to feed themselves, especially if their trees are old and not of a higher-yielding variety. This is at times referred to as "slaughter tapping".

The techniques of tapping rubber and collecting and transporting rubber latex have remained highly labour-intensive, making the industry less competitive as standards of living and wages rise.

Consumption of Natural Rubber

Although the world's consumption of natural rubber is increasing in absolute terms, there is, however, a fundamental shift in the distribution of consumption. Diagrams 4.1 and 4.2 show the share of consumption by major countries in 1960 and 2003–2005 respectively. Asia's share of consumption has been increasing over the years and western countries' shares are falling. In 1960, USA alone consumed 23% of the world's rubber output, but this has declined to 14% in 2003–2005. Conversely, Japan's share of

Diagram 4.1
Percentage of Natural Rubber Consumption by Countries, 1960

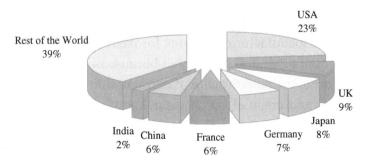

Source: International Rubber Study Group, *Rubber Statistical Bulletin,* various issues.

Diagram 4.2

Percentage of Natural Rubber Consumption by Countries, 2003–2005 (Average)

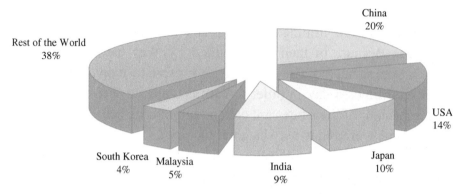

Source: UNCTAD, *infocomm* website, www.unctad.org/infocomm. (Data: International Rubber Study Group).

consumption increased from 8% in 1960 to 10% in 2003–2005. China and India have emerged as the fastest-growing consumers of natural rubber and are now among the top four consumers of natural rubber. China's share of consumption increased from 6% in 1960 to 20% in 2003–2005, making her by far the most important consumer of natural rubber in the world. India's share increased from 2% to 9%. Of note is that, comparing Diagrams 4.1 and 4.2, European countries like the United Kingdom, Germany and France have disappeared from the conspicuous consumer countries list, presumably being substituted by synthetic rubber.

The largest user of natural rubber is the tyre industry, with tyres and tyre products accounting alone for over 50% of natural rubber. Truck and bus tires represent the largest single outlet for natural rubber, followed by automobile tires. The manufacturing of tyres for passenger cars only requires a very small amount of natural rubber, but because of the large quantities of car tyres produced, the market share of consumption is quite significant.

With the advancement of mechanical knowledge, the natural rubber industry may be losing some of its major customers. Conventional way of retreading worn tyres consumes substantial amount of natural rubber. However, the growing use of new retreading technique, known as procured retreading, largely has done away with the need for natural rubber.

However, the healthcare industry is becoming a major user of natural rubber (latex). This is due to the increased incidence of the AIDS epidemic. The manufacturing of surgical and examination gloves has now constituted an important demand for natural rubber. Other products manufactured from latex include prophylactics, catheters, rubber threads, adhesives, and moulded foams. Natural rubber is also used in the production of general rubber goods such as transmission and elevator belts, hoses and tubes, industrial lining, golf balls, footballs, erasers, footwear as well as seismic materials.

Prices of Natural Rubber

Diagram 4.3 shows the price of natural rubber was on a general downward trend from 1980 to 2001. The depressed price of natural rubber was catalytic in the disbandment of the International Natural Rubber Organization, a rubber cartel. The depressed price of natural rubber also cemented the belief that the rubber industry was a sunset industry.

The price of natural rubber, however, made a speedily recovery from the beginning of 2002. In June 2008, the price of natural rubber hit a high of

Diagram 4.3

Price of Natural Rubber (US Cents Per Pound), 1980 Jan.–2008 Nov.

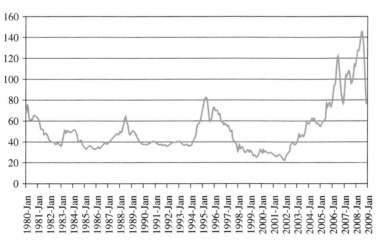

Source: IMF Primary Commodities Prices, 9 Dec. 2008,
http://www.imf.org/external/np/res/commod/index.asp

Note: Prices used refer to the Rubber, No. 1 Rubber Smoked Sheet, FOB Malaysian/Singapore.

US$1.47 per pound, an increase of 5.6 times over the recent low of US$0.22 recorded in December 2001. There were two important drivers behind the price surge. Firstly, the booming economies of China and India, in particular their dramatic increase in trucks and passenger cars, greatly increased the demand for natural rubber. Secondly, the sharp increase in fossil oil prices since 2002 has pushed up the production cost of synthetic rubber, which in turn pushed up the prices of natural rubber.

Going forward, price of natural rubber is expected to weaken from its peak in June 2008. Downturn in the U.S. and Europe has resulted in a negative growth in global demand for vehicles. In addition, the price of fossil oil was falling rapidly from its peak in July 2008. This would help lower the production cost of synthetic rubber. The economies of China and India are also expected to be adversely affected by the ongoing financial crisis. The significant increase in planted area of natural rubber in ASEAN in response to the sharp price increase in the last six years means that supply is unlikely to be reduced even in face of a weakening demand, thus putting more downward pressure on the prices of natural rubber.

Competition from Synthetic Rubber

One important reason for the relative decline in natural rubber consumption is the competition posed by the introduction of synthetic rubber in the early 20th century and its spread after WWII. The synthetic rubber industry is currently enjoying about 57% market share of the world's total rubber consumption (International Rubber Study Group, *Rubber Industry Report*, 8(1–3), Jul.–Sep. 2008). In 1950, the percentage of synthetic rubber to total rubber consumption was only a paltry 25%. It peaked at 70% in 1980. The share has been hovering around the 60% mark in recent years.

Even though the first synthetic rubber polymer was created as early as 1910 and important technical advancements were made in 1930, large-scale production of synthetic rubber only started around middle of 1940s. During the WWII, worldwide natural rubber supplies were limited and by mid-1942 most of the rubber-producing regions were under Japanese control. The importance of rubber for production of tires for military trucks and various war machines spurred the U.S. government to launch a major effort to develop and refine synthetic rubber. By the early 1960s, synthetic rubbers had overtaken natural rubber in volume.

The presence of synthetic rubber as a good substitute for natural rubber increases the price elasticity of demand for natural rubber. The increased price elasticity has a contributing effect on price stability of natural rubber, which was very volatile particularly before the advent of synthetic rubber, in decades before WWII (Lim, 1967: 87–92).

In the face of synthetic rubber competition as a substitute, Malaysia can move and has moved to palm oil cultivation and industrialisation. This is diversification strategy, which Malaysia has carried out very successfully. The law of comparative advantage has compelled Malaysia to make this paradigm shift, so that she can continue to improve the standards of living for her people. However, at lower levels of per capita income, rubber cultivation is still profitable, as the opportunity cost is lower. However, when the costs of production of synthetic rubber go up in line with the costs of fossil oil, which supplies the synthetic rubber inputs, the glimmer of hope in the competitive environment for natural rubber has become brighter, though the industry has remained as a highly labour-intensive one. Similarly, the rapid increase in demand by any large emerging countries like China and India has also been very encouraging to the natural rubber industry in Southeast Asia.

Rubber Cartel

With the highly volatile prices of natural rubber, from time to time, it was felt that there was a need for some organisational body to stabilise the price of natural rubber. In 1979, an International Natural Rubber Agreement (INRA) was adopted in Jakarta. An intergovernmental commodity body, the International Natural Rubber Organisation (INRO) was subsequently set up in 1980 to administer the Agreement. INRO comprised 6 producing countries and 17 consuming countries. The 6 producing countries were Thailand, Indonesia, Malaysia, Sri Lanka, Nigeria and Cote d'Ivoire. The 17 consuming countries were the US, UK, Japan, China, Germany, France, Austria, Belgium, Luxembourg, Finland, Ireland, Greece, Denmark, Italy, the Netherlands, Spain and Sweden.

Under the INRA, an international buffer stock of 550,000 tonnes was established. The buffer stock consists of two parts,

(1) A normal buffer stock of 400,000 tonnes, and
(2) A contingency buffer stock of 150,000 tonnes.

The operations of INRO were funded by member countries, with the costs of stocks being shared equally among them. The cost contributions of members within each group were more or less proportional to their production or consumption of natural rubber and also determined by their voting power.

The sole way of intervention was through the buying of rubber stock when prices were too low and selling the buffer stock when prices were too high. This was done by setting upper and lower "price bands" in relation to a "reference price". There were two sets of "price bands". A set of "may sell" and "may buy" bands allowed the prices to fluctuate within 15% of the reference price. A further set of "must sell" and "must buy" bands was determined to be at a 20% band. The agreement was revised in 1987 and 1995.

However, in 1998, Malaysia complained that INRO was not effective in supporting the prices of the natural rubber. On 15 October 1999, Malaysia ceased to be a member of INRO. With the pull out of Thailand, the largest producer of rubber, INRO announced in September 1999 the termination of its 1995 Agreement (INRA III). At the same time, the INRO was disbanded.

The cessation of the INRO does not spell the end for natural rubber price fixing for the three major producers of natural rubber. In December 2001, Indonesia, Malaysia and Thailand met in Bali and signed a Joint Ministerial Declaration pledging to work collectively to support rubber prices. Arising from the Bali Declaration, International Tripartite Rubber Council (ITRC) was formed as the body responsible for coordinating and overseeing the implementation of the agreement to cut productions and exports. In August 2002, the three countries met again in Bali to sign the MOU on setting up of the International Rubber Consortium Limited (IRCo). The IRCo was officially registered in April 2004 with an authorized capital of US$225 million, to be fully subscribed by Thailand, Indonesia and Malaysia at the ratio of 4:3:2. The main task of the consortium is to buy natural rubber from farmers at times when export prices are depressed and withhold the rubber from the market.

Actually, the rubber commodity agreement has a long history. Before World War II, there was the Stevenson Scheme in the 1920s and the various International Rubber Agreements in the 1930s. None had been able to help the rubber industry. The *modus operandi*, however, has remained the same: the use of buffer stock and export control to regulate supply. Before the War, synthetic rubber was not there, consequently natural rubber prices fluctuated more violently. But when supply was controlled by the agreement countries, this encouraged the non-agreement countries to become more important rubber producers. For example, the Netherlands East Indies was not part of the Stevenson Scheme, and soon became a very important producer of natural rubber, as there was no control over the production and export of rubber by the Netherlands East Indies (Lim, 1967: 76–78). With synthetic rubber dominating the scene after the War, any control of natural rubber production and export and prices would only help the synthetic rubber to compete better. The solution must be found elsewhere, such as researching into the increasing uses of natural rubber and reduction of costs of natural rubber production. The shifting comparative advantage of the natural rubber industry has to be recognised, and other better forms of stabilization measures be looked into.

Also of note is that the case of commodity agreement on tin or fossil oil is different from that for natural rubber, as tin and oil are non-replaceable assets, whereas natural rubber is a replaceable resource, besides the ready availability of a very good substitute in synthetic rubber. Indeed, for most rubber products, synthetic rubber is a perfect substitute for natural rubber, and in some cases, synthetic rubber is a much-preferred substitute.

In Malaysia, true enough, with industrialisation and the shift to oil palm and cocoa cultivation, there is falling export value and export volume of rubber. In the past, short trees with short maturation period were preferred to the original high trees with low latex yield. However, in recent years, with technological advance in furniture making with rubber trees, there is the reversal to the old bigger trees again for wood pulp for furniture making.

Oil Palm

The oil palm tree, which originated from West Guinea, was introduced into other parts of the world in the 15th century. However, in the earlier days, the tree was used for ornamental purpose only. The oil palm fruit (*Elaeis guineensis*) is made up of three parts: the pericarp, the shell and the seed (kernel). The palm fruit grows in large bunches containing up to 2000 individual fruits. When the fruit ripens, it turns yellowish red. In a year, there can be 12 bunches each weighing 20–30 kg and each bunch containing 1000–3000 fruits. Oil can be extracted from the pericap (known as palm oil) and the kernel (known as palm kernel oil). Although the two types of oil are derived from the same oil palm fruit, their properties and chemical composition differ. Palm kernel oil is very similar to coconut oil while palm oil shares many common characteristics with those of whale oil.

Palm oil is used for making soaps, candles, cooking oil and cosmetics. Recently, attempts are being made to turn it into a viable biofuel as a substitute or partial substitute for fossil oil. Palm oil has an advantage as an oil-based product because it is not a wasting asset and the crop is perennial, not annuals or semi-annuals. However, its use as a biofuel depends much on its price relative to the price of fossil oil. When fossil oil price is high, palm oil usage as a biofuel increases and vice-versa. Diagram 4.6 below shows the very close relationship between palm oil price and fossil oil price.

Production and Export

Due to the losing competitive advantage to lower cost rubber producers, Malaysia has steadily shifted a significant portion of its resources to the cultivation of oil palm. The harvested area of oil palm fruits in Malaysia increased by 24 times between 1970 and 2007 (see Diagram 4.4). In comparison, the production of oil palm in Indonesia picked up steam only after *circa* 1990. Between 2000 and 2007, the compound annual growth rate of harvested area in Indonesia was an impressive 12.5%. The harvested area of oil palm fruits in Indonesia has overtaken that of Malaysia since 2005. In comparison, the harvested area in Thailand lagged behind those of Malaysia and Indonesia significantly.

Diagram 4.4

Oil Palm Fruit Harvested Area, 1970–2007

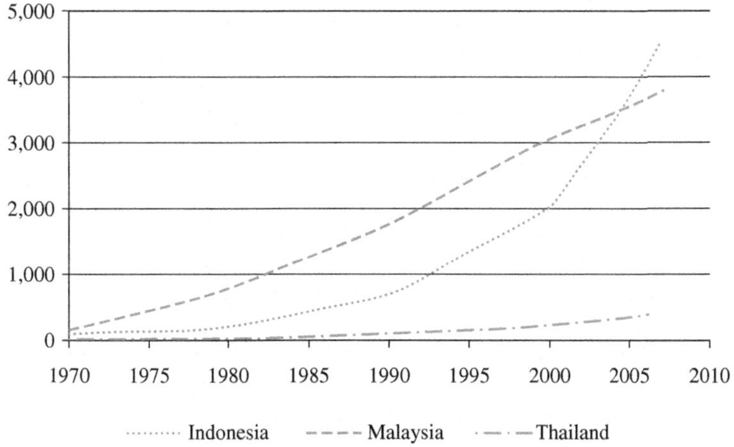

········ Indonesia   – – – – Malaysia   — · — Thailand

Source: Food and Agriculture Organization of the United Nations, FAOSTAT,
12 Oct. 2008, http://faostat.fao.org/.

As shown in Table 4.4, Malaysia was the leading producer of palm oil in the world in 2005, producing 44% of the world's output[1]. Malaysia was also the leading exporter of palm oil with a market share of almost 50% in 2005. This was closely followed by Indonesia, whose share of the world's palm oil production increased from 21% in 1990 to 41% in 2005. Indonesia's share of the world export market has also increased significantly over the 15 years, from 14% in 1990 to 39% in 2005.

As for world palm oil imports, as shown in Table 4.5, of importance to note is that emerging countries, particularly China and India, are among the most important importers, China being the world's most important importer, with the US hardly playing any important importing role. Palm oil trade reflects the positive shifts in complimentarily between land-resource rich tropical Southeast Asia and warm temperate Northeast Asia and the very high population density countries of the Indian Sub-Continent.

Prices of palm oil were fairly volatile in the last 28 years, fluctuating between a very wide range of US$163/Mt (in August 1986) and US$1147/Mt (in March 2008) around a mean of about US$400/Mt (see Diagram 4.5). There were prolonged periods when palm oil prices remained depressed,

---

[1]Indonesia edged out Malaysia, and was the top producer of palm oil in 2007.

Table 4.4

Palm Oil Production and Export ('000 Metric Tons), 1970–2005

		1970	1980	1990	2000	2005
World	Production	1,937	5,083	11,444	22,039	34,298
	Export	906	3,617	8,072	14,162	26,565
Malaysia	Production	431	2,573	6,095	10,842	14,962
	Export	402	2,136	5,656	8,141	13,193
Indonesia	Production	217	721	2,413	6,855	14,070
	Export	159	511	1,097	4,110	10,376
Thailand	Production	1	19	226	525	700
	Export	0	0	<1	37	81

Source: Food and Agriculture Organization of the United Nations, FAOSTAT, 12 Oct. 2008, http://faostat.fao.org/.

Table 4.5

World Palm Oil Imports ('000 Metric Tons), 2004/05–2007/08

	2004/05	2005/06	2006/07	2007/08
World	26,130	28,146	29,585	32,640
China	4,319	5,182	5,543	6,150
EU-27	4,489	4,534	4,777	5,060
India	3,342	2,820	3,664	4,500
Pakistan	1,683	1,728	1,743	1,700
Bangladesh	860	823	871	815
Egypt	723	669	876	760
Russian Fed.	594	581	495	600
Japan	486	497	516	528
Turkey	429	542	366	480

Source: Development Prospects Group, The World Bank.

such as between 1989 and 1993 when palm oil prices averaged less than US$290 per tonne. Palm oil prices were buoyant between 1994 and 1998 on the back of rising consumption, averaging US$510 per tonne. Palm oil prices collapsed in the aftermath of the Asian Financial Crisis, and hit a low of US$185 in early 2001.

Diagram 4.5

Price of Palm Oil (US$ Per Metric Ton), 1980 Jan.–2008 Nov.

Source: IMF Primary Commodities Prices, 9 Dec. 2008,
http://www.imf.org/external/np/res/commod/index.asp.

Note: Prices used refer to palm oil futures (first contract forward), 4–5 percent
FFA, Bursa Malaysian Derivatives Berhad.

The recent run-up of the palm oil prices can be largely attributed to the surging price of fossil oil and the development of biofuel as a substitute of fossil oil. Biofuel has been promoted as a renewable energy source that reduces net emissions of carbon dioxide into the atmosphere. In addition, biofuel is also viewed as a way of diversifying energy supplies in face of increasingly tighter supply of fossil oil in the future. Palm oil can be used as a feedstock for biofuel and has comparatively high yield among the vegetable oils. It is evident from Diagram 4.6 that, as stated earlier, there exists a high level of correlation between fossil oil price and palm oil price. Price of palm oil has fallen sharply since the middle of 2008 on the back of an equally sharp decline in fossil oil prices. In view of the global financial crisis in 2008, if fossil oil price is adversely affected in the foreseeable future, price of palm oil is likely to remain depressed. However, in the medium and long-term, the prospect of the industry appears very bright. Palm oil uses have in addition the important biofuel use. But other producers can join the production and export competition.

During the 1997–1998 Asian financial crisis, Indonesia, against IMF's advice, banned the export of palm oil, thus depriving itself of the much-needed foreign exchange, the lack of which constituted the basis

Diagram 4.6

Prices of Palm Oil and Fossil Oil, 2006 Jan.–2008 Nov.

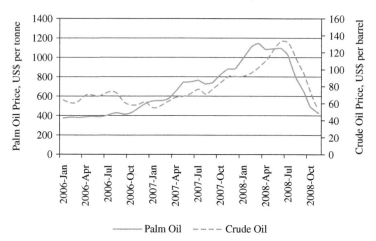

———— Palm Oil   – – – – Crude Oil

Source: IMF Primary Commodities Prices, 9 Dec. 2008,
   http://www.imf.org/external/np/res/commod/index.asp.
Note: Prices for palm oil refer to palm oil futures (first contract forward),
   4–5 percent FFA, Bursa Malaysian Derivatives Berhad. Prices for
   fossil oil refer to U.K. Brent (light), spot price, FOB U.K. ports,
   International Petroleum Exchange, London.

of the exchange rate generated crisis. The decision was later reversed. Indonesia still has plentiful supply of land suitable for oil palm cultivation, and attempts should be made, like Malaysia, to develop the industry not just for domestic consumption but also for exports. This development can be accelerated through the encouragement of foreign investment, particularly from Malaysia and Singapore, in this area.

One feature of the oil palm industry is that its output per hectare is very much higher than coconuts, and thus should be used to replace coconuts in plantations where soil and climatic conditions permit. Palm kernel oil and coconut oil have almost perfectly indistinguishable characteristics. Coconut palms, however, are useful in individual and small clusters to supplement the food and fuel supply of villages and subsistence farmers.

But even in palm oil cultivation, constant upgrading through replanting is necessary. Research has produced plants of shorter height to ease harvesting, plants that bear fruits earlier and plants that bear more fruits. A recent newspaper article reported that London Sumatra, an Indonesia plantation company part of the Indofood Group, has researched and developed a hybrid variety of oil palm seeds that could boost yields by at least 350 percent (*Financial Times*, 7 October 2008). Although the commercial roll-out of the new seeds is still a decade away, the successful adoption of the new seeds would have a huge impact on palm oil production.

Other Crops

Over the past decades, other than promoting industrialization and international tourism, the various Southeast Asian Governments have made efforts to diversify the agricultural base of their respective economies. While Southeast Asia was once well known as the rice bowl of Asia, since the 1960s, the region has also claimed new achievements in grabbing a slice of the world's market share of exports other than rubber and palm oil, but also those not commonly associated as the main agricultural produce from the region such as coffee, cocoa, tea, cassava, pepper and banana.

Southeast Asian farmers too have to be encouraged to grow vegetables to supplement their meagre income and the varieties of vegetables suitable for growth in Southeast Asia are enormous. Similarly, the rearing of poultry and fish and other types of animal husbandry to supplement their income should also be actively encouraged. The State should play an active supportive role in this direction of development.

Coffee and Tea

Vietnam is the world's second largest exporter of coffee after Brazil, surpassing other traditional coffee producers such as Colombia. The emergence of Vietnam as a formidable exporter of coffee is extraordinary. Vietnam was only exporting a meagre 4000 tonnes of coffee in 1980. In a short period of 25 years, exports grew by 220 times (see Table 4.6). Indonesia was the world's fourth largest exporter of coffee. Indonesia was also the world's fifth largest exporter of tea in 2005, after Kenya, Sri Lanka, China and India.

Cocoa

Cocoa production and exports have traditionally been dominated by the African countries and Brazil. Indonesia has emerged as a major producer and exporter of cocoa beans since 1990. In 2005, Indonesia was the world third

Table 4.6

Coffee Production and Export ('000 Metric Tons), 1970–2005

		1970	1980	1990	2000	2005
World	Production	3,850	4,837	6,071	7,555	7,133
	Export	3,282	3,747	5,043	5,927	6,265
Brazil	Production	755	1,061	1,465	1,904	2,140
	Export	963	784	853	968	1,356
Vietnam	Production	7	8	92	803	752
	Export	2	4	90	734	892
Colombia	Production	507	724	845	637	693
	Export	390	660	811	509	617
Indonesia	Production	185	295	413	555	640
	Export	104	239	422	339	446

Source: Food and Agriculture Organization of the United Nations, FAOSTAT, 12 Oct. 2008, http://faostat.fao.org/.

Note: Production refers to green coffee beans while export refers to both green coffee beans and roasted coffee products.

Table 4.7

Cocoa Beans Production and Export ('000 Metric Tons), 1970–2005

		1970	1980	1990	2000	2005
World	Production	1,543	1,671	2,532	3,380	3,992
	Export	1,136	1,065	1,896	2,503	2,932
Côte d'Ivoire	Production	179	417	808	1,401	1,286
	Export	143	285	676	1,113	991
Ghana	Production	406	277	293	437	740
	Export	367	195	249	360	535
Indonesia	Production	2	10	142	421	643
	Export	0	5	104	334	367
Malaysia	Production	3	35	247	70	28
	Export	2	31	163	11	9

Source: Food and Agriculture Organization of the United Nations, FAOSTAT, 12 Oct. 2008, http://faostat.fao.org/.

largest producer and exporter of cocoa beans after Côte d'Ivoire and Ghana (see Table 4.7). Malaysia followed some distant behind as the world's fourteenth largest producer and sixteenth largest exporter of cocoa beans. While Indonesia exports almost 80% of its cocoa production in 2000, the ratio decreased to 57% in 2005. This could imply the intensified development of downstream activities that use cocoa as an intermediate input in Indonesia.

Cassava

Thailand, Vietnam and Indonesia were the world top three exporters of cassava, jointly exporting 94% of total cassava exports in 2005 (see Table 4.8). Thailand alone has a market share of 80%. In terms of world's production of cassava, Thailand, Indonesia and Vietnam were the world's third, fourth and seventh largest producers of cassava. Cassava itself is a staple in many parts of the developing world but in the international realm, it is used as a substitute for grains in animal feeds. The major export market for cassava is the European Union.

Pepper

Pepper was traditionally an important cash crop in Southeast Asia. During the 17th and 18th centuries, pepper trade was already flourishing Sumatra.

Table 4.8

Cassava Production and Export ('000 Metric Tons), 1970–2005

		1970	1980	1990	2000	2005
World	Production	98,590	124,136	152,474	178,471	207,437
	Export	5,201	17,198	26,598	15,755	18,352
Thailand	Production	3,431	16,540	20,701	19,064	16,938
	Export	3,675	13,662	21,592	13,438	14,732
Vietnam	Production	945	3,323	2,276	1,986	6,646
	Export	—	—	70	338	1,335
Indonesia	Production	10,478	13,726	15,830	16,089	19,321
	Export	869	977	3,260	444	1,134

Source: Food and Agriculture Organization of the United Nations, FAOSTAT, 12 Oct. 2008, http://faostat.fao.org/.

Table 4.9
Pepper Production and Export ('000 Metric Tons), 1970–2005

		1970	1980	1990	2000	2005
World	Production	103	179	288	311	433
	Export	103	167	208	255	312
Vietnam	Production	0	1	11	51	80
	Export	—	—	9	36	109
Brazil	Production	14	63	78	39	79
	Export	9	32	29	20	38
Indonesia	Production	17	37	70	69	94
	Export	3	30	48	48	35
India	Production	26	29	55	59	73
	Export	20	27	29	19	21
Malaysia	Production	32	32	31	25	19
	Export	26	32	29	24	18

Source: Food and Agriculture Organization of the United Nations, FAOSTAT, 12 Oct. 2008, http://faostat.fao.org/.

Southeast Asian countries are still important producers and exporters of pepper in the present days. In 2007, Indonesia, Vietnam, Malaysia, Thailand, the Philippines and Cambodia were the world's first, second, sixth, eighth, tenth and fourteenth largest producers of pepper respectively. Together, these six countries produced 45% of the world's pepper output.

Maize

In Southeast Asia, Indonesia, the Philippines, Thailand and Vietnam are the major maize producers in the region. Together, these four countries accounted for 4% of global output of maize in 2005. The bulk of the maize is grown for own consumption. Output has grown over the last three decades in all the four countries, but most dramatically in Vietnam. However, Southeast Asia's export market share was low and remains low. In fact, these four countries were all net importers of maize in 2005.

In contrast to the application of new technology in the planting of rice, rubber and palm oil, there has, however, been no major technological breakthrough in maize production in Southeast Asia. Much of the increase in output has been made possible by an expansion in area rather than through productivity improvement. Output productivity has increased by leaps and bounds in the United States, for example, mainly because of the use of better seeds. Incidentally, maize too is being used as a partial substitute for fossil oil in the U.S. and Western Europe, but maize is not a perennial crop like oil palm. Maize is bi-annual.

Sugar

The major sugar producers in the region are Thailand, the Philippines, Indonesia, and Vietnam. However, only Thailand has significant sugar exports. In 2005, Thailand's share of world export market of sugar was 6.1%. Malaysia, the second largest sugar exporter in Southeast Asia, had a market share of only 1.1%. Sugar faces protectionist barriers in the temperate developed areas, particularly in the EU. International forums that place pressure on the developed countries to remove protectionist measures will be important. On their part, Southeast Asian sugar producers and their Governments have to increase their effort to provide irrigation facilities and improve cultivation practices to enhance the cost-effectiveness of their sugar cane industry.

Banana

The Philippines, Indonesia, Thailand and Vietnam are significant producers of bananas. They were the world's third, sixth, ninth and twelfth largest producers of bananas in 2007. However, only the Philippines has significant banana exports. In 2005, the Philippines was the world's second largest exporter of bananas after Ecuador, with a market share of 11%. The main export market is Japan. After a long period of decline since early 1980s, Philippine production of bananas increased significantly in the 1990s. The production of bananas in 2007 is 2.4 times the production level in 1990.

Key Points

1. Plantation crops such as rubber and oil palm, unlike rice, are mainly grown to earn income and foreign exchange for their countries. Thailand, Indonesia, Malaysia and Vietnam are the four largest natural rubber exporters in the world, cornering 89% of the world export market. Palm oil industry has great potential, and more and more resources have been devoted to the development of this industry, particularly in Indonesia and Malaysia.

2. The majority of the rubber farmers in Southeast Asia are smallholders. They suffer from low productivity and have low incomes. Research in the areas of reducing the costs of natural rubber production and increasing the uses of natural rubber should intensify. These efforts may go a long way in improving the livelihood of the rubber farmers and the natural rubber industry as a whole.

3. The development of synthetic rubber since the Second World War has posed serious competition to natural rubber. Currently, synthetic rubber has enjoyed around a 57% market share of the world's total rubber consumption. The introduction of synthetic rubber has also capped the increase in the prices of natural rubber but reduced the volatility of price fluctuation.

4. The volatility of the prices of natural rubber has prompted the setting up of various price stabilisation schemes from as early as the 1920s. However, none of these schemes had been of real help to the rubber industry. Even though some of the schemes, especially the earlier schemes, were able to artificially hold up the prices of natural rubber, it was done at the expense of severe curtailment of rubber production and inviting new comers from other countries to the market. The lack of success of the rubber agreements is attributable to the fact that rubber is a replaceable resource with a ready availability of substitute in synthetic rubber and natural rubber from new sources of supply.

5. Until recently, Malaysia was the most important producer and exporter of rubber. She has, however, lost her comparative advantage of producing natural rubber to Thailand and Indonesia. Countries such as Vietnam and the Philippines are also fast catching up to be significant producers and exporters of natural rubber. In response to the changing

comparative advantages, Malaysia has, however, directed her resources into the production of palm oil due to the more lucrative returns from the industry, and into the production and export of manufactured goods and international tourism.

6. Malaysia and Indonesia are the world's leading producers and exporters of palm oil. Palm kernel oil and coconut oil have very similar characteristics, but the output per hectare of oil palm is very much higher than that of coconuts palm. In addition, both Indonesia and Malaysia still have plentiful supply of land suitable for oil palm cultivation. Thus attempts should be made to further develop the industry for domestic consumption and exports. Attempts should continue to be made for the wider use of palm oil as a biofuel.

7. Other crops in Southeast Asia that are grown for export include coffee, cocoa beans, cassava, pepper, sugar and maize. However, crops such as maize are grown mainly for own consumption. Maize and cassava are a major source of carbohydrates for most developing countries, including those in Southeast Asia.

8. Governments should play an active role in encouraging Southeast Asian farmers to grow vegetables to supplement their meagre income. Similarly, the rearing of poultry and fish and other types of animal husbandry to supplement their income should also be encouraged. Much more effort can be done and should be done in promoting income and productivity and in agricultural diversification in Southeast Asia.

Suggested Discussion Topics

4.1 In the face of synthetic rubber competition, is there a future for the rubber growing industry in Southeast Asia, in particular in Malaysia? Discuss.

4.2 Is it true that other than rubber and palm oil, Southeast Asian dominance of the world market for primary products is not there? Discuss. Also discuss ways and means of augmenting farm incomes in Southeast Asia and the role of the State.

4.3 Why is it that there are less compelling reasons to have international commodity agreements on natural rubber than to have them on tin or petroleum? Do you agree? Discuss with reference to Southeast Asia.

4.4 Do you think Agriculture Ministers in Southeast Asia should meet more often to highlight the importance of agricultural diversification and development in Southeast Asia? What should they discuss at such meetings? Discuss.

References

BARLOW, Colin, S. K. JAYASURIYA and C. S. TAN, 1994, *The World Rubber Industry*, London, New York: Routledge.

LIM, Chong Yah, 1967, *Economic Development in Modern Malaya*, Kuala Lumpur: Oxford University Press.

Further Readings

BASIRON, Yusof, 2007, "Palm oil production through sustainable plantations", *European Journal of Lipid Science and Technology,* 109(4), 289–295.

BAUER, P.T., 1984, *Reality and Rhetoric: Studies in the Economics of Development*, London: Weidenfeld and Nicolson.

GHATAK, S. and K. INGERSENT, 1984, *Agriculture and Economic Development*, Brighton, Sussex: Wheatsheaf Books.

GRIFFIN, Keith, 1979, *Political Economy of Agrarian Change: An Essay on the Green Revolution*, London: MacMillan.

LIM, Chong Yah, 1960, "Export taxes on rubber in Malaya — A survey of post-war development", *Malayan Economic Review*, 5(2), 46–58.

LIM, Chong Yah, 1961, "The Malayan rubber replanting taxes", *Malayan Economic Review*, 6(2), 43–52.

MYINT, Hla, 1972, *Southeast Asia's Economy: Development Policies in the 1970s*, New York: Praeger Publishers.

SCHULTZ, T. W., 1964, *Transforming Traditional Agriculture*, New Haven and London: Yale University Press.

Sime Darby Berhad, 2008, *Annual Report 2008*.

Wilmar International Limited, 2007, *Annual Report 2007*.

Chapter 5

Agriculture: Prospects and Policy Options

Give a man a fish and he eats for a day.
Teach the man to fish and he eats for a lifetime.

Old Proverb

Objectives

✓ Point out the economic unfeasibility of self-sufficiency in food.
✓ Highlight the situation of unfair land ownership and its implications.
✓ Discuss issues relating to trade policy.
✓ Discuss international commodity stabilisation agreements.
✓ Describe and evaluate the success of price stabilisation agreements of tin and rubber.
✓ Show the effects of government policies on agricultural development.

Introduction

Agricultural development in Southeast Asia is not even. On the one hand, subsistence farming is technologically outdated. Rice yields in most Southeast Asian countries are relatively low. Further, many of the Southeast Asian countries grow rice with the objective of becoming self-sufficient in food. On the other hand, plantation crops such as rubber and oil palm are cultivated using more advanced technologies. Extensive research and large amount of money are committed to the development of better species. Moreover, these plantation crops are direct earners of foreign exchange for the countries.

Government plays a critical role in determining the path of agricultural development. In accordance with Ricardo's theory of comparative advantage, a country should only produce goods that it has a comparative advantage in. A country that produces rice, whatever the comparative disadvantage, just to satisfy the objective of being self-sufficient will be doing it to the detriment of the overall economy. This is true too with other food crops, such as wheat or sugar. Conversely, the cultivation of suitable cash crops for exports should be encouraged. However, international trade comes with its own set of problems. For example in 2008, global rice shortage prompted rice-exporting countries to ban export so as to secure sufficient stock for their domestic consumption. The ban aggravated the increase of rice price and sent the rice-importing countries scrambling to find other sources of rice. Another important issue that the Government should address is the problem of land ownership and tenancy. Without an amicable settlement of the land issue, economic progress in the agricultural sector will not take off. Last but not least, the price policies implemented by the Government, if not appropriate, will have dire consequences on the development of the agricultural sector.

Food Self-Sufficiency

The growing demand for food is of major economic significance in all Southeast Asian countries. Firstly, high rates of domestic population growth exceeding 2% characterise many of these countries (see Table 3.4). Growth of demand for food arising from population growth alone is, therefore, substantial. Secondly, the income elasticity of demand for food in the low-income countries and lower middle-income countries of Southeast Asia is likely to be considerably higher than in the high-income nations[1].

---

[1]JOHNSTON, and MELLOR (1961) suggested that the income elasticity of demand for food in LDCs is probably of the order 0.6 or higher in the low-income countries as against 0.2 or 0.3 in Western Europe, the United States and Canada.

Thus, a given rate of increase in per capita income has a considerably stronger impact on the demand for food in most of Southeast Asian countries. The supply of food will have to be domestically produced or imported. Although rice is not the only food consumed, it is the staple of Southeast Asian countries.

With the projected population growth rates for the Southeast Asian countries, and assuming even a modest rise in per capita income, the annual rate of increase in demand for food can easily exceed 3%. Rice production, on the aggregate, however, has been able to keep pace at least with population growth in the last four decades in all the Southeast Asian rice-producing countries except Brunei, Malaysia and Cambodia. The argument assumes that there is free trade between food producers and non-food producers within the same country. The non-food producers should include rubber and palm oil producers, tin miners, the petroleum-producing sector and the increasingly important manufacturing and international tourism sectors. With increasing industrialisation, pressure for increased demand for food will also come from the expansion of the urban population. Thus, there will be additional problems in developing transportation links and marketing facilities in order to satisfy the requirements of the increasingly growing non-agricultural population.

If food supplies fail to expand in tune with the growth of demand, the result will be a substantial rise in food prices. It is further argued that food imports can strain balance of payments, cause currency depreciation and further aggravate domestic inflation. Moreover, because higher food prices are likely to result eventually in higher industrial wages, industrial product prices can also be expected to rise. With both food and industrial product prices higher, inflation is the result. The inflationary impact of a given percentage increase in food prices is likely to be much more severe in a low-income country than in a developed country, since food occupies a dominant position as wage good in the budgets of the consumers of the low-income countries.

Another problem that arises from food price increases follows from the fact that the price elasticity for "all food" must be considerably low. Cheap starchy staple foods — rice and other cereals — make up a significant portion of total calorie intake for the Southeast Asian populace so that there is relatively limited scope for offsetting a rise in food prices by shifting from expensive to less costly food. The pressure to resist a reduction in calorie intake is also strong. However, if the factors of production are diverted from food production to higher value-added economic pursuits, the resultant outcome on prices, including food prices could be very different. This argument assumes that there is international trade.

However, for those countries that are in a favourable position to shift to other higher value-added economic pursuits, that may bring in the foreign exchange for various imports. In view of the potential that exists for increasing agricultural productivity, it may nevertheless be argued that it is likely to be advantageous to obtain the additional food supplies by increasing domestic output rather than by relying solely on expansion of exports of industrial products to finance enlarged food imports. Another popular reason often cited in favour of food self-sufficiency, in particular rice self-sufficiency, is food security. Nonetheless, the case for autarky in food supply for every country regardless of factor endowment may be a sure road to immiserising the country, as it ignores all the benefits of international trade and the theory of comparative costs. Resources are scarce and should be put to use where the returns are the highest. In the case of food security, the question would then be whether food security can be attained in any other ways, such as stockpiling, diversification of sources of food supply, and agreements with various countries for long term supply. Self-sufficiency in food production holds water, if there is no international trade, and domestically, there is free trade. If domestically there is no free trade, every family will have to be self-sufficient in food production. Services like medical and health care, education, transportation and communication cannot exist, and if they exist, will be at a very low level.

Agricultural Exports and Imports

There is some variation among the Southeast Asian countries in the extent to which agricultural exports contribute to foreign exchange earnings. In 1985, agricultural exports of Malaysia and the Philippines earned about 25% of these countries' gross foreign exchange income from merchandise trade, while Thailand and Myanmar earned 45% and 43% respectively. Agricultural exports contributed a substantial 76% of export earnings in

Table 5.1
Agricultural Exports as a Percentage of Total Merchandise Exports
(by Value in US$), 1985 and 2005

	1985	2005
Indonesia	13.3	12.8
Thailand	45.0	11.2
Vietnam	30.4	11.1
Malaysia	24.3	7.6
Myanmar	43.1	7.0
Philippines	25.1	6.2
Laos	21.4	3.8
Singapore	8.0	1.6
Cambodia	76.3	1.3
Brunei	0.2	0.0

Source: Derived from data from Food and Agriculture Organization of the
United Nations, FAOSTAT, 4 Nov. 2008, http://faostat.fao.org/.

Cambodia. In Indonesia, the share is lower, comprising about 13%, largely
due to the dominance of oil exports then. In 2005, all the Southeast Asian
countries earned less than 13% of their export earnings from agriculture
(see Table 5.1). The decline in agricultural exports of Southeast Asia countries reflects their successful industrialisation after WWII. In some cases
the relative decline also reflects the emergence of petroleum oil exports.
Brunei, Malaysia and Vietnam have significant oil exports in their export
compositions. With the completion of two large offshore gas field projects in late 1990s, Yadana and Yetagun, gas export is currently Myanmar's
largest single export earner.

It has been argued that in a country with a lagging agricultural sector and
a large food import bill, food production should be expanded for the domestic market rather than to encourage agricultural exports. This policy is called
import-substitution. This policy is sound, if hitherto unutilised resources are
thus utilised. It is unsound, if utilised resources including land, labour and
capital are diverted to achieve this end and at the expense of other exports.
The trouble with an import-substitution policy is that it often leads to the
misallocation of scarce resources. Export-orientation, on the other hand,

ensures efficient utilisation of scarce resources, be they land, labour and capital, and if the policy is successfully carried out, the balance of payments position will be improved, incomes will be increased, and standards of living enhanced.

Among the Southeast Asian countries, the largest relative import bill for cereals is borne by Indonesia, the Philippines and Brunei (see Table 5.2).

Table 5.2

Agricultural and Cereals Imports as a Percentage of Total Merchandise Imports (by Value in US$), 1985 and 2005

		1985	2005
Brunei	Agricultural	18.6	13.4
	Cereals	1.5	1.5
Cambodia	Agricultural	14.7	10.8
	Cereals	13.3	0.2
Indonesia	Agricultural	8.8	9.0
	Cereals	2.7	1.8
Laos	Agricultural	1.9	19.1
	Cereals	1.2	0.9
Malaysia	Agricultural	12.0	5.2
	Cereals	2.8	0.8
Myanmar	Agricultural	5.9	25.6
	Cereals	0.0	1.4
Philippines	Agricultural	11.2	8.4
	Cereals	5.3	1.7
Singapore	Agricultural	9.3	2.5
	Cereals	0.6	0.1
Thailand	Agricultural	5.9	3.6
	Cereals	0.3	0.2
Vietnam	Agricultural	9.4	6.4
	Cereals	4.9	0.7

Source: Derived from data from Food and Agriculture Organization of the United Nations, FAOSTAT, 4 Nov. 2008, http://faostat.fao.org/.

Table 5.3

Per Capita Cereal Imports (US$), 1985 and 2005

	1985	2005
Brunei	41.8	58.9
Singapore	53.7	41.5
Malaysia	22.2	34.1
Philippines	5.3	10.0
Indonesia	1.7	4.5
Thailand	0.6	4.4
Vietnam	1.5	3.0
Laos	0.7	1.3
Cambodia	2.0	0.6
Myanmar	0.0	0.5

Source: Food and Agriculture Organization of the United
Nations, FAOSTAT, 4 Nov. 2008,
http://faostat.fao.org/.

On a per capita basis, Brunei is most dependent on imported cereals, followed by Singapore and Malaysia (see Table 5.3), and yet these three countries have the highest per capita income in Southeast Asia. A close analysis of the exports of Southeast Asian countries shows that the comparative advantage of the countries most dependent upon cereal imports lies in non-food products: petroleum and petroleum products in Brunei; manufactured goods, palm oil and petroleum in Malaysia; and services and manufactured goods in Singapore.

It is claimed that there are some disadvantages of heavy reliance on agricultural exports. Trade in the Southeast Asian countries tends to be concentrated in a few key commodities. Geographic or market concentration also prevails, that is, most of the major exports are sold in a few markets of the industrialised countries, namely Japan, Western Europe and North America. Such a geographic concentration has the implication that the economic fortunes of the Southeast Asian countries are strongly related to the rise and fall of the domestic and economic activities of these industrialised countries. That is the price paid for specialisation and international division of labour. That too does not mean that domestic stabilisation measures cannot be adopted or implemented. Neither does the argument takes into consideration the emergence of other important markets in emerging countries such as China and India. In the chapter on rubber and palm oil, the statistics show that both rubber and palm oil in Southeast Asia have found their way to China and India as their most important importers.

It has also been argued that the degree of fluctuations in the export prices of agricultural and other primary commodities is higher than the extent of fluctuations in the export prices of manufactured goods. The income and price elasticity of demand for agricultural products are usually less than unity. Given a low-income elasticity, with economic growth and a rise in per capita income in the developed countries, the increase in demand for agricultural products will tend to decline in proportional terms. This will have an adverse effect on the export earnings of the agricultural economies. Similarly, with low price elasticity of demand, an increase in supply of agricultural products in the international market will sharply reduce prices. Moreover, the additional demand generated by the decline in price of agricultural exports will be unable to prevent a decline in total revenue. Policies toward primary commodity price stabilisation wherever feasible are clearly important, but more often than not they have failed miserably, as is the case of natural rubber.

Another point that has been made in the literature on economic development concerns the problem of a secular downward trend in the terms of trade of agricultural economies, where the terms of trade are defined as the ratio of export price received to import price paid by the agricultural economies in their trade with the developed nations. Analysis of agricultural commodity prices over the past 40 years reveals that real prices of agricultural commodities, relative to prices of all manufactured goods, have declined significantly, even as nominal prices have risen (FAO, 2004). The adverse effect of a declining terms of trade on economic welfare that arises from economic growth that is biased in favour of the agricultural export sector can be diagrammatically illustrated.

Before discussing the adverse effect due to the decline in terms of trade, the production and consumption patterns of a closed economy are analysed. In Diagram 5.1, industrial goods are measured on the vertical axis and agricultural goods on the horizontal axis. The domestic production possibility frontier is given by P_0P_0', and the relative price line, also

Diagram 5.1
Production and Consumption in a Closed Economy

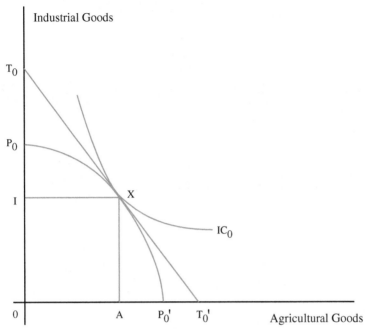

known as the budget line, is given by T_0T_0'. Since it is a closed economy which is not involved in international trade, the relative price line is governed by the domestic price levels of the industrial and agricultural goods. Optimal production takes place at the point of tangency (point X) of the relative price line and the production possibility frontier. OA units of agricultural goods and OI units of industrial goods are produced. Consumption is determined by the point of tangency (also the point X) of the relative price line and the indifference curve IC_0. Thus, without international trade, consumption is equal to production at X on the production possibility frontier.

In Diagram 5.2, the case of an open economy is illustrated. Before growth takes place, the production possibility frontier is P_0P_0', and production takes place at X where the relative price line, T_0T_0', is tangent to P_0P_0'. With international trade, the relative price line also measures the terms of trade between the two commodities in the international markets. Consumption is now at Y where the indifference curve IC_0 is tangent to the relative price

Diagram 5.2

Production and Consumption in an Open Economy

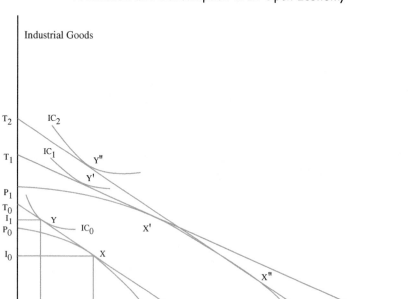

line, T_0T_0'. The economy produces OA_0 units of agricultural goods and OI_0 units of industrial goods.

It consumes OA_1 units of agricultural goods and OI_1 units of industrial goods. The diagram shows that $OA_1 < OA_0$ and $OI_1 > OI_0$. This implies that A_1A_0 units of agricultural goods are exported to finance the import of I_0I_1 units of industrial goods.

With a growth that is biased towards agriculture, the production possibility frontier shifts outward from the origin to P_1P_1', with the shift on the horizontal axis farther away. *Ceteris paribus*, as more agricultural goods are produced relative to industrial goods, the international terms of trade for agricultural goods deteriorate. The new relative price line is T_1T_1', and production takes place at X', which is above and to the right of X. Therefore, the economy produces more of both kinds of goods, although the agricultural goods increase more than the industrial goods. Consumption is at Y' on IC_1. More agricultural goods and more industrial goods are consumed. Since IC_1 is above and to the right of IC_0, there is a gain in welfare.

Now, consider the case where the terms of trade remain the same despite the growth in the agricultural sector. This new situation is illustrated by the tangency of the relative price line T_2T_2' to P_1P_1'. T_2T_2' is parallel to T_0T_0' which implies unchanged terms of trade. It is to the right of T_0T_0' which means an increase in income. Production takes place at X". Here, more agricultural goods are produced at the expense of industrial goods. Consumption takes place at Y" on IC_2, which is higher than IC_1. Thus, consumers' welfare increases significantly since they consume more of both goods than in the situation before growth takes place. Consumers' welfare in this case is also higher than the case where international terms of trade for agricultural goods deteriorate. In the latter case, less industrial goods are consumed. This is the result of the substitution effect as industrial goods are now much more expensive. Thus, it can be seen that deterioration in the terms of trade leads to a smaller increase in welfare than the situation where the relative prices remain the same. It can also be shown that in extreme cases of the deterioration in the terms of trade, growth in the agriculture sector actually leads to lower welfare than before growth takes place. This is known as immiseration (Bhagwati, 1958).

However, with more and more countries, especially huge nations like China and India, successfully joining the industrialization bandwagon, the terms of trade moving in favour of agricultural exports cannot be ruled out. Besides, the full utilization of the land and labour resources and factor endowment should be factored in in the degree of priority for agricultural exports.

Problems of Land Ownership and Land Tenure

Apart from some of the oil palm and rubber plantations that are large estates and that are most prevalent in Malaysia, most of the other crops are raised on smallholdings in Southeast Asia. Some countries also show a high concentration of operating units in a few large farms. This is especially so in the Philippines, where tenancy is also important while partial ownership (partly owned and partly rented) is also quite common.

Control of large land size often gives the landlord ease of access to other resources as well, in particular, to the capital market. Such landlords have idle cash balances upon which they can draw to finance purchases of material inputs and make wage payments. Moreover, they can obtain capital easily in the organised credit market. They have ready access to commercial banks outside the farming locality and can obtain loans at preferential interest rates since their wealth, income and status make the risk of lending to them minimal. The small peasant, in contrast, has little working capital and restricted access to credit.

Unequal access to land and capital frequently is accentuated by unequal access to water and technical knowledge. The large landowners, in effect, are able to exercise some control over all the material inputs in their locality, and because of their greater literacy, social status and political influence they are invariably the first to learn about and adopt new methods of production. The whole process of agricultural growth, therefore, tends to increase inequality of income and wealth. Furthermore, in an agrarian economy, control of land, credit and water enables landowners to influence the local labour market as well. That is, monopoly of material resources gives the landlords monopsony power over labour. This tends to undercut rural wages and further acts to increase inequalities.

The bias in the imperfect factor markets that is in favour of the large landowners has implications for the techniques of cultivation used in agriculture. The alternative methods of cultivating a particular crop, say, rice can be represented in terms of a discontinuous isoquant which indicates the various combinations of labour and material inputs which can be used to produce a given quantity of rice. Each farmer will try to minimise the cost of producing any given quantity of food grains. The most economical method of cultivation will depend on relative factor prices. It can be argued that since material inputs are relatively more expensive to small peasants than to large landowners, the two types of farmers would adopt different techniques of production. The peasant farmer will adopt a relatively labour-intensive method of production, while the large landowner will adopt a relatively capital-intensive method. In comparison with the socially optimal combination of inputs, the small farmer, therefore, tends to be insufficiently capital-intensive and the large farmer tends to be insufficiently labour-intensive. Neither of these achieves technical and allocative efficiency in production, and the consumer and the society pay for the inefficiency.

There are some specific advantages of owner cultivation related to productivity considerations as well as the more obvious effects on income distribution. Although in principle, investments in land improvement that are profitable will be made by the landowner, by the tenant, or under some joint agreement, the division of responsibility in decision-making is likely to delay or prevent investments even though they would be to the advantage of both parties. Owner cultivation also avoids the difficulties that arise when landlords, responding to higher yields, raise the percentage share of output that they demand as rent. It seems, therefore, that there is a strong case for both land reform and tenancy reform in the Southeast Asian countries.

The record of achievement of land reforms in Southeast Asia on the whole, however, has not been encouraging. This is explained partly by the lack of serious commitment on the part of policy makers as well as weaknesses in the land reform legislations and cumbersome administrative procedures.

A case in point is the Philippines. It had one of the highest farm tenancy rates in Asia, especially in Central Luzon. The country had also experienced more peasant unrest than other Southeast Asian countries and consequently, had the most comprehensive experience of land reform practices in the region. The Agricultural Tenancy Act in 1964 provided a formula for crop sharing, for the promotion of resettlement of public lands, and for the expropriation of landed estates to provide family-size farms for landless tenants. An unrealistic ceiling for landlords, however, prevented the Act from producing effective results. This led to the passing of the more comprehensive and formal Land Reform Code in 1963. The Code shifted the emphasis away from expropriation to a two-stage conversion of share-croppers into leaseholders and leaseholders into owner-operators. Again implementation had not been effective. In 1972, after martial law was declared, it was announced that all rice and maize tenants were to be emancipated, and the whole country was to be covered by land reforms. Redistribution of land, however, has been hindered by landowners' political influence, harassment of tenants and protracted litigation (Dorner and Thiesenhusen, 1990). The program was generally considered a failure. By 1985, only 25 percent of the expected beneficiaries had become owner-cultivators. In 1988, the Philippine Congress passed the Comprehensive Agrarian Reform Law. Under the Reform Law, landowners were allowed to retain up to five hectares plus three hectares for each heir at least 15 years of age, the amount of land that could be retained was to be gradually decreased, and a non-land-transfer, profit-sharing program could be used as an alternative to actual land transfer. Proponents of land reform considered the stock-ownership provision a loophole in the law.

Trade Policy

Two important questions of trade policy are: (1) whether countries exporting agricultural goods should continue to raise government revenue through the imposition of export taxes on their agricultural goods or should export taxes be eliminated/reduce to boost export, and (2) whether countries without comparative advantage in food crop production, in particular rice, should adopt measures to protect domestic food crop production.

Export taxes are mainly used by developing and least-developed countries (LDCs); only a few OECD countries use export taxes. Table 5.4 shows selected Southeast Asian countries that impose export taxes. Among the objectives for which export taxes have been used are to increase tax revenue, stabilize prices (via progressive export tax rates) and improve terms-of-trade. Export taxes are sometimes used to discourage exports with the aim to secure adequate domestic supply and to lower domestic prices. Export taxes on unprocessed commodities, such as crude palm oil, are also used to encourage downstream value-adding processes to take place in the home countries.

Generally speaking, export taxes imposed by a "large" country, i.e. country with large market share, would depress the domestic price of the taxed commodity, increase the international price and reduce the volume of trade. Thus, if a "large" country implements an export tax, there will be an efficiency loss, an improvement of the terms-of-trade for the exporting country, but a worsening of the importing country's terms-of-trade. However, increase in international prices will encourage other producers to expand output, and weaken the leading position of the "large" countries over the long term. If the country imposing the export tax is a "small" country, i.e. country with small market share, domestic price of the taxed commodity would be depressed but impact on international price and trade volume is negligible. In this case, there is no terms-of-trade gain for the "small" countries (Piermartini, 2004).

Table 5.4

Export Taxes in Selected Southeast Asian Countries

Country	Year	Commodity	Tax Rate
Indonesia	2007	logs	10%
		rattan	5%
		crude palm oil and (depending on price per tonne)	10%, 15% or 20%
Malaysia	2006	petroleum oil	10% *ad valorem*
		crude palm oil (depending on price per tonne)	10–30%
		logs	15%
		cockles (molluscs), live cattle, buffaloes, goats, and wild animals and birds	5%
Philippines	2005	logs	20%
Thailand	2003	hides of bovine animals	B0.4–B5 per kg
		wood, sawn wood and articles made of wood	0–40%

Sources: WTO, Trade Policy Review: Indonesia, 2007.
WTO, Trade Policy Review: Malaysia, 2006.
WTO, Trade Policy Review: Philippines, 2005.
WTO, Trade Policy Review: Thailand, 2003.
Jakarta Post, February 5, 2008.

Note: Export taxes applied to crude palm oil in Indonesia change frequently, often in reaction to international palm oil prices. In April 2008 when palm oil prices skyrocketed, Indonesia imposed a 20 percent tariff on export of crude palm oil, in an attempt to reduce prices in local Indonesia markets. In November 2008 when palm oil prices plummeted and Indonesia faced an oversupply situation, the Indonesian government announced a national crude palm oil export tax exemption aimed to stimulate exports.

Consider the dilemma facing the two rice-exporting nations Myanmar and Thailand. One option is to continue to impose export taxes on rice; the Government can raise revenue from this source. Myanmar and Thailand have both adopted such a policy at least in the immediate post-war period, although Thailand has shifted away from taxing rice exports since 1986. The level of applied export taxes in Thailand has in fact been very low for the last two decades, and their contribution to the government revenue is almost negligible. Thailand, however, could in principle reintroduce statutory export taxes on rice (10%), rubber (40%), and several other commodities without the need for legislative approval. Imposition of export taxes tends to encourage other rice exporting countries to increase their share of the market; moreover, it encourages rice-deficit countries to seek self-sufficiency in rice by planting the new HYVs. Local farmers are also discouraged from adopting the modern seed-technology in rice production. Instead, the export tax had induced rice farmers in Thailand to shift to other food crops.

Another alternative would be for Thailand and Myanmar to exploit their comparative advantage in rice by eliminating export taxes, and hence expand production and regain some of the markets lost to other competitors and to import-substitution in the rice-deficit countries. This is the policy which has been adopted by Thailand. Such a policy is, however, not without problems. The loss of export markets may be irreversible at least in the short run since countries that have adopted a policy of import-substitution in rice, for example, Indonesia and the Philippines, might not abandon their policies. Moreover, the new rice technology tends to be biased against the rice-exporting countries that grow rice under conditions of uncontrolled river flooding. Thus, in the long run, the costs of cultivation in the importing countries may fall relative to costs in the traditional exporting countries.

Thailand and Myanmar, however, remain relatively low cost producers. Despite problems that will be encountered by a policy of vigorous price competition and export promotion, it may be in the interest of both countries to enlarge and strengthen their positions in the global rice export market. Thailand, indeed, has been successful in increasing rice exports. Over the period 1980–2005, rice exports grew at a compound annual growth rate of 2.9% in Thailand. On the other hand, rice exports in Myanmar have fluctuated widely over the years between a high of 939,100 tons in 2001 and a low of 28,300 tons in 1997. Comparison over the last 25 years shows that rice exports have fallen from an annual average of 520,000 tons in the 1980s to 244,000 tons in the 1990s, and then increased to an annual average of 435,000 tons between 2000 and 2005. Much more impressive is Vietnam's rice export performance; between 1980 and 2005, the compound annual rate of growth of rice exports was 16%.

The new agricultural technology offers the rice-deficit Southeast Asian countries not only the physical possibility of self-sufficiency but also the economic opportunity of lowering the cost of production of rice and other agricultural products. In focusing excessively on the former, these countries are in danger of neglecting the latter. A rice-deficit country may easily encourage the substitution of imported rice by domestically produced rice through agricultural protection and subsidy. The real issue, however, is the extent to which it can reduce the price of rice and allow the imported rice to compete freely with the domestically produced rice.

Indonesia has cut export taxes in recent years in bid to bolster exports and increase its foreign-exchange reserves. It reduced export taxes by 20% at end 1998 and another 25% at end 2000. The commodities covered paper pulp, wood chips, veneer, railroad sleepers, rattan, logs, sawn timber and natural sand, and the raw materials for producing these products. Export taxes on these goods had been as high as 200% for logs but have now fallen to just 10%. The export tax on rattan fell to 5% (WTO, 2007).

Another issue to be considered here concerns the trade policies adopted by the developed countries toward the agricultural products of LDCs. Here, it should be noted that various tropical agricultural products such as rubber, palm oil, coffee, cocoa and pepper do not compete with temperate agricultural products, and do not suffer significantly from agricultural protection in the temperate developed countries. An exception is sugar, which is an important export of Thailand. Sugar can be produced either from cane in tropical countries or from beet in temperate countries, and the tropical sugar producing countries have undoubtedly suffered from the protection of beet sugar production in Europe and North America. As for the tropical non-food agricultural products, the competition faced by the agricultural economies is not from agriculture in the developed countries but from industry, which produces, for example, synthetic rubber. Restricting the development of these synthetic substitutes would help the exporting countries, but clearly, would be hard to implement. What can be done, however, is for the Governments of developed countries to refrain from subsidising the production of synthetic commodities and beet sugar. But, for whatever reasons, countries in Southeast Asia that have lost their competitiveness in the production of a particular commodity should shift to the production of other commodities, as Malaysia has ably and successfully done in the shifting from rubber to palm oil.

In our view, Southeast Asian nations should look into the removal of all export taxes on agricultural products in order to enhance their competitive position in the world markets. This move is far from the opposite polar position of heavily subsidising agriculture, including agricultural exports, in developed countries.

Commodity Stabilisation

Policy Instruments

Two policy instruments can be used for the purpose of price stabilisation: buffer stock and export control. These two instruments can be used as a stand-alone measure, or together as a package. Contribution to the buffer stock is generally made in a combination of both cash and the commodity. A Buffer Stock Manager will use cash to buy the commodity if the market price is falling towards the floor price, and will sell the stockpiled commodity if the market price is too high. The buffer stock scheme is most workable and can be best defended if the prevailing market price is around the mean price of the buffer stock floor and ceiling price, or that the foreseeable market price is likely to remain in the middle range. If the objective of the commodity agreement is to maintain the highest possible price for the commodity, with the floor price being set unrealistically high, defending the scheme using buffer stock will not be viable.

Such a situation would point toward the use of export control as a policy instrument. The Organisation of Petroleum Exporting Countries (OPEC) has successfully utilised export control in raising petroleum prices. Export controls were also used in various other commodity agreements. For example, the International Tin Agreement had restricted export resulting in the curtailment of production to the tune of 30% to 40% during 1957 to 1958. However, the effectiveness of export control would be undermined if member nations cheat on their export quotas or if non-member nations start to gain bigger market shares, especially in cases where the exports are producible and are not wasting assets, such as natural rubber, palm oil, coffee and tea or bananas.

Commodity agreement is most successful when the commodity is irreplaceable and non-substitutable. A good example would be petroleum. Using the same argument, tin, being an irreplaceable asset, its commodity agreement is likely to enjoy a higher degree of success than that of natural rubber, which can be easily substituted with other products, like synthetic rubber. While both tin and petroleum are both non-substitutable in the short run, they are substitutable in the long run. Solar energy, nuclear energy, and hydro energy are all substitutes of petroleum as energy sources, although these substitutes are not comparable to petroleum in terms of ease of usage and/or cost efficiency. Lately, biodiesel is also increasingly used as a substitute. On the other hand, tin cans and tin containers have already given way to plastic and paper products, which are cheaper substitutes of tin products.

Price Stabilisation Agreements

Southeast Asia is a major producer and exporter of raw materials, notably rubber and palm oil, and used to be a major producer and exporter of tin. As most of these raw materials have high price volatility, there appears to be a need for commodity agreements to stabilise prices through the maintenance of a buffer stock and/or export control.

The first International Tin Agreement (ITA) came into operation from 1931 to 1933, the second from 1934 to 1936, and the third, 1937 to 1941 (Lim C. Y., 1967). The Second World War broke out in late 1941. With the Japanese forces occupying Southeast Asia, which produced about 70% of the world's tin supply, an international tin-control scheme (1942–1946) though in existence, was not meaningful. In the post-Second World War period, the first scheme operated between mid 1956 and mid 1961. There were five successive Tin Agreements, but they had all retained essentially the same provisions.

The main device used in all the Tin Agreements was export control, although buffer stock operations also played an important role as part of the supply adjustment mechanism. While buffer stocks were mere adjuncts to the Tin Agreements in the pre-war scheme, and set up only when export control operations failed, or seemed likely to fail, buffer stocks have become part and parcel of the Tin Agreements in the post-war schemes.

The International Tin Council, representing most of the exporting nations, set the policy for these schemes. The producers contributed to the buffer stock based on their share in production. A lower and an upper price were agreed and the manager of the buffer stock was given directives on purchasing and selling tin from the stock in accordance with the price range. These limits were adjusted many times in the course of the several tin agreements, with the range constantly moving upwards. The financial resources required to operate the stock were, until the late 1970s, almost entirely supplied by the exporters and there was no obligation on importing members to buy exclusively from exporting members. Their sole responsibility was to assist with the administrative costs.

On the whole, the ITA had succeeded in holding the tin price above the agreement's floor price in most years, but doing so required that the buffer stock be buttressed by the imposition of export quotas. The ITA resources had never been enough to enable it to hold large enough stocks to even out the swings in the market. The ITA collapsed in October 1985.

The first international effort to stabilise rapidly declining rubber price was put into operation in 1934 using export control as a policy instrument. The International Rubber Regulation Scheme, together with the expansion of the world economy helped to raise rubber price between 1934 and 1940. The subsequent outbreak of Second World War saw the whole of Southeast Asia, which produced about 90% of world's natural rubber supply, fall into the hands of the Japanese. This resulted in a serious shortage of natural rubber in the Allied nations, and propelled the United States Government to turn to synthetic rubber as a substitute. Synthetic rubber usage became more wide spread in the 1950s as a result of its technological superiority, and has helped to stabilise the prices of natural rubber.

A renewed effort to stabilise prices of natural rubber led to the setting up of the International Natural Rubber Organisation in 1980. However, Malaysia pulled out from the organisation in 1998 citing ineffective price support as the main reason. Thailand followed suit in the following year. This led to the termination of the International Natural Rubber Agreement III and the dissolution of the International Natural Rubber Organisation in 1999. In September 1999, Malaysia and Thailand agreed to co-operate in pushing up the prices of natural rubber. In July 2000, Indonesia joined in, and the three countries signed a rubber industry cooperation pact. In August 2002, Thailand, Indonesia and Malaysia, the three largest rubber-producing countries in the world, formally established the International Rubber Consortium Limited (IRCo). The main task of the IRCo is to buy natural rubber from farmers at times when export prices are depressed and withhold the rubber from the market.

One great disadvantage in price control over natural rubber is that it has no control over its close substitute synthetic rubber, which has become the dominant component of total rubber consumption. Beside, a high price of rubber will encourage other non-agreement countries to increase rubber production and exports, thus unintentionally introducing a self-defeating and a self-destructive element in the commodity agreement. However, if the buffer stock scheme can be well managed, with profit maximization as an objective, the scheme may still be able to kill two birds with one stone: stabilization and profit maximization. Thus, the buffer stock scheme need not be international. Incidentally, the stockpile concept can also be applied to exchange rates and international exchange reserves.

Other Government Policies

A common feature in Southeast Asia has been the important role of Government in directing agricultural production and influencing agricultural incomes. Government intervention in agricultural markets is largely explained by the economic and political significance of certain agricultural commodities. Subsistence crops like rice, for instance, are important wage goods, and their availability and price carry important political implications in the countries of Southeast Asia. In a number of countries in Southeast Asia, exports of certain crops critically affect the balance of payments position.

The policy-makers in the region have tended to work towards similar basic goals in regard to agriculture. These include achieving food self-sufficiency, diversification of cropping patterns and all-round rural development. While policy instruments to achieve these goals have differed in individual countries, government intervention in agriculture has taken the form of land reform, credit supply, public investment in agricultural infrastructure and supporting systems, as well as modification of the economic environment through systems of incentives and deterrents, mainly in the areas of price and trade policies.

One important aspect that may be singled out is agricultural price policies. The tendency among Governments in the region has been to raise output prices in the hope of creating a favourable environment for more rapid diffusion of modern agricultural technologies on the one hand, and subsidised retail prices to ensure the availability of cheap food to urban consumers, on the other. In retrospect, such a policy stance has proved difficult to manage and too costly. In practice, therefore, the producer-oriented and consumer-oriented objectives of price policy were not given equal weight by Governments of the region. Where the bias was in favour of consumers, the financial inability of Governments to absorb the additional cost of a production incentive programme via high prices, meant that producer prices were made relatively low (Timmer, 1993). For instance in Myanmar, farmers were required to sell a portion of every rice harvest (620 kg/ha) to Myanmar Agricultural Products Trading, an agency under the Ministry of Commerce. However, the procurement price in the past had typically been around half the free-market price or less. In response, farmers tried to pass on their lowest-quality rice to the agency. This in part explains the low export prices and the low export quantities (with the exception of 2001 when market price fell below the procurement price) of Myanmar's rice. This 40-year long policy of government directly purchasing rice from farmers was put to an end in 2004; a new rice trading policy that permits free trade of rice was adopted in the interest of the farmers and to help develop the market oriented economy.

As pointed out earlier, countries aiming to attain rice self-sufficiency could jeopardise the economy. A possible solution is the implementation of a rice-stockpiling scheme. This can be supplemented by long-term purchase agreements with a member of rice exporting countries. Any shock caused by a sudden disruption of rice supply can be and will be absorbed. Singapore, for example, has a 3-month rice stockpiling rotation programme and long-term rice supply agreements with several countries.

Southeast Asian Governments should also consider the abolition of export taxes. The taxes had been a very important source of government revenue, although its importance has declined over the years. The imposition of export taxes has detrimental impact on the competitiveness of the agricultural sector. Malaysia still levies taxes on the export of primary commodities such as crude and semi-processed palm oil; rubber and tin are also subject to research and development cess in Malaysia. Myanmar levies taxes on rice and Indonesia levies taxes on palm oil.

In fact, Indonesia and some other countries in Southeast Asia have developed very sophisticated techniques of what constitute an export substitution policy. This policy eschews exports. Domestic consumption comes first. Only surpluses are exported. Price distortions set in. Foreign exchange earnings are curtailed. The ability of the country to import much-needed technology and other important imports becomes restricted. The balance of payments position is often threatened. Exchange rate depreciation is to be expected. We recommend the removal of the export substitution policy, where it exists. All industries, including agricultural industries, must be free to compete and be encouraged to compete in the international markets and the prices of such products for domestic consumption should not be artificially suppressed.

Where economic incentives have been suppressed by pricing agricultural products below competitive equilibrium levels, some consequences must follow: an adverse effect on employment opportunities in farming, processing and rural industries; disincentive to produce food and export crops; lack of inducement to make new technological discoveries as well as the adoption of these techniques by farmers; and lack of private investment in inputs like labour, land and irrigation. The lesson is clear — if government intervention is not to improve efficiency and to raise productivity, it is better not to intervene.

Besides, governments in Southeast Asia should look into the possibility of inviting foreign investors to invest in various sub-sectors in the agricultural industry, including rice-growing, cocoa-growing, coffee cultivation, maize cultivation, animal husbandry, fish-rearing, and fruits and vegetables growing. The injection of new capital and enterprise is likely to make the industry more dynamic, more invigorated and more modernized with likely good spread effects for the industry and the economy as a whole.

The focus of the government then will be in agricultural extension services, to help to raise productivity of the farmers and to enhance export competitiveness with a view to raise the standard of living of rural farmers. Extension services include not just the training and retraining of farmers in the use of new seeds, new methods of cultivation, new choice of fertilizers, crop rotation, crop storage, the handling of crop diseases and in all areas that will enhance productivity and above all the quality of life and the standards of living of the farmers. In other words, the State is a friend and a helper of first and last resort. Farmers cannot be neglected and unsupported.

Key Points

1. With Southeast Asia's population growing at a rapid rate, it is imperative to ensure that the supply of food is sufficient to meet the growing demand. However, it is not advisable for countries to be self-sufficient in food, particularly in all types of food. If all scarce resources are devoted to the production of food inefficiently, other sectors will not be able to function properly, if at all. The country as a whole suffers.

2. In most Southeast Asian countries, the factor markets are biased towards the large landowners. This leads to inefficiency in agricultural production by small cultivators, particularly tenant farmers.

3. The rice exporting countries are facing a quandary in their trade policy. By increasing export taxes, their foreign market share will decline further. However, such taxes are still being imposed. Nonetheless, it is important and prudent to increase rice productivity, eliminate export taxes and encourage exports.

4. Due to the Green Revolution, rice-deficit countries are able to reduce their reliance on rice imports. They implemented import-substitution policy. However, these countries should not just focus on being self-sufficient in rice. Their policy must be guided by their resource endowments and comparative advantages.

5. Plantation crops face the risk of being substituted by other agricultural products or those manufactured by industries. The bottom line is fair competition among these substitutes. If countries are not able to compete in certain products, they should consider shifting their scarce resources to more profitable production and exports.

6. Given that Southeast Asia is a major producer and exporter of primary commodities, and that these primary products have volatile prices, there

appears to be a need for commodity agreements to stabilise prices through the maintenance of a buffer stock and the regulation of supply through export control. ASEAN member countries had participated in both the now defunct International Tin Agreement and International Natural Rubber Organisation. In truth, these measures often serve to increase the production and exports of non-agreement countries, and if the prices are persistently high, even the search for substitutes, such as synthetic rubber.

7. The price policies implemented by most Southeast Asian Governments are, on one hand, to encourage rapid diffusion of modern agricultural technologies and on the other, to ensure a cheap source of food for the urban population. These policies, where applicable, may be too costly for the Government to undertake. The deliberate suppression of food prices will have adverse consequences on the agricultural sector.

8. Where export substitution policy exists such as in palm oil and rice production, it should be removed. International prices should prevail for these produces as well.

Suggested Discussion Topics

5.1 "The lesson is clear — if Government intervention is not to improve efficiency and to raise productivity, it is better not to intervene." Discuss this statement in the book in relation to agricultural development policy in Southeast Asia.

5.2 Do you agree that self-sufficiency in rice production as an objective is not a sound policy even for countries in Southeast Asia? Discuss. How to ensure adequate rice supply, if the self-sufficiency principle is abandoned?

5.3 Discuss the use of export taxes as a stabilization devise and its disadvantages in enhancing export competitive in the agricultural sector in Southeast Asia.

5.4 Appraise the use of buffer stock and export control to stabilise the price of a primary export, using natural rubber and tin as examples.

5.5 Discuss the advantages and disadvantages of import substitution and export substitution policy for the agricultural sector in Southeast Asia using rice, palm oil, and other crops as examples.

References

BHAGWATI, Jagdish, 1958, "Immiserising growth: A geometrical note", *Review of Economic Studies*, 25(3), 201–205

DORNER, P. and W. C. THIESENHUSEN, 1990, "Selected land reforms in East and Southeast Asia: Their origins and impacts", *Asian-Pacific Economic Literature*, 4(1), 65–95.

Food and Agriculture Organization (FAO), 2004, *The State of Agricultural Commodity Markets 2004*, Rome: Publishing Management Service, FAO.

JOHNSTON, B. and J. W. MELLOR, 1961, "The role of agriculture in economic development", *American Economic Review*, 51(4), 566–593.

LIM, Chong Yah, 1967, *Economic Development of Modern Malaya*, Kuala Lumpur: Oxford University Press.

PIERMARTINI, Roberta, 2004, "The role of export taxes in the field of primary commodities", *WTO Discussion Papers, No. 4*, Geneva: World Trade Organization

TIMMER, P. C., 1993, "Rural bias in the East and Southeast Asian rice economy: Indonesia in comparative perspective", *Journal of Development Studies*, 29(4), 149–176.

World Trade Organization, 2007, *Trade Policy Review: Indonesia, 2007*, Geneva: WTO Secretariat.

Further Readings

GHATAK, S. and K. INGERSENT, 1984, *Agriculture and Economic Development*, Brighton, Sussex: Wheatsheaf Books.

GRIFFIN, Keith, 1979, *Political Economy of Agrarian Change: An Essay on the Green Revolution*, London: MacMillan.

MEARS, Leon, 1981, *The New Rice Economy of Indonesia*, Yogyakarta: Gadjah Mada University Press.

MYINT, Hla, 1972, *Southeast Asia's Economy: Development Policies in the 1970s*, New York: Praeger Publishers.

SCHULTZ, T. W., 1964, *Transforming Traditional Agriculture*, New Haven and London: Yale University Press.

World Bank, 2007, *World Development Report 2008: Agriculture for Development*, Washington, D.C.: The World Bank.

Chapter 6

Industrialisation: Comparative Strategy

By the labour of your hands, you shall eat.
Old Injunction

Objectives

✓ Present trends in manufacturing development.
✓ Explain how distorted factor price structure hampers the creation of employment.
✓ Describe various tax policies and their impacts on industrialisation and FDI promotion.
✓ Describe regional development policy and Export Processing Zones.
✓ Evaluate import-substitution and export orientation strategies.
✓ Discuss policies necessary for industrial development.

Introduction

Industrial activities are normally defined to comprise mining, manufacturing, construction, and utilities. Except in countries that are endowed with large deposits of mineral resources, manufacturing activity is typically the largest constituent within the industrial sector. In Myanmar, the Philippines, Singapore and Thailand, the manufacturing sector typically contributes 65% or more of total industrial output. In Indonesia and to a lesser extent Malaysia, both of which are important producers of petroleum, the manufacturing share is somewhat smaller.

After World War II, industrialisation has occupied an important place in overall economic development in many LDCs. Industrial growth and the accompanying urban development are considered necessary to relieve pressures on agricultural land, permit increased agricultural productivity, provide markets for farm products, and supply competitively priced manufactured goods for rural and urban consumers as well as for exports. In practice, many LDCs, including the Southeast Asian economies, began the drive to industrialise shortly after attaining their political Independence. At that time, industrialisation was seen to be synonymous with economic development. The manufacturing sector was believed to be capable of providing new employment opportunities for a fast growing population. Furthermore, policy-makers in these countries held the view that their economies, being heavily dependent on primary commodity exports, would not be able to achieve sustainable economic growth, especially since the long run terms of trade for primary exports were believed to be unfavourable.

The principal focus of this chapter is industrialisation. The trade-off between output growth and employment growth will be discussed, followed by the choice between import-substituting and export-oriented industrialisation. Taxation policies, and in particular, policies that promote private foreign investment are considered, along with some discussion of trade policies and policies that affect the choice of technology. We conclude with a discussion of the growth prospects of manufacturing in Southeast Asian countries.

Trends in Manufacturing Development

Structure of Manufacturing

During the last 40 years, the manufacturing sector of Southeast Asian countries, with the exception of the Indo-Chinese states and Myanmar, has grown at relatively high rates. As was shown in Chapter 2: Economic Diversity, agriculture's share in GDP has declined in these countries, with a corresponding increase in the share of manufacturing.

In Malaysia and Thailand, manufacturing accounted for 30% and 35% of GDP in 2006 respectively, up from 8% and 13% in 1960 (Table 6.1).

Table 6.1

Manufacturing Share in GDP (%), 1960–2006

	1960	1970	1980	1990	2000	2006
Thailand	13	16	22	27	32	35
Malaysia	8	12	22	24	33	30
Singapore	n.a.	20	29	27	27	29
Indonesia	9	10	13	18	26	28
Philippines	20	25	26	25	23	23
Vietnam	n.a.	n.a.	n.a.	12	19	21
Laos	n.a.	n.a.	n.a.	10	17	21
Myanmar	8	10	10	8	7	10[a]
Cambodia	n.a.	n.a.	n.a.	5	n.a.	19
Brunei	n.a.	n.a.	12	n.a.	n.a.	10

Source: World Bank, *WDI Online*, 8 Sep. 2008, http://publications.worldbank.org/WDI/
    a: Data refers to 2003/04 figure.

In Singapore, the share increased from 20% in 1970 to 29% in 1980. However, its share declined steadily in the last two decades as a result of the rapid growth of the service sector. The Philippines, an early starter in manufacturing with its share of GDP at already 20% in 1960, had only a marginal increase to 23% in 2006. The share of manufacturing in GDP in Myanmar is still relatively low, at 10% in 2003. In Vietnam, on the other hand, manufacturing's share of GDP grew rapidly since 1990, reaching 21% in 2006.

The share of value-added in manufacturing in the GDP indicates a country's level of industrialisation. The measure, nevertheless, is fraught with some difficulties. Countries with heavy protection for manufacturing will over value their manufacturing output in relation to non-protected activities and in relation to other countries with lower protection; the under-pricing of agricultural products to keep the urban cost of living down similarly tends to depress agriculture's share of GDP and exaggerate the share of manufacturing. These difficulties are further exacerbated due to differences in the measurement of the value-added in the services sector among countries (Hughes, 1978). Notwithstanding this caveat, Malaysia, Thailand, Indonesia, Singapore and the Philippines can be regarded as the relatively more industrialised economies in the region; Laos, Cambodia and Myanmar the less industrialised. Diagram 6.1 shows the manufacturing share of GDP in the ASEAN-5 countries.

Diagram 6.1

ASEAN-5 Manufacturing Share in GDP, 1970 and 2006

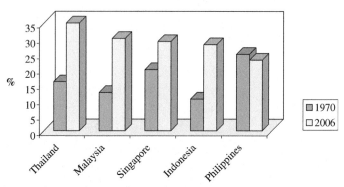

Source: World Bank, *WDI Online*, 8 Sep. 2008,
http://publications.worldbank.org/WDI/

Table 6.2 presents the structure of manufacturing in the five Southeast Asian countries. One important feature is that the share of total manufacturing value-added contributed by the agro-industries is significantly larger in traditionally agricultural economies. In Indonesia and the Philippines, the share of food, beverages and tobacco value-added in 2003 was 23%. In Thailand, it was 18%. In contrast, the share was only 4% in Singapore and 8% in Malaysia.

Because the income elasticity of demand for the processed agricultural products is usually higher than that for the raw materials themselves, agriculture-based industries tend to be important in the early stages of the industrialisation process of the traditionally agricultural economies. Moreover, the food and agricultural processing industries constitute the logical "downstream" industries of the agricultural sector and their development is a fairly straightforward step in the overall process of industrialisation. Also of interest is that the share of the food, beverages and tobacco value-added in total manufacturing value-added declines in the process of economic growth. In Malaysia, for instance, in 1970, this sub-sector was 26% and this had declined to 9% by 2000.

By way of contrast, in 2003 the machinery and transport equipment sub-sector contributed about 50% of total manufacturing value-added in Singapore, and 39% in Malaysia. The share of this sub-sector was 13% for the Philippines and 18% for Indonesia. Such a structure of manufacturing

Table 6.2
Structure of Manufacturing (Sectoral Breakdown), 1970, 1990 and 2003

	Manufacturing Value-Added (%)											
	Food, Beverages and Tobacco			Textile & Clothing			Machinery & Transport Equipment			Chemicals		
	1970	1990	2003	1970	1990	2003	1970	1990	2003	1970	1990	2003
Indonesia	66	28	23	14	15	13	2	12	18	6	9	9
Malaysia	26	13	8	4	7	3	8	31	39	9	11	10
Philippines	39	39	23	8	11	5	8	13	13	13	12	2
Singapore	12	4	4	5	3	1	28	53	50	4	10	24
Thailand	23	24	18[a]	14	30	12[a]	4	19	24[a]	25	2	6[a]

Source: World Bank, *WDI Online*, 8 Sep. 2008, http://publications.worldbank.org//WDI/
a: Data for Thailand is 2000, latest figure available from source.

production suggests that countries like Indonesia and the Philippines are still largely natural resource-based and labour-abundant. The emphasis of manufacturing is on the production of agro-based and labour-intensive goods.

For Singapore, the 1960s saw severe unemployment problems — an offshoot of the post-war baby boom. It launched an industrialisation pro-gramme designed to attract labour-intensive industries. As the economy rapidly grew over the years, it accumulated both human and physical capi-tal, resulting in a shift of production pattern toward more skill-intensive and capital-intensive goods. Thus, Singapore has been gradually experiencing a shift in its comparative advantage from labour-intensive industries such as textiles and garments to skill-intensive industries such as computer com-ponents and precision instruments. A similar shift is also taking place in Malaysia.

The Informal Sector

Within the industrial sector of most Southeast Asian countries, one finds "modern", "small" and "cottage" sub-sectors. The modern sub-sector con-sists of wage earners in formal employment and is characterised by modern management and modern techniques of production. It is often favoured by government policies and incentives, notably tariff protection and tax con-cessions. In contrast, the small and cottage or informal sub-sectors com-prise the self-employed, the artisans, and small-scale traditional crafts, and generally do not enjoy any policy benefits. The informal sub-sector is sometimes the larger sub-sector in terms of employment. For example, in Indonesia, a study revealed that in the early 1980s, the informal sec-tor's share of employment in manufacturing was 48% (Sethuraman, 1997). During the mid-1970s in the Philippines, of the manufacturing sector's 1.6 million jobs (10% of total national employment), as many as a million were in the cottage sub-sector (De Vries, 1980).

Employment opportunities in the informal sub-sector are partly need-driven: necessity drives people to work in every conceivable occupation. Workers in the informal sub-sector may often work long hours under extremely difficult working conditions, with low productivity, and a meagre and vari-able income. With extensive rural-urban migration and the incapacity of the urban modern sub-sector to absorb all the migrants, the informal sub-sector has served to absorb the surplus labour. Despite the impressive performance of most countries in achieving high rates of growth of manufacturing output, the manufacturing sector's share of total employment remains low, between 10 and 15% in 2005 in Indonesia, Myanmar, the Philippines and Thailand. It is higher only in Singapore (23%) and Malaysia (30%).

Employment Issues

Most Southeast Asia cities suffer from high rates of unemployment and underemployment. This is inconsistent with what had been postulated by Arthur Lewis (1954). The essence of the Lewis model is that wages in the modern sector are based on the average product of labour in the traditional rural sector, but somewhat higher in order to attract labour into the sector and to compensate for the higher cost of urban living and other non-pecuniary factors. The model further posits that wage rates would not rise with rising productivity, but instead capital formation in the capitalist sector would raise the share of profits in national income. With the profit ratio increasing, there should then be capital-widening investment in the industrial sector causing the demand for labour to continue to rise so that more industrial workers are employed at a constant real wage. Finally, when all the available surplus labour has been absorbed, wages begin to rise.

However, what actually happens is that those formerly in disguised unemployment in the rural sector have, in effect, been transferred into urban unemployment and underemployment. Urban unemployment problems in the Southeast Asian countries are due to the low labour absorption in the manufacturing sector. This can be traced to the choice of policy measures which favoured the use of capital rather than labour via subsidised interest rates, concessions in the form of tax holidays, accelerated depreciation allowances, and low or no duties on import of industrial machinery.

Such encouragement of capital-intensive methods of production tends to distort the price of capital. This is sometimes intensified by inflation, which lowers the real rate of interest below the nominal rate. In addition, there is a bias toward more capital-intensive production methods when a country's currency is overvalued, and the true cost of importing machinery is hence undervalued. Governments have also lowered the relative price of producers' equipment by measures such as allowing duty-free importation of equipment, a preferential exchange rate, and making foreign exchange available for servicing loans from overseas machinery suppliers. Moreover, when domestic enterprises are protected by tariffs and import quotas, the pressure to economise on capital is also less than in more competitive markets.

A more general argument would be that there exists some "undistorted" set of factor prices — wage rates, interest rates and prices of investment goods — which would reflect the true opportunity cost of the various resources, and which would ensure full employment of all resources. Unemployment and/or underemployment are then attributed to various market imperfections distorting the factor prices and thus preventing full employment of resources. Hence, for example, subsidies on investment, designed to raise the rate of investment, artificially lower the cost of investment; similarly, overvalued exchange rates artificially depress the costs of imported machinery.

Assuming a production function that permits alternative methods to produce a given product, it is possible to choose methods of varying labour and capital intensity, thus allowing alternative levels of capital to be associated with different levels of employment. Diagram 6.2 illustrates the existence of unemployment arising from distorted factor prices (Stewart, 1978). Full employment of resources would occur with price line, PP', given capital stocks, OI and labour supply OL. However, distortions of the type mentioned earlier, together with insufficient resources for investment, result in the actual price line of DD'. Given limited capital stocks, OI, unemployment UL results. The solution is clear from the diagram: if the price line is allowed to shift to QQ' — reflecting a higher relative price of capital — full employment of labour can be restored. Thus, an important prerequisite for solving unemployment problems in the industrial sector may be the correction of the distortion in the factor prices.

Policies Toward Manufacturing

Tax Policies

Various taxation instruments are available to the Government, for example, corporate income taxes, consumption taxes, expenditure taxes and personal

Diagram 6.2
Unemployment Arising from Distorted Factor Prices

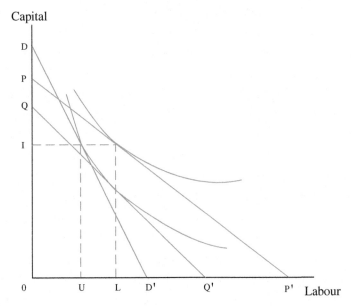

income taxes. Practically all taxes have an impact on resource allocation. The effect of a corporate income tax is such that it produces a bias in the allocation of resources against the sector in which the tax is applied. Thus, if the tax is imposed only on manufacturing firms, resources will tend to move into sectors where profits are not so heavily taxed, for example, agriculture. Also, where corporate and personal income taxes are progressive, the imposition of such taxes will result in resources being shifted to other uses, or firms being broken down into less economic but separately taxed units, and possibly, workers shifting toward more leisure. In an increasingly globalised world, resources, particularly capital, enterprise and skilled labour can also move with increasing speed from high-tax countries to low-tax countries.

With regards to consumption-based taxes, they may be levied at a single point at the manufacturing, wholesale or retail level, or at multiple points as in the case of turnover and value-added taxes. In terms of the neutrality of impact, the retail sales tax is preferred to either the wholesale or the manufacturing sales tax since the point of impact in this case is the same whatever the production and marketing system, so that firms have no incentive to shift their activities. For example, the imposition of a manufacturing sales tax encourages some manufacturers to artificially push to the wholesale level as much of their manufacturing activities and costs as possible. Moreover, this tax discriminates against those manufacturers who have valid economic reasons for vertically integrating their production and wholesale activities. While the wholesale sales tax eliminates such distortions, it nevertheless introduces distortions of its own. It encourages a manufacturer or wholesaler to shift his activities to the retail level and thus integrate backwards.

The diverse effects of the different forms of taxes suggest that it is not possible to provide an unambiguous ranking of different taxes for industrial development purposes. Moreover, there is a need for tax systems to attain several objectives such as provision of government revenue, income redistribution and export competitiveness. The problem of judging the impact of taxes on industry is further compounded in an LDC because the inefficiency of the tax collection machinery provides another constraint on the decision making process. Most countries, however, have in fact gone beyond the passive and indirect use of taxes in their industrialisation programmes. They have made active and direct use of taxes as instruments of industrial policy in the form of exemptions from taxation as incentives for the acceleration and direction of industrial development.

Another method used by policy-markers to promote the manufacturing sector is by granting tax incentives. These tax instruments include tax holidays and depreciation allowances. Complete elimination of the tax liability is achieved by granting tax holidays whereby firms are totally exempted from the prevailing corporate tax for a given period. The tax holiday provides greater liquidity to firms that make profits in the early stages of operation and reduces the element of risk involved, thereby encouraging investment. With depreciation allowances, a firm is permitted to write off the cost of its capital investment in a relatively shorter period, against its gross revenue. Accelerated depreciation allowances often reduce a firm's effective future tax liability, encourage it to change its capital stock often, modernise, and stay on top of technological trends. In Thailand, for instance, since 1959 the Board of Investment has been providing incentives in the form of exemptions of import duties on machinery and capital equipment and exemption from corporate income tax for a certain period. In the Philippines, the Board of Investment provides duty exemptions on imported capital equipment, accelerated depreciation allowances and preferences in access to government loans. In Indonesia, fiscal incentives given to favoured industries consist of exemptions of import duties, tax holidays, and other tax concessions, including accelerated depreciation allowances. In Malaysia, the major fiscal incentive was the granting of "pioneer status" to investors whose projects were approved by the Government. These investors are exempted from paying company tax for a period of between two to five years depending upon the amount invested (Amjad, 1981). In Singapore, incentives include the granting of tax holiday for pioneer firms, lowering of the tax rate on profits from exports earned by approved manufacturing companies, and complete tax exemption on interest received by overseas enterprises or individuals on approved loans to Singapore enterprises for the purchase of capital equipment.

Tax concessions have an impact not only on the level of investment but also on the composition of investment. The granting of a tax holiday is traditionally aimed at affecting the level of investment. Nevertheless, a tax holiday whose duration varies with the scale and the capital-intensity of specific industries clearly has a bias toward the composition of investment. Moreover, when the duration of tax holidays depends on the number of workers employed, the type of product manufactured, and the use of local raw materials, they affect both the total level as well as the composition of industrial investment.

An argument against tax incentives is that they may be redundant (Lim D., 1983). Most beneficiaries are likely to invest without incentives. For example, the profit-based tax holiday provides little assistance where it is most needed — for firms making little or no profits — and a great deal of assistance where it is least needed — for firms making high profits. It is likely that the latter would have invested even if no incentives had been offered. It is also possible that subsidised firms may have displaced other potential new firms or the investment planned by existing firms. The above argument, however, is difficult to test empirically with the existing methods of assessing the effectiveness of incentive programmes (Cody, Hughes and Wall, 1980).

Foreign Direct Investment (FDI)

The ASEAN market economies have a generally positive attitude towards the role of private investment from abroad. During 1994–2006, Thailand, for instance, approved foreign investment to the tune of US$89 billion. In the case of Singapore, the cumulative total foreign investment in manufacturing for the same period amounted to US$177 billion (see Diagram 6.3). The policies adopted by the individual countries in Southeast Asia vary and reflect different perceptions of foreign investment as well as differences in development objectives and options. Generally, Singapore's policies are more liberal, with the absence of restrictive conditions governing the entry and operation of foreign enterprises, while the policies of Indonesia, Malaysia and the Philippines are relatively more restrictive. The countries also vary in the consistency of foreign investment policy over time, but all countries have become more selective in their approach (Chia S. Y., 1980).

From the standpoint of national economic benefit, the essence of the case for encouraging inflows of foreign capital is that the increase in real income resulting from foreign investment is greater than the resultant increase in the income of the investor (Meier, 1985). So long as foreign investment raises labour productivity, and this increase is not entirely appropriated by the investor, the increased productivity will be shared by the host country. These benefits can take the form of increased tax revenue, lower

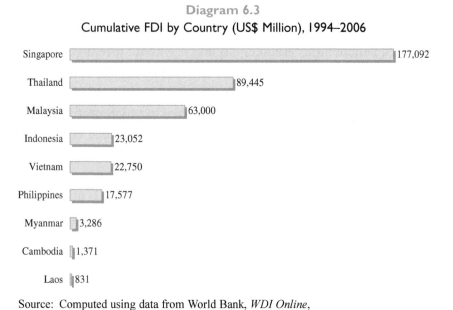

Diagram 6.3
Cumulative FDI by Country (US$ Million), 1994–2006

Singapore	177,092
Thailand	89,445
Malaysia	63,000
Indonesia	23,052
Vietnam	22,750
Philippines	17,577
Myanmar	3,286
Cambodia	1,371
Laos	831

Source: Computed using data from World Bank, *WDI Online*, http://publications.worldbank.org/WDI/

consumer prices and higher real wages for domestic labour. Beyond this, there are also likely to be indirect gains through the realisation of external economies.

In an LDC, the inflow of foreign capital may not only lead to an increase in labour productivity, but also an increase in employment. In the context of a labour-surplus economy, this point is of considerable importance. A shortage of capital in a heavily populated country limits the transfer of labour from the rural sector to the advanced sector where wages are higher. However, this is not observed in Indonesia. Contribution of foreign investment to employment creation has been minimal (Akrasanee and Vichit-Vadakan, 1979). Foreign investment, particularly from transnational corporations, typically flows into large scale and capital-intensive projects. Employment effects are likely to be limited to secondary effects. Foreign capital inflow, however, may make it possible to employ more labour in the advanced sector. The social benefit from foreign investment thus exceeds profits, since the wages received by the newly employed in the advanced sector exceed their former real wage in the rural sector.

Another, and perhaps most significant, contribution of foreign investment, is the external economies that it brings to the host country in terms of "managerial ability, technical personnel, technological knowledge, administrative organisation, and innovations in products and production techniques" (Meier, 1985). Moreover, private foreign investment may serve as a stimulus to additional investment in the host country. Where foreign investment is channelled to develop the host country's infrastructure, it may directly facilitate more investment, both foreign and domestic.

To encourage foreign investment, the host country Government often provides special services and facilities, offers special tax concessions, and extends financial assistance or subsidies. In Singapore, for instance, foreign investment policy has generally been liberal in the last two decades. This is evident from the availability of various investment and export incentives and especially from the absence of restrictions governing the entry and operations of foreign firms. Fiscal incentives apart, Singapore also offers stable industrial relations, orderly wage rises, and efficient government administration and infrastructural support. Furthermore, there are no exchange controls and more generally, no restrictions pertaining to repatriation of capital and remittance of profits, dividends and interest; no import restrictions; no requirement regarding local equity participation; no requirement on the use of domestic materials or domestic value-added content; and relatively fewer restrictions on the employment of foreign personnel. Similarly like Singapore, fiscal incentives augmented Malaysia's relatively good infra-structure, political stability, bureaucratic efficiency and literate labour force in its export-oriented industrialisation (Jomo, 2001). In the last two years, the investment climates in both Malaysia and Thailand have deteriorated, following uncertainty and disunity in the political arena.

Sometimes, problems arise when different countries compete to attract foreign capital. Each may offer more inducement than is necessary, thus creating a "redundancy" problem. Without some form of understanding among the countries competing for foreign investment, regarding the maximum concessions that will be made, it is possible to have more con-cessions than required to attract foreign investment. It is also likely that countries encouraging foreign direct investment will face balance of pay-ments problems, because foreign capital inflows and foreign debt may become complementary. For instance, in order to attract foreign invest-ment, a country may have to develop roads, ports, power plants, and other infrastructure which may require external borrowing. If the amount of for-eign exchange needed to service the debt becomes larger than the amount of foreign exchange being supplied by new foreign investment, the country will have to earn a surplus on current account equal to the debit amount on the payment of interest, dividends, profits and amortization on the foreign borrowings and investments. Where this is not feasible, the country may turn to currency devaluation or restrictive import policies. These measures have their own adverse consequences. This problem, however, can be overcome by having more foreign investment and the export-orientation of foreign investments.

Recent trends in net FDI inflows are shown in Table 6.3 and illustrated in Diagram 6.4. Indonesia registered a marked improvement in the inflow of foreign direct investment from 1990 onwards up to the onset of the financial crisis in 1997. Malaysia did not do well in the mid-1980s in maintaining the amount of inflow. However, the FDI inflow situation in Malaysia took off from 1990 onwards. The large infrastructural and privatisation proj-ects undertaken by the Mahathir Government attracted much international attention.

Table 6.3

Net FDI Receipts (US$ Million), 1975–2006

	1975	1980	1985	1990	1995	2000	2006
Singapore	292	1,236	1,047	5,575	8,788	5,407	15,560
Thailand	86	190	163	2,444	2,068	3,366	7,971
Philippines	98	–106	12	530	1,478	1,241	1,983
Vietnam	n.a.	n.a.	0	16	2,336	1,298	2,315
Malaysia	351	934	695	2,333	4,178	3,788	6,084
Myanmar	0	0.4	0	161	277	255	279
Cambodia	n.a.	n.a.	0	0	151	112	483
Laos	0.2	0	–1.6	6	95	34	187
Indonesia	476	180	310	1,093	4,346	–4,550	5,580

Source: World Bank, *WDI Online*, 8 Sep. 2008,
http://publications.worldbank.org/WDI/

Diagram 6.4

Trend of Net FDI Inflows into the ASEAN-5, 1985–2006

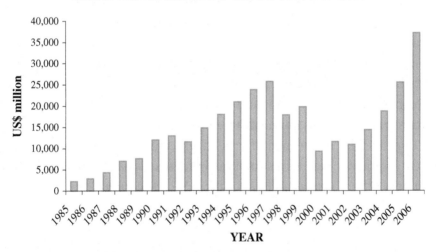

Source: World Bank, *WDI Online*, 8 Sep. 2008, http://publications.worldbank.org/WDI/.
*Note that the figures are in nominal US dollars. There are some temporal comparability problems to be overcome.

The political and economic uncertainties of the 1982–1985 period in the Philippines led to a sharp drop in FDI. It began to pick up in 1987 and reached almost a billion US dollars by 1988. The 1989 November coup attempt, however, scared away the investors once again, for a short while at least. The Philippines slowly began to regain the confidence of investors after the election of General Fidel Ramos. The closure of the US military bases in Subic Bay and its transformation into civilian and industrial use in itself may have further raised its investment opportunities. However, the instability of the Estrada and Arroyo Governments has again dampened the investment climate for foreign investors in the Philippines. Similarly, fears of instability under Presidents B J Habibie, Abdurrahman Wahid, Megawati Sukarnoputri, and to a lesser extent, Susilio Bambang Yudhoyono have had a detrimental effect on foreign investment in Indonesia.

Singapore, as noted earlier, has always been an attractive destination for foreign investment, except when high wages and high government service costs temporarily slowed down investment inflows in 1985–1986. The wage reforms (mainly the introduction of flexible wage policies) and reduction in costs (for utilities, telecommunications, and other services) triggered the resumption of capital inflows. Singapore has managed to maintain strong flows of direct investment despite rising wage costs and keener competition for FDI. This is partly because over the last two decades, the republic has developed a pool of highly skilled technical and managerial manpower that complements a high value-added type of production, research and development and marketing process that is higher up the technological production ladder than in the other countries of the region.

Thailand became a very attractive place for foreign investment since 1988 and there was a general optimism about future inflows. However, Thailand's attraction for FDI has waned after a strong spurt in 1990. Unstable coalition Governments and infrastructural bottlenecks have dented Thailand's investment attractiveness. While all the ASEAN countries provide tax and non-tax incentives, *ceteris paribus*, political stability and economic dynamism are certainly determinants of foreign investment inflows — as indicated by the case of Singapore in most years, and Malaysia, the Philippines and Thailand in the 1980s. This explains why the 1990s Malaysia and Singapore received the lion's share of FDI within ASEAN. On the other hand, FDI in transitional economies such as Myanmar and Laos remains negligible. The recent political uncertainties in Thailand and in Malaysia are likely to have detrimental effects on investment inflows into these two countries. Even in the Philippines under President Arroyo and in Indonesia under

President Yodhoyono, there are political tensions that are quite detrimental to FDI inflows.

Regional Development

Another facet of industrial policy that is important in the context of the Southeast Asian countries, particularly in Indonesia, the Philippines and Thailand, is regional industrial development. Taking into account the cost of infrastructure and the existence of economies of scale in infrastructure as well as in industry, the application of a multi-pronged regional development policy is often recommended for Thailand (Balassa, 1980a). This would involve a shift away from industrial concentration in the Bangkok metropolitan area, allowing for continued industrial expansion of the Central and other regions, establishing new industrial growth poles linked to ports, improving existing infrastructural facilities in outlying regions, and providing technical assistance to the establishment of agro-processing and other resource-based industries.

In 1973, the Board of Investment (BOI) identified ten Investment Promotion Zones located beyond the 50-km radius of Bangkok for preferential treatment. BOI's preferences, however, did not affect the regional distribution of investment, with Bangkok's share in BOI-promoted firms being greater than the share of all other regions. The limited effectiveness of BOI's regional preferences has led to a reduction in the number of Investment Promotion Zones. However, existing regulations on minimum capital investment and on duty and tax exemption as well as reductions for machinery continue to discriminate against small- and medium-size firms that are of greater importance in the outlying regions. Discretionary decision-making, too, tends to favour large, well-established firms in the Bangkok area. The limited effectiveness of regional tax incentives may partly be explained by the fact that they do not compensate for the additional costs of locating in outlying areas. Transport costs are high, in particular, in cases where materials have to be obtained from Bangkok; small volume production for local markets raises the cost of materials purchased in small quantities; access to public utilities is more limited in other regions; and although wages are lower than in Bangkok, differences in labour effectiveness are said to be even greater due in part to lack of industrial experience and in part to absenteeism during planting and harvesting time.

Export Processing Zones (EPZs)

Another set of policies relates to the development of EPZs in a number of the Southeast Asian countries. Usually, EPZs engage in production primarily for world markets. They are heavily dependent on imported material inputs. Foreign investment is predominant in the industries in these zones whereby firms located in these zones receive a wide range of investment incentives: a major component being the exemption from the normal corporate taxes as well as the granting of other special incentives such as accelerated depreciation allowances and exemption from the usual import tariffs and quotas.

The primary reason for establishing EPZs is to increase manufactured exports, increase foreign exchange earnings and increase employment opportunities. The almost 100% export orientation of firms that operate in the EPZs helps to ensure that they contribute significantly to foreign exchange earnings. In addition, it is mainly labour-intensive industries that are attracted into the EPZs. This is because the major motivation for off-shore production by foreign firms is to transfer labour-intensive operations to LDCs in order to take advantage of lower labour costs. As such, employment creation is likely to be an important outcome of EPZs. Additional long run benefits are expected from FDI and these include transfer of technology, skills and in particular external linkage effects.

Within Southeast Asia, EPZs have produced some success. The development of EPZs has been important in employment creation for the Malaysian economy. According to the Fourth Malaysian Plan, industrial development during the 1970s generated 416,000 new jobs, representing 24.5% of total additional employment, with more than a fifth of these jobs coming from firms located within EPZs (Lee, 1984). However, the firms located in the zones have little inter-industry linkages with the rest of the economy. Nevertheless, the essentially export-oriented firms operating in the EPZs have contributed significantly to Malaysia's export success.

The Malaysian EPZ experience, however, is not free from subtle problems. An issue that confronts the Malaysian authorities is the termination of the tax holidays granted to the foreign inventors for limited periods at the time of setting up of the plants within the zones. These tax incentives could have been important in attracting the multinational corporations to set up processing units in Malaysia. With an increasing number of other LDCs offering similar incentives, the withdrawal of tax advantages in Malaysia may induce these firms to relocate their processing units to the other countries (Lee, 1984). Increasing globalisation of the world economy means increasing capital and enterprise mobility globally. Export competitiveness thus cannot take the back-seat but move to the front seat in the central stage. Countries that ignore global competition for FDI will lose out in global economic rankings and global standards of living.

Import-Substitution versus Export Orientation

In many of the Southeast Asian countries, with the exception of Singapore, the dominant strategy of industrialisation, at least in the early stages, had been the production of consumer goods to substitute for imports. For instance, during the 1960s, the industrial policies of Malaysia and Thailand followed an import-substitution strategy supported by tariff barriers. While protection continued to increase in the 1970s, both countries shifted their industrial policies towards their export sectors. In contrast, Indonesia continuously pursued an import-substitution strategy throughout 1960s and 1970s.

In the mid-1970s, ASEAN witnessed a substantial increase in the average rates of effective protection of import-competing sector for consumer goods, machinery and transport equipment. Import-substituting sectors are highly protected while export sectors are not.

Import-substitution is not without its problems. The Philippines is an example of an economy which, after following a successful import-substitution strategy, found itself faced with all the major problems inherent in such a strategy, and despite attempts to break into the global export markets, had achieved only limited success. In the Philippines, the 1950s was a period of rapid industrial growth behind tariff barriers and import controls but once the domestic market had been exhausted, the industrial sector suffered a sharp reduction in growth rates in the 1960s.

In the case of Singapore, the initial phase of import-substitution that prevailed in the context of it's being part of Malaysia, was short-lived. In light of its separation from Malaysia in August 1965 and the ensuing loss of Malaysian-wide protected domestic market and the British withdrawal of its troops from Singapore, new growth strategies were adopted. The mild import-substitution industrialisation programme was quickly replaced by a strategy that emphasised export-oriented industries.

But what is obvious over the last 30 years is that the economies of Southeast Asia had become gradually more export-oriented and more open, and as such, there was an increasing demand for imports and in particular, for intermediate inputs. While there was an increasing trend towards lower tariff protection levels throughout Southeast Asia, on the other hand, non-tariff barriers still remain high. With respect to the former (see Table 6.4), there had been a dramatic decrease in tariff rates over the last decade in the ASEAN-5 countries. The reduction of tariff levels during the 17 year period amounted to 77% on average.

What is the rationale for an import-substitution strategy? Given domestic demand for imported consumer goods, it is easy to plan for industrialisation on the basis of replacing imports. In fact, most new industries may import components and engage in assembling, rather than manufacturing, in the hope of eventually progressing to the production of intermediate and capital goods. Import-substitution is also believed to reduce the developing country's adverse balance of payments by saving foreign exchange. If we accept that the income elasticity of demand for imports is relatively high and that industrial imports are essential, then they must be either imported

Table 6.4

Effective Tariff Rates of ASEAN-5 (Trade Weighted Average) 1989 and 2006

	Effective Tariff Rates		% Change
	1989	2006	
Indonesia	14.7	6.4	−56.5
Thailand	34.1	6.2	−81.8
Singapore	0.6	0	−100.0
Malaysia	10.6 (1988)	4.4	−58.5
Philippines	23.1	3.3	−85.7

Source: United Nations Conference on Trade and Development, *Handbook of Statistics Online*, 8 Sep. 2008, http://stats.unctad.org/

or domestically produced. In such circumstances, if the capacity to export is somewhat limited thus restraining the capacity to import, then there is a case for import-substitution in certain industries. In particular, this argument applies to primary-commodities exporting countries like the traditionally agricultural economies of Southeast Asia, which face low-income elasticity of demand for their primary commodity exports.

It can be argued, however, that what is relevant for individual primary commodities exporting countries is not the overall income elasticity of demand for primary products, but the prospects for their own exports. It is unrealistic to assume that export prospects are equally unfavourable for food crops, minerals, and other raw materials, or for all commodities in each of these broad categories. Moreover, although the elasticity of demand for a commodity may be low in world markets, it might be high for the commodity from a particular source of supply. Furthermore, the future demand of industrial countries for imports will depend not only on their income elasticity of demand for imports but also on their income growth rate, and on the degree of liberalisation in the importing countries' trade policies. These considerations limit the validity of an import-substitution strategy.

Another often cited rationale for replacing industrial imports with domestic production is the creation of employment outside agriculture. The promotion of new employment opportunities is certainly a crucial component of economic development policies, and a significant potential benefit of industrialisation. The issue, however, is whether investment should be directed towards import-replacing industries, and whether protection is the appropriate policy to facilitate the expansion of non-agricultural employment. The distorted price structure that often accompanies an import-substitution industrialisation strategy makes capital relatively cheaper and leads to highly capital-intensive methods of production that limit the extent of employment creation. One can even argue that there is, in fact, no need for protection at the first stage of import-substitution, which involves replacing the imports of non-durable consumer goods. Such commodities are labour-intensive, the efficient scale of output is relatively low, costs do not rise substantially at lower output levels, production does not require the use of sophisticated technology, and a network of suppliers of parts, components and accessories is not required for efficient operations. For all these reasons, little or no protection is needed for such industries.

In the course of first-stage import-substitution, domestic production will rise more rapidly than domestic consumption, since it not only provides for increases in consumption but also replaces imports. The rate of growth of output, however, declines to that of consumption, once the process of import-substitution has been completed. Henceforth, maintaining high industrial growth rates requires either the exportation of manufactured goods or moving to second-stage import-substitution. The latter involves replacing the imports of intermediate goods and producer and consumer durables with domestic production. These goods have different characteristics from those replaced at the early stage. Intermediate goods such as petrochemicals and steel tend to be highly capital-intensive. They are also subject to significant scale economies, with efficient plant sizes being large compared to the domestic needs of most LDCs and costs rising rapidly at lower output levels. Accordingly, the establishment of these industries to serve the small domestic markets is predicated on high protection. Moreover, the rates of protection need to be continually escalated as countries embark on the production of commodities that do not conform to their comparative advantage.

A consequence of the policies that favour import-substitution is that the development of manufactured exports is hindered. The typically slow growth of primary exports combined with the lack of manufactured exports, leads to a shortage of foreign exchange. The situation is aggravated as net foreign exchange savings of the import-substitution strategy decline due to the increased need for foreign materials, machinery, and technological know-how. Consequently, economic growth is constrained by the limited availability of foreign exchange, and intermittent foreign exchange crisis may occur as attempts are made to expand the economy at rates exceeding that permitted by the growth of export earnings.

In Southeast Asia, as elsewhere, interest has been shifting toward export promotion as a development strategy. A growing number of countries have successfully promoted their manufactured exports, in particular the Asian "Newly Industrialising Economies" that is, the Republic of Korea, Taiwan, Hong Kong, and Singapore. The adoption of an export-oriented industrialisation strategy involves certain policy prescriptions (Balassa, 1980b):

1. While infant-industry considerations call for the preferential treatment of manufacturing activities, such treatment should be applied on a moderate scale, so as to avoid the establishment and maintenance of inefficient industries and to ensure the continued expansion of primary production for domestic and foreign markets;

2. Equal treatment should be given to exports and to import-substitution in the manufacturing sector so as to ensure that resources are allocated according to comparative advantage. The provision of equal incentives, moreover, contributes to efficient exportation and import-substitution through specialisation in particular products and in their parts, components, and accessories;

3. Infant-industry considerations apart, variation in incentive rates within the manufacturing sector should be kept to a minimum. This implies that firms are allowed to decide on the activities to be undertaken, and in particular, to choose their export composition in response to changing world market conditions; and

4. In order to minimise uncertainty for the firm, the system of incentives should be stable and automatic.

One of the ASEAN countries that have shifted from early import-substitution to export promotion is Thailand. Import-substitution in Thailand in non-durable consumer goods and their inputs significantly contributed to industrial growth following the end of the Second World War. By the early seventies, however, the replacement of those imports by domestic production practically came to an end. With the completion of the first stage import-substitution, the strategy ceased to contribute to industrial growth. During the export expansion phase, exports of processed goods, including processed materials such as rubber and tin, and traditional processed foods, as well as textiles and clothing, have been particularly important.

In the case of Malaysia, the early period of import-substitution was nearly completed by 1973. In the early seventies, the rise in exports of manufactures was basically driven by largely labour-intensive industries such as electrical machinery, footwear, clothing and textiles. Similarly, as the tariff and tax disincentives for export industries in the Philippine have been partly offset since the early 1970s by giving free-trade status to approved export producers, non-traditional export growth has come primarily from garments, electrical and electronic equipment, and handicrafts. A more detailed discussion of international trade is presented in Chapter 7: Economic Inter-Dependence: External Trade.

Growth Prospects

Productivity

The value-added per employee in manufacturing in 2004 was US$76,580 in Singapore and US$23,706 in Malaysia. Latest statistics show that in 2003, the value-added per employee in manufacturing was US$8,914 in Indonesia and US$13,628 in the Philippines. In 2000, the value-added per employee in manufacturing was about US$8,276 in Thailand and US$2,623 in Cambodia. This divergence in labour productivity is largely a reflection of the differences in the overall relative factor intensities (i.e. capital/labour ratios) within the industrial sector of the Southeast Asian countries. Countries like Myanmar, Laos, Cambodia, Indonesia, and the Philippines are relatively labour abundant, while Singapore and Malaysia have become labour scarce. This suggests that the future industrial development of the relatively labour-abundant countries should focus on the continued development of labour-intensive manufacturing. In fact, for Cambodia, Indonesia, the Philippines, Vietnam and Myanmar, an industrial development strategy that emphasises production of labour-intensive goods for export should be recommended. In the past, such an export-oriented industrialisation strategy was successfully adopted by Hong Kong, South Korea, Singapore, Taiwan, Malaysia and Thailand.

How can the growth of labour-intensive exports in the Southeast Asian countries carry over to other sectors and lead to economy-wide development? Different export commodities tend to provide different stimuli according to the technological characteristics of their production. The nature of the export good's production function has an influence on the extent of secondary changes elsewhere in the economy. Essentially, the development of labour-intensive exports will have significant employment creation effects, which stimulate demand for a wide variety of domestic products, thus expanding the size of the domestic market.

In countries like Malaysia, the Philippines and Thailand where labour productivity is in the middle of the range within the region, stimulus to development may also come from the growth in exports that require new skills and more productive combinations of the factors of production. Favourable linkages may stem from exports that are intensive in skilled labour. The use of skilled labour may help the economy in various ways: greater incentives for human capital formation may channel resources into education, on-the-job training in the export sector may be disseminated at little cost through the movement of workers into other sectors, and skilled workers may save more of their wage incomes than unskilled workers and thus promote overall national savings. However, relatively more developed infrastructure and markets, and extensive development of human resources are vital in order for the development of labour-intensive exports to spill over to other sectors and lead to economy-wide development.

Other appropriate industrial policies are also helpful in developing the labour-intensive export sector in Southeast Asian countries. Positive incentives to facilitate rapid export expansion could include reforming the duty and tax systems; giving incentives to compensate for the burden of custom duties and indirect taxes on export production; introducing or reforming export credit schemes; abolishing export taxes and limiting export controls, and employing various institutional measures of export promotion such as simplifying export procedures.

The higher productivity in Singapore reflects the shifting overall relative factor ratio in the process of economic growth. In mid-1979, the Government stepped up policies to raise the level of labour productivity. Industrial development, therefore, took on a different character from that in the 1960s and 1970s. The trend has been towards the creation of higher value-added activities largely through the attraction of foreign investment, with multinational corporations providing the expertise, technology and markets. Local manufacturers and entrepreneurs, however, have also been encouraged to upgrade their operations through automation, computerisation, robotisation and rationalisation of labour use. To provide the necessary skills to achieve the operational upgrading, the Government, through the National Wages Council, operates a Skill Development Fund (SDF) to which employers contribute a small percentage of their total wage bills and from which funds can be used by workers for training and re-training. Perhaps, it is not out of place to report that the author of this book was also the initiator of the SDF and was for three years its first chairman. Malaysia too followed closely the footstep of Singapore in this area as a longer-term sustainability move through the raising of labour productivity and export competitiveness.

International Competitiveness

As a country's overall capital/labour ratio increases in the process of economic growth, the structure of its production as well as trade changes. The growing country will continuously be breaking into new markets and becoming dislodged in others; its resources will steadily shift into sectors requiring more capital-intensive means of production.

A country like Singapore in the 1960s would have a low capital/labour ratio (K/L) and so produce and export to the rest of the world goods which are relatively labour-intensive. In turn, it imports from the rest of the world more capital-intensive goods. However, in the process of economic growth, the labour market becomes tight, and both human and physical capital accumulates so that the overall capital/labour ratio rises. In the process, the country shifts from producing labour-intensive goods to more capital-intensive goods. Accordingly, the country gets displaced in the markets for labour-intensive goods.

In the process of growth, the ratio of labour cost to capital cost rises. Thus, not only is there a change in the industrial pattern of production and trade, labour becomes increasingly more expensive. Consequently, as Singapore and other newly industrialised countries gradually lose their comparative advantage in labour-intensive goods, countries like Malaysia and Thailand break into these markets. Therefore, relatively labour abundant countries must initially adopt policies that encourage the development of labour-intensive industries.

Notwithstanding the potential for export development of labour-intensive commodities, rising protectionism in the rest of the world may limit the scope for export expansion. If exports are confined to a slow rate of growth, then there can be little scope for development through trade even if domestic obstacles are removed. This suggests that for many of the Southeast Asian countries, raising agricultural productivity in order to ensure that their primary exports remain competitive in world markets continues to be important. Furthermore, policies should be pursued to allow specialisation in exports with the highest growth prospects. To do so, a country must have the capacity to reallocate resources — to shift, for instance, from exporting a foodstuff with slow demand growth to exporting non-industrial raw materials or minerals with faster demand growth. Instead of import-substituting industrialisation, an industrialisation strategy that emphasises export-substitution is likely to be more relevant for the Southeast Asian countries. Export-substitution refers to the exports of non-traditional products such as processed primary products, products of semi-manufactures, and manufactured goods that substitute for the traditional exports of primary products. Malaysia and Thailand appear to have carried out this export-substitution strategy very successfully.

In other words, the resources used in export-substitution could have earned a greater amount of foreign exchange through export expansion than the foreign exchange saved in import-substitution, which relies on high effective rates of protection. Even though import-substitution is profitable in terms of local currency, because of high protection, the opportunity cost in terms of real resource usage is very high. This is because the value of exports that could be produced with a given amount of scarce factors is greater than the value of imports that have been replaced. Furthermore, to the extent that it rests on exogenous world demand, industrialisation through export-substitution is not limited by the size of domestic market, as is import-substitution.

Exporting to global markets also entails the benefits of economies of scale and learning effects. A strategy that emphasises trade may also help to attract foreign direct investment. An inflow of foreign capital to support export-substitution is not dependent on home market protection but is guided by considerations of efficiency. In addition, foreign investment for export-substitution tends to have more linkages to agriculture when such investment involves the processing of primary goods.

Other Constraints

The constraints to industrial growth may be classified into internal constraints and external constraints. The implementation of the specific industrial policies discussed above, which are instrumental in industrial development, is predicated upon sound macroeconomic policies for internal and external balance, appropriate interest rate policy and the development of efficient credit markets, and measures to increase the availability of skilled labour. For instance, policies to reduce the existing bias in the incentive system in favour of import-substitution and against exports would contribute to improvements in the balance of payments. Macroeconomic policies to reduce balance of payments deficits and maintain internal balance may also be important. In addition, modern industrial development requires the availability of technical and skilled labour. This purpose would be served by taking measures to promote both vocational and in-plant training — the former involving technical education at the tertiary and high school levels as well as special training courses for skilled workers. Unsound macroeconomic policies and inadequate institutions for training workers will hamper industrial development.

Industrial development tends to be concentrated in and around certain urban centers. Such concentration entails overcrowding in these centers with consequent economic and social costs, and more importantly, the problems associated with urban unemployment as well as rural-urban migration. In as far as creating industrial employment is an important policy objective, a successful regional dispersion of manufacturing activities will be important. A long-term solution to the problems of regional disparities is the provision of infrastructure and key industrial services to all regions.

Turning to external constraints, it should be noted that the potential for industrialisation via exports of labour-intensive goods depends on continued growth of world trade. Increasing protectionism in the industrial countries and the slowdown of world trade growth, however, might constrain industrialisation via export promotion. The nature of protection in the industrial countries has changed dramatically over the years. Under the auspices of the General Agreement on Tariffs and Trade (GATT) which later became the World Trade Organisation (WTO), the tariff levels in the industrial countries have declined during the past four decades. This trend creates the impression that developing country exporters will find little difficulty in exporting to the developed countries. However, this is not true. A number of non-tariff barriers have been erected against developing countries exports, and the dismantling of these barriers should be a high-priority agenda item in the on-going multinational trade negotiations. However, nearly all developed countries give most favoured nation (MFN) status to most developing countries, and this means that the latter's exports to the former enjoy one of the lowest import tariffs. This provision is, however, for non-sensitive goods and services only. Southeast Asian countries too are likely to increase their demand for the manufacturing and other exports of their neighbours during their development process.

With globalisation, competition for FDI has become more intensified. More and more countries are joining in the competition for FDI. The recent entry of China into the global market economy greatly intensifies the competition for FDI. This has resulted in the re-location of some industries from Southeast Asia to China, which offers not just cheaper labour and land cost but also more importantly a large and growing domestic market. By contrast, the ASEAN markets are fragmented into ten separate markets. Even the largest market is relatively very small when compared with China. Furthermore, China's economy is growing significantly faster than ASEAN economies.

Finally, export-oriented industrialisation does not only mean exports to the developed economies. If ASEAN can achieve an effective ASEAN-wide Free Trade Area, this would promote intra-ASEAN trade in manufacturing goods as well as trade in other goods and services. In other words, other ASEAN countries can become significant markets for ASEAN exporters. Besides, other fast developing Asian economies, including China and India, provide potential markets for ASEAN exports. The export potential is bright, not bleak.

Key Points

1. Industrialisation is a main feature of most economies in Southeast Asia since Independence. Many have made impressive gains in this area.
2. The Philippines was an early starter of industrialisation. However, over the years, its leadership position was taken over by the other ASEAN-5 countries.
3. In primarily agricultural economies, a significant portion of manufacturing value-added comes from the agro-industries. As the country develops, the share of this sector tends to fall.
4. Tax concessions are given out by Governments to promote manufacturing industries. However, if inappropriately structured, such policies may

distort factor prices. As a result, countries with a large labour force may not get to enjoy the full benefits of industrialisation in terms of employment creation.

5. From 1980s onwards, FDI in the region grew rapidly, with Singapore attracting the largest amount of investment. On the other hand, the transitional economies of Myanmar, Cambodia and Laos are still lagging behind in attracting FDI.

6. Export Processing Zone (EPZ) has been instrumental to the export industrialisation success of many Southeast Asian economies. Not only do they help to increase manufactured exports, they also increase foreign exchange earnings and provide employment.

7. Most ASEAN countries have implemented import-substitution policy one time or another. However, this is no longer the case. The ASEAN countries are instead pursuing export-oriented strategies to promote economic growth.

Suggested Discussion Topics

6.1 With reference to Southeast Asia, discuss the advantages and disadvantages of adopting an import-substitution strategy as opposed to an export promotion strategy in the industrialisation process. Is foreign direct investment important in either of the two strategies?

6.2 The rates of post-war industrialisation differ substantially among the Southeast Asian countries. Discuss the reasons for the divergent performance. Also, discuss the factors that help or hinder industrialisation in any country in Southeast Asia.

References

AKRASANEE, Narongchai and Vinyu VICHIT-VADAKAN (eds.), 1979, *ASEAN Cooperation in Foreign Investment and Transnational Corporations*, Bangkok, 125–128.

AMJAD, Rashid (ed.), 1981, *The Development of Labour-intensive Industry in Asian Countries*, International Labour Organisation, 15–16.

BALASSA Bela, 1980a, "Industrial development strategy in Thailand", *A World Bank Country Study*, Washington, D.C.: The World Bank.

BALASSA, Bela, 1980b, "The process of industrial development and alternative development strategies", Princeton University, International finance section, *Essays in International Finance*, No. 141.

CHIA, Siow Yue, 1980, "Direct foreign investments in ASEAN", *The Philippines Economic Journal*, No. 43, Vol. XIX, No. 1.

CODY, John, Helen HUGHES and David WALL (eds.), 1980, *Policies for Industrial Progress in Developing Countries*, World Bank, New York: Oxford University Press, 179–180.

DE VRIES, B. A., 1980, *Transition Toward More Rapid and Labour-intensive Industrial Development: The Case of the Philippines*, Washington, D.C.: The World Bank, World Bank Staff Working Paper No. 424.

JOMO, K. S., (ed.), 2001, *Southeast Asia's Industrialization: Industrial Policy, Capabilities and Sustainability*. New York: Palgrave.

HUGHES, Helen, 1978, "Industrialisation and development: A stocktaking", UNIDO, *Industry and Development*, No. 1.

KRAUS, W. and W. LUTKENHONST, 1986, *The Economic Development of the Pacific Basin: Growth Dynamics, Trade Relations and Emerging Cooperation*, New York: St. Martin's Press.

LEE, Eddy (ed.), 1984, *Export Processing Zones and Industrial Employment in Asia: Papers and Proceedings of a Technical Workshop*, International Labour Organisation.

LEWIS, Arthur W., 1954, "Economic development with unlimited supplies of labour", *Manchester School*, Vol. 22, 132–191.

LIM, David, 1983, "Fiscal incentives and foreign investment in LDCs", *Journal of Development Studies*, Vol. 19(2), 207–212.

MEIER, Gerald M., 1985, *Leading Issues in Economic Development*, 4th Edition, Singapore: Oxford University Press, 322–330.

SETHURAMAN, S V., 1997, *Urban Poverty and the Informal Sector: A Critical Assessment of Current Strategies*. Geneva: International Labour Organization.

STEWART, Frances, 1978, *Technology and Underdevelopment*, 2nd Edition, London and Basingstokes: MacMillan, 46–50.

Further Readings

CHOWDHURY Anis and Iyanatul ISLAM, 1993, *The Newly Industrialising Economies of East Asia*, London, New York: Routledge.

HOFFMAN, Lutz and Siew Ee TAN, 1980, *Industrial Growth, Employment, and Foreign Investment in Peninsular Malaysia*, Kuala Lumpur: Oxford University Press.

HUGHES, Helen, 1988, *Achieving Industrialisation in East Asia*, New York: Cambridge University Press.

KRONGKAEW, Medhi (ed.), 1995, *Thailand's Industrialisation and its Consequences*, New York: St. Martin's Press; Basingstoke, Hampshire: Macmillan Press Ltd.

LEE, Eddy (ed.), 1981, *Export-led Industrialisation and Development*, Geneva: International Labour Office.

LIM, Chong Yah et. al., 1988, *Policy Options for the Singapore Economy*, Singapore: McGraw-Hill Book Company.

LIM, Linda, Y. C. and Eng Fong PANG, 1991, *Foreign Direct Investment and Industrialisation in Malaysia, Singapore, Taiwan and Thailand*, Paris: Development Centre of the OECD.

MASUYAMA, Seiichi, Donna VANDENBRINK and Siow Yue CHIA (eds.), 1997, *Industrial Policies in East Asia*, Tokyo, Japan: Nomura Research Institute; Singapore: Institute of Southeast Asian Studies.

NGUYEN, Anh Tuan, 1996, *Prospects for Vietnam's Industrialisation: Lessons from East Asia*, Petaling Jaya: INSAN; Singapore: Friedrich-Ebert-Stiftung.

RAJAH, Rasiah, 1995, *Foreign Capital and Industrialisation in Malaysia*, New York: St. Martin's Press.

TEOFILO C. DAQUILA (2005), "The industrial sector in Southeast Asia: development experiences and policies", in *The Economies of Southeast Asia: Indonesia, Malaysia, Philippines, Singapore and Thailand*, New York: Nova Science Publishers.

Chapter 7

Economic Inter-Dependence: External Trade

If a foreign country can supply us with a commodity cheaper than we ourselves can make it, better buy it of them with some part of the produce of our own industry employed in a way in which we have some advantage.

Adam Smith, *The Wealth of Nations*

Objectives

✓ Provide theoretical explanation of relationship between export and economic growth.

✓ Ascertain relationship between per capita income and export orientation.

✓ Describe services trade.

✓ Assess whether concentration in primary exports has led to export instability.

✓ Examine export diversification trends.

✓ Evaluate intra-ASEAN trade.

✓ Discuss role of trade centre.

✓ Present Southeast Asian countries' export promotion strategies.

✓ Discuss whether ASEAN countries should pursue export-led industrialisation.

✓ Describe trade barriers and protectionism.

✓ Present new international economic order.

Introduction

This chapter deals with issues connected with economic development through trade. Recent trends in export performance in the Southeast Asian countries and exports diversification are first examined. One principal issue is whether Southeast Asian countries should emulate the Asian Newly Industrialising Economies (NIEs), which have been able to experience very rapid economic growth and transformation based largely on export-led industrialisation. With most of the Southeast Asian economies being largely primary producing countries, issues relating to trade in primary products will receive special attention.

Trade is exchange of goods and services through the medium of money, which enables complex multilateral trading arrangements to take place. Freely and willingly entered into, trade benefits both transaction parties, thus indirectly contributes to wealth creation. Trade also enables specialisation and division of labour to take place. International trade enables international specialisation and international division of labour. Malaysia, for example, produces palm oil mainly for export, and unless there is international trade in palm oil, Malaysia cannot specialise in palm oil production on the scale she does today. Neither can Brunei specialise in the production of petroleum oil, if there is no external demand or trade in this commodity. International trade also helps in the integration of the global economy. As James A. Garfield, the 20th President of the United States had once said, "Commerce links all mankind in one common brotherhood of mutual dependence and interests."

Export Orientation

Contribution of Export to Economic Growth

The classical and neoclassical economists held the view that foreign trade can be a propelling force in development. Adam Smith's 'vent for surplus' view, for example, holds that resources are not fully employed prior to external trade, and that exports can be increased without a decrease in domestic consumption, with the consequence that the level of economic activity is raised through external trade.

More generally, classical economists held the view that comparative advantage determined the pattern of trade. Resource reallocation rather than the use of surplus resources allows trade to benefit countries by promoting a more efficient international division of labour. Each trading country is able to enjoy a higher real income through specialisation in production according to its comparative advantage. More recently, management guru Michael Porter developed the Theory of Competitive Advantage that measures international competitive advantage by "the presence of significant and sustained exports to a wide array of other nations and/or significant outbound foreign investment based on skills and assets created in the home country" (Porter, 1990). According to Michael Porter, "internationally competitive industries are those whose firms have the capacity and will to improve and innovate in order to create and sustain a competitive advantage". While the basis of trade in the Theory of Comparative Advantage hinges on differences in labour productivity and/or factor endowments, Michael Porter's Theory of Competitive Advantage emphasises the importance of successfully developing and commercialising new technologies, new products, and new processes. In present day's jargon, some would say that comparative advantage is applicable to the old economy, while competitive advantage is relevant in the new economy.

Apart from static benefits of trade, there are also dynamic benefits of international exchange through economies of scale — widening the extent of the market, inducing innovations and raising productivity through international trade. These allow a country to overcome the diseconomies of scale of the domestic market and domestic resource endowment. In addition, trade helps the transfer of technology, skills and entrepreneurship. For these reasons, the gains from trade do not result merely in an once-over improvement in resource allocation, but they in fact can promote impetus for higher levels of economic growth.

In the context of the primary producing countries of Southeast Asia, the staple theory of growth, an export-based model of growth formulated to present a macro-dynamic view of how an economy's growth can be determined by expansion in its exports, also has relevance (Meier, 1985: 491). The term 'staple' refers to a raw material or resource-intensive commodity occupying a dominant position in the country's exports. It argues that there will be an expansion of resource-based export commodities with the discovery of a primary product or increase in demand for the commodity in which the country has a comparative advantage. This, in turn, will result in higher rates of growth in per capita income. Resources hitherto left idle or not yet discovered are brought into use, thus creating a return on investment in the use of these resources. The export of a primary product has effects on the rest of the economy through reducing underemployment and unemployment, inducing a higher rate of domestic savings and investment, and inducing a flow of factor inputs from other sectors of the economy. Thus, a rise in exports induced by greater demand leads to supply responses within the economy that increase the productivity of the exporting economy. However, the extent of the impact depends much on the nature of the primary resource. For tin and rubber exports, for example, the economic infrastructure has to be built, thereby benefiting the economy as a whole. The impact will be less, if oil is the primary export. Only pipelines will be necessary, not railway lines and roads. The pre-War history of economic development of present day Peninsular Malaysia proves this point beyond the shadow of a doubt (Lim C. Y., 1967).

Empirically, a positive relationship has been found between the rate of growth of exports and that of GNP in the LDCs. Michaely (1977) estimated the relationship between the change in the proportion of exports in GNP and GNP growth for 41 LDCs over the period 1950–1973, and established a positive and significant relationship between the two variables. Balassa (1978) also found a similar positive relationship for a smaller group of countries over the period 1960–1973. Subsequently, he confirmed this positive relationship for a group of 28 LDCs over the period 1963–1979. The latter study included Indonesia, the Philippines, Singapore and Thailand (Ariff and Hill, 1985: 38–40).

However, Ahmad and Harnhirun (1995) using annual export and GDP data for the period 1966–1990 found that there was no long-term relationship between exports and GDP growth for Indonesia, Malaysia, the Philippines and Thailand. Singapore, on the other hand, was found to have a long-run relationship between exports and GDP growth but the causality between these two economic variables was bi-directional. This means that for Singapore, economic growth and exports mutually reinforces each other. Thus, it would appear that the theory of circular cumulative causation (Lim, 1996) operates at least in Singapore.

Table 7.1 shows that all the countries in Southeast Asia, except Cambodia and Myanmar, displayed exceptionally high export growth rates for the period 1960–2006. Nearly all of these were certainly much higher than the global annual growth rate of 10.4% achieved over the same period, with Thailand for example achieving an average growth rate of 13.8% per annum. These very high growth rates in part also reflect their corresponding high growth rates in GDP. Indonesia, the star performer in the 1970s, was not able to sustain the high export growth rates throughout the period, registering an annual growth rate of only 6.1% in the period 1980 to 2006, although her export growth rates over the longer period of 40 years could still be considered very respectable by world standard. Myanmar, by way of contrast, grew at a much slower pace of 5.5% per annum because of the adoption of the socialist policy of autarky and self-reliance. The export performance of Myanmar was highly erratic over the years, with negative growth experienced in the 1960s and the 1980s. The pariah status of Myanmar also hampers its ability to export. Myanmar, however, managed to increase its merchandise exports steadily throughout the 1990s. Its exports surged in 2000 largely due to the commencement of gas exports in 1999.

Table 7.1

Annual Growth Rate of Value of Merchandise Exports (%), 1960–2006

	1960–2006	1960–1979	1980–2006
Thailand	13.8	14.4	13.3
Singapore	11.9	14.2	10.2
Malaysia	11.2	12.5	10.3
Indonesia	10.6	16.6	6.1
Philippines	10.9	11.0	8.4
Laos	10.1	4.0	14.6
Cambodia	9.8	−13.4	23.3
Myanmar	5.5	2.9	7.5
Vietnam	n.a.	n.a.	20.2
Brunei	n.a.	n.a.	−2.0

Source: Computed from data from ADB, *Asian Development Outlook*, 2007 and World Bank, *WDI Online*, 23 Sep. 2008, http://publications.worldbank. org/WDI/

Another interesting piece of information is also revealed in Table 7.1: the top Southeast Asian exporters from 1980 to 2006 are Cambodia and Vietnam. Their annual export growth rates are twice that of other ASEAN economies. Problem over data reliability aside, the strong upward trend signals the development orientation and the growth potential of these two countries.

Table 7.2 shows that in terms of exports per capita. Singapore, Malaysia and Thailand lead the way. Exports per capita in Brunei is also very high, although the level of exports per capita has fallen significantly over the years. We have to bear in mind that Brunei is a small and richly endowed nation, whose fortune is closely tied to the prices of petroleum. It has achieved a very high per capita GNI even though its manufacturing and financial sectors are still not well developed. Brunei is unique, and its path to wealth is not possible to be replicated in other Southeast Asia nations. Singapore, Brunei, Malaysia and Thailand are the most export-oriented economies in Southeast Asia in 2006. Laos and Myanmar are the least export-oriented economies in Southeast Asia in terms of per capita exports. They also displayed much lower per capita income growth levels.

If we take exports to GDP ratio as a criterion of export orientation, Table 7.3 shows Singapore followed by Malaysia are the most

Table 7.2
Per Capita Exports (US$), 1980 and 2006

	1980	2006
Singapore	8,027	60,627
Brunei	23,736	20,051
Malaysia	942	6,022
Thailand	139	2,058
Philippines	120	550
Indonesia	148	452
Vietnam	6	440
Cambodia	2	248
Laos	9	70
Myanmar	14	73

Source: Author's estimates from data in World Bank, *WDI Online*, 23 Sep. 2008, http://publications.worldbank. org/WDI/

Table 7.3

Exports/GDP Ratios (%), 1980 and 2006

	1980	2006
Singapore	165	253
Malaysia	52	117
Thailand	20	74
Brunei	93	71
Vietnam	5 (1985)	73
Cambodia	3 (1987)	69
Philippines	18	46
Indonesia	28	31
Laos	3 (1984)	36

Source: Author's estimates from data in World Bank,
WDI Online, 23 Sep. 2008, http://publications.
worldbank.org/WDI/

export-dependent economies in Southeast Asia. Indonesia and Laos are the least export-dependent. This, however, was not the case for Indonesia in 1980. Inter-temporally, most of the Southeast Asian countries have become increasingly export-oriented, particularly Vietnam, Cambodia and Laos. However, we have to be very careful in interpreting the information in presented Table 7.3, as the high exports to GDP ratio in countries such as Vietnam, Cambodia and Laos could be the result of a large informal sector that leads to the GDP figures of these countries being under-reported in 1980. Thus, the computed exports to GDP ratios of these countries in 1980 could be higher than what they actually were.

As can be seen from Table 7.4, there is a perfect ranking relationship between per capita income on the one hand and export orientation as measured by per capita exports and exports to GDP ratio on the other among the ASEAN-5. Singapore tops the list followed by Malaysia, Thailand, the Philippines and Indonesia in all the three columns.

International Trade in Services

The International Monetary Fund (IMF) defines trade in commercial services as those items that cover transportation, travel and other commercial

Table 7.4

Ranking Relationship between GDP Per Capita (A), Per Capita Exports (B) and Exports/GDP Ratio (C), 2006

	Ranking on A	Ranking on B	Ranking on C
Singapore	1	1	1
Malaysia	2	2	2
Thailand	3	3	3
Philippines	4	4	4
Indonesia	5	5	5

Source: Author's estimates from data in World Bank, *WDI Online*, 23 Sep. 2008, http://publications.worldbank.org/WDI/

services but excludes labour income. Transportation covers all land, air and sea services that are performed by residents of one economy for those of another that involves the carrying of passengers and freight, the rental of carriers and related services. Travel includes services and goods acquired by personal travellers, for health, education or other purposes, and by business travellers. The most common goods and services covered are lodging, food and beverages, entertainment and transportation, gifts and souvenirs. Other commercial services correspond to communication services, construction services, insurance services, financial services, computer and information services, royalties and licences fees, other business services and personal, cultural and recreational services. In other words, tourism is an important part of ASEAN's invisible exports.

According to Peter Lloyd (1994), between 1980–1991, the broader Asian region "is less important as a trader of services than as a trader of merchandise and it has been increasing its share of world trade less rapidly in the service trade". As Table 7.5 shows, the Philippines has shown decline in the global trade in services. Only Singapore and Thailand seem to have both increased their services trade share. Nonetheless, some ASEAN countries run surpluses, others deficits in the balance of trade in services and some of these deficit countries include Indonesia and the Philippines. In 2003, for example, Indonesia imports of services were 3.3 times that of her services exports.

In the city-state of Singapore, export of services is of great importance. Singapore is ranked by the World Trade Organisation as the world's

Table 7.5

Value of Commercial Services Trade (US$ Billion), 1985 and 2006

	Imports		Exports	
	1985	2006	1985	2006
Singapore	3.9	60.8	6.3	57.0
	(0.9)	(2.3)	(1.5)	(2.1)
Malaysia	3.9	21.0	2.0	23.0
	(0.9)	(0.8)	(0.5)	(0.9)
Thailand	1.7	24.0	1.9	32.0
	(0.4)	(0.9)	(0.5)	(1.2)
Indonesia	5.0	17.0*	0.8	5.0*
	(1.2)	(1.0)	(0.2)	(0.3)
Philippines	0.8	6.0	1.9	5.3
	(0.2)	(0.2)	(0.4)	(0.2)

Source: World Trade Organisation, *International Trade Statistics*, 2007.
Note: Values in (parenthesis) show percentage share in world services trade.
*refers to 2003 figure, the latest data available.

16th leading exporter in world trade in commercial services, constituting 2.1% of world services exports in 2006. Singapore's role as a transportation hub is reflected in her transportation exports, which are nearly three times as important to her as her important tourism trade.

In all ASEAN countries, the emerging services industry is tourism; regional and international tourism. Thailand leads the way in terms of the value of tourist export, followed by Malaysia and Singapore. There is much more potential in this area for Indonesia, the Philippines and the new ASEAN-4. In an important sense, all countries have important natural, historical and cultural unique comparative advantages in tourism export. More investment to enhance these advantages should take place to promote more employment opportunities, to increase foreign exchange earnings and state revenue.

When economists speak of the balance of trade, they mean the balance of merchandise trade and the balance of services trade. Services trade also refers to as invisible trade and the balance is referred to as the balance of invisible trade which includes tourist trade. A trade surplus that includes only visible or merchandise trade is thus not complete when the balance of total external trade is considered. Most trade statistics published in the media refer only to balance of visible trade. It thus shows an incomplete picture of trade statistics and the balance of payments on current account, which also includes the balance of invisible trade and the balance of transfers.

Export Instability

As is true in most LDCs, trade in Southeast Asian countries tends to be concentrated in a few key commodities. In 1985, for instance, the contribution of just three major commodities in total merchandise exports was more than 50% for six out of the ten Southeast Asian countries (see Table 7.6). Export concentration was still high in 2006, and has gone up substantially in some countries. Cambodia, for example, showed a sharp increase in export

Table 7.6

Percentage of Three Most Important Commodities Exports
to Total Exports, 1985–2006

	1985	2006
Brunei	99	98
Laos	88	54
Indonesia	69	33
Myanmar	67	72
Malaysia	54	42
Cambodia	53	69
Vietnam	43	47
Singapore	40	45
Thailand	29	26
Philippines	27	61

Source: Based on information from Statistics Canada, International Trade Division, *World Trade Analyser (computer file)*, 2002, and World Bank, *World Trade Indicators* 2008.

Note: Based on 3-digit SITC code.

concentration from 53% in 1985 to 69% in 2006, and the Philippines, from 27% to 61%. On the other hand, export concentration in Indonesia has declined significantly from 69% in 1985 to 32% in 2006.

Table 7.7 is also interesting. Important new export products appeared in 2006, when they were not found in 1985. In Thailand, for example, the three main exports in 2006 were office machines, semiconductor devices and integrated circuits, and telecommunication equipment, whereas in 1985, they were rice, vegetables and roots, and rubber. In Malaysia, office machines and telecommunication equipment have taken the places of petroleum and palm oil. In the Philippines, automatic data processing machines and office machines have replaced coconut oil and fruits and nuts. The profile of the main export commodities given in Table 7.7 reflects the successful industrialisation of these countries in Southeast Asia. In 2006, electronic and electrical products are the dominant export commodities in the much more market-oriented older ASEAN 5 economies of Singapore, Malaysia, Thailand, the Philippines, and to a lesser extent, Indonesia. On the other hand, primary products are still the main export commodities in the less market-oriented new ASEAN 4 economies of Cambodia, Laos, Myanmar and Vietnam. However, garment, a labour-intensive manufacture, is featured prominently in the new ASEAN 4 countries in 2006, particularly Cambodia and Laos. This reflects the later industrialisation progress of these countries. They are the late-comers in the industrialisation process in Southeast Asia. Also of note is that Brunei continues to display export concentration in just petroleum. Whatever the export instability in exporting more or less one commodity, statistics show that Brunei has one of the highest per capita income levels in Southeast Asia (Table 2.2).

Geographic or market concentration also exists in Southeast Asia. It implies that most of the major exports are usually sold to a few markets of the industrialised countries. Merchandise exports sold to Japan, the United States and the European Union accounted for 44% of extra-ASEAN exports in 2006.

It has long been held that export instability is a serious problem in LDCs because of the belief that certain products, mainly primary commodities, were exported mostly by the developing nations of the world (Knudsen and Parnes, 1975). *A priori* reasoning has led to the view that a high concentration of trade in primary products together with a geographic concentration

Table 7.7

Three Main Export Commodities, 1985 and 2006

	1985	2006
Brunei	Petroleum & products	Petroleum & products, gas
Cambodia	Rubber Iron and steel Oil seeds and oleaginous fruits	Garments Veneers and plywood Rubber
Indonesia	Petroleum & products Veneers & plywood Rubber	Petroleum & products Coal Palm oil, rubber
Laos	Coffee Wood Rubber tyres	Copper Wood products Garments

Malaysia	Petroleum & products
	Palm oil
	Semiconductor devices, integrated
	   circuits, electronic valves & tubes
		Semiconductor devices, integrated
		   circuits, electronic valves & tubes
		Office machines
		Telecommunication equipment

Myanmar	Wood Base metals Rice	Gas Wood Beans

Philippines	Coconut oil
	Semiconductor devices, integrated
	   circuits, electronic valves & tubes
	Fruits & nuts
		Semiconductor devices, integrated
		   circuits, electronic valves & tubes
		Automatic data processing machines
		Office machines

Singapore	Petroleum & products
	Semiconductor devices, integrated
	   circuits, electronic valves & tubes
	Automatic data processing machines
		Semiconductor devices, integrated
		   circuits, electronic valves & tubes
		Automatic data processing machines
		Petroleum & products

Thailand	Rice
	Vegetables and roots
	Rubber
		Office machines, microcircuits
		Semiconductor devices, integrated
		   circuits, electronic valves & tubes
		Telecommunications equipment,
		   auto parts

Vietnam	Frozen shrimps Oil seeds and oleaginous fruits Coal	Petroleum & products, oils Footwear Seafood

Sources: Derived from information from Statistics Canada, International Trade Division, *World Trade Analyser* (*computer file*), 2002, and World Bank, *World Trade Indicators* 2008.

Note: Based on 3-digit SITC code.

of trade are important causes of export instability. As demand and supply elasticities of primary commodities are much lower than those of manufactures, it would therefore appear that much of the export instability in LDCs is attributable to their specialisation in primary products. The production of natural rubber, an important produce of Thailand, Indonesia, Malaysia and Vietnam, for example, is inelastic in the short run since it involves a gestation period of about four to seven years between planting and maturity. Variations in the level of output are too negligible in the short run to have any appreciable effect on the short-run supply elasticity. Due to heavy capital investment, exit from the rubber industry is also extremely difficult. The case of tin is similar. Its low output elasticity is attributable to the fact that it generally takes about three years to set up a dredge mine and begin operations and the fact that the resources used in tin mining are industry-specific. The low variable costs relative to fixed costs imply that production has to continue even in the face of falling prices.

The price elasticities of demand for primary commodities are also usually low. Given the low elasticities of supply and demand, any change that affects either supply or demand or both will inevitably generate extreme price instability. In the case of natural rubber, palm oil and tin, output variability due to weather and similar factors is small. Hence, it is largely the changes in demand that lead to price instability. Furthermore, supply being inelastic in the short-run, there are stockholdings of commodities in the world market that give rise to intensive speculative activities that tend to amplify the price oscillations. Given the high degree of fluctuations in prices, export earnings are also expected to fluctuate. However, national rubber prices have fluctuated much less consequent on the availability of synthetic rubber. Demand for natural rubber has become much more price elastic.

The susceptibility of the export proceeds to externally induced fluctuations is exacerbated by a heavy concentration of export markets in a limited number of industrial countries. Primary export commodities, being dependent on derived demand (and having low supply elasticities), are characterised by cycles in the prices in line with the cycles in the industrial output of the advanced countries. In a world of normally growing production and consumption of primary commodities, it does not require a severe reduction in the imports of the industrialised countries to cause a marked fall in the prices of these products. Given a normal rate of growth of the productive capacity of the export sector, a slowdown in the growth of the industrial countries' demand could lead to a temporary excess supply, causing prices to decline.

Although the more industrialised countries of Southeast Asia no longer depend heavily on exports of primary products, export concentration remains high. Countries such as Singapore and Malaysia have now come to depend heavily on the exports of electronic and electrical products. In addition, most of these electronic and electrical products are exported to the United States. The export concentration together with the geographical concentration has not untied the economic fortunes of Singapore and Malaysia to that of the United States, despite the successful industrialisation process. In the past, the dependence was on rubber and tin exports.

The current discussion on decoupling in the world economy following the rapid expansion of China and India does not seem to hold true in many ASEAN countries, certainly not Singapore and Malaysia. However, that China and to a much lesser extent India have become added locomotives of growth in the world, including in Southeast Asia is without doubt. Much of the palm oil exports from Southeast Asia have been shifted to China and India, for example.

Export Diversification and Promotion

Diversification Trends

Chapter 2 analysed the significant structural changes that have occurred in the Southeast Asian economies. There has been a continuous and relatively substantial decline in the share of agriculture in GDP, accompanied by an increase in the share of industry, although in terms of employment, agriculture is still the largest sector in Southeast Asia. There have also been important changes in the position of exports and imports of the Southeast Asian countries. On exports, as expected, the main trends were a rapid decline in the relative importance of agricultural products, an increase in the importance of manufactures and, in the case of Indonesia and Vietnam, increased fuel oil export as well.

Oil export in Indonesia rose very sharply in the 1970s, in response to increased prices. However, since the mid 1980s, the Indonesian Government has been actively promoting non-oil exports in the face of declining oil prices and revenues. By 2008, Indonesia however has become a net oil importer and at the time of writing, she has left OPEC, the international oil exporting cartel.

The increase in manufactured exports in Southeast Asia is attributable mainly to the increase in processed foods, chemicals, electrical electronics and various other manufactures. Textiles and clothing particularly grew in importance in Indonesia, Cambodia and Myanmar. Most of these goods may be classified as products of the unskilled labour-intensive variety. In the ASEAN-5, the share of machinery and transport equipment also assumed greater importance. Consequently, the shares of agricultural products in total exports in Southeast Asia declined substantially.

The change in commodity composition of exports has also been accompanied by changes in the direction of manufactured exports. Between 1985 and 2006 (see Table 7.8), the industrial economies were the most important markets for the primary exports of Southeast Asian countries. This came to, for example, as much as 76% in Indonesia in 1985. As they industrialised, they have also exported their manufactures to the other developing countries. Note that this increase in exports is noticeable in all the ASEAN

Table 7.8
Direction of Merchandise Exports (%), 1985 and 2006

	Industrial Countries		Developing Countries	
	1985	2006	1985	2006
Cambodia	n.a.	76	n.a.	24
Brunei	69	56	24	44
Philippines	74	55	25	45
Vietnam	27	64	65	29
Thailand	57	46	41	53
Indonesia	76	47	24	53
Malaysia	55	44	44	56
Singapore	47	31	52	69
Myanmar	20	13	75	85
Laos	20	15	80	65

Source: International Monetary Fund, *Direction of Trade Statistics Yearbook*, 2007.

economies except Vietnam. Together with the increase in intra-ASEAN trade, China and the Northeast Asian NIEs comprising Hong Kong, South Korea and Taiwan also increased their share of manufactured imports from the Southeast Asian region, reflecting the largely market-led integration of the East Asian economies.

Intra-ASEAN Trade

Total intra-ASEAN merchandise trade increased by 12 times over the period 1990 to 2006 from US$27.6 billion to US$336 billion. The 2001 economic slowdown has dealt a severe blow to intra-ASEAN trade. Intra-ASEAN exports fell by 12.3% in 2001, compared to the previous year. In terms of percentage share of total exports, intra-ASEAN exports increased from 20.1% in 1990 to 25.1% in 2006, which is still lower than the 25.5% share achieved in 1995 (see Table 7.9). On the other hand, the share of intra-ASEAN imports has increased steadily over the years, from 16.2% in 1990 to 23.1% in 2006. The steady increase in intra-ASEAN trade reflects a steady increase in the economic integration of the ASEAN economies.

As Table 7.10 shows, intra-ASEAN exports for all ASEAN countries except Vietnam have increased over the period 1985–2006. The formation of ASEAN Free Trade Area (AFTA) in 1992 helped to reduce trade tariffs within ASEAN, which in turn encouraged intra-ASEAN trade.

Singapore with her strategic location and deep seaport has endeared herself to international traders since the 1870s, serving as a major port of call for ships plying between Europe and East Asia. Entrepot trade has boomed in Singapore, and remains a dominant segment of Singapore's

Table 7.9

Intra-ASEAN Trade Compared to Total ASEAN Trade (%), 1990, 1995 and 2006

	1990	1995	2006
Intra-exports	20.1	25.5	25.1
Intra-imports	16.2	18.9	23.1

Source: World Trade Organisation, *International Trade Statistics*, 2007.

Table 7.10

Intra-ASEAN Exports Compared to Country's Total Exports (%), 1985 and 2006

	1985	2006
Brunei	21	25
Cambodia	n.a.	7
Indonesia	11	18
Laos	18	72
Malaysia	26	26
Myanmar	20	61
Philippines	11	17
Singapore	23	31
Thailand	15	22
Vietnam	22	17

Source: ASEAN Secretariat, *ASEAN Statistical Yearbook*, 2006.

total trade. In 2006, re-exports accounted for 25% of Singapore's total exports. Table 7.11 shows that Singapore remains an important distri-port in the region, accounting for 16% of Malaysia's total exports and 12% of Indonesia's total exports.

With a hub-and-spoke transportation network, transhipment business in Singapore, which includes extra-ASEAN business, has been expanding. There were 128,922 vessel calls with a shipping tonnage of 1.46 billion gross tons in 2006, making Singapore the world's busiest port in terms of shipping tonnage. Singapore is also one of the world's busiest container ports, handling 24.8 million TEUs in 2006.

The high usage of Singapore's port by Malaysia is partly historical, as Singapore was a trading centre for both Peninsular Malaysia and East Malaysia. It is in part geographical, because of the location of Singapore between Peninsular Malaysia and East Malaysia and Singapore's geographical position as a Southern terminal of the important Straits of Malacca trade route. Malaysia, however, is trying hard to limit and to reduce its usage of the Singapore port, thus the statistics show a decline of Malaysian exports to Singapore, from 20% in 1985 to 15% in 2006. Cambodia and Myanmar show a more spectacular decline between 1985 and 2006.

Table 7.11

Exports to Singapore Compared to Country's
Total Exports (%), 1985 and 2006

	1985	2006
Brunei	7.9	3.0
Cambodia	21.9	3.9
Indonesia	3.4	11.8
Laos	17.4	0.05
Malaysia	20.0	15.4
Myanmar	17.1	1.4
Philippines	5.4	7.3
Thailand	7.8	6.4
Vietnam	17.2	3.8

Source: IMF, *Direction of Trade Statistics Yearbook*,
2007.

Most big cities function both as a thru(through)-port and a distri-port. Examples are Kuala Lumpur's Port Klang in Malaysia, Jakarta's Tanjong Priok in Indonesia, Manila in the Philippines, Bangkok in Thailand, and Hong Kong and Shanghai in China, Tokyo and Osaka in Japan and Singapore in Asia. A thru-port is one where vessels make a port call to unload part of the cargo while on the way to the next thru-port or distri-port. Even though a thru-port undertakes the distribution of goods to the hinterland, the volume of cargo handled by a thru-port is generally smaller. On the other hand, a distri-port is the final destination of calling vessels, where the calling vessels unload all the cargo. A large portion of the cargo would then be distributed to other parts of the country or region using smaller vessels. Ports located in countries with large hinterland, for example Indonesia, China and India, usually handle large amount of national distribution, while much smaller countries, like Singapore, handle largely international distribution.

Economic efficiency normally results in the creation of a distribution hub within a country or a region. Diagram 7.1 depicts the scenario where there is no distribution centre playing the role of a middleman. In this scenario, manufacturers from London or Tokyo will have to ship their goods directly

Diagram 7.1
Shipment of Goods in the Absence of a Middleman

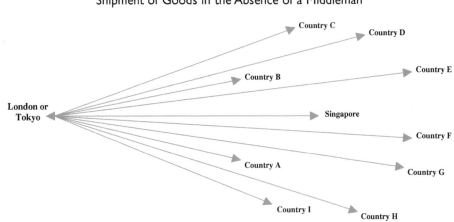

to customers in each country. Due to the smaller individual load to each country, manufacturers cannot reap economies of scale by utilising vessels of larger tonnage in the transportation of goods. In addition, the frequency of vessels making a port call at the intended country is limited by the total demand from the country. Shipment schedules for the manufacturers thus become infrequent and irregular. Similar argument could apply to shipment of goods from these countries to London or Tokyo. Only the directions are reverse.

Diagram 7.2 depicts a second scenario where Singapore serves as a distribution centre for the region. Manufacturers from London or Tokyo are able to ship their goods to Singapore, and Singapore undertakes the distribution of the goods to the neighbouring countries. The first advantage is in economies of scale where the manufacturers are able to deploy vessels of bigger tonnage to ship their consolidated goods to the region. Secondly, manufacturers are able to ship goods to the region more frequently and regularly as a result of a larger aggregate order. Thirdly, total distance travelled will also be significantly reduced in the second scenario. Similarly, manufacturers from the cluster of countries would find it economically more efficient to consolidate their goods in Singapore before shipping them to London or Tokyo. The presence of a middleman can therefore be said to facilitate the flow of trade.

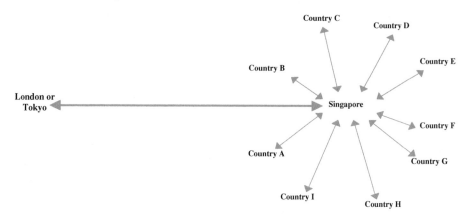

Diagram 7.2
Shipment of Goods in the Presence of a Middleman

Singapore's role as the distri-port in the region has helped her neigh-bouring countries to link up with the rest of the world more efficiently. Singapore has, over the years, developed strong trade and investment link-ages with her neighbouring countries, functioning as one of the important growth centres of the region. Singapore's strategic location has not only helped in the development of Southeast Asia, but has also enabled Singapore to prosper and stay relevant. This view is contrary to that of an investment analysis firm Independent Strategy. Independent Strategy has mentioned in a report saying that "Singapore is blessed with brilliant governance and cursed with doing all the right things in the wrong place. There is a price of being located near some of Asia poorest-reforming states and its most politically-volatile ones." The report further says that "the island would be better served (and so would investors) if it were somewhere south of Hawaii. Instead, it is moored in a sea of troubled nations and that will affect investment and economic policy.... The biggest challenge of all is location. Singapore is in the wrong place." The view of Independent Strategy is neg-ative. It has ignored the mutual benefits that could arise from the positive cumulative causation through trade and factor flow. Besides, Singapore has neither the inclination nor indeed the ability to sail out of Southeast Asia. She has to accept and should proudly accepts her destiny as a Southeast Asian nation, at the cross-roads between Europe and India in the West and China, Japan and Korea in the East. Singapore might take comfort from a stanza by a great American poet, Henry Wadsworth Longfellow, running as follows:

"Footprints, that perhaps another,
Sailing o'er life's solemn main,
A forlorn and shipwrecked brother,
Seeing, shall take heart again."

The emphasis is for Singapore to be of service and help to her sister nations in Southeast Asia, if she does not want to be a shipwrecked sailor herself. Singapore has to be able to perform a trading service, a useful trading service, otherwise other ports will compete for its role as an important trading centre in Southeast Asia and beyond. As Singapore does not have a national hinterland, her options to earn a living are much more limited; being an international trading centre becomes a natural and expected option.

Policies Towards Export Promotion

As noted in Chapter 6, the industrialising Southeast Asian countries began to adopt export-oriented industrial strategies beginning with Singapore and Malaysia in the mid 1960s, followed by the Philippines, and Thailand in the late 1960s and by Indonesia in the early 1980s. And since then, Vietnam, Cambodia, Laos and Myanmar have followed this well-trodden path: trade-oriented and outward-looking industrialisation. A number of factors were responsible for the shift in policy reorientation in Southeast Asia. Firstly, the record of import-substitution was generally poor: direct resource cost ratios tend to be high; the establishments of these industries to serve the narrow domestic markets is predicated on high protection; discrimination in favour of import-substitution and against export hinders the development of manufactured exports; net foreign exchange savings from import-substitution quickly decline due to the increased need for foreign materials, machinery, and technological know-how; and consequently, economic growth is constrained by limitations in the availability of foreign exchange.

Secondly, the spectacular success of the Asian NIEs (Newly Industrialising Economies which are Hong Kong, Singapore, South Korea and Taiwan) in achieving rapid economic growth by adopting export-oriented industrialisation strategies amidst a relatively free international trading environment (until the late 1970s) provided important examples to the Southeast Asian countries. Moreover, rising real wages led to a shift in comparative advantage away from the traditional labour-intensive exports and into more skilled and technology-intensive activities in the NIEs. The Southeast Asian countries are, therefore, in a position to break into the export markets being vacated by the NIEs.

Moreover, it is not unreasonable to expect that the NIEs may develop as export markets for low technology, unskilled labour-intensive products from the Southeast Asian countries, in the same way a similar relationship emerged between Japan and the present NIEs in the 1970s. The relationship between the Northeast Asian NIEs on the one hand, and the rest of Southeast Asia on the other, including Indonesia, the Philippines, Vietnam, Thailand and Myanmar on the other, has developed into one of complementality, given the differences in their factor endowments. The spectacular economic ascendancy of China has provided an added impetus for the 10 ASEAN nations to cooperate more closely to meet the challenges of global competition for markets and for FDI flows.

To promote export-oriented industrialisation, Singapore relied on a wide range of tax incentives, including tax concessions and export incentives. Consistent with Singapore's outward-looking policy, mild tariffs introduced in the import-substitution phase of the early 1960s were also either reduced or removed. Furthermore, export industries in Singapore have access to a number of special benefits such as a concessionary corporate tax rate on profits from exports. The concessional rate was 4% as against the normal corporate tax rate of 40% for the years 1986 and before. Corporate tax rate has been steadily declining since 1987. The corporate tax rate for the Year of Assessment 2008 is 18%.

In Malaysia, the Philippines and Thailand, however, export orientation did not imply an abandonment of import-substitution. Thus, the policy reorientation in the 1970s was not accompanied by a withdrawal of government support for industries oriented toward the domestic market, although emphasis was placed on export orientation. The various national industrial promotion agencies such as the Malaysian Industrial Development Authority (MIDA) in Malaysia and the Boards of Industry (BOI) in the Philippines and Thailand have deliberately channelled sizeable proportions of the new investments into export-oriented manufacturing activities.

While these countries also extended incentives to promote exports ranging from exemption from corporate income tax to exemption from import duties and business taxes on imported machinery and equipment, raw materials and other intermediate products, protection continues to be extended to import-substituting industries. For example, while Thailand implemented a major revision of its tariff structure in 1974, with significant reductions in tariff rates on 'necessary' consumer goods, raw materials, intermediate products, machinery and mechanical appliances, changes were made in the business tax structure — mainly reductions for domestically produced goods — which resulted in additional protection. These changes reflect the commitment of the Thai Government to protect import-substituting industries even in the period of an intensive export drive.

In Myanmar an 'export task force' was formed in early 1979 to promote exports by co-ordinating, streamlining and supervising export activities. Exports are seen to be necessary by the Government to increase its foreign exchange reserves.

How effective have been the export-promotion policies in the industrialising countries of Southeast Asia? Several empirical studies in the ASEAN context question the effectiveness of government policies designed to promote manufactured exports (Ariff and Hill, 1985: 53). There is empirical evidence showing that various incentives given to exporters of manufactures have only partially compensated for the anti-export bias in the tariff structure in Malaysia, the Philippines, and Thailand. Several manufactured exports, in fact, receive negative effective protection in spite of implicit subsidies in the form of export incentives. The reason is that protected domestic inputs are used, and import duties and tax refunds are frequently insufficient to compensate for the effects of input protection. Policies adopted, therefore, conflict with the policy prescriptions suggested in an earlier chapter for an export-oriented industrialisation strategy, namely, equal incentives should be given to export- and to import-substitution in the manufacturing sector. Such a policy not only ensures resource allocation according to comparative advantage but also contributes to efficient exportation and import-substitution through specialisation in particular products and in their parts, components, and accessories. In the Southeast Asian countries, market penetration has been particularly favourable for two main types of products: labour-intensive manufactures, and several resource-based products. Moreover, increased competitiveness emerged as the essential explanatory factor for the countries' good export performance. The increased competitiveness reflects that the comparative advantage of the Southeast Asian countries, except Singapore, is in labour-intensive and resource-based products. Comparative advantages, however, do not remain static for all times. They change. There are already strong indications too that Malaysia is losing its comparative advantage in labour-intensive exports.

Obstacles to Diversified Export Growth

Export-oriented industrialisation has resulted in closer integration of the Southeast Asian economies with the global economy and also with themselves. Their economies have performed fairly impressively. It may be asked, however, whether the slow growth in the developed economies and the spate of protectionism will limit imports from the LDCs, in particular, the industrialising Southeast Asian countries. Arthur Lewis (1980) has posed the question in a wider context:

"For the past hundred years the rate of growth of output in the developing world has depended on the rate of growth of output in the developed world .... (the) world has just gone through two decades of unprecedented growth, with world trade growing twice as fast as ever before, at about 8 percent per annum in real terms... During these prosperous decades, the less developed countries (LDCs) have demonstrated their capacity to increase their total output at 6 percent per annum... But what is to happen if the more developed countries (MDCs) return to their former growth rates, and raise their trade at only 4 percent per annum: is it inevitable that the growth of the LDCs will also fall significantly below their target?"

Lewis' own prescription is that assuming industrial production in MDCs grows more slowly than before 1973, and that the imports of these countries grow only at 4% per annum, over the next two decades, LDCs can continue to maintain a high growth rate by following the customs union route, with LDCs giving preferential treatment to intra-LDCs' trade. The ASEAN Free Trade Area could be one of the routes to take, in our opinion.

In the context of an uncertain international environment, the future growth of export-oriented industries in Southeast Asia will depend, to a large extent, on the role that OECD countries play in terms of a market for the region's export of manufactures. In turn, the extent to which OECD markets will remain open depends on the extent of structural change and adjustment that occurs in the OECD countries (Bradford, 1982). From the point of view of an international division of labour in accordance with shifting comparative advantage, it is clear that the traditionally labour-intensive industries get relocated, and accordingly, a change in the pattern of trade must result. ASEAN has rightly chosen the route of either having FTAs with other countries as a group or with them individually, as Singapore has done with the USA and China.

Given the slow structural adjustment that is occurring within the OECD countries, it may also be asked whether the Southeast Asian industrialising countries can emulate the Japan-NIE model of development. A simulation exercise concludes that the generalisation of the Japan-NIE model of export-led development across all developing countries would result in untenable market penetration into industrial countries (Cline, 1982), and that it would be inadvisable for authorities in LDCs to depend their long-term plans upon the same kind of export results that have been obtained by the five East Asian economies. To the extent that the five East Asian economies have followed open trade policies and realistic exchange rates, other LDCs should follow suit (on grounds of general efficiency), but should not expect free-market policies to yield the same results that were achieved by the five East Asian economies, which took advantage of the outward-looking strategy before the OECD markets became crowded by competition from other developing countries such as China and India, and did so when the world economy was in a phase of prolonged buoyancy.

For a number of reasons, it may be asserted that the prospects for continued rapid export growth are not particularly promising (Ariff and Hill, 1985: 62–65). One reason is that the high export growth rates of the past were from a very low base. Continued growth rates of the same magnitude will imply a much larger absolute increase, something that will be more difficult to achieve. Another reason is that the rapid export growth was, in the early stages, facilitated by preferential market access arrangements. However, such arrangements, most notably the implementation of the Generalised System of Preferences (GSP) by some developed countries had only once-and-for-all effects on the growth of Southeast Asian manufactured exports. Moreover, the GSP stimulus appears to have dwindled, as a consequence of the low quota ceilings and the stringent rules governing GSP exports. Finally, rapidly rising real wages, especially in Singapore and Malaysia, will erode their comparative advantage in the labour-intensive manufactured exports. Continued export orientation based on international competitiveness requires sustained productivity growth and industrial restructuring. However, the rapid growth of the East Asian economies themselves will also provide new markets for other economies in the region through the circular cumulative causation process. This is a case of circular causation to the benefit of all. The very rapid expansion of China will provide a further impetus through a rapidly expanding market for the Southeast Asian exports. With China joining the World Trade Organisation (WTO) in 2001, the probability of this happening is much greater in scope. Nearly all countries in Southeast Asia have penetrated this important enlarged market. The rise of India too would provide another locomotive for Southeast Asian growth.

Protectionism

With the slowdown in economic growth over the 1980s, the growth of international trade has retarded. World exports increased at an annual growth rate of 15.3% per annum during 1960–1980 as against the low 6.0% during 1980–1990. Annual growth rate of world exports climbed to a slightly higher 6.9% during 1990–2006. Coming together with the slowdown in international trade in the 1980s, is the rising tide of protectionism. From the point of view of the advanced countries, the costs of adjustment to a growing volume of imports are difficult to shoulder when exports are also slowing down. Workers displaced in import-competing sectors could not be readily absorbed in the export industries. Moreover, the rate at which resources can be transferred is limited by various rigidities — inertia in switching jobs, problems of retraining, and limits to the creation and expansion of business units — as well as by the changes in macro-economic management causing a move away from policies of full employment due to the fear of inflation or an external deficit. Once such a move takes root, Government will give more attention to the demands for protection, either on grounds of market disruption and higher unemployment prospects or because the external deficit would be aggravated by continued imports.

So far, new pressures of this kind have, with important exceptions, largely been held at bay. Multilateral trade negotiations under the auspices of the General Agreement on Tariffs and Trade (GATT), and after 1994, the World Trade Organisation (WTO), have generally helped improved market access. However, in a joint study by the IMF and the World Bank (IMF and World Bank, 2001), it was highlighted that although tariff and non-tariff measures have declined substantially over the past thirty years, they remain significant in both industrial and developing countries. In particular, industrial countries, through an array of very high tariff, tariff peaks and escalation, and restrictive tariff quotas, have maintained high protection in agriculture. Average tariff in agricultural is about nine times higher than in manufacturing. Moreover, agricultural subsidies in industrial countries also undermine developing countries' agricultural sectors and exports by depressing world prices. And while industrial countries' border protection in manufacturing is generally low, it remains high on labour-intensive products where developing countries have comparative advantage. For example, applied tariffs on textiles and clothing are three times the average in manufacturing, and the bulk of restrictive quotas under the Multifiber Arrangement (MFA) will not be phased out until 2005. In addition, the adoption of tariff escalation by industrial countries where tariffs increase with the level of processing, also inhibit the developing countries from diversifying their exports towards higher value-added products.

Table 7.12 compares the incidence of applied tariffs across different product groups. In a report by the World Bank and IMF (2001), developing countries in general face higher tariffs (3.4%) than industrial countries (2.0%) on manufactured goods. And while the average tariff faced by developing countries on agricultural goods is lower than industrial countries, the weighted average tariff is still very high (21.9%).

Table 7.13 gives the frequency of non-tariff barriers (NTBs) faced by developing countries in developed countries. The frequency of NTBs is lowest for exports of copper and copper products, aluminium and aluminium products, furniture, precious stones, ores, diamond, wood and wood products. Both mines and forests are very valuable natural resources of

Table 7.12

Trade-Weighted Average Tariff Faced by Developing and Industrial Countries (%), 1997

	Industrial Countries (Importer)
Manufactures	
Industrial countries	2.0
Developing countries	3.4
Agricultural goods	
Industrial countries	32.0
Developing countries	21.9
All goods	
Industrial countries	4.2
Developing countries	4.6

Source: World Bank and IMF report, "*Market Access for Developing Countries' Exports*", 27 Apr. 2001.

Note: The report used 1997 applied tariff and trade weights, excluding intra-EU trade.

the developing countries in general and Southeast Asia in particular (e.g. Indonesia, Malaysia and the Philippines). Exhaustion of mineral deposits and environmental concerns arising from the depletion of forests act as natural restraints on the exports of mineral and forestry products. Moreover, industrial countries naturally like to obtain resource based (and preferably unprocessed) products at as low a price as possible to drive their industrial enterprises. All these considerations result in low or no barriers for the imports of such products into the industrial countries.

In sharp contrast to the low NTBs on mineral and forestry products, in the categories of fishery products, fruits and nuts, coffee, cereals, garments and motor vehicles, 30% or more of the export commodities are subject to NTBs in the industrial country markets. The prospects for Southeast Asia's labour-intensive exports thus are not very bright as a result of the NTBs imposed by the potential importers.

Trade preferences granted by developed countries to LDCs, extended on a non-reciprocal basis, go some way towards ameliorating the trade barriers

Table 7.13

Frequency of NTBs Faced by Developing Countries (in Developed Countries)

Agricultural and fishery products	48.24
Fish, crustaceans, molluscs and aquatic invertebrates	63.82
Edible fruit and nuts	53.95
Coffee and substitutes with coffee	32.25
Cereals	65.46
Other agricultural and fishery products	42.92
Minerals and fuels	6.72
Ores, slag and ash	1.74
Crude petroleum oil	22.73
Refined petroleum oil	31.03
Other fuel and oils	17.28
Other minerals and fuels	7.27
Manufactures	10.67
Wood and wood articles	17.33
Knitted or crocheted articles and accessories	30.46
Non-knitted or non-crocheted articles and accessories	30.89
Diamonds	9.09
Other precious stones	1.55
Iron and steel	12.95
Copper and copper products	0.75
Aluminium and aluminium products	0.64
Machinery and mechanical appliances	11.15
Electronic integrated circuits	15.50
Other electric, machinery and parts	14.99
Motor vehicles for transporting persons	40.91
Other motor vehicles and parts	10.83
Furniture, bedding and lamps	2.01
Other manufactured articles	12.35

Source: Bacchetta and Bora (2001).

that would otherwise present a more serious obstacle to the exports of LDCs, including the Southeast Asian countries. However, they are greatly circumscribed by product exclusion, and by limitations on the preferences granted through tariff quotas, ceilings and maximum country amounts. Most schemes have a restricted coverage of agricultural products and either exclude or severely limit the preference granted to 'sensitive' products, those in which import penetration tends to be strong and in which therefore beneficiary countries have a substantial interest. All agreements also provide for unilateral termination or alteration by the implementing country without compensation for the affected countries.

Since the formation of ASEAN Free Trade Area (AFTA) in 1992, tariff levels within ASEAN have been declining. By the beginning of 2002, only 3.8% of products in the CEPT Inclusion List of the first six signatories, or 1,683 items out of 44,060, have tariffs above 5%. The current average tariff on goods traded under the AFTA scheme is about 3.8%. In order to bring their tariff policies in line with their AFTA and WTO obligations, various ASEAN countries have implemented tariff reduction policies from around mid 1990s.

While the levels of extra-ASEAN tariff and non-tariff barriers in Southeast Asia are falling, such barriers still exhibit significant variation among the different economies. Laos' weighted average tariff for manufactured goods, ores and metal was 14% in 2005, while Thailand's average tariff was lower at 4.9%.[1] Indonesia and the Philippines have seen significant tariff reduction over the period 1990–2005. Indonesia's weighted average tariff fell from 15.1% in 1990 to 6% in 2005; the Philippines' average tariff sharply declined from 14.8% to 3.1% in 2005. In addition, Indonesia also has a 10 to 40% Sales Tax on "luxury items". Import duties in Malaysia range from 0–300%, with the trade-weighted average tariff being 4.4% in 2005. In Malaysia, particularly high level of protection is granted to the national automobile industry through import tariffs of up to 300%. Apart from such import restrictions, non-automatic import licensing for import-sensitive industries and export subsidies still add to the cost of trade. Singapore pursues a free trade policy. Other than a 7% Goods & Services Tax effective for the sale of goods and services, very few goods are dutiable in transaction.

Southeast Asia is not much different from the rest of the world when it comes to the imposition of non-tariff barriers (NTBs). According to APEC (1995), "NTBs are used frequently in some sectors, for example, agriculture,

---

[1]Information in this section is obtained from The Heritage Foundation website, *Index of Economic Freedom*, (http://www.heritage.org).

labour intensive manufactures, steel and automobiles". The highest incidences of NTBs are found in agriculture followed by manufacturing and
then mining. Overall, NTBs are found almost across all the sectors (based on
the 2-digit International Standard of Industrial Classification (ISIC)) for the
Philippines and Thailand. In the Philippines, coal mining, petroleum, paper
products, metal products and machinery sectors have frequency ratios in
excess of 50%. Thailand's frequency ratio of NTBs is below 40%. Indonesia,
Malaysia and Singapore have very minimal NTBs imposed on their economies. However, Malaysia protects her forestry and logging sector with an
NTB frequency ratio of almost 100%. The same report (APEC, 1995,
section 5) also reveals that ASEAN members of the APEC forum imposed
"an extensive array of impediments to trade and investment in services".
Using a frequency-type of measure for NTBs affecting services, almost all
the relevant service sectors in Southeast Asia have frequency scores of close
to or exactly 100 (denoting no commitments to open up market access nor
to relax national treatment). With strong growth in the services sector, it is
likely that the Southeast Asian countries would impose impediments and
expectedly many service sectors are the subject of very detailed regulations,
most of which act to impede international service provision.

New International Economic Order

While the economic performance of the developing countries were fairly
good on an aggregate level in the 1960s and the early 1970s (at least in
comparison to the experience of the developed countries at a similar stage),
dissatisfaction was widespread and growing in the developing countries.
A number of factors contributed to this dissatisfaction: (i) the perception
that the gap between the developing and developed economies would continue to grow and widen; (ii) some of the poorest among the developing
countries had been faring particularly poorly, although the aggregate LDC
performance had been good; and, most importantly, (iii) the developing
countries had little impact on the international economic environment in
which they operated. UNCTAD and other international organisations thus
had provided forums for expressing this dissatisfaction and for promoting
proposals for improving the lot of the developing countries. Until the early
1970s, however, such discussions were mostly fragmented and rhetorical.

Then came the sudden and unexpected rise in some developing nations' economic power in the wake of the Organisation of Petroleum Exporting Countries' (OPEC) 1973 oil embargo and subsequent pricing policies. The ability of the oil-producing countries of OPEC in increasing petroleum prices served as a catalyst to pull together the LDCs in support of a call for a New International Economic Order (NIEO) in which the interests of the LDCs would be better represented. This call integrated many of the proposals that had been discussed previously at UNCTAD and elsewhere. The proposals for an NIEO, as adopted at the Sixth Special Session of the United Nations General assembly, in April 1974 included the following:

(a) An 'integrated' programme of price supports at levels higher than historic trends for commodities exported by developing countries.
(b) The indexation of prices of exports of developing countries to prices of these countries' imports from developed countries.
(c) The attainment of the target of 0.7% of gross national product (GNP) of developed countries for official development assistance.
(d) The linkage, in some form, of development aid to the creation of international reserves in terms of special drawing rights (SDRs) on the International Monetary Fund (IMF).
(e) The target for shifting manufacturing capacity from the developed to developing countries to the extent of 25% of world industrial output by the year 2000.
(f) Mechanisms for the transfer of technology to developing countries and codes of conduct for multinational enterprises.

A major proposal was made pertaining to international commodity agreements. This proposal was formalised in the resolution in favour of an integrated commodity programme at UNCTAD IV, in Nairobi in 1976. The resolution places primary and immediate emphasis on two objectives for ten core commodity markets (including sugar, rubber and tin, which are important for Southeast Asia): (i) stabilisation and (ii) improvement in the real income developing countries received from commodity exports. Subsequent international meetings reaffirmed the need for the development of international commodity agreements under the auspices of UNCTAD.

The New Order attracted diverse reactions: some saw the New Order as giving exemptions to the developing countries from established rules thereby providing them with some short-term benefits like more aid and trade concessions. Others identified it with long-term changes in the distribution of power and wealth across nations.

The establishment of the World Trade Organisation (WTO) in January 1995, after 9 years of Uruguay Round negotiations, had opened up a new chapter in the globalisation of world trade. Using the original General Agreement on Tariffs and Trade (GATT) as the WTO's principal rule-book for trade in goods, the Uruguay Round also created new rules for dealing with trade in services, various aspects of intellectual property, dispute settlement, and trade policy reviews. The main function of the *WTO is to ensure that trade flows as smoothly, predictably and freely as possible.* Apart from serving as a forum for trade negotiations, the WTO also administers WTO trade agreements, handles trade disputes, and monitors national trade policies. As at July 2008, total membership stands at 153 countries, with 30 other countries, including Laos participating as observers.

The global trading system advocated by the WTO is the multilateral trading system. Decisions and agreements are made by the entire membership, ratified in all member countries' parliaments, and apply to all members. Special concessions are made for developing countries, which include longer time periods for implementing agreements and commitments, and measures to increase trading opportunities for these countries.

Traditionally, Southeast Asian countries have been closely interwoven with the international economy. Increasing internationalisation and international inter-dependence may be regarded as a positive force for the future growth of Southeast Asia because it promotes further efficiency, specialisation and competition. However, there are some negative effects too: vulnerability of each nation to developments elsewhere increases; and domestic autonomy in policy-making is, at times, subordinated to international policy considerations. When the economic objectives of two or more nations clash, regional and global tension and conflict may result. The conflicts may arise, for instance, when a nation seeks to acquire a larger share of the gains from trade or foreign investment or when a country wishes to maintain domestic autonomy in policy-making when confronted with a destabilising external event. ASEAN nations in general have been well aware of the need to cooperate among themselves and within the framework of growing global integration. More discussion on trade and trade-related issues for Southeast Asia will be done in Chapter 8 under "Economic Regionalism".

In the last few years, less is talked about the New International Economic Order. In ASEAN, interest has been on ASEAN FTAs with themselves and with other non-ASEAN countries. Most ASEAN countries are major fossil oil importers and suffer under the deteriorating terms of trade with the oil exporters. But this setback is shared by other oil importers outside ASEAN and as the European Union, India, China, Japan and the United States which has become an important oil importer.

Key Points

1. Singapore followed by Malaysia and Thailand are the most export-oriented countries in Southeast Asia, and the extent of export orientation of the ASEAN-5 exhibited perfect ranking relationship with their per capita income.

2. The ASEAN-5 except the Philippines have all increased their share in world services trade over time, but some countries in Southeast Asia run deficits in the balance of trade in services. All countries in Southeast Asia have placed tourism as an important export with Thailand and Malaysia leading the way in terms of export value.

3. Heavy concentration in export markets and specialisation in export of primary products are reasoned to have led to export instability in the LDCs. However, export concentration has declined for every ASEAN country over time.

4. Relative importance of agriculture exports has declined while the importance of manufacture exports has increased in Southeast Asia. This shift in trading pattern has led to an increase in exports to the developing countries.

5. Intra-ASEAN trade is of continuing and increasing importance in ASEAN countries. At the same time, Singapore has maintained her importance as the regional distribution hub.

6. Singapore and Malaysia adopted export-oriented strategies in the mid 1960s, followed by the Philippines and Thailand in the late 1960s, and by Indonesia in the early 1980s, and the trend spread to the other new

ASEAN–4 of Vietnam, Cambodia, Laos and Myanmar. All ASEAN countries have relied on a wide range of tax incentives to promote export-oriented industrialisation.

7. Southeast Asian countries should emulate the NIEs in areas of open trade polices and realistic exchange rates. However, due to the increasingly crowded OECD market, LDCs should not expect free-market policies to yield the same results as achieved by the Asian NIEs in earlier decades.

8. The emergence of China and India provide other important markets to ASEAN which is trying to help itself with intra-ASEAN FTAs as well as with non-ASEAN countries.

Suggested Discussion Topics

7.1 Discuss and evaluate the relationship between GDP per capita on the one hand, and per capita exports and exports to GDP ratio on the other among Southeast Asian countries. How to achieve highexport orientation? What are the limits in this policy and strategy?

7.2 Discuss the export concentration of Southeast Asian countries. Does it mean that export concentration ensures economic instability and low per capita income? Or, does it mean that countries should concentrate in the exports in which they have the competitive advantage? Discuss.

7.3 Discuss the role of Singapore as a trading centre for Southeast Asia? What other option can Singapore have, other than being a trading and service centre, without a national hinterland?

References

AHMAD, Jaleel and Somchai HARNHIRUN, 1995, "Unit roots and cointegration in estimating causality between exports and economic growth: Empirical evidence from the Asean countries", *Economics Letters*, 49(3), 329–334.

APEC, 1995, *Survey of Impediments to Trade and Investment in the APEC Region*, PECC.

ARIFF, Mohammed and Hal HILL, 1985, *Export-Oriented Industrialisation: The ASEAN Experience*, Sydney: Allen and Unwin.

BACCHETTA, Marc and Bijit BORA, 2001, *Post-Uruguay Round Market Access Barriers for Industrial Products*, UNCTAD Policy Issues in International Trade and Commodities, Study Series No. 12 (New York and Geneva: United Nations), UNCTAD/ITCD/TAB/13.

BALASSA, Bela, 1978, "Exports and economic growth: Further evidence", *Journal of Development Economics*, 5(2) 181–189.

BRADFORD, Colin I., 1982, "Newly industrialising countries in an interdependent world", *The World Economy*, 5(2), 171–185.

CLINE, William R., 1982, "Can the East Asian model of development be generalised?", *World Development*, 10(2), 81–90.

International Monetary Fund, 2001, *Market Access for Developing Countries' Exports* (Washington). Available via the Internet: www.imf.org/external/np/madc/eng/042701.htm.

KNUDSEN, Odin and Andrew PARNES, 1975, *Trade Instability and Economic Development*, Lexington: Lexington Books, D.C. Heath and Co.

LEWIS, Arthur W., 1980, "The slowing down of the engine of growth", *American Economic Review,* 70(4), 555–564.

LIM, Chong Yah, 1967, *Economic Development in Modern Malaya*, Kuala Lumpur: Oxford University Press.

LIM, Chong Yah, 1996, "Trinity growth theory: The ascendency of Asia and the decline of the west", *Accounting and Business Review*, 3(2), 175–199.

LLOYD, P. J., 1994, "Intra-regional trade in the Asian and Pacific region", *Asian Development Review*, 12(2), 113–143.

MICHAELY, Michael, 1977, "Exports and growth: An empirical investigation", *Journal of Development Economics*, 4(1), 49–53.

PORTER, Michael E., 1990, *The Competitive Advantages of Nations*, UK: The Macmillan Press Ltd.

Further Readings

CAIRNCROSS, Alec *et al.*, 1982, *Protectionism: Threat to International Order*, London: The Commonwealth Secretariat.

RAZEEN Sally and Rahul SEN, 2005, "Whither trade policies in Southeast Asia? The wider Asian, and global context". *Asean Economic Bulletin*, 22(1), 92–115.

SPENCE, MICHAEL, (Ch.), 2008, *The Growth Report: Strategies for Sustained Growth and Inclusive Development* by Commission on Growth and Development, Washington, D.C.: The World Bank.

TOH, Thian Ser, 1996, "Regionalism, sub-regionalism and regionalisation", in LIM, Chong Yah, (ed.), *Economic Policy Management in Singapore*, Singapore: Addison-Wesley Publishing Company, 419–444.

WONG, John, 1990, *ASEAN Economies: Will It Be the Fastest Growing Region of Asia in the 1990s?*, Kuala Lumpur: Malaysian Institute of Economic Research.

Chapter 8

Economic Regionalism

The vision is of ASEAN as a concert of Southeast Asian nations, outward looking, living in peace, stability and prosperity, bonded together in partnership in dynamic development and in a community of caring societies.

ASEAN VISION 2020

Objectives

✓ Describe the various levels of regional economic co-operation.

✓ Discuss the motivations, benefits and costs of economic co-operation.

✓ Describe and assess the success of various ASEAN economic co-operation projects.

✓ Explore the nature and extent of intra-ASEAN trade.

✓ Assess the success of various growth triangles launched within ASEAN.

✓ Discuss Asia Pacific organisations and ASEAN's participation in PECC and APEC.

✓ Present the emergence of Asian regionalism.

Introduction

With the world becoming more and more globalised, individual countries have to liberalise their markets in order to stay internationally competitive. But some countries fear that a complete liberalisation could seriously jeopardise the survival of their own industries. The formation of regional trading blocs, despite its shortcomings, provides some respite to countries that are not ready for the powerful 'invisible hand' of global market forces to have full rein. They are prepared to have market-friendly systems but not market-only systems.

ASEAN's formation in 1967 had its priority in the prevention of the infiltration of Communists in the region. With the subsequent global containment of the spread of Communism, ASEAN's focus shifted to cooperation in the arenas of culture, economics, tourism, environment and science and technology, just to name a few.

The promotion of economic development through co-operation is one of the main objectives of ASEAN. However, most of the projects undertaken under the various ASEAN industrial schemes were unsuccessful, if not outright unworkable. ASEAN's first experiment with trade liberalisation through the implementation of Preferential Trading Agreement (PTA) in the 1970s did not succeed in boosting intra-ASEAN trade. Two reasons for the low intra-ASEAN trade were mentioned (Yeung, Perdikis and Kerr, 1999). First, reduction in tariffs was not broad based. Second, items that enjoyed significant tariff reductions were not heavily traded. Given the low intra-ASEAN trade, the potential benefits brought about by the formation of ASEAN Free Trade Area were also questioned. Other forms of economic co-operation include the establishment of growth triangles among regions of different countries and ASEAN PTAs with other regional countries like China, Japan and Korea.

Levels of Economic Co-operation

A preferential trading arrangement exists when a group of countries reduces or eliminates trade barriers such as tariffs that were previously imposed on the member countries. There are four levels of economic co-operation, ranging from the least restrictive Free Trade Area to

Economic Union, where there is complete harmonisation of fiscal, monetary and socio-economic policies. In between, there are Customs Union and Common Market. As the member countries of these economic groupings are usually located within a geographical region, they are also often called 'regional arrangements'. In a Free Trade Area (FTA), tariffs among member countries are abolished. However, member countries are free to erect their own trade barriers for non-member countries. Examples of FTAs include the North American Free Trade Agreement (NAFTA) consisting of USA, Canada and Mexico, European Free Trade Association (EFTA) comprising Iceland, Liechtenstein, Norway and Switzerland, and the ASEAN Free Trade Area (AFTA). A common misconception of FTA is that as each member country sets its own tariff structure, there is a possibility of imports from non-member countries to enter through the lowest tariff country and then transport to the other parts of the FTA, thus avoiding countries with higher tariffs. This fallacious concept has even resulted in objections to formation of FTA by some member countries. One must however be mindful of the fact that preferential tariff rates among member countries within a FTA are only applicable to products that have a certain minimum percentage of local content. In the case of AFTA, the required minimum ASEAN content is 40%.

Customs Unions are similar to FTAs; tariffs among member countries are eliminated. On top of that, member countries adopt a common external tariff structure. A Common Market not only encompasses all the characteristics of a Customs Union, it also allows free movement of labour and capital between countries, resulting in an integration of both the factor and product markets. The highest level of economic co-operation is the Economic Union. In an Economic Union, there are no restrictions on the flow of goods, services, labour and capital. Further, economic activities and policies relating to currency, interest rates and taxation are harmonised. The best-known example is the European Union.

However, not all types of economic co-operation are discriminatory in nature. Some economic groupings practice outward looking regionalism. The objective of these groupings is to encourage the exchange of products and factors not only among member nations but also with non-member nations. An example would be the Asia-Pacific Economic Cooperation (APEC), which was formed in 1989, based on the philosophy of the antecedent Pacific Economic Cooperation Council (PECC), which the author had the privilege of helping to form. APEC member countries work to sustain economic growth through a commitment to open trade and investment by progressively reducing tariffs and other barriers to trade, APEC member economies have become more efficient and exports have expanded dramatically.

Motivations, Effects and Costs

There are many reasons why countries within a region co-operate economically. The main motivator is to achieve greater welfare through the promotion of less restrictive if not free trade. This concept has its roots in the theory of comparative advantage. The benefits of free trade are best exhibited in small countries. Free trade allows countries with small domestic market to enlarge their market size, and in the process, achieve economies of scale. Another way to explain the formation of trade organisations is that industries in some countries are simply too inefficient and are unable to compete globally. Such a scenario often, though not necessarily, applies to infant industries. The usual argument is that these industries need time to build up their competencies and could eventually compete in the global markets. Thus the formation of regional trading blocs would provide these industries with limited competition, and at the same time, breathing space for them to grow.

There are two possible effects when countries form trade organisations, namely trade creation and trade diversion (Viner, 1950). Trade creation occurs when, after the eradication of tariffs within a region, more efficient producers from member countries outmatch domestic producers in terms of cost of production, and this is followed by an increase in the volume of trade between the countries. Conversely, trade diversion occurs when less competitive producers from member countries replace more efficient producers from non-member nations.

For that reason, trade creation is beneficial not only because consumers get to enjoy cheaper imports, scarce resources are also being put into more productive uses. In the case of trade diversion, the standard of living deteriorates, as regional consumers now have to pay a higher price for their goods. Regionalism becomes a wider form of protectionism.

The following guidelines help to determine whether a formation of trade organisation will be predominately trade creating or trade diverting (Robson, 1980: 19–20).

1. The larger is the trade organisation, the greater will be the scope for trade creation.
2. Trade creation occurs when post-formation 'average' tariff level is lower than pre-formation 'average' tariff level; trade diversion occurs when it is higher.
3. When member countries' economies are more competitive, trade creation is more likely. However, each member must also be the most efficient producer of goods that were protected and inefficiently produced by its partners.
4. When there is an overlap of competitive industries due to protection, trade creation is more likely, as there is a greater difference in the unit costs between the member countries.

Apart from the trade-creating and trade-diverting effects that arise from resource reallocations, welfare improvements may also arise through scale of economies, favourable terms of trade and enhanced factor productivity. To reach an efficient scale of output, a modern manufacturing plant may have to produce an amount larger than that can be absorbed by domestic demand. With a sufficiently large market, economies of scale can be achieved.

The possibility of a larger market also attracts foreign direct investment. Over time, there is the further possibility that new industries can become increasingly competitive in world markets and eventually be able to export manufactured goods to non-member countries. Improvement in terms of trade arises when there is an increase in the supply of exports, or a reduction in the demand by member countries for imports from non-member countries, or if the members' bargaining power in trade negotiations is strengthened. This argument, however, depends on the member countries being major suppliers in the world market or constitutes a large part of the world market for imports, so that they are able to exercise sufficient market or non-market power to influence terms of trade.

Regional co-operation is also beneficial in encouraging competition among the member states. Technical efficiency in existing industries is improved as marginal firms are forced to reduce costs, resources are reallocated from less efficient to more efficient firms, and monopolies previously established behind tariff walls will no longer be sheltered. Moreover, the stimulation of competition within member countries may yield not only a better utilisation of given resources, but may also raise the rate of growth of the usage of productive resources. The latter may result from stronger incentives to adopt new techniques of production, to replace obsolete machinery more readily, and to innovate more rapidly with higher investment.

ASEAN Co-operation

A major purpose of economic co-operation within a region is to facilitate division of labour across the member countries so that gains from trade can be achieved. Thus, the successfulness of ASEAN economic co-operation will be reflected in its intra-ASEAN trade figures. In 2006, intra-ASEAN trade comprised 25.1% of total ASEAN trade. This is low when compared to trade within the European Union. In 2006, 71% of European Union's trade were conducted among member countries. Moreover, the bulk of intra-ASEAN trade is between Singapore and Malaysia.

ASEAN Preferential Trading Arrangement (PTA)

PTA was started in 1977. Tariff preferences were extended on a product-by-product basis through voluntary offers and negotiations. However, this process was slow and cumbersome. In 1980, the across-the-board approach was introduced. Under the agreement, preferences would be given to items below a certain import-value ceiling. The margin of preferences (MOP) was also raised from 10% to a minimum of 20–25% in 1981, and later on to 40% or more. By May 1984, the total number of items granted tariff preferences amounted to over 18,000 (Chng, 1985). However, there was a flaw in the across-the-board approach. Its potential was effectively negated by the extensive national exclusion lists. An examination of the trade flows for 1981 covered by some 9,000 preferences in 1982 showed that they accounted for only about 2% of intra-ASEAN trade (Chng, 1985: 33).

Various factors stood in the way of greater and more effective trade liberalisation in Southeast Asia. One is that the industrial structures of the member countries are broadly similar, with member countries producing or planning to produce similar goods. In other words, the economic complement of the ASEAN countries is limited. This non-complementary nature is further reinforced by the policy of import-substitution pursued by some of the ASEAN countries during the 1960s and the 1970s. However, it should be pointed out that one positive effect of the similarity in the economic structure of ASEAN is that the countries involved have common interests in entering into joint approaches to international economic problems. Varying perceptions of the gains from regional co-operation also hamper trade liberalisation within ASEAN. The problem is compounded by differences in the tariff levels among member countries. From the point of view of a high tariff country, a given percentage reduction in its tariff may be regarded as a greater concession than a similar reduction in a low tariff country. As all preferences granted under the PTA are multi-lateralised on a 'most favoured nation' basis to all member countries, high tariff countries are reluctant to reduce tariffs due to perceived inadequate reciprocity from low-tariff countries. In practice, actual negotiations also encounter serious difficulties as political problems take precedence, with countries guarding against a sacrifice of their sovereignty.

Differences in the perception of gains from regional co-operation among the ASEAN members also arise because primary commodities comprise a major proportion of total exports of the ASEAN countries (except Singapore). Given that these countries have a strong comparative advantage in certain primary products, a member country can sell to other members only goods that it could readily export to outside countries as well. At the same time, the location of manufacturing industry and ancillary activities may become localised within one member country, and 'polarisation' results. A less industrialised member country may also argue that in buying from a more industrialised partner, instead of importing from outside, it is losing revenue equal to the duty on outside manufactures.

In 1995, the ASEAN Free Trade Area (AFTA) Council decided to phase in all PTA products into the CEPT scheme. AFTA and CEPT scheme will be discussed in the latter section of this chapter.

ASEAN Industrial Projects (AIP) Scheme

The AIP concept was initially proposed as early as 1973 in a UN study (United Nations, 1974), and officially adopted in 1976. Each of the five ASEAN members was allocated a first-line industrial project, with several other second-line industrial projects also being identified. The first-line industrial projects include the ASEAN Urea Projects in Indonesia and Malaysia, the ASEAN Rock Salt-Soda Ash Project in Thailand, the ASEAN Phosphate Fertiliser Project in the Philippines and the ASEAN Diesel Engine Project in Singapore. In each case, the host country would take up 60% of the equity, with the rest shared equally among the then four countries. The AIPs would enjoy ASEAN-wide marketing preferences, which could include guaranteed pre-agreed purchases.

Of the five projects, only the Urea Projects of Indonesia and Malaysia took off. The other projects were unsuccessful due a multitude of difficult technical and economic issues and problems in the implementation of an AIP. The basic problem seems to be the reluctance of national Governments to grant others the exclusive rights of production in specific areas even if these are part of an exchange arrangement. All ASEAN Governments have ambitious industrial plans; and for many ASEAN Governments, the receipt from a specific AIP often seems unequal to the apparent sacrifice of industrial plans in various areas. Hence, each Government attempted to restrict as much as possible the scope of AIPs hosted by the other countries so as to give themselves the greater freedom for future courses of action, even to the point of rendering such projects non-viable. Thus, when AIPs were agreed upon and implemented, non-host member countries often adopt the narrowest interpretation of their commitment to these projects. For example, Indonesia found that its domestic diesel-engine plants would probably be adversely affected by the proposed Singapore's ASEAN plant. It changed it mind by requesting that Singapore should limit the proposed ASEAN diesel-engine production to engines of above 500 horsepower (Lim, 1981: 110–115). Singapore responded that this would make its ASEAN diesel-engine plant not viable, as most of the diesel engines used in ASEAN were below 500 horsepower. A great deal of discussion thus centred on resolving problems of this nature. However, while the issue over the engine horsepower waited to be resolved, Indonesia, the Philippines and Thailand continued to develop their diesel-engine industries, thus sealing the fate of Singapore's ASEAN diesel-engine plant. Singapore eventually opted out of full equity participation in the other AIPs, but in the interest of ASEAN solidarity, agreed to participate in the other AIPs by a token contribution of 1% of the cost of the projects. This participation would enable ASEAN to approach Japan as a group for soft loans.

A similar problem also plagued the ASEAN Phosphate Fertiliser Project in the Philippines. Under the AIP plan, the ASEAN plant in the Philippines was to produce 105,000 metric tons of superphosphate in full production. However, the proposed project was undermined by Indonesia's plan to expand its own superphosphate production. It was reported that the petroleum plant in East Java and the fertiliser plant in Palembang were geared towards the production of superphosphate to the tune of about 320,000 metric tons each. Another difficulty encountered by the Philippines' superphosphate plant was the sharp decline of the price of superphosphate. At the time when the Philippines put forward the proposal in 1974, the price of superphosphate was about U$308 per metric ton. The price tumbled to only US$96 in 1978, casting further doubts on the viability of the project.

The progress of AIPs has also been adversely affected by differences in economic philosophy. A difficult issue concerns the nature and extent of market support to be given to AIPs. Singapore, in particular, due to its open economy and free market experience, holds the view that barriers to entry and other restrictions on competition tend to promote inefficiency. Accordingly, it remains unenthusiastic about any form of exclusive arrangements. ASEAN countries also differ in their view on the balance between protection and international competitiveness.

Another area of controversy centred on whether infrastructure costs should become a part of the cost of the projects. The problem of future pricing of the products too has engaged the attention of ASEAN negotiators. The price of the ASEAN products has also to be jointly agreed upon since the other partners are obliged to give market access besides giving guaranteed purchases. The immense intervention and intrusion in the free market mechanism have contributed to make the AIP scheme controversial and non-viable.

ASEAN Industrial Complementation (AIC) Scheme

The AIC scheme was launched in 1981 on the principles of resource pooling and market sharing. The first project under the AIC scheme is the production of the 'ASEAN car'. The rationale is to obtain greater economies of scale through dividing different production stages of vertically integrated industries among ASEAN countries. However, the scope for co-operation under the AIC scheme was limited as most ASEAN members have their own domestic automotive industries in collaboration with multinational corporations. The problem was further compounded by the incompatibility of production facilities in different ASEAN countries (Rao, 1996).

Due to its shortcomings, the AIC scheme was replaced by the Brand-to-Brand Complementation (BBC) scheme. There would be no specification problem since the scheme was implemented within the same brand. The scheme helped in providing incentives to some of the multinationals in the automotive industries to relocate their production facilities to lower cost ASEAN centres and take advantage of the reciprocal element of the scheme whereby components are exchanged between countries. The BBC scheme was relatively more successful except that the non-participation of Indonesia has reduced the potential gains from economies of scale. This scheme was later superseded by the ASEAN Industrial Cooperation (AICO) scheme.

ASEAN Industrial Joint Venture (AIJV) Scheme

Introduced in 1983, the AIJV scheme aimed to encourage intra-ASEAN investment among private investors. AIJV could be any scale with participation of at least two ASEAN members. Joint ventures with foreign partners are encouraged. The AIJV requires a minimum of two ASEAN countries equity participation contributing at least 51% to the total equity of the AIJV entity, and that each participating ASEAN partner must hold a minimum of 5%. The 51% total ASEAN equity requirement was subsequently relaxed to 40%. The main incentive for the AIJVs is reduced tariffs. Member countries in the schemes levy only a tariff of 10% of the normal rate on goods produced by AIJVs. However, the scheme did not have any major impact on intra-ASEAN trade and investment. Two probable reasons for the lack of progress are lack of awareness of the scheme, and the lengthy bureau-cratic application process. Besides, the scheme was not ASEAN-wide, thus it lacked the ASEAN-wide regional interests and push.

ASEAN Industrial Cooperation (AICO) Scheme

With the implementation of AICO scheme in 1996, the Brand-to-Brand Complementation scheme and AIJV scheme ceased to exist. The AICO scheme is based on the Common Effective Preferential Tariff (CEPT) Scheme for ASEAN Free Trade Area and is to promote resource sharing and to increase the competitive position of ASEAN's manufacturing indus-tries by means of cross-border production integration. The new scheme is less stringent compared to the AIJV scheme. Interested parties must first form an AICO Arrangement. Upon approval, companies will enjoy prefer-ential tariff rates of 0–5%. An AICO Arrangement consists of a minimum of two participating companies from two different ASEAN countries, and each company only needs a minimum 30% national equity. A total of 145 AICO applications have been approved within ASEAN, amounting to US$1,802 million in 2007. Most of the participating companies are from the automotive sector, with a handful from the electronics sector.

ASEAN Free Trade Area (AFTA)

AFTA was mooted at the 1992 Fourth ASEAN Summit in Bangkok. Initially the plan was to remove all tariffs currently existing within a time frame of 15 years (i.e. by the year 2008) from 1 January 1992 by means of the Common Effective Preferential Tariff (CEPT) scheme. However, this move to achieve the realisation of a free trade area in ASEAN was continu-ously moved forward.

In terms of trade in goods, the AFTA has been effectively realised. As of 1 January 2005, tariffs on 98.98% of the products in the CEPT Inclusion List (IL) of the ASEAN-6 have been reduced to the 0–5% tariff range. Products in the IL which continue to have CEPT tariffs of above 5% are those which have been transferred from the Temporary Exclusion List (TEL), Sensitive List (SL) and General Exception List (GEL) after 2003. For the CLMV, 86.91% of the products traded in the region have been moved into the IL, up from 80% in 2003/04. Tariffs on 81.35% of these items have been brought down to within the 0–5% band. As the CLMV acceded to ASEAN and the CEPT agreement at a later stage, they were given longer deadlines to phase down tariffs of products in their respective ILs to the 0–5% level: Vietnam in 2006; Lao PDR and Myanmar in 2008; and Cambodia in 2010. Overall, 92.99% of all products in the IL of the ten ASEAN member countries have tariffs between 0–5%.

The ASEAN-6 have also committed to eliminate tariffs on 60% of their products in the IL by the year 2003. Currently, 64.12% of products in the IL of the ASEAN-6 have zero tariffs. The average tariff for ASEAN-6 under the CEPT scheme is now down to 1.93% from 12.76% in 1993. The present target for full completion of AFTA is 2015.

The free trade area covers all manufactured and agricultural products, although the timetables for reducing tariffs and removing quantitative restrictions and other non-tariff barriers differ. There are four categories of products, each subject to different tariff barriers.

Inclusion List (IL) — Products in the Inclusion List are those that have undergone immediate liberalisation through reduction in CEPT tariff rates, removal of quantitative restrictions and other trade barriers. Import duties on products in the Inclusion Lists of Brunei, Indonesia, Malaysia, Philippines, Singapore and Thailand shall be eliminated not later than 1 January 2010. Import duties on products in the Inclusion Lists of Cambodia, Laos, Myanmar and Vietnam shall be eliminated not later than 1 January 2015, with flex-ibility however allowed for import duties on some sensitive products to be eliminated not later than 1 January 2018.

Temporary Exclusion List (TEL) — Products in the Temporary Exclusion List can be shielded from trade liberalisation only for a tempo-rary period of time. However, all these products would have to be trans-ferred to the Inclusion List and begin a process of tariff reduction so that tariffs would come down to 0–5%. Starting on 1 January 1996, annual instalments of products from TEL have been transferring to the Inclusion List.

Sensitive List (SL) — This contains unprocessed agricultural products, which are given a longer time frame before being integrated with the free trade area. The commitment to reduce tariffs to 0–5%, remove quantitative restrictions and other non-tariff barriers is extended up to the year 2010.

The new members of ASEAN have up to 2013 (Vietnam), 2015 (Laos and Myanmar) and 2017 (Cambodia) to meet this deadline.

General Exception List (GEL) — These products are permanently excluded from the free trade area for reasons of protection of national security, public morals, human, animal or plant life and health and articles of artistic, historic and archaeological value. The GEL represents about 1% of all tariff lines in ASEAN.

The move to set up a free trade area has been made easier within ASEAN partly because in recent decades, all the ASEAN economies have, in varying degrees and in varying stages, implemented an outward-oriented development strategy. For instance, Indonesia, which has the largest market in ASEAN and was the most closed, has undergone considerable trade liberalisation. The further lowering and eventual abolition of tariffs would make the progression so much easier. However, it was changes in the international trading arena that catalysed the dramatic move by the ASEAN countries to liberalise their economic and trading environment. Firstly, the formation of the Single European Market and subsequently the North American Free Trade Agreement (NAFTA) brought out concerns in ASEAN of growing trade protectionism against ASEAN exports to these regional economic blocs. Secondly, the disintegration of the Soviet Union and the subsequent dismantling of the communist regimes in Eastern Europe were expected to divert foreign direct investments from Western Europe and North America away from East Asia to these newly independent socialist states in the course of rebuilding these previously command economies towards free market policies. Thirdly, China's decision to designate selected coastal cities as Special Economic Zones, India's cautious but steady efforts to deregulate and liberalise her economy, as well as Vietnam's rapprochement with the United States gave special impetus in re-examining ASEAN's overall competitiveness and attractiveness in an era of global economic competition for the investors' capital.

ASEAN trading relations have generally been oriented more towards extra-regional rather than intra-regional trading. Intra-ASEAN trade rose by 13 times between 1990 and 2006 from US$27.6 billion to US$352.7 billion, with most of the intra-ASEAN trade taking place between Singapore and Malaysia. Although intra-ASEAN exports inched up from 20.1% of total exports in 1990 to 25.2% of total exports in 2006, it is still very low as compared with the experience within the European Union. For AFTA to be successful, greater economic co-operation and integration will be required.

Currently, a major feature of ASEAN economic interdependence is the relocation and rationalising of production activities along the commodity value chain from the more developed ASEAN countries to the less developed members. Akamatsu's and Kojima's (1970) 'flying geese' model of economic development appears to be unfolding in the larger context of East Asia starting from Japan to the NIEs and down to the ASEAN countries. The crux of the 'flying geese' model is that economies of countries on the receiving end of foreign direct investment, usually in the form of relocating manufacturing plants, would have a easier take off and an easier flight, as depicted by the V-formation of the migrating geese. Of greater interest would be why some countries like North Korea and Mongolia in Northeast Asia, the Philippines in Southeast Asia did not join the 'flying geese' formation. In other words, what are the endogenous policies developing countries should adopt in order to join the 'flying geese' club? Also, why some geese have been able to fly faster and others not so fast? Lastly, foreign investments flow out not just from Japan, but also from the US and Western Europe, and recently, also from the four Asian NIEs. Differences in the rates of growth in Southeast Asia will be dealt with in greater detail in Chapter 13.

A positive spin-off from AFTA could be a larger inflow of foreign direct investment into the region. According to Menon (1996), the main type of intra-ASEAN trade that is occurring is the type of intra-industry trade where multinational corporations (MNCs) pursue 'efficiency seeking' type of foreign direct investments (or factor-based FDI). This type of investment is driven by the premise that the factors of production found in ASEAN have attributes that are superior to that found in one home country alone. Free movement of goods would encourage regional division of labour where vertical integration of a production process is spanned across ASEAN according to the comparative advantages of each ASEAN country. Positive developments have been taking place in this aspect. Singapore and Malaysia thus have in place financial incentives to encourage MNCs to set-up operational headquarters for their ASEAN and Asia Pacific operations in Singapore and Kuala Lumpur respectively. Such strategic moves serve to take advantage of the phenomenon in the new international trading and production environment by plugging into MNCs' global value-added chain of production operations. Foreign investors could access the better transport and financial facilities available in the more developed countries, and at the same time minimise their production costs by setting up production facilities in the labour and land abundant countries. Moreover, the strong economic growth experienced by the ASEAN economies over the past two decades has fuelled demand for consumer goods and services in these countries. Investors would likely want to take advantage of this new vast market now laid open with tariffs being reduced.

However, whether ASEAN through AFTA would be able to attract tariff-jumping investments is still not clear (Athukorala and Menon, 1996). Partly, the ASEAN countries have undertaken various unilateral tariff reduction exercises that are not ASEAN-wide. Secondly, the more important concern would be the existence of non-tariff barriers at the borders (including investment policies, product and technical harmonisation, macroeconomic co-operation and consultation) that requires attention. Notwithstanding the attractiveness of a larger AFTA market, the likely pull for a larger inflow of FDI would be the flexibility open to investor in undertaking vertical specialisation (trade based on division of labour).

AFTA, however, is not immune to adjustment pangs. Concerns about Indonesia's ability to adjust because of the dominance of large protected state-owned monopolies and well-connected private enterprises in the economy would put a drag to the overall pace of trade liberalisation. The same concerns are also evident for the newer members of ASEAN, namely Vietnam, Myanmar, Laos, and Cambodia. These countries are still in the throes of learning what a free market environment is; the state owned enterprises in these countries would probably have to downsize, if not to corporatise and privatise, in order to survive in the presence of competing foreign and domestic privately owned enterprises.

ASEAN should be concerned about the perceived sense of unequal benefits that flow among the various members of the free trade area. It would also be detrimental to the future prospects of ASEAN economic growth, if ASEAN decides not to adopt open regionalism whereby membership is open to those outside the grouping. Once the necessary harmonising of policies and rules have been in place, greater intra-regional trade can be expected as a buffer against rising trade protectionism and ever-expanding markets in China and India. In addition, higher levels of income can be expected, as AFTA would boost the region's appeal to foreign investors who might otherwise relocate their funds to other parts of the world, including if not particularly to China and India as well.

Initiative for ASEAN Integration (IAI)

Amid the slow progress of ASEAN integration effect, the association was criticised by some quarters to be of all talk and little action. With a view to assisting the newer members in the process of economic development and regional integration, ASEAN has launched the Initiative for ASEAN Integration (IAI) in 2000 during the 4th ASEAN informal Summit, and formally endorsed the six-year IAI Work Plan (2002–2008) (with 48 projects) in 2002. The Plan focuses on four priority areas: infrastructure including energy; human resource development; information and communication technology; and capacity-building for regional economic integration. Currently, there are 203 projects in the IAI Work Plan, at various stages of implementation.

As part of the IAI, ASEAN has adopted the ASEAN Integration System of Preferences (AISP) scheme whereby preferential tariffs are offered to the newer members by the older members on voluntary and bilateral basis starting on 1 January 2002. At the sub-regional level, activities within the framework of Mekong Basin development mechanisms have been strengthened to assist the integration of the four CLMV Countries (Cambodia, Laos, Myanmar, and Vietnam). On bilateral basis, older Member Countries have extended several technical assistance programmes to CLMV, particularly in the area of human resource development. Singapore increased its scholarship grants from 30 to 60 places, and has undertaken training courses for IT trainers. Singapore has also established 4 training centres in the CLMV Countries. Thailand has organized technical assistance projects in the form of training projects, seminars, courses, and sending of experts to CLMV. Malaysia has announced a special human resources development package for CLMV countries under the Malaysian Technical Cooperation Programme (MTCP). Japan has also actively supported ASEAN efforts to bridge the development gap among the countries in the region. Several Japan-funded technical assistance projects for CLMV have been carried out.

Also pushing ahead during the 4th Informal Summit was the collective effort by the 10 ASEAN nations to plug ASEAN into the global networked economy. The e-ASEAN Framework Agreement signed during the Summit constitutes a broad framework to develop a free trade area for goods, services and investments for the info-communications and telecommunications industries within ASEAN. Apart from binding themselves to facilitate interconnectivity and technical interoperability among their information and communication technologies (ICT) system, the ASEAN Governments also committed themselves to create a seamless favourable legal and regulatory environment in order to foster the growth of electronic commerce in the region.

Growth Triangles

Growth Centre Theory

The Growth Centre Theory postulates a positive cumulative causality between a growth centre and the peripheries. A growth centre rises initially from certain advantages, such as factor endowments, favourable location, fertile land, transportation convenience, and other natural strategic advantages. As the growth centre develops, it develops its own internal growth momentum. As it grows, it reaps certain economies of concentration. The peripheries benefit from the centre by being suppliers of raw materials, foodstuff and labour, thus spreading the wealth from the centre to the peripheries. This circular cumulative causation process in turn helps to further develop the centre which can become a high metropolis like Bangkok, ho Chi Ming City, Jakarta, Kuala Lumpur, Manila or Singapore. The spread of wealth will narrow the differences in the standards of living between the centre and the peripheries over time, and it is conceivable that the peripheries may one day overtake the centre such as Penang overtaking Malacca and Singapore in turn overtaking Singapore. The last three growth centres are all located along the strategic trade and shipping route of the Straits of Malacca and all came under British rule during the colonial period.

An important ingredient for this mutual beneficial relationship to flourish is a reasonably free movement of goods and factors of production. The lesser the barriers, the greater will be the benefits. An example will be within a nation where there are no legal barriers for the flow of goods and factors of production. Better job opportunities will speedily attract people from the smaller surrounding towns to flock to the bigger booming industrialised towns, thus equalising the average earnings of the neighbouring towns. Of course, geographical distances and artificial segregation of population could also hinder the spread of wealth within a country. On the other hand, a country completely isolates itself from the rest of the world would see its economy stagnating or even declining, despite having rapidly developing neighbours. One extreme example left would be North Korea. Other examples given in the earlier versions of this book were Myanmar and Mongolia. Their interconnectivity with the outside world has been minimal.

At the global level, Growth Centre Theory would suggest developing countries to establish linkages with the developed countries so as to achieve development through the flow of goods, services, factors and knowledge. At the regional level, Growth Centre Theory would propose the lowering of barriers between neighbouring countries or cities of neighbouring countries to facilitate the spread of wealth. Examples are Hong Kong and Shenzhen and the various growth triangles launched within ASEAN. Of course, connectivity can also usher in the reverse process, should the centre decelerates for whatever reason.

Of note meanwhile is that the Growth Centre Theory is a part of the Triple C Theory that will be more fully dealt with in Chapter 13.

SIJORI

The first growth triangle that was launched in Southeast Asia was the Singapore-Johor-Riau Growth Triangle that was mooted by Mr Goh Chok Tong in 1989, when he was Singapore's Deputy Prime Minister. Also known as SIJORI, this sub-regional economic co-operation covers Singapore, the Riau Islands of Indonesia and the Johor State of Malaysia. The economic rationale of the growth triangle lies mainly on the comparative as well as competitive advantages arising from the differences in factor endowments, natural and built-up, among the three participating ASEAN partners. However, some would have seen the formation of SIJORI as a desire by the three for a quicker pace in ASEAN economic co-operation.

The SIJORI growth triangle was marketed initially to interested investors as an opportunity to tap into Singapore's advanced communication, transport and financial infrastructure and high quality human capital; Batam's relative inexpensive industrial land and large pool of unskilled labour; and Johor's semi-skilled labour force and relatively accessible large industrial land. The formation of the growth triangle merely formalised a long established traditional link between Singapore and Malaysia, in particular the State of Johor. The Southern leg of the triangle between Singapore and Batam (and the surrounding Riau islands) is, however, a recent development. Basically, SIJORI works on bilateral relationships with Singapore playing the pivotal role to Johor and Batam. There is no formal link between Johor and Batam (see Diagram 8.1).

Under the framework of the Growth Centre Theory, Singapore functions as the growth centre of SIJORI, where capital and entrepreneurship would flow from Singapore to Johor and Batam. The centre and the peripheries are both the markets and the suppliers. While Singapore supplies capital and entrepreneurships to the factories in Johor and Batam, Singapore purchases foods and water from Johor and Batam. In addition, Johor and Batam also tap on the transportation facilities available in Singapore and import and export through Singapore to the outside world, which includes the USA, Japan and Western Europe, and China and India. These three participants are in many ways mutually interdependent.

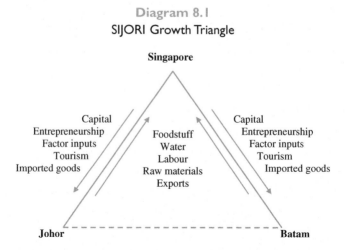

Diagram 8.1
SIJORI Growth Triangle

The Riau Islands linkages with Singapore have brought about faster growth in the former. Over the past two decades, Singapore based MNCs have relocated their labour-intensive operations to Batam's various industrial parks that were jointly developed by Singapore's government linked companies and Indonesia's large conglomerates. Among which are the Batamindo Industrial Park and the Bintan Industrial Estate jointly developed by Singapore's Sembcorp Industries and JTC International, and Indonesia's Salim Group. These two industrial parks total 430 hectares in size and are staffed by over 92,000 workers. In 2002, the two industrial parks attracted over US$300 million in foreign direct investment, generating export value of more than US$6 billion. The nearby Indonesian Bintan Island has also been earmarked as an eco-tourist economy with several international class resort hotels and golf courses and marinas being developed.

However, the progress is accompanied by associated problems. The creation of new job opportunities has attracted many Indonesians from other parts of the huge Indonesian Archipelago to flock to the Riau Islands. This has created bottlenecks in the provision of suitable housing, transportation, social and recreational facilities in Batam. There is concern of the rising costs of living and higher incidences of land speculation in Batam. Locals are also resentful that the benefits of economic growth are not seen to be fairly distributed among the people but rather to the big Jakarta-based business conglomerates. For Johor, the concern was the resentment in the marketing of them as being providers of cheap labour. Another perennial complaint is the strong purchasing power of the Singapore dollar has driven up the costs of housing, food and other necessities for the residents of Johor. For Singapore, her participation has helped in restructuring her economy away from labour intensive activities. And with rising affluence, demand for leisure and recreational facilities is met by just a short ferry ride across the Straits of Singapore or a drive up north towards Johor. A New Strait Times (Malaysia) news article dated 2006 reported that 7.1 million Singaporeans entered Johor in the first ten months of 2005 and that some 23,500 Singaporeans visit Johor on a daily basis, spending RM5.3 million daily, with approximately RM 225 spent per visitor. However, the links between Batam and Johor are less well developed than those with Singapore, as the factor endowment between these two areas are more competitive than complementary. It will take a longer time to develop the economic links between these two legs of the triangle.

IMT-GT and the BMIP-EAGA

The development of growth triangles or sub-regional economic zones must be seen as a form of co-operation where all participating players benefit equitably from the outcome. Despite the problems mentioned, the SIJORI is viewed as a success. It provided a useful learning model that was being replicated in the other parts of Southeast Asia. Two other regional growth triangles were also being pushed. The first was the Indonesia–Malaysia–Thailand Growth Triangle (IMT-GT) or Northern Growth Triangle launched in July 1993. It included North Sumatra, the Northern states of Malaysia (Penang, Kedah, Perlis) and Southern Thailand. The second was the East ASEAN Growth Area (EAGA), which was launched in March 1994. It included oil rich Brunei, the Malaysian States of Sabah and Sarawak, Southern Philippines and the Indonesian provinces of Kalimantan and Sulawesi.

The expectations from the formation of these growth triangles are to quicken the pace of growth and economic development while at the same time increase the level of economic co-operation between cross border economic participants that are located away from each country's major metropolitan centres. The IMT-GT has a potential market of 21 million people while EAGA covers one million square kilometres in area and has a population of 31 million. However, while there are ambitious plans on the drawing board, the Asian Development Bank (ADB) has cautioned that the challenges in making the two growth triangles as successful as SIJORI may not be free from hurdles. In particular, there is a lack of resource complementarities within the EACA. The participants have similar production mix in the agriculture, fishery and forestry sectors that make them competitors rather than partners. The region is made up of poorer and less developed areas of three out of the four major participants. In addition, the EAGA also suffers from poor infrastructure and transport facilities and the lack of financial services. The success of the IMT-GT and the EAGA is also perceived to be limited due to the lack of a well established strategically located growth centre. Penang could play the role of the growth centre within the IMT-GT.

However, very close geographical proximity between Penang and other participants is not there.

In spite of these innate problems, the proposed areas of co-operation that were identified for the EAGA included marine fishing joint ventures, forestry conservation, tourism, expansion of air linkages, improvement of sea transport and services, and the simplification of tax and investment laws. For the IMT-GT, likely projects to be implemented included the setting up of an export processing zone, an inland cargo dry port and a power plant in Southern Thailand; the production of automobile parts and concrete poles in Sumatra; and the construction of hotels and tourist facilities in Medan. Other areas of co-operation that were targeted included telecommunications, agricultural and human resource training projects.

It is important that these sub-regional growth zones should not be seen as competing with each other. Rather, such sub-regional economic co-operation should be viewed as a catalyst to hasten the pace of region-wide trade liberalisation. While these major initiatives have generally been pushed by senior government officials, it would be the task of the private sector to follow-up on the development plans once the Governments have removed trade and investment barriers and simplified administrative procedures. Lastly, the momentum and enthusiasm for sub-regional growth cooperation in Southeast Asia, including the Sijori, the IMT-GT and the BMIP-EAGA projects, appears to have subsided in recent years.

Asia Pacific Community

In recent years, increasing attention and study have centred on the Pacific Basin and the possibilities of establishing an institutional arrangement encompassing the littoral states. However, considerations of differences in political and economic systems have limited most Pacific Community proposals to a narrower group of countries, at least in the initial stages. Generally, the 'core' countries include the five advanced Pacific economies of the United States, Canada, Japan, Australia, and New Zealand, the original five ASEAN economies and the three Northeast Asian NIEs. China joined the grouping, following the opening up of its economy since late 1978. This 'core' group of countries embraces great diversities in terms of population, land area, GDP, as well as in levels and rates of economic development.

Armed with the motive of "establishing an independent, regional mechanism to advance economic co-operation and market-driven integration", the Pacific Economic Cooperation Council (PECC) was born in 1980, at the initiative of Masayoshi Ohira and Malcolm Fraser, then Prime Ministers of Japan and Australia. An important characteristic of PECC is its independent, unofficial status that would permit it to address economic issues and measures free from constraints of formal government policies and relationships. Another unique characteristic of PECC is its tripartite nature, where senior representatives from the Governments, business sector and academic research institutes are all active participants. The regional organisation since then has been headquartered in Singapore, in response to an invitation by the author as the Head of the Singapore Committee for Pacific Economic Co-operation (SINCPEC). PECC currently has 26 Member Committees from economies in the Pacific region, including the United States, Japan, Australia, New Zealand, China, Taiwan, and ASEAN (with the exception of Myanmar and Laos). The objectives of PECC are to serve as a regional forum for co-operation and policy co-ordination to promote economic development in the Asia-Pacific region, in areas such as trade, investment, finance, human resource development, and all major industrial sectors.

Nine years after the formation of the PECC, the government-based Asia-Pacific Economic Cooperation (APEC) was established in Australia in 1989 in response to the growing interdependence among Asia-Pacific economies. Similar to PECC, APEC begun as an informal dialogue group among government representatives, but has since become the primary regional vehicle for promoting open trade and practical economic co-operation. APEC currently has 21 members, which includes all the major economies of the region. Its member economies had a combined Gross Domestic Product of US$19.3 trillion in 2007 and over 50% of global trade. APEC is a governmental organisation. It brings together all the Heads of Governments in the region. The initial membership is modelled on that of PECC, together with other PECC practices.

Both PECC and APEC serve as useful forums that have provided significant boost to advance global trade and investment liberalisation. However, formal institutional arrangement aims at closer-integrating the Pacific Basin economies, such as the European Union, is widely considered to be infeasible, at least in the foreseeable future. Firstly, the Pacific Basin countries represent too diverse a group of countries with diverse goals, perceptions, potentials and constraints, to conform to set objectives, schedules, co-ordinated policy measures and rigid institutional framework. Secondly, the experience of the European Union shows a long period of ideological, polit-ical and bureaucratic gestation, preparation, and step-by-step progressions are needed. The Pacific Basin countries have yet to establish the required economic and non-economic preconditions for closer economic integration. Thirdly, it has been argued that trade liberalisation and improved resource flows are not dependent on regional integration. Thus, the emphasis of the Pacific Community concept has been on the consultative rather than for-mal integrative aspects of regionalism. At any rate, they have the vision of a Pacific Basin Free Trade Area. Currently, Singapore, Brunei, New Zealand and Chile have joined into a free trade arrangement with the USA, Australia, Peru and Vietnam actively exploring the possibility of joining the group. This FTA, known as the "Comprehensive Trans-Pacific Strategic Economic Partnership" agreement — the first trade pact involving a group of Pacific Rim countries — has the broad objective of tearing down trade barriers among participants by 2020.

The various proponents of the Pacific Community have generally regarded ASEAN as a key member of the regional organisation. It is situ-ated in the Asia-Pacific region; the original ASEAN-5 is a dynamic group of market-oriented economies; it has substantial trade, investment and other economic relationships with major countries of the Pacific Basin; and it is generally committed to an open international economy. The com-modity structure of ASEAN's trade with the other 'core' Pacific Basin countries shows a preponderance of resource exports and manufactured imports. Its major export and import markets are the United States, Japan and China, the three most important Pacific economies. ASEAN is also heavily dependent on the United States and Japan, and to a lesser extent, China, as sources of foreign direct investment and official development assistance. Both the United States and Japan are leading investors in many ASEAN countries.

With the United States and Japan accounting for a large proportion of ASEAN's trade as well as inflows of direct foreign investment and offi-cial development assistance, ASEAN's economic relations with these two countries have a dominant position. In trade, ASEAN seeks stable prices and export earnings for primary exports, and improved market access for manufactured exports. ASEAN's bilateral negotiations with the United States and Japan have not, however, been one of unqualified success. For instance, ASEAN's requests for better market access for manufactured exports have only been partly met by improvements in the Japanese and American Generalised System of Preferences (GSP) and the American extension of GSP benefits to Indonesia. Improved market access has been partly hindered by the protectionist lobby in the American economy and the peculiar internal distribution network of the Japanese economy, as well as by ASEAN's concentration of exports in processed materials and labour-intensive manufactures.

Besides APEC, ASEAN has taken the initiative to establish a FTA with China, Japan and Korea. ASEAN's economic relations with the Northeast Asian countries have expanded rapidly in both trade and direct investments. Complementary relationship exists in most industries between Northeast and Southeast Asia (Akrasanee, 1984). As ASEAN countries continue to produce more and more labour-intensive and resource-intensive goods according to international shift in comparative advantage, the more advanced countries in East Asia are losing comparative advantage in those industries. One can therefore see that Japan-NIEs have been restructuring to allow labour-intensive and resource-intensive industries to be phased out, and at the same time, turning more towards the production of higher value-added products. For example, Japan-NIEs will specialise in upper end production of electronic and electrical products, and high technology parts and components, while other Southeast Asian countries will specialise in lower-end products and assembly of parts and components. The vertical division of labour appears to be developing between Japan and the Asian NIEs on the one hand and the rest of ASEAN on the other.

A new and increasingly important player has been China (the People's Republic of China). She became a full member of PECC and later an increasingly important member of APEC. She has played and will continue to play an increasingly important role in the evolution of the Asia-pacific Community. This is mainly because of her spectacular economic growth, particularly outward-looking economic expansion including trade expansion and the rapid accumulation of foreign exchange reserves, the largest in the world.

Overall, Asian economies are getting more integrated through trade and investment. The center of gravity of the global economy is shifting to Asia and with the rise of this new regionalism, economies in Asia are increasingly becoming more vital to one other — and to the world. The 1997/98 Asian financial crisis, in particular, was an important catalyst for this new regionalism and gave rise to a range of new initiatives including the Chiang Mai Initiative (CMI) which have focused on enhancing cooperation in the region in the event of another exchange rate crisis through pre-arranged exchange-swap agreement. Under the CMI, there were 16 bilateral swap agreements in place with a magnitude of about USD83 billion as of July 2007.

While regional integration is viewed as benefiting Asia through faster economic growth, deeper integration with the world economy and a stronger Asian voice in global economic forums, the potential costs of integration and the loss of some autonomy in national economic policy making, are judged to be substantially smaller than its benefits. Indeed, a dynamic and outward-looking Asian regionalism is likely to bring huge benefits not just to Asia but to the world. According to a recent study by ADB, an integrated Asia could help sustain the region's growth, underpin its stability, and with the right policies, reduce faster the incidence of poverty. In addition, it could also contribute to the efficiency and stability of the global financial markets by making Asian capital markets stronger and safer, as well as providing leadership to help sustain open global trade and financial systems.

Asian regionalism could help marshal a common response to major new challenges that often arise suddenly and unexpectedly. An integrated Asia does not imply a fortress Asia, but creates a network of bridges to deepen economic integration and foster regional growth. As markets interconnect the region, governments need to work together more closely to sustain economic development, grasp common opportunities, and manage shared risks and problems. Ultimately, Asian regionalism is likely to follow a distinctive blueprint, building on the countries' economic priorities and based on an Asian vision for establishing a regional community. The rapid economic ascendancy of China and India in recent decades has added a fuller meaning to Asian economic cooperation with China, India and Japan playing a strategic role in it. But it cannot be over-emphasised that Asian cooperation in regional self help has to be an outward looking one and as a block in the Asian-Pacific grouping and in greater global cooperation and mutual support.

Bilateral Free Trade Agreement (FTA)

Against the backdrop of a faltering global trading system, where plans for a new round of global trade talk progress very slowly, several Asia-Pacific countries including Australia, Canada, South Korea, Mexico, Singapore, and New Zealand are adopting bilateral FTAs as an alternative strategy to kick-start the stalled trade liberalisation momentum in the World Trade Organisation (WTO). Similar attempts at regional trading blocs, such as AFTA and APEC, have also exhibited slow progress. Within ASEAN, Singapore has taken the first step in forging bilateral FTAs with a large number of countries. It has started with signing a bilateral FTA with New Zealand in 2000, followed by Japan and EFTA[1] in 2002, and Australia and the US in 2003. Singapore is also working towards bilateral free trade pacts with Mexico, Canada, Republic of Korea, India, Ukraine and Pakistan. Malaysia too is attempting to have an FTA with the US after its FTA with Japan took effect in 2006. There is also a growing number of countries and regions either expressing interest in entering into an economic framework agreement with ASEAN as a group or actually in the process of negotiating one. These countries include China, Japan, India, the United States, the European Union, Australia and New Zealand. Hopefully this will eventually lead to the formation of a free trade area in the Asia-Pacific region, spanning across the US and Canada, Southeast Asia and Northeast Asia, and Australia and New Zealand.

However, several ASEAN members had expressed their reservations about the push for bilateral FTAs, fearing that bilateral FTAs would hinder ASEAN integration effort and affect AFTA's credibility. There are also fears that countries that are unattractive FTA partners may be left behind in a global trading environment dominated by FTAs.

Despite the various arguments against bilateral FTAs, bilateral FTAs do have their merits. One of which is that bilateral FTAs or sub-regional FTAs such as between Singapore and developed countries would help to

---

[1]EFTA is an arrangement consisting of Switzerland, Iceland, Liechtenstein and Norway.

retain the interest of the foreign investors in AFTA. The commitment of all ASEAN nations towards the establishment of AFTA would help ASEAN to be seen as a single market by investors. Bilateral FTA also allows countries that are prepared to embrace trade liberalisation to proceed faster. To quote then Singapore Prime Minister Mr Goh Chok Tong, "Those who can run faster should run faster. They shouldn't be restrained by those who don't want to run at all." Despite fears from Singapore's neighbours that non-ASEAN countries may use FTAs as a back door to get into ASEAN markets without providing reciprocal access, Singapore was sure that its efforts to strike bilateral free trade deals with non-ASEAN economies would benefit its neighbours; ultimately, these bilateral or sub-regional FTAs are building blocks that provide stimulus to a new round of multilateral trade negotiation, thereby lifting the WTO out of the doldrums. However, conscientious efforts must be invested towards the launch of a new round to ensure that the gap between FTAs and the WTO does not grow so wide that it becomes irreconcilable.

Key Points

1. There are four levels of regional economic co-operation ranging from least restrictive to complete harmonisation of policies, they are: Free Trade Area, Customs Union, Common Market, and Economic Union. Mooted in 1992, ASEAN Free Trade Area (AFTA) is scheduled to be realised in 2015. The creation of AFTA would encourage greater trade flow among member countries and could bring about larger inflow of foreign direct investment. It is one of the most important ASEAN economic co-operation projects currently underway.
2. Potential benefits that could arise from regional economic co-operation include trade creation, economies of scale, improved terms of trade, enhanced factor productivity, and larger inflow of foreign direct investment. However, if member countries were to erect higher trade barriers for non-member countries after the formation of regional trading blocs, this could result in trade diversion.
3. Intra-ASEAN trade comprised 25.1% of total ASEAN trade in 2006. This is significantly lower than the 71% intra-regional trade within the EU. One reason is the lack of complementary relationship among ASEAN members, as most of the countries have strong comparative advantage

in only primary commodities. Greater economic interdependence and co-operation would be required to boost intra-ASEAN trade.

4. ASEAN member countries have co-operated in various ASEAN industrial projects, including ASEAN Industrial Projects Scheme, ASEAN Industrial Complementation Scheme, ASEAN Industrial Joint Venture Scheme, and ASEAN Industrial Co-operation Scheme. Most of the projects were unsuccessful.

5. Singapore, the Riau Islands of Indonesia, and the Johor state of Malaysia have launched the first growth triangle in South East Asia in 1989. Also known as SIJORI, the attractiveness of this sub-regional economic zone lies in the different and complementary resource endowments of the partners. The SIJORI is considered as a success in terms of attracting FDI and generating growth.

6. Asia-Pacific Economic Cooperation (APEC) and Pacific Economic Cooperation Council (PECC) were established in response to the growing interdependence among Asia-Pacific economies. Both organisations have served as useful forum to advance global trade and investment liberalisation. The earlier members of ASEAN are also members of these two Asia-Pacific organisations.

7. Economies in Asia are getting increasingly integrated through trade, capital and investment. Attempts at state-sponsored regional self help can be a positive force if this cooperation removes further barriers to trade and investment flow and as a move to wider global economic cooperation and integration.

Suggested Discussion Topics

8.1 Evaluate the various attempts at ASEAN economic cooperation, particularly the AIP, AIC, AIJV and AICO schemes. Does the AFTA scheme hold a better promise of future success?

8.2 Discuss the Growth Centre Theory and its applicability in economic cooperation in the SIJORI region. If SIJORI is successful, why cannot IMT-GT and BMIP-EAGA schemes be equally successful?

8.3 Discuss the desirability of having individual free trade agreements with countries within and outside the East Asian region in the context of the ASEAN Free Trade Agreement and the APEC Free Trade proposal.

References

AKRASANEE, Narongchai, 1984, "Industrialization of ASEAN and structural adjustments in the Pacific", in Benjamin ROGER and Robert T. KUDRLE (eds.), *The Industrial Future of the Pacific Basin*, London: Westview Press, Chapter 4.

ASEAN Secretariat, 2003, *ASEAN Annual Report, 2002–2003*, Jakarta: ASEAN Secretariat.

ATHUKORALA, P. C. and Jayant MENON, 1996, "Foreign direct investment in Asean: Can Afta make a difference", in *AFTA in the Changing International Economy*, TAN, Joseph (ed.), ISEAS.

CHNG, M. K., 1985, "ASEAN economic co-operation: The current status", *Southeast Asian Affairs*, Singapore: Institute of Southeast Asian Studies.

KOJIMA, K., 1970, "Towards a theory of agreed specialization: The economics of integration". In W. A. ELTIS, M. F. G. SCOTT, & J. N. WOLFE (eds.), *Induction, Growth and Trade, Essays in Honour of Sir Roy Harrod*, 305–324. Oxford: Clarendon Press.

LIM, Chong Yah, 1967, *Economic Development of Modern Malaya*, Kuala Lumpur: Oxford University Press.

LIM, Chong Yah, 1981, *Economic Development in Southeast Asia*, Singapore: Federal publications.

MENON, Jayant, 1996, "The dynamics of intra-industry trade in ASEAN", *Asian Economic Journal*, 10(1), 105–115.

RAO, Bhanoji, 1996, *ASEAN Economic Co-operation and the ASEAN Free Trade Area: A Primer,* Institute for policy research.

ROBSON, Peter, 1980, *The Economics of International Integration*, London: George Allen and Unwin.

United Nations, 1974, "Economic cooperation among member countries of the Association of Southeast Asian Nations", *Journal of Development Planning*, No. 7.

VINER, Jacob, 1950, *The Customs Union Issue*, Carnegie Foundation of International peace, New York.

YEUNG, May T., Nicholas PERDIKIS and William A. KERR, 1999, *Regional Trading Blocs in the Global Economy: The EU and ASEAN*, Cheltenham: Edward Elgar.

Further Readings

Asian Development Bank, May 2008, *Emerging Asian Regionalism: A Partnership for Shared Prosperity.* Softcopy of book available at www.adb.org website.

BEHRMAN, Jere R., 1978, *Development, the International Economic Order and Commodity Agreements*, USA: Addison-Wesley Publishing Company.

CHIA, Siow Yue and Joseph L. H. TAN, 1996, *ASEAN in WTO: Challenges and Responses*, Singapore: Institute of Southeast Asian Studies.

ESMARA, Hendra (ed.), 1988, *ASEAN Economic Cooperation: A New Perspective*, Singapore: Chopmen publishers.

ISEAS, 2008, *The Asean Community: Unblocking the Roadblocks*. Singapore: Institute of Southeast Asian studies.

KAO, Kim Hourn and Sarah KANTER, 1997, *ASEAN Free Trade Agreement: Implications and Future Directions,* London: ASEAN Academic Press.

LIM, Chong Yah, 1960, "A re-appraisal of the 1953 tin agreement", *Malayan Economic Review*, 5(1), 13–24.

LIM, Chong Yah, 1979, "Singapore's position in ASEAN co-operation", conference paper presented in joint research program series, No. 14, Institute of developing economies, Tokyo, Japan. Also appeared in *ASEAN Business Quarterly*, 111(1), 9–19, and *Economic Bulletin*, 1979, 17–21.

TAN, Joseph (ed.), 1996, *AFTA in the Changing International Economy*, Singapore: Institute of Southeast Asian studies.

TOH, Mun Heng and Linda LOW, 1993, *Regional Co-operation and Growth Triangles in ASEAN*, Singapore: Times Academic Press.

Chapter 9

Fiscal Policy

There are always two tax rates that yield the same revenues.

Arthur Laffer

Objectives

✓ Provide theoretical support behind fiscal policy.
✓ Assess fiscal positions of Southeast Asian countries.
✓ Analyse sources of government revenue of Southeast Asian countries.
✓ Examine Southeast Asian countries' government expenditure patterns.
✓ Discuss issues concerning deficit financing.
✓ Discuss issues concerning tax capacity.
✓ Examine tax reforms in Southeast Asian countries.

Introduction

According to orthodox neo-classical theory, the problem of development, like most important economic problems encountered by industrial countries, is best resolved by the market mechanism. There may, however, be reasons for active government participation, particularly in the LDCs. One reason for such intervention is the generally recognised fact that market forces operate less effectively in these countries than in developed economies. Secondly, the market mechanism may lead to a pattern of resource allocation that is highly biased towards the higher income groups and the more prosperous regions. The absence of government intervention in the allocation of investment resources could result in a more lopsided development. A third reason for government intervention in the economy is the presence of externalities or factors leading to divergence between private and social costs and benefits of investment projects. Ports, electric power distribution, education, healthcare, water supply, sanitation and public parks are some examples of sectors where social benefits are larger than private benefits. Government investment (and intervention) in such sectors is necessary, especially in the early stages of economic development of a country.

Keynesian and neo-Keynesian economists, in particular, assign special importance to the use of fiscal tools in the management of an economy. They hold the view that active fiscal and monetary policies are needed to attain full employment and economic growth with price stability. Expansionary fiscal policies aimed at stimulating aggregate demand through tax cuts or stepped-up government spending could stabilise an economy during a recession. Naked market forces do not guarantee a recession-free economy. Indeed, they constitute a part of the ups and downs, the booms and the bursts.

To achieve sustainable economic development in the LDCs, capital formation, technological progress, and changes in the social and institutional framework are all required. The public sector has a vital role to play in all these components of development (Musgrave and Musgrave, 1984: 781–784). In the early stages of development, public investment in physical and social infrastructure takes on particular importance since it sets the framework for further investment in the private sector. In a market economy, internal resources for capital formation must come from public or private savings. To some extent, if conditions are conducive, a higher savings rate may be generated voluntarily in the private sector. The Government then plays the role of securing reasonable monetary stability so that saving habits are not discouraged by continuing inflation. Furthermore, the Government may play a part in facilitating, or itself creating, the appropriate financial institutions to attract household savings and direct them into productive uses. These monetary policies are aimed at creating and sustaining an effective system of financial intermediation. Issues on monetary policy will be discussed in greater detail in Chapter 10: Financial Policy.

At an early stage of development, voluntary private savings though useful and important, may not be sufficient. An economic setting that encourages private savings takes time to develop. In the interim, the government budget appears to be the most promising source of finance for development purposes. However, just like a business or household, a Government also faces budget constraints. The ability of a Government to generate revenue to finance desired expenditure is of utmost importance for the effective running of the Government. In the case of the LDCs, given the importance of tax revenue as a source of government revenue, it is thus critical for the Government to put in place an effective system for tax collection. Weak fiscal management has often been a major cause of macroeconomic instability in the LDCs: weak tax administration coupled with expansionary fiscal policy often lead to a large fiscal imbalance which requires central bank financing of the budget deficit.

There are many ways of financing a government budget deficit. One easy-to-implement way is to print more money. However, this method of deficit financing has often resulted in domestic runaway inflation and serious exchange rate depreciation. Alternatively, the Government may opt to issue government bonds, or in another word, borrow. The borrowing does not have to be confined to domestic sources. However, Governments of developing countries that are already facing large fiscal imbalances and/or serious balance of payment deficits may find themselves having to pay exorbitant interest rates for their borrowings. Moreover, debt burden is being shifted to the next generation, which may not be justifiable if the bulk of the money is spent on current consumption expenditure. In addition, while domestic borrowing might lead to crowding out of private investment as a result of rising interest rates, overseas borrowing could precipitate a foreign debt crisis. Issues concerning deficit financing will be further discussed in a later section.

Government Fiscal Balance

The fiscal balances of various Southeast Asia countries are shown in Table 9.1. During boom periods, most governments are able to cumulate surpluses, with revenue collected exceeding expenditure. In 1980, with the exception of Singapore, the Philippines and Myanmar although most of the Southeast Asian countries have budget deficits, these deficits are relatively

Table 9.1

Total Revenue and Expenditure as a Percentage of GDP, 1980 and 2006

	1980			2006		
	Revenue	Expenditure	Balance	Revenue	Expenditure	Balance
Singapore	25.4	20.0	5.4	24.7	22.0	2.7
Thailand	14.3	18.8	−4.5	17.6	19.9	−2.3
Myanmar	16.0	15.8	0.2	2.0	8.7[a]	−3.4
Indonesia	21.3	22.1	−0.8	20.6	24.1	−3.5
Philippines	14.0	13.4	0.6	15.4	19.4	−4.0
Vietnam	n.a.	n.a.	n.a.	20.0	24.2	−4.2
Malaysia	25.8	28.0	−2.2	23.9	29.5	−5.6
Cambodia	n.a.	n.a.	n.a.	11.4	17.7	−6.3
Laos	n.a.	n.a.	n.a.	12.8	20.0	−7.2

Source: World Bank, *WDI Online*, 1 Oct. 2008, http://publications.worldbank.org/WDI
Asian Development Bank, *Key Indicators 2007*,
http://www.adb.org/Documents/Books/Key_Indicators/2007/.
a: Figures refer to year 2000.

smaller than those incurred during the recession year of 2001. A particularly noteworthy point is that Myanmar's revenue share of GDP has fallen drastically over the years, from 16.0% of GDP in 1980 to only 3.0% in 2006. Myanmar's government expenditure has also fallen, albeit not as much as its revenue. A budget deficit is thus unavoidable.

In 2006, among the Southeast Asian economies, Singapore is the only Southeast Asian country that has a budget surplus. Even Malaysia has a budget deficit exceeding 5% of GDP, Cambodia 5.6% and Laos, 7.2%. En passant, to be a member of the European Union, a member cannot have a fiscal deficit of 3% of more. This target is part of the concept of fiscal stability or responsible fiscal policy.

Government Revenue

Tax Revenue

There are basically two sources from which a Government can obtain its revenue, namely tax and non-tax. Common tax sources include corporate and individual income taxes, withholding taxes on interests, dividends and royalties, sales and value-added taxes (VAT), customs and excise duties and inheritance taxes (estate duties). In countries that have a more elaborate and sophisticated tax administration and collection system, property taxes, stamp duties, anti-pollution, anti-congestion taxes, foreign workers' levy, skills development fund, among others, are also collected. Table 9.2 shows

Table 9.2

Components of Current Revenue (%), 1980 and 2006

		1980	2006
Vietnam	Tax	n.a.	94.5
	Non-tax	n.a.	5.5
Thailand	Tax	92.6	89.1[a]
	Non-tax	7.4	10.9
Philippines	Tax	87.9	88.3
	Non-tax	12.1	11.7
Laos	Tax	13.1	85.0
	Non-tax	86.9	15.0
Cambodia	Tax	n.a.	78.8
	Non-tax	n.a.	21.2
Malaysia	Tax	86.6	70.1
	Non-tax	13.4	29.9
Indonesia	Tax	96.9	64.3
	Non-tax	3.1	35.7
Singapore	Tax	74.8	63.7
	Non-tax	25.2	36.3[b]
Myanmar	Tax	59.3	56.5[c]
	Non-tax	40.7	43.5[c]

Source: Asian Development Bank, *Key Indicators of Developing Asian and Pacific Countries*, various issues; *Key Indicators 2007*, http://www.adb.org/Documents/Books/Key_Indicators/2007/.

a: Figures refer to year 2003.
b: Figures refer to year 2005.
c: Figures refer to year 2000.

the various components of Government's current revenue. In all the Southeast Asian countries, tax revenue contributed more than 50% of the Government's current revenue. In 2006, the percentages ranged from a low of 57% for Myanmar to a high of 95% for Vietnam.

The old ASEAN countries such as Malaysia, Singapore, Indonesia and Thailand seem to have a long-term decline in tax-revenue to GDP ratio, whereas the opposite trend appears evident in the new ASEAN countries such as Vietnam, Cambodia, Laos and Vietnam. Please see Table 9.2. The tax revenue to GDP ratios of the Southeast Asian countries are also generally lower than that of the developed countries. For instance, tax revenue to GDP ratio was 24% for the Netherlands and 29% for the United Kingdom in 2006, contrasting with 16% for the Philippines and 13% for Singapore (see Table 9.6).

As Table 9.3 shows, also of interest is the importance of income taxes as a source of government revenue. In Malaysia, Singapore, Thailand and the Philippines, individual and corporate income taxes made up the largest portion of tax revenue. In all the countries shown except Singapore, income tax collection is on the rising trend. Singapore has deliberately lowered her income taxes in order to enhance her competitive position for FDI inflow, particularly vis-a-vis Hong Kong.

At low levels of development, most of the revenues from income taxes are derived from large, and often foreign corporations. The share contributed by individuals is relatively small as wage and salary levels are low. As income levels increase, the share of revenue from income tax on individuals in total revenue from income taxation should increase due to (a) the broadening of the tax base, (b) the reduction in the level of exemptions, and (c) the improvement in tax administration (Tanzi, 1986). However, as stated earlier, in the case of Singapore, competition for foreign direct investment has seen corporate and income tax rates falling in the past years, resulting in a shrinking income tax revenue to GDP ratio.

As countries become more developed, some basic changes in the structure of tax revenue should be expected. Initially, tax is collected through excises limited to a few products (tobacco, alcohol and gasoline). Services are normally exempted, and the excises will be specific rather than ad valorem. The first change will be an expansion in the number of taxable products; and the second will be some conversion from specific to ad valorem rates

(Tanzi, 1986). A time will come when the need for additional tax revenue will force the countries to expand the scope of domestic indirect taxation. Indirect taxation on goods and services for domestic use also replaces some taxes on foreign trade as trade liberalisation gains pace. Table 9.3 shows

Table 9.3

Components of Tax Revenue as a Percentage of GDP, 1980, 1990 and 2006

		1980	1990	2006
Malaysia	Tax Revenue	23.1	19.1	21.6
	Taxes on Income	9.7	8.1	11.1[a]
	Taxes on Goods and Services	4.3	5.3	5.1
	Taxes on International Trade	8.5	4.7	1.3
Singapore	Tax Revenue	17.5	15.4	13.2
	Taxes on Income	8.2	6.9	6.2[b]
	Taxes on Goods and Services	4.0	4.3	4.6[b]
	Taxes on International Trade	1.7	0.5	0[b]
Thailand	Tax Revenue	13.2	17.1	17.6
	Taxes on Income	2.5	4.5	8.1
	Taxes on Goods and Services	6.6	7.7	1.3
	Taxes on International Trade	3.7	4.1	1.8
Philippines	Tax Revenue	12.5	14.1	16.2
	Taxes on Income	3.0	4.6	6.2
	Taxes on Goods and Services	5.9	5.0	4.1
	Taxes on International Trade	3.4	4.1	3.3
Indonesia	Tax Revenue	20.2	17.8	19.1
	Taxes on Income	16.6	11.6	16.9
	Taxes on Goods and Services	1.8	4.4	8.1
	Taxes on International Trade	1.5	1.2	1.8
Myanmar	Tax Revenue	9.6	6.2	n.a.
	Taxes on Income	0.5	1.8	2.1
	Taxes on Goods and Services	6.8	2.9	2.5
	Taxes on International Trade	2.4	1.4	0.2

Source: World Bank, *WDI Online*, 1 Oct. 2008, http://publications.worldbank.org/WDI and Bank Negara Malaysia, *Monthly Statistical Bulletin*, April 2003, http://www.bnm.gov.my.

a: Figures refer to year 2003.

b: Figures refer to year 2005.

that the revenue from domestic taxes on goods and services as a percentage of GDP has increased in Indonesia and Singapore. However, the percentage has declined in Thailand and the Philippines. In all countries except Thailand, taxes on goods and services are relatively more important than taxes on foreign trade, which show a declining trend in all countries except Indonesia. In Malaysia, Thailand and Myanmar, this declining trend is particularly conspicuous. Does it reflect declines in tariffs consequent on membership of ASEAN Free Trade Agreement?

Previously, foreign trade taxes (import duties and export taxes) were important sources of revenue in many countries in Southeast Asia, including Malaysia, the Philippines and Thailand. Over time, however, the importance of foreign trade taxes has declined in all Southeast Asian countries. Malaysian export duties on rubber and tin fell most significantly, reflecting the new economic structure with a sizeable manufacturing sector that has emerged in the country. While the Philippines imposes export duties on a wide range of wood, mineral, plant, and animal products, Thailand has concentrated on taxing rice exports, even though their importance has fallen drastically through the 1970s. Such export taxes in Southeast Asia should now be minimal if not negligible, and as liberal export promotion takes place, the revenue from export taxation would be expected to become less and less significant. Incidentally, export taxes have been banned in the USA under its Constitution. Sometimes, however, export taxes are temporarily imposed to ensure adequate domestic supplies in a supply crisis situation, as in the 1998 global rice shortage. Thailand neither imposed a ban nor increased export taxes on rice supply.

Non-Tax Revenue

As shown in Table 9.2, non-tax revenue contributed less than 40%, some very much less than 44%, of the Government's current revenue in all the Southeast Asian countries. An interesting point to note is that non-tax revenue is a relatively more important source of revenue in the transitional economies than their more developed Southeast Asian neighbours. Non-tax revenue constituted 21% of Cambodia's current revenue, 15% of Laos's current revenue and 44% of Myanmar's current revenue in 2006. These percentages are much higher than those of Thailand (11%) and the

Philippines (12%). One likely explanation of the above observation is that effective tax collection systems are not yet in place in the transitional economies, resulting in lower amounts of tax revenue collected, and thereby a higher percentage of non-tax revenue. Returns from investments made by a Government constitute a substantial proportion of non-tax revenue, especially when public enterprise plays a significant role in an economy. In the case of Myanmar, the availability of natural resources such as gas could add to fiscal revenue, as a non-tax source.

Among the ASEAN-5, Singapore and Indonesia have the highest ratios of non-tax revenue to total current revenue. 36% of total current revenue is derived from non-tax sources in both Singapore and Indonesia. While Singapore obtains her non-tax revenue largely from fees, charges, and particularly investment income, earnings from oil and gas is the main source of non-tax revenue for Indonesia.

Government Expenditure

Government expenditure is categorised under current expenditure and development expenditure. Current expenditure includes wages and salaries of civil servants, expenditure on goods and services, interest payments, and subsides. Development expenditure, on the other hand, consists of infrastructure and other capital outlays. Development expenditure is normally associated with physical capital formation.

On the whole, ASEAN countries spent an average of 79% of total expenditure on current expenditure and 21% on capital expenditure. In Indonesia, capital expenditure came to only 8.9% and the Philippines 8.2%. While the average capital expenditure ratio may appear low as compared to the current expenditure ratio, it is significantly higher than the 2% to 5% average observed in the developed countries (see Table 9.4). This higher-level ratio partly reflects the much lower state of infrastructure development of the ASEAN nations but in part it also explains the higher income growth rates of these countries, with higher rates of capital formation. Note that the rates of capital formation of Myanmar and Vietnam are particularly high, and that of Singapore has declined considerably.

Although capital expenditure is important for building up a strong foundation for achieving long-term growth, capital spending has often come

Table 9.4

Components of Government Expenditure (%), 1990 and 2006

	1990		2006		
	Current	Capital	Current	Capital	
Myanmar	71.1	28.9	57.3	42.7	(2000)
Vietnam	n.a.	n.a.	70.3	29.7	
Singapore	76.4	23.6	87.1	12.9	(2005)
Indonesia	56.5	43.5	91.1	8.9	
Malaysia	76.2	23.8	75.5	24.5	
Thailand	81.8	18.2	81.1	18.9	(2004)
Philippines	84.3	15.7	91.8	8.2	(2001)
France	94.0	6.0	95.7	4.9	
United Kingdom	90.0	10.0	96.1	2.2	
Netherlands	94.2	5.8	96.5	5.5	
Sweden	97.5	2.5	98.0	4.1	

Source: Asian Development Bank, *Key Indicators of Developing Asian and Pacific Countries*, various issues (http://www.adb.org/Documents/Books/Key_Indicators/2007) and IMF, *Government Finance Statistics Yearbook*, various issues.

under pressure as a result of budgetary deficit. In Malaysia, as current expenditure could not be significantly reduced in the short run, major development projects had to be either postponed or abandoned. Furthermore, the capital expenditure to total expenditure ratio was on the low side in the early 1970s. It peaked around 40% in 1980 reflecting the increased priority for public investment needed to fulfil the targets of various Malaysian development plans. The ratio declined in the mid-1980s as budgetary imbalances mounted and in 2006, the ratio stood at 24.5%. The Philippines is another country where the capital expenditure ratio came under tremendous budgetary pressure (see Table 9.4), reducing it to only 8.2% in 2006. In Chapter 13 of this book, it is noted that the Philippines is the only country left in low-income Southeast Asia that has exhibited very low long-term economic growth rates. Can this be partly reflected in its very little emphasis on capital formation in the public sector?

As shown too, on the other end of the spectrum are Myanmar and Vietnam. They spent an estimated one-third to 43% of their total

Diagram 9.1

Public Sector Capital Formation (as a Percentage of Total Government Expenditure), 2006

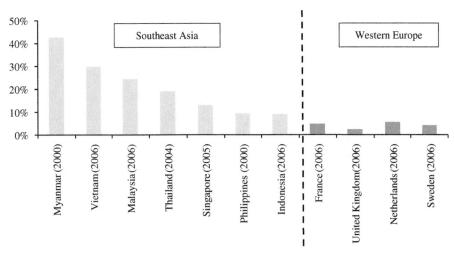

Source: Table 9.4

expenditures on infrastructure development and capital outlay, reflecting that higher rates of economic growth at the initial transformation process.

Another interesting point to note is the use of capital spending for the purpose of pump priming during an economic downturn. An example can be taken from Singapore. Though limited in scope in terms of effect, the capital expenditure ratio in Singapore shot up significantly in 1985 and most notably in 1986, as the Government embarked on expenditure programmes to help combat the 1985–1986 recession. This is an example of Keynesian ism in operation.

Expenditure policy in economic development has not been explored as extensively as that of tax policy, and comparative data are more difficult to obtain (Musgrave and Musgrave, 1984: 804). One most disappointing feature in the composition of State expenditure in Southeast Asia as shown in Table 9.5 is the perceptible decline in the proportion devoted to education, to human capital formation, in recent years. In Indonesia, this dropped from already a very low percentage of 9.1% in 1990 to 4.0% in 2004. Even Malaysia shows a decline from 18.3% in 1980 to 13.2% in 2004. Only in Singapore has education expenditure gone up to 21.6% in 2006, by far the highest rate among the Southeast Asia nations. This reflects at least in the

Table 9.5

Expenditure by Function as a Percentage of Total Expenditure, 1980, 1990 and 2006

	Indonesia			Malaysia			Philippines			Singapore			Thailand		
	1980	1990	2004p	1980	1990	2004p	1980	1990	2006	1980	1990	2005p	1980	1990	2005p
Defence	13.5	6.7	6.6	14.8	8.7	5.0	15.7	11.0	5.0	25.2	24.0	31.1	21.7	17.3	24.1
Education	8.3	9.1	4.0	18.3	18.9	13.2	13.0	16.9	13.7	14.6	19.9	21.6	19.8	20.1	19.6
Health	2.5	2.4	1.4	5.1	5.1	7.5	4.5	4.1	1.3	7.0	4.6	5.8	4.1	6.8	8.8
Housing and Community Amenities	1.8	1.8	0.8	3.0	7.0	n.a.	5.2	0.6	0.3	6.2	6.1	12.0	2.4	2.2	2.7
Economic Affairs Services	21.8	17.2	6.2	20.9	18.8	30.9	27.4	14.4	10.4	7.6	11.8	11.6	14.1	15.6	20.1
General Public Services	33.3	36.2	74.1	5.4	7.6	40.0	20.1	8.7	56.4	9.8	6.3	24.1	3.4	5.5	23.2
Transportation and Communications	18.4	9.9	2.0	9.1	7.0	4.6	29.5	9.2	6.8	10.1	5.0	2.8	10.1	6.5	4.1

Source: IMF, Government Finance Statistics Yearbook, various issues.
   p: IMF preliminary figures from Government Finance Statistics Yearbook, 2007.

Singapore case the need to have more and better education in a country that depends almost completely on human capital for growth and development, having hardly any natural capital including land intensive agriculture or fossil oil to speak of.

On the other hand, the expenditure on 'General Public Services' has skyrocketed in all the five ASEAN countries. The Indonesian and the Philippine cases are of most concern. In Indonesia, this rises up to 74% of total State expenditure. In the Philippines, it has gone up to 56.4%. Even in Malaysia, General Public Services have gone up to 40% from a low of 7.6% in 1990 while in Singapore, the ratio rose to 24.1% from 6.3% in 1990. This rise in expenditure is mainly attributed to a re-classification of 'General Public Services' by the IMF starting from 2004. General Public Services now include public debt transactions, i.e. interest payments and outlays for underwriting and floating government loans, as well as transfers between different levels of government.

As Table 9.5 shows, Singapore is the only country among the ASEAN 5 that spends about one-third of her total expenditure on defence, as against the 5% to 24% in the other ASEAN countries. The fragility of Singapore as a new small nation with very little land resource must have heightened her concerns for national security. In addition, the small population size of Singapore has led to a greater substitution of expensive military equipment for the limited manpower.

Also of significant interest is the general decline in high spending on defence, except in Thailand and Singapore. Perhaps, this reflects the declining fear of international conflicts in Southeast Asia. Unlike some categories of government expenditure like education, health and infrastructural development, defence expenditure makes little or no direct contribution to development and can only be rationally justified by threats or fear of threats of external aggression and perceived security by investors. Clearly, this category of expenditure should be kept to the minimum that is consistent with the requirements of external stability of the individual countries. Here, the ASEAN countries appear to be moving in the right direction.

Economic services also command a disproportionately high share of total expenditures compared to the industrial market economies. This category of public expenditure covers outlay on the maintenance of economic infrastructure, such as transport, communication, water and power, which in most LDCs are owned and managed by the public sector. In addition, the authorities often offer, at no cost to the recipients, technical advice to industry, commerce and agriculture, which constitute part of economic services. Clearly, expenditure on economic services can play an important part in the promotion of development and should have a fairly high claim on the resources available for government expenditure purposes. The relatively high share of economic services in total expenditures in the Southeast Asian countries reflects the fact that these Governments play a relatively large role in promoting economic development. The proportions for economic services for Malaysia, Singapore and Thailand have shown encouraging increases whereas for Indonesia and the Philippines discouraging decreases. For the Philippines, it went down from 27.4% in 1980 to only 10.4% in 2006.

A way for Governments to improve their capability and effectiveness is to boost competition for and within the civil service (World Bank, 1997). Civil servants can be motivated to perform effectively through adequate compensation together with a merit-based recruitment and promotion system. In addition, eradication of corruption is also vital to ensure an effective civil service. But as the well-known Chinese proverb goes, if the top is corrupt, the bottom will be corrupt (上梁不正下梁歪).

James D. Wolfensohn, former President of the World Bank, has pointed out that there is increasing evidence that corruption undermines development and hampers the effectiveness with which domestic savings and external aid are used in many developing countries. Ways to reduce opportunities for corruption include cutting back on discretionary authority, establishing formal checks and balances, reforming the civil service, restraining political patronage, and improving civil service pay. Introducing more competition in the provision of public goods and services through contracting out services via competitive bids and auctions could also bring about a more effective use of government expenditure.

Fiscal Policy Issues

Deficit Financing

Government investment in infrastructure and other capital outlays during the early stages of development could be instrumental in getting an LDC out of its low-level equilibrium trap. However, weak tax administration and limited means of obtaining revenue from other non-tax sources could imply that a Government might not have the financial resources to implement the economic development programmes. One way out of this financial constraint is to resort to deficit financing. At any rate, as Table 9.1 shows, all the ASEAN governments except Singapore run budget deficits.

There are many ways of financing a government budget deficit. One of the simplest but highly unsafe way is the printing of more money. A second method of deficit financing that will also be considered here is the sale of public asset. Financing from accumulated reserves, especially foreign exchange reserves, is by far the best method, if in normal times, there is a budget surplus.

Printing of more money is equivalent to increasing the money supply. Under the situation where an economy is producing under-capacity and supply is elastic, an increase in government expenditure accompanied by an increase in money supply could lead to an increase in aggregate demand and bring the economy back to full employment. However in reality, deficit financing has often resulted in runaway domestic inflation and excessive exchange rate depreciation. Some examples in Southeast Asia include Vietnam in the 1980s, and Indonesia during the 1960s. The supply curve in LDCs is very often inelastic, due to a shortage of entrepreneurs, knowledge, skills and bad management. The inelastic supply hinders the economy's ability to respond to the increase in aggregate demand. Domestic inflation then follows as a result of "too much money chasing after too few goods". In addition, the increase in aggregate demand is likely to lead to an increase in imports, resulting in a balance of payments deficit, which in turn brings about an exchange rate depreciation. Thus, governments often are forced to printing more money most reluctantly and as a last, last resort such as in meeting badly needed war expenditure or maybe in financing a general election. What a risk to take?

On the other hand, sale of public assets could circumvent the inflationary problems faced by printing more money. The selling of public assets could take many forms. The Government in the United Kingdom, under Mrs Margaret Thatcher, when bogged down by too many unprofitable government enterprises started selling public assets. The Singapore and the Hong Kong Government have both resorted to "selling" state land to finance government spending. Not many governments, however, can do this. There must be a great demand for the land for development, and the government has legal ownership of the land.

There are many benefits associated with the selling of public assets. Firstly, if an enterprise is making losses as a result of inefficient bureaucracy, selling the enterprise to the private sector can reduce cost and improve overall efficiency. Secondly, sale of public assets bring in much-needed finance for the Government, easing the Government's reliance on tax revenue. Hong Kong's corporate tax rate of 16.5% is one of the most competitive in the world, and is made possible largely because the land sales programme in Hong Kong.

Of course there are also many concerns associated with the selling of public assets. The chief concern is the loss of sovereignty, especially in the case of land sale. It must be emphasised that selling of State land for development does not mean that the Government has given up its sovereign right over the land, or its proper utilisation and other developmental control. Both the Hong Kong and the Singapore Governments have strict rules and conditions governing the utilisation of the land sold under their land sale programmes. In fact, both Governments do not "sell land", what they sell is the "right to develop the land for stipulated uses". Unless the sale conditions are satisfied, the land cannot be utilised.

The blind sale of public assets may bring about disastrous results. But when accompanied by proper rules and conditions set with the intention of promoting efficiency and safeguarding public's interest, selling of public assets can be a desirable source of government revenue. It means a transfer of much-needed funds to the public sector. It can also mean the development of areas that would otherwise be underdeveloped. It should be added that since the Asian financial crisis (1997–1998), some Governments in Southeast Asia including Indonesia and Malaysia have wisely sold off some government enterprises on a competitive basis, foreigners included. These enterprises like the land sales in Singapore operate under stipulated conditions laid down by the Government. Here, all governments will have to avoid fire sales.

Less Is Better

As pointed out in the earlier section, most of the Southeast Asian countries rely heavily on taxes as a source of government revenue. A simple way for

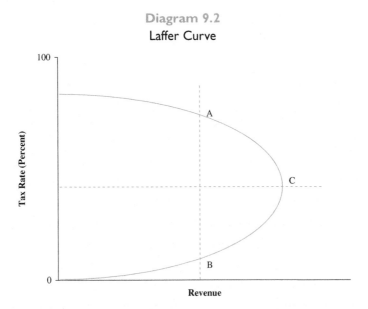

Diagram 9.2
Laffer Curve

a Government to raise tax revenue is to increase tax rates. However, Arthur Laffer noted in the 1970s that reducing tax rate could lead to an increase in tax revenue. Arthur Laffer's idea is presented in Diagram 9.2.

When tax rate is at 0%, logically there will be zero tax revenue. When the tax rate is at 100%, the Government receives every cent that a person earns. The incentive to work is zero, and tax revenue is again zero. Production activities would still take place when tax rate is at 100%, but transactions would go underground and people would resort to underground trading in order to evade taxation.

At point A, the tax rate is still relatively high. When choosing between leisure and work, people would choose to work less and enjoy more hours of leisure. In addition, the incentive to evade taxes is high resulting in a decrease in officially reported economic activities. On the other hand, the tax rate at point B is substantially lower while generating the same amount of tax revenue. The incentive to work is high at point B and people might find that the cost of tax evasion (paying accountants to identify tax loopholes; not purchasing big-ticket items for fear of scrutiny from the tax authority) outweighs the cost of paying taxes. The lowering of the tax rate at point A and increasing tax rate at point B will both result in higher tax revenue.

Point C is the optimal point. It is the magic tax rate that maximises both tax revenue and production. It is a variable that varies from country to

Table 9.6

Tax Revenue as a Percentage of GDP, 2006

	2006
Philippines	16
Thailand	18
Singapore	13
United Kingdom	29
France	23
Netherlands	24

Source: World Bank, *WDI Online*, 1 Oct. 2008,
http://publications.worldbank.org/WDI/.

country, during wartime and peacetime. A country that values social security and a country that is facing aggression will have higher tolerance for tax.

Using tax revenue as a percentage of GDP as a proxy for tax burden, and 25% as a yardstick, Table 9.6 compares the tax burden in the Southeast Asian countries with some of the developed nations. It could tentatively be concluded that the tax burden in most of Southeast Asian countries are well below the optimal point and increasing tax rates might generate higher tax revenue. However, countries must also bear in mind the global competition for capital. A lesser-taxed country, particularly with respect to direct taxes, is generally favoured when compared to a country with higher tax rates. Besides, the Southeast Asian economies are generally at a very much lower level of per capita income than their developed counterparts. Their taxable capacity too is likely to be more limited.

Singapore, however, has drastically cut down direct income taxes in order to compete with Hong Kong for FDI and for talents. Malaysia too has taken the first step in this direction. But those who cut income taxes will have to find other alternative tax revenues or trim unnecessary expenditure or both.

Nothing Is Even Better

It has just been shown that a lowering of tax rates could result in higher tax revenue. In some instances, a zero specific tax rate can be desirable even in the eyes of the Government. One example is death duties. The chief concern in these instances would no longer be tax revenue, but rather to encourage activities that are perceived to be beneficial to the economy or society to take place. In the case of death duties, it is competition for the dead man's money. In an increasingly globalised economy, a country with high death duties may encounter capital-outflow problems, as rich people migrate or move their assets overseas with the intention of avoiding death duties. Besides, there is also the problem of double taxing the wealth owners: income tax as they earn their income and death duties for the remaining unspent income. Malaysia is probably the first country in Southeast Asia that has abolished death duty. Singapore in early 2008 also finally announced this abolition.

Another example where a low tax rate can benefit the society as a whole is royalties on intellectual products. The tax rates of royalties in the ASEAN-5 lie within the range of 0 to 10% substantially lower than the individual taxes rates. The argument for lower royalties is to encourage more writers and artistes to engage in intellectual activities in the country and to encourage foreign talents to do likewise by positioning themselves in the country concerned. If lower royalties encourage more local and foreign writers/artistes to publish/produce their work in the country, tax revenue may in fact go up, as intellectual activities increase.

Bigger Is Not Necessarily Better

This chapter has repeatedly discussed the importance of government investment in physical and social infrastructure projects especially during the early stages of development. However, it must be emphasised at this point that a large and likely to be incompetent Government is not being encouraged, but rather, a small, efficient, and development-oriented Government. A big and cumbersome Government plagued by corruption and inefficiency would do more harm to a country than a small Government that may not afford to invest enough but could uphold the rules of law and justice in a country. Studies have shown that Governments are more efficient, if they are meritocratic in recruitment and promotion, and if compensation is not grossly inferior to the counterparts in the private sector.

Some Governments in Southeast Asia have attempted to reduce the size of the Government through the establishment of publicly listed

Government-linked companies. These companies are run on a completely private basis. But since the Government is a substantial owner of the shares, benefits, in the form of profits, go to the Government and therefore to the people. A good example is the Singapore Airlines (SIA) in Singapore. However, if the companies are not well run or not run on a commercial basis, they can be a great drag on the Government and the economy.

Complete privatisation of state enterprises is another way to reduce the size of Government, but there are several potential pitfalls. For one, private ownership does not automatically bring about an efficiently run enterprise. In addition, a state's interest and that of an individual may not coincide. Small economies also have to be wary of the situation where wealth and control of previous national enterprises are in the hands of a few persons. The problems are compounded if these few persons are foreigners. Extreme income inequality could result from the sale of these national enterprises and cronyism could manifest itself under these conditions. Inequality of opportunities for its citizens could also be a serious problem. Indonesia under President Suharto provided a good example that private ownership is not always the best solution. Good and competent Government is the best solution and it is not easy to have good and competent government. Besides, if high growth rates are to be sustained, must it follow that the sustainability of growth and competent government must also be a sine quo non?

Tax Reforms

Fiscal measures can be used to increase domestic savings by restricting the growth of private consumption. This is so because private consumption accounts for a considerably larger proportion of national income than investment. A relatively small reduction in its rate of growth can have a significant impact on the rates of growth of voluntary savings and investment. Taxation measures, in particular, affect consumption through their influence on the purchasing power of private disposable incomes. Direct taxes reduce the amount of private disposable income while indirect taxes affect purchasing power by raising the prices of goods and services on which taxes are imposed. Taxation, on the one hand, restrains the growth of private consumption in order to increase the volume of resources available for investment purposes, and on the other hand, transfers resources from the private to the public sector. All things being equal, the larger the ratio of taxation to GNI, the higher will be the share of resources available to Governments to meet their current and capital expenditures. Compared to the industrial countries, the ratio of tax revenue to GDP for the Southeast Asian countries is relatively low. Among the ASEAN-5, Malaysia has the highest ratio (22%) and Singapore the lowest (13%).

Since the early 1950s, the Governments of newly independent countries in various parts of the world felt the need to guide economic development of their economies. They made use of fiscal incentives and disincentives in various sectors of economic activity to promote or discourage certain types of investment. Governments also invested heavily in physical and social infrastructure, industry, agricultural research, extension services, energy and a wide variety of other areas. In the course of time, these investments and increasing complementary government current expenditures brought forth the challenge of resource mobilisation. Most Governments respond by taking steps in recent years to increase tax collection efforts and implementing fairly far-reaching tax reforms. Table 9.7 shows the tax rates for various Southeast Asian countries in 2008.

Most Governments tend to undertake tax reforms when the tax system's revenue productivity is falling or when it becomes inadequate for the mounting government current and capital expenditures. While there are bound to be differences in regard to the scope and depth of tax reforms across countries, the experience of tax reforms in various countries indicates the following guideposts.

Firstly, the tax base should be as broad as possible. This helps to bring a large part of the economy under the tax net, and thus allows the average tax rate to be lowered. If tax collection also improves, tax revenue would automatically increase as various sectors expand. Moreover, the elasticity of a broad-based tax system would be greater, implying that tax revenue could be significantly increased with a relatively small upward adjustment in the tax rate.

Secondly, the tax mix is important: not all taxes should be direct or only indirect taxes. For most Southeast Asian economies desiring to compete internationally, the tax system should move to a stage where indirect taxes (other than export and import duties) provide a significant portion of total revenue. Several key points should be taken into account when imposing

Table 9.7

Tax Rates, Selective Countries 2008

	Malaysia	Indonesia	Philippines	Singapore	Thailand	Vietnam
Corporate Taxes						
— Resident	26	10–30	10–35	18	30	28–50
— Non-Resident	26	10–30	35	18	30	28–50
Individual Taxes						
— Resident	0–28	5–35	5–32	4–22	10–37	0–40
— Non-Resident	28	5–35	5–32	20	10–37	25
Withholding Taxes						
— Interest	0 or 15	15	15	Nil	15	10
— Dividend	Nil	10 or 20	25–35	Nil	10	5–10
— Royalties	0–10	10	10	Nil	10	10
VAT/Sales Taxes	n.a.	0–10	12	7	7	0–10

Source: Economist Intelligence Unit, *Country Commerce Reports*; 2008, Price Waterhouse Coopers, PWC online, http://www.taxsummaries.pwc.com.

Note: Due to the complexities of the tax structure, this table only attempts to give a general overview of the tax rates.

n.a.: The Malaysian government announced in the 2006 Budget speech that the GST tax will be implemented in Malaysia from 1 January 2007. However, the implementation date was later postponed to a date which has yet to be announced.

indirect taxes: (a) sales or value-added taxes are preferable; (b) a single rate of taxation minimises price distortions; (c) all material inputs should be tax free; (d) some taxes can be at rather high rates to discourage consumption, for examples alcohol and tobacco; (e) for very poor countries, luxury goods too may be taxed relatively heavily.[1]

Thirdly, concession, rebates and exemptions should be minimised, if they cannot be entirely eliminated.

Lastly, globalisation has provided additional challenges to the government administration in implementing tax reforms. To encourage and retain foreign investment and skilled labour, it is important to maintain an overall low tax burden. However, this may drain the Government of fiscal revenue to build adequate economic and social infrastructure to facilitate future economic growth. On another note, globalisation precipitates rising income inequalities both within each ASEAN nation and across the Southeast Asian region. Fiscal measures to strike a fine balance between those who do not gain from globalisation and those who are actively involved in the globalisation process is an important issue that all Governments need to manage with care (Asher, 2002).

Export Duties

Export duties on principal export commodities had been a very important source of government revenue in Southeast Asia. It is conceivable that as early as the 1860s, at the beginning of the tin export boom in Malaya, Malay chiefs had positioned their men at river mouths to collect tin export duties. In the post-war period, between 1946 to 1962, export duties remained an important but wildly fluctuating component of Malayan government tax revenue, ranging between 19% to 43%, with rubber and tin contributing to more than 90% of total export tax revenue every year (Lim, 1967: 266–268). Until today, although the importance of export duties as a component of

---

[1]It is true that the argument for treating a dollar as a dollar to whomsoever it goes in specific policies, leaving the pursuit of equality to the general tax/transfer system by Ng (1984) may cast doubts on the efficiency of taxing luxury goods as such. However, Ng (1987) himself also argues that goods with diamond effects (goods valued for their values) should be highly taxed simply on efficiency grounds. Since many luxury goods have high degrees of diamond effects, our proposed higher taxes on luxury goods may be efficient after all.

total tax revenue has declined substantially, Malaysia still levies export duties on rubber and palm oil, and Thailand levies export duties on rice. Indonesia too has export duties on palm oil exports.

Theoretically, export taxes imposed on a monopolist supplier, serves to extract consumer surplus. But, in reality, most products have substitutes. With the advancement of science and technology, even primary products such as natural rubber, tin, rice and palm oil are not precluded from the availability of substitute products. In other instances, the presence of monopoly power is counterbalanced by monopsonies. In Southeast Asia, export duties on raw materials (eg. unprocessed logs) have been used with mixed success to promote industrialisation. Export duties in the form of *ad valorem* tax have also been used as anti-inflationary and stabilisation devices when commodity prices skyrocket. Against these arguments for export duties, there are several points of contention against export duties. Firstly, export duties undermine the competitiveness of the commodities in the world market. Secondly, export duties levied on agriculture products but not manufactures create distortion that favours manufacturing exports. Last but not least, tax rates of commodity exports are usually variable with the prices of the commodities, and not related to the "ability to pay". Thus, export taxes could bring about real hardship to smallholders.

In the early days when the newly independent Governments in Southeast Asia were confronted with mounting development expenditure needs but had relatively few sources of tax revenue, export duties were justifiable. However, as the ASEAN nations develop large industrial bases, income taxes, which have a better correlation to the ability to pay, should be favoured over export duties. An exception to this would be the export duty on irreplaceable assets, such as petroleum and natural gas. But this can be more efficiently collected through excise duty and royalties than through the export mechanism.

Indirect Taxes — Goods and Services Tax

Most of the Southeast Asian Governments rely heavily on the collection of income tax to generate significant tax revenue. As compared to broad-based indirect taxation, direct taxation is easier to implement, and the successful collection of income taxes from a relatively small number of big corporations and rich individuals generate substantial tax revenue. However, excessive direct taxation nowadays is a problem, if the intention of the Government is to attract foreign investment and foreign talents. Direct taxation also has a detrimental effort on savings and enterprise. As the competition for foreign direct investments heated up amongst the Southeast Asian countries, corporate tax rates in these countries started to come under downward pressure. The corporate tax rate in Singapore was at 40% in 1986 and before. Gradual reduction since 1987 saw the corporate tax rate in Singapore reducing to 18% for the Year of Assessment 2008. Malaysia has also followed suit, with her corporate tax rate declining to 26% in the latest revision. In addition, globalisation together with freer movement of labour has implied that high income tax rates could lead to an outflow of talented and skilled workers.

The reduction in income tax revenue has to be compensated by an increase in other revenue, and one obvious choice is domestic indirect taxation on goods and services. There are many arguments against goods and services taxes. One of which is the regressive nature of goods and services taxes as compared to income taxes. While progressive income tax ensures people who earn more pay a higher tax rate, and only profit-making companies pay corporate tax, goods and services tax is levied on the whole population. Everybody pays the same tax rate, regardless of whether he is rich or poor, regardless of ability to pay.

However, there are some attractive features of goods and services tax. It taxes consumption and not production; it does not "penalise" a person for working hard and engaging in higher value-added activity, and thus earning a higher income. Secondly, as goods and services tax is broad-based, tax revenue can be substantially increased through a small percentage point increase in tax rate.

Indonesia, the Philippines, Thailand, Singapore and Vietnam have all introduced Value-added Tax (VAT) or Goods and Services Tax (GST) in the 1980s and 1990s. Exemptions on basic necessities and rebates are sometimes given in attempts to minimise the inequity effects of the taxes. However , when GST is first introduced, it can be extremely unpopular. Much care is needed to have a smooth and acceptable introduction. The introductory rate should be as low as possible, say, at 2% only.

Electronic Filing of Tax Returns

With the advent of the internet and the advantages associated with its use, a few Southeast Asian countries have implemented electronic filing of tax returns. In the long run, there will be substantial reduction in administrative costs when tax returns and payments are electronically submitted. Taxpayers in the Philippines were encouraged to file and pay their taxes via the internet as part of the administrative reforms in 2002 to improve tax collection. Thailand had set a target to electronically file all types of tax returns by end of 2003. To meet this objective, electronic filing of VAT was introduced in April 2001 and personal income tax in January 2003. In Singapore, as much as 90% of personal income tax returns were filed electronically in 2007, partially a result of incentives provided by the Inland Revenue Authority of Singapore to encourage e-filing as a beneficial alternative for submitting tax returns.

Oil Subsidy

Some Southeast Asian countries are fossil oil exporters. To ensure that the people benefit from oil production, they keep the domestic prices well below international level. Lately when international prices skyrocketed, they found that their subsidy burdens became unbearable. In part, low domestic prices of oil discourage oil exploration. It promotes oil consumption and car population explosion. Besides, the need to improve public transport becomes less pressing. Budget deficits too soon become very burdensome when imports of oil become necessary. Reduction of subsidy is very unpopular, for what has been given is difficult to be taken back. At any rate, oil consumption subsidy has contributed to fiscal problems like fiscal deficits. Reforming the subsidy scheme is underway in Southeast Asia. The move is highly unpopular and unacceptable, especially if the removal of the subsidy is high, for it can create hardship for the poor and lower-income groups. This is particularly so if the removal also results in the raising of other related prices such as electricity prices and bus fares. The timing of the removal becomes of utmost importance.

Expenditure Control Options

For ASEAN, while it is important to scout around for other suitable taxes to finance government expenditure, it appears to be much more important to reduce government unproductive spending. Earlier we have noted with dismay (shown in Table 9.5) that a large part of government spending in Southeast Asia appears to be on "General Public Services", not on education, health, economic services and infrastructural development. There is tremendous potential for the axing of this explosive item which accounted for 74% of the Indonesian Budget, for instance, before any thinking of raising any tax or the introduction of any new tax be contemplated. The task ahead is very challenging indeed. Trimming of such a huge State expenditure to balance the budget, however, can immediately increase the unemployment rate through retrenchment. This problem has to be prudently handled.

Key Points

1. Southeast Asian countries have generally shown budget deficits, making the balancing of the budget an important anxiety of the government.
2. Due to the re-classification of 'General Public Services' by the IMF, the government expenditure on this particular item has risen. General Public Services now include public debt transactions, i.e., interest payments and outlays for underwriting and floating government loans, as well as transfers between different levels of government.
3. All the Southeast Asian countries rely heavily on tax revenue to finance its expenditure. The proportion can vary from a low of 57% for Myanmar and a high of 95% for Vietnam.
4. Of the tax revenue, by far the most important source is that on income; company income and individual income. Indirect taxation, such as goods and services tax, is gaining importance as a source of government revenue.
5. Taxes on international trade have shown a declining trend in Southeast Asia consequent on the desire to have Free Trade Agreement within ASEAN and outside the region.
6. Non-tax revenue is also an important source of government finance, varying from a low of 6% in Vietnam to a high of 44% in Myanmar. The average is 23%.
7. Public sector fixed capital formation as a part of overall government expenditure is much higher in every country in Southeast Asia

when compared to West European countries. The higher proportion country-wise in Southeast Asia appears to be correlated with the higher growth rate. There is some validity in this seemingly causal factor even when comparison is made over time in the same country.

8. The proportion of the government budget devoted to education appears to have declined considerably in countries like Indonesia, Malaysia and the Philippines.

9. Deficit financing through the printing of money has often resulted in domestic inflation and exchange rate depreciation. Southeast Asian countries facing budget constraints could consider the option of "selling" of public assets. The Hong Kong and the Singapore Governments have been selling "the right to develop state land for stipulated uses" to the private sector and have generated substantial government revenue over the years.

10. A Government could increase its tax revenue by lowering tax rate if the tax rate is above the optimal tax rate suggested by the Laffer Curve. Using tax revenue as a percentage of GDP as a proxy for tax burden, and 25% as a yardstick, it could be concluded that the tax burden in all the Southeast Asian countries are below the optimal point.

11. Most Southeast Asian countries have undertaken tax reforms in the last twenty years. The experience of tax reforms in various countries indicates that tax base should be as broad as possible with consumption taxes providing an important part of the revenue, and concessions, rebates and exemptions should be minimised. The shift away from very heavy reliance on direct taxes is likely to contribute to the international competitiveness of the Southeast Asian economies.

12. One important option to consider in Southeast Asia before raising taxes further is to drastically cut down on unnecessary and unproductive bureaucratic expenditure.

Suggested Discussion Topics

9.1 The book claims that "The ability of a Government to generate revenue to finance deserved expenditure is of utmost importance for the effective running of the Government". Do you agree? Do you think that the prudent management of public expenditure is also important in public finance? Discuss.

9.2 The government development expenditures of Southeast Asian countries are very much higher as percentages of total government expenditure when comparable with Western European countries. Why is it so? Does it mean that Southeast Asia should follow the West European model of having very low government development expenditure?

9.3 Evaluate the sale of State assets as a way of financing government expenditure in Southeast Asia. Like all sources of revenue, what are the limits to this modus operandi?

9.4 Do you think export taxes and death duties should be abolished in Southeast Asia? Discuss.

References

ASHER, Mukul G. and David G. Newman and Thomas P. Snyder (eds.), 2002, *Public Policy in Asia: Implications for Business and Government*. Westport, Connecticut, Quorum Books.

Economic Intelligence Unit, 2008, *Country Commerce Report*, various issues, http://www.eiu.com.

LIM, Chong Yah, 1967, *Economic Development of Modern Malaya*, Kuala Lumpur: Oxford University Press, Chapter 9: Taxation.

MUSGRAVE, Richard A. and Peggy B. MUSGRAVE, 1984, *Public Finance Theory and Practice*, New York: McGraw-Hill Book Company, 4th Edition.

NG, Yew-Kwang, 1984, "Quasi-pareto social improvements", *The American Economic Review*, Vol. 74(5), 1033–1050.

NG, Yew-Kwang, 1987, "Diamonds are a government's best friend: Burden-free taxes on goods valued for their values", *The American Economic Review*, Vol. 77(1), 186–191.

TANZI, Vito, 1986, "Economic development and tax structure", in SHOME, Parathasarati (ed.), *Fiscal Issues in Southeast Asia: Comparative Studies of Selected Economies*, Singapore: Oxford University Press, 9–24.

World Bank, 1997, *World Development Report 1997: The State in a Changing World*, New York: Oxford University Press.

Further Readings

ASHER, Mukul G., 1989, *Fiscal Systems and Practices in ASEAN: Trends, Impact and Evaluation*, Singapore ASEAN Economic Research Unit, ISEAS.

ASHER, Mukul G. *et al.*, 1992, *Fiscal Incentives and Economic Management in Indonesia, Malaysia and Singapore*, Singapore: Asian-Pacific Tax and Investment Research Centre.

ASHER, Mukul G. and Amina Tyabji (eds.), 1996, *Fiscal System of Singapore: Trends, Issues and Future Directions*, Singapore: Centre for Advanced Studies, NUS.

BOOTH, Anne, 1997, *Indonesian Economy in the Nineteenth and Twentieth Centuries: A History of Missed Opportunities*, Basingstoke: Macmillan.

LIM, Chong Yah, 1997, "The low-income trap: theory and evidence", *Accounting and Business Review*, Vol. 4(1).

MANASAN, Rosario G., 1990, *A Review of Fiscal Policy Reforms in the ASEAN Countries in the 1980s*, Manila: Philippines Institute for Development Studies, No. 90–14.

SHOME, Parthasarathi (ed.), 1986, *Fiscal Issues in Southeast Asia: Comparative Studies of Selected Economies*, Singapore: Oxford University Press.

STIGLITZ, Joseph E., 2000, *Economics of Public Sector*, New York: W. W. Norton.

Chapter 10

Financial Policy

"Money is too important to be left to central bankers."

Milton Friedman

Objectives

✓ Highlight the various stages of financial development.
✓ Show the importance of good money and credit supply management.
✓ Illustrate how technology affects innovations in the banking sector.
✓ Point out some of the salient features of banking development.
✓ Describe some pre- and post-crisis banking sector reforms undertaken.

Introduction

The financial system plays a critical role in the development of a country's economy. First, it provides for the use of money as a medium of exchange, a unit of account and a store of value. The use of money as a medium of exchange lowers the cost of transactions by eliminating the high search and information costs associated with barter. Money enhances transactions as there is no need for 'double coincidence of wants'. With money as a standard unit of account, decision-making is expedited. No wonder money is considered as one of mankind's most important early inventions.

The role of banks in economic development is that of an intermediary between savers and investors. Funds from surplus units are channelled to deficit units. This function is shared with a number of other financial institutions, including finance companies, savings and loan associations and insurance companies. In many parts of Southeast Asia, particularly in Singapore and Malaysia, forced domestic savings are also a significant source of funds. The presence of a sound banking system permits the mobilisation of scarce resources and their subsequent efficient allocation. In all Southeast Asian countries, the banking system dominates the financial sector, although in the better developed market-oriented economies such as Malaysia, Singapore and Thailand, direct financing is increasingly being utilised. The increase in the level of financial instrument utilisation relative to real output is referred to as financial deepening.

At the core of the financial system lies the central bank (known as monetary authority in Singapore). Besides supervising and regulating the financial sector, the central bank influences economic growth through the design and implementation of monetary policies. The central bank regulates the money supply using various common instruments such as open market operations, reserve requirements, discount windows and selective credit controls. In developing countries, the central banks may take on the additional role of actively developing the financial sector.

In the 1970s, some Southeast Asian countries started liberalising their financial sector. Interest rates in these countries were no longer determined by the Government or a banking cartel. Credit controls were also eradicated to various degrees. Selective liberalisation of the capital accounts was also on the agenda. Notwithstanding the liberalisation, the financial sectors in Southeast Asian countries still had a strong government presence. Foreign ownership of banks was still highly regulated. In 1997–1998, the Asian financial crisis swept across Southeast Asia damaging some of the promising economies in the region. Financial liberalisation was listed as one of the many contributory factors of the crisis. This led Governments of the region to take diverse stances towards financial reforms. Some countries continued to liberalise their financial sectors, some chose to close their capital accounts temporarily, while some others had no choice but to further open up.

Another interesting development is how technology affects the banking industry. Three innovations are highlighted in this chapter. First, more and more banking services are being automated. Second, the payment system is revolutionised. Many countries in Southeast Asia are moving towards a cashless society. The use of the internet to conduct banking transactions online and to access banking products and services are also increasingly gaining acceptance.

Financial Development

Money is uniquely risk- and default-free for short-term transactions. The cost of buying and selling money for real goods is low, both for the owner of cash balances and for the banking system. Since creditors often know little or nothing about the repayment capability of potential debtors in developing countries, financial instruments other than money cannot easily be marketed. Thus, in early stages of economic development when the financial system is still in its rudimentary stage, money as a means of payment and its sanction by the state greatly enhances its value as an instrument of private capital accumulation. If M1 is defined as narrow money constituting currency and coins in active circulation plus demand deposits, then the ratio of M1 to GNI will be higher in the initial stages of economic development. With economic progress, credit markets become better organised, and financial assets other than those classified under M1 are created. In the various phases of economic development, the structure of assets and liabilities of banks changes, causing a rising trend in the M2/GNI ratio, where M2 includes M1 and savings and fixed deposits. Table 10.1 shows the level of monetisation and its relation to economic development. Cambodia has one of the lowest M2 per capita and GNI per capita of US$120 and US$490 respectively. On the other extreme, Singapore with the highest GNI per capita also has the highest M2 per capita.

Despite the benefits associated with monetisation, in practice, they are seldom realised fully in the developing countries since barter still prevails in some parts. In the larger ASEAN countries such as Indonesia, the Philippines, and Thailand, monetisation is somewhat incomplete in the rural sector where the bulk of the population still live. Barter is even more predominant in the rural areas in the Indochinese countries.

The next phase of financial development sees an increase in the utilisation of banking services. The degree of financial intermediation in any

Table 10.1

Levels of Monetisation and Economic Development, 2006

	Per Capita M2		Per Capita GNI	
	US$	Index with Singapore as 100	US$	Index with Singapore as 100
Myanmar	43*	0.1	n.a.	n.a.
Cambodia	120	0.3	490	1.7
Laos	125	0.3	500	1.7
Vietnam	625	1.7	700	2.4
Indonesia	676	1.8	1,420	4.9
Philippines	773	2.1	1,390	4.8
Thailand	3,601	9.8	3,050	10.6
Malaysia	7,532	20.0	5,620	19.6
Singapore	36,670	100.0	28,730	100.0

Source: World Bank, *WDI Online*, 20 Oct. 2008, http://publications.worldbank.org/WDI/.
*Denotes 2005 figure.

country can be gauged by the ratio of deposit money to GDP. The ratio is expected to be low in less developed countries and high in developed ones (see Table 10.2).

It would be interesting to point out that in 1965 among the ASEAN-5 countries, Indonesia had the lowest deposits to GDP ratio. This could be attributed to the hyperinflation in the country in the 1960s, relatively low rate of returns arising from imposition of interest ceilings and the inclination of many Indonesian individuals and businesses to hold deposits abroad, especially in Singapore. The absence of any retractions on transferring funds in and out of both Indonesia and Singapore and the considerable amount of commerce between the two countries had resulted in the very close link between the two financial systems. Because of the strength and stability of the Singapore's currency, in contrast with continuing inflation, spate of devaluation and negative real interest rates in Indonesia, it was understandable why so many Indonesians avail themselves of Singapore's financial services then.

The credit market in LDCs is dichotomised into formal and informal sub-sectors. The formal sub-sector usually consists of the commercial banks, the

Table 10.2

Savings and Time Deposits as a Percentage of
GDP, 2006

Cambodia	6
Laos	6
Indonesia	10
Philippines	13
Myanmar	14
Thailand	86
Malaysia	89
Singapore	94

Source: World Bank, *WDI Online*, 20 Oct. 2008,
http://publications.worldbank.org/WDI/
and EIU, Economist Intelligence Unit
(http://www.eiu.com).

co-operatives, the insurance companies and other financial institutions such as development banks, agricultural and industrial finance corporations. On the other hand, the informal sub-sector chiefly consists of moneylenders, indigenous bankers, pawnbrokers, traders, rotating savings and credit associations (ROSCA), and wealthy landowners. Unlike the formal sub-sector, there is no division of labour in the informal sub-sector. The presence of the informal sub-sector is most conspicuous in countries with an underdeveloped formal credit market. Furthermore, with the bulk of the population still engaging primarily in subsistence farming, countries with a large agricultural sector provide a fertile ground for the growth of the informal sub-sector. In a study by Ng Beoy Kui, it was shown that funds from the informal sub-sector were an important source of credit to the rural areas in the 1970s. For example, in Malaysia, informal sources accounted for 75% of the credit in the rural sector while in Thailand, it was 53% and the Philippines, 68% (Ng, 1985). As these countries further developed, the role played by the informal sub-sector as a financial intermediary diminishes. Table 10.3 shows the amount of domestic credit provided by the banking sector. Over the years, with the exception of Myanmar and Indonesia, the amount of credit provided by the formal sector has increased. This indicates the development of the formal credit market. Further, transitional economies

Table 10.3

Domestic Credit Provided by the Banking Sector (% of GDP), 1990 and 2006

	1990	2006
Laos	5.1	7
Cambodia	n.a.	9
Myanmar	32.8	28*
Indonesia	45.5	42
Philippines	26.9	49
Singapore	75.6	73
Vietnam	n.a.	75
Thailand	91.1	101
Malaysia	75.7	119

Source: World Bank, *WDI Online*, 20 Oct. 2008, http://publications.worldbank.org/WDI/. *Denotes 2005 figure.

such as Cambodia and Laos have a lower percentage of credit provided by the banking sector. This could signify the presence of a large informal credit market. On the other hand, Singapore, Malaysia and Thailand have a significant portion of credit provided by the banking sector. The slightly lower percentage seen in the case of Singapore could be due to the raising of funds from other sources such as the equity market and to a lesser extent the bond market.

Many Southeast Asian economies still rely heavily on indirect financing as the major source of funds. In Malaysia and Singapore, the amount of funds raised through direct financing as a percentage of GDP is comparatively higher than the other countries in the ASEAN-5. This is nothing peculiar as in all economies, it is the banking system that develops first. As economies develop, more and more funds are raised through the money and capital markets. Seiichi Masuyama attributes this pattern of financial development to information asymmetry (Masuyama, Vandenbrink and Chia, 1999). In the initial stages of economic development, lenders possess relatively less information than their counterparts in the more advanced stages of economic development than borrowers. Given this asymmetry of information, banks have the capability and resources to process the necessary

Table 10.4

Market Capitalisation of Listed Companies in ASEAN-5, 2006

	US$ Million	As a Percentage of GDP
Indonesia	138,886	38
Philippines	68,382	58
Thailand	141,093	68
Malaysia	235,356	156
Singapore	276,329	209

Source: World Bank, *WDI Online*, 20 Oct. 2008, http://publications.
   worldbank.org/WDI/.

information and are in a better position to diversify the risk. As economies develop, transparency improves due to better disclosure policies. And with the emergence of large corporations, direct financing is utilised more often. Table 10.4 also shows the level of financial deepening in the ASEAN-5 countries.

Monetary Policy

The main function of a central bank is to ensure the country's economy is able to grow at a sustainable rate with reasonable price stability. This is achieved through the manipulation of the money supply and interest rates in the economy using various instruments. A major consideration of the central bank when designing and implementing monetary policies is to control inflation. Although an increase in money supply is necessary as an economy develops, excessive increases will lead to high inflation.

The link between money supply and inflation is demonstrated by the Equation of Exchange, which is as follows:

$$MV \equiv Py$$

In the above equation, M is the quantity of money, V is the income velocity of money, which measures the number of times the average dollar is used in transactions involving current output, P is the price index for currently produced goods, and y is the level of current output. This identity postulates that price level varies directly with the quantity of money in circulation, directly with the velocity of money in circulation, and inversely with the volume of trade done by it.

Assuming that output is supply-determined, and that money velocity is fixed in the short run, we have:

$$M\bar{V} = P\bar{y}$$

$$\Rightarrow P = \frac{\bar{V}}{\bar{y}}M$$

Take proportionate change, the equation becomes:

$$\pi = \dot{m} - \dot{y} + \dot{v}$$

where π: inflation rate

$\dot{m}$: growth rate of money supply

$\dot{y}$: real GDP growth rate

$\dot{v}$: change in velocity of money.

As the economy is on a steady state ($\dot{y} = 0$), velocity of money will remain constant. The above equation implies that it is the quantity of money that determines inflation rate in an economy in the long run. A simplified version of this relationship is observed in the ASEAN member countries. Table 10.5 shows that Cambodia, Vietnam, Myanmar and Laos have higher M2 growth than the other more market-oriented economies in ASEAN, thus resulting in higher inflation rates.

To the extent that the Central Banks have control over the inflation rates, the ASEAN-3 Central Banks, namely Singapore, Malaysia and Thailand have done a good job in every decade since the 1960s, except Thailand in the 1970s, as can be seen in Table 10.6. Indonesia recovered from a very high inflation rate of 210.6% per annum in the 1960s to a much less infla-tionary rate throughout the decades since the 1960s. The Philippines, how-ever, deteriorated from a comfortable position in the 1960s. Myanmar shows increasing inflationary pressures since the 1960s, reaching a height of nearly 25% per annum during the 1991–2000 period and from 2001 to 2006. While good control over the growth rate of money supply has helped to preserve the internal value of money in the ASEAN-5, the same, however, cannot be said for the external value of money. The erosion of the external value of

Table 10.5

Average Annual Growth in Money Supply (M2) and
CPI (%), 1990–2006

	M2	CPI
Singapore	10.2	3.7
Thailand	11.6	4.7
Malaysia	12.2	6.9
Philippines	15.7	10.3
Indonesia	21.2	9.4
Cambodia[a]	26.8	37.2
Vietnam[a]	27	19.3
Myanmar[b]	32.6	20.9
Laos	38.1	28.0

Source: Derived using figures from World Bank, *WDI Online*, 20 Oct. 2008,
  http://publications.worldbank.org/WDI/.
  a: Values are obtained from a shorter time series (1994–2006).
  b: Values are obtained from a shorter time series (1990–2005).

Table 10.6

Average Annual Growth Rate of CPI (%), 1961–2006

	1961–1970	1971–1980	1981–1990	1991–2000	2001–2006
Singapore	1.1	6.7	2.3	1.6	0.8
Malaysia	0.9	6.0	3.2	3.6	2.2
Thailand	2.3	10.0	4.4	4.6	3.0
Philippines	5.7	14.9	13.7	8.2	5.5
Indonesia	210.6	17.5	8.6	14.1	10.7
Myanmar	3.3	11.3	11.8	25.0	24.8
Laos	n.a.	n.a.	n.a.	34.1	10.5
Brunei	n.a.	n.a.	2.8	2.1	0.2
Cambodia	n.a.	n.a.	n.a.	38.0	3.2
Vietnam	n.a.	n.a.	191.2	13.4	5.0

Source: Computed using figures from World Bank, *World Development Indicators*. Online and
  ADB, Asian Development Bank, *Asian Development Outlook* (various issues).

ASEAN currencies during the East Asian financial crisis (1997–1998) will be appraised in Chapter 12: The Asian Financial Crisis.

There are basically two types of inflation, domestically generated inflation and world (imported) inflation. Domestically generated inflation can be due to an increase in domestic credit from the banking system. Increase in domestic credit can generally be traced to government budgetary deficits, where the deficits must either be financed through borrowing or direct money creation. On the other hand, world inflation originates from a monetary expansion abroad. In this case, prices of internationally traded goods rise relative to prices of domestic non-traded goods. Inflation will be then imported to countries that have a fixed exchange rate regime and to countries with a weak currency. A variety of contractionary monetary policies are available to control inflation. The central bank can conduct open-market operations, increase the reserve requirements of commercial banks, or increase the discount rates. Unlike developed countries, open-market operation is rarely used in Southeast Asian countries due to the absence of a developed government debt market. Another difficulty faced by the open economies of Southeast Asia, especially Singapore, in the implementation of monetary policies, is that it is difficult for domestic targeting of interest rates to be independent of foreign interest rates (and exchange rate expectations). The demand and supply of money cannot be fully influenced by the domestic central banks since they have to depend on external forces such as the present and expected levels of external interest rates, and exchange rates. Therefore, central banks have to resort to adopting exchange rate policy and setting targets either for the exchange rate or the amount of foreign reserves.

Banking Innovations

The impact of automation, technology and internet on the banking industry is enormous. First, automation affects the way we conduct our banking transactions. The introduction of ATMs, for instance, not only brings greater convenience to the bank customers, but also improves productivity in the banking sector. The main benefit of automation is that customers enjoy longer banking hours. Furthermore, over the years, more and more services are made available on these machines. Besides performing the usual functions of cash withdrawals and cheque book request, ATMs nowadays are capable of transferring funds, applying and paying for shares and Initial Public Offerings (IPOs), bidding for Certificate of Entitlements (in Singapore), just to name a few. The rapid automation process can be seen from the exponential growth in the number of ATMs in Singapore. In 1985, there were only 283 ATMs but by 2004, there were 1,609 ATMs. In other Southeast Asian countries, notably Malaysia, Thailand, Indonesia and the Philippines, the utilisation of ATMs is also very ubiquitous.

Technology has also revolutionised the payment and settlement system. There is a clear indication that some Southeast Asian countries are moving towards a cashless society. In Singapore, consumers have the option to pay for their purchases electronically. It is commonly known as Electronic Fund Transfer at Point of Sale (EFTPOS). Like ATMS, the benefit this system offers is convenience. Shoppers no longer need to carry with them large amounts of cash. Furthermore, the use of EFTPOS is safer for both consumers and retailers. The payment system is further enhanced with the introduction of cash card. The card is no different from other plastic cards except it has features of a smart card and it allows consumers to make low value payments. The greatest difference between cash card and other payment cards is that cash card requires no personal identification. Different forms of cash card exist in Southeast Asian countries.

In a speech by Mr. Koh Yong Guan, the then Managing Director of Monetary Authority of Singapore (MAS), at the 26th Annual Dinner of the Association of Banks in Singapore, he pointed out that internet technology is changing the way banks compete. First, the internet has reduced the cost of providing banking services. The cost per transaction on the internet has been estimated at one cent, compared to 27 cents for ATM transactions and more than a dollar for a branch transaction. Second, the internet has the potential to make banking borderless. A customer can access a website anywhere in the world. Third, the traditional relationship between banks and their customers is being transformed. Major international banks are leveraging aggressively on technology to build extensive databases on their customers. Through data warehousing and mining, more and more banks can better access customers' needs and thus offer relevant products and services at various stages of a customer's life cycle. Instead of viewing retail customers as just cheap sources of funding, the more progressive banks are seeing them as purchasers of products and services that yield fee income.

However, in most of the Southeast Asian countries, internet banking has yet to take off. Several reasons can be identified. Security of internet banking is still a major concern among bank customers. The higher user fees and costs impede the widespread use of internet in developing countries. Table 10.7 shows the internet penetration rates in the Southeast Asian countries. Furthermore, after badly savaged by the Asian financial crisis, countries in the region have their priority in handling the non-performing loans and the re-capitalisation of the banks; bringing their business to the virtual world can take a back seat in the meantime.

Notwithstanding the need to use the internet to leverage a bank's business, there are not many banks that really offer online banking services such as balance inquiry, bill payment and fund transfer. There are also virtual banks, which exist side-by-side with their brick-and-mortar counterparts, merely use the internet as an avenue to advertise their products and services.

Table 10.7
Internet Penetration Rate (%), 2007

Singapore	70.0
Malaysia	59.7
Brunei	41.7
Thailand	21.0
Vietnam	17.5*
Philippines	6.0
Indonesia	5.6
Laos	1.7
Cambodia	0.5
Myanmar	0.1
USA	72.0
Japan	68.9
Sweden	77.0

Source: International Telecommunication Union, www.itu.int/net/home.
*Denotes 2006 figure from World Bank, *WDI Online*, 20 Oct. 2008, http://publications.worldbank.org/WDI/.

With the advent of the telecommunication age, Wireless Application Protocol (WAP) technology, which allows internet access via mobile phones, is used with increasing frequency to add banking features to mobile phones. This has resulted in the increasing widespread use of the internet as a platform for business transactions. A survey, conducted by Citibank and reported in *The Straits Times* on 5 June 2003, showed that 80% of internet users in Singapore carry out their banking transactions online. This has placed Singapore third after South Korea and Australia in online banking usage. As soon as consumers gain sufficient confidence in online security measures, e-banking may become the next wave in the development of financial services.

Financial Reforms and Development

Southeast Asian economies started liberalising their financial sectors as early as the 1970s (Ng, 1985). Several areas of liberalisation were identified, namely interest rates, credit controls, capital accounts and exchange rates. The benefits of financial liberalisation came under closer scrutiny when the region was hit by the Asian financial crisis in 1997–1998.

Indonesia

Modern banking in Indonesia dates back to 1827. The Dutch colonial administration encouraged the establishment of a private bank, the De Javasche Bank. The Government gave the Bank the authority to circulate paper money and coins. Until the Second World War, Dutch, British, Japanese, Chinese and also a few Indonesian banks operated in the country. The operations of the banks were disrupted during the Japanese Occupation, but soon resumed after the proclamation of Independence in 1945.

The banking system comes under the jurisdiction of Bank Indonesia, Indonesia's *de facto* central bank. Under the Central Banking Act of 1968 (amended in 1992), Bank Indonesia was required to take on all the customary functions of a central bank, namely, the issue of notes and coins, holding of foreign reserves, and the regulation of domestic money and credit expansion in line with Government's policies. The Bank regulates the operation of all financial institutions except the insurance companies.

To improve the mobilisation of domestic savings in the country, Bank Indonesia introduced a series of reforms to the banking sector in the 1980s. The way the Bank conducted its monetary policy was changed from direct controls to a more indirect and market-oriented approach. From 1983, for example, banks are allowed to set their own deposit rates. In addition, credit ceilings set by the central bank were removed. Nevertheless, a few priority sectors continued to be assisted with subsidised interest rates covered by Bank Indonesia's subsidised re-financing facilities. To better manage the money supply in the economy, the central bank created two new financial instruments, namely Bank Indonesia Certificates (Sertifikat Bank Indonesia, SBI) and Surat Berharga Pasar Uang (SBPU). SBIs are discount instruments with different denominations and maturities. They can be traded within the banking system prior to their redemption on maturity by the central bank. Similarly, SBPUs are short-term money market securities that can also be traded within the banking system. The SBIs and SBPUs are auctioned and sold weekly by Bank Indonesia like any normal open market operation to vary the level of liquidity in the banking system. The introduction of a lender-of-last resort facility further instilled depositors' confidence in the banking system.

Further deregulations were carried out by the central bank in 1988. The easing of entry requirement and the reduction of reserve requirement as well as the lifting of restrictions on bank and non-bank activities led to the proliferation of new banks. Notwithstanding these developments, stricter regulations governing the banking sector were implemented. Related-party lending and capital requirements were tightened. Banks' external borrowings were also restricted to a foreign-exchange equivalent of 25% of banks' equity.

Another wave of banking sector reforms occurred in the 1990s. Subsidised credit to priority sectors was further reduced. Measures to improve banking regulations and supervision were also announced. In order to strengthen the banks' capital base to meet the capital adequacy ratio of 8% recommended by the Bank for International Settlements, banks were encouraged to merge. This was achieved through the introduction of new tax regulations. In addition, the minimum paid-up capital requirement for banks seeking foreign exchange licence was raised from 50 billion rupiah to 150 billion rupiah. In 1996, Bank Indonesia increased the reserve requirement of commercial banks from 3 to 5%. Measures with the objective of increasing transparency of the banking industry were announced.

In 1996, there were 240 commercial banks, of which seven were state-owned commercial banks, 166 were private commercial banks, 30 were joint venture banks, 10 foreign banks and 27 were regional government banks. Historically, the state-owned commercial banks had specialised roles. For example, Bank Negara Indonesia lent to industrial companies, Bank Dagang Negara to mining companies, Bank Bumi Daya to companies in the agriculture and forestry sector, Bank Rakyat Indonesia to co-operative farms and fisheries and Bank Ekspor Impor Indonesia to export companies.

Despite the prudent measures and supervision, the weakness of the banking system was revealed when the Asian financial crisis erupted in the second half of 1997. It was reported that most banks violated their capital adequacy ratios, their loan/deposit ratios, legal lending limits and limits on their net open positions. The calling on of the IMF and its subsequent order to close 16 banks without providing support of a deposit insurance scheme led to a massive bank run. In 1998, the Government announced that it would guarantee all national banks' deposits and liabilities. The Indonesia Bank Restructuring Authority was also set up to restore the ailing banking system.

To re-capitalise the affected banks, the Government would put up four rupiah for every rupiah of fresh capital injected into qualified banks. The funds would be raised through bond issues backed by the sales of bank assets under IBRA. The Government would receive equity stakes in the banks. Banks owners then have three years to redeem part or the entire government stake. There were also more mergers and acquisitions. Four of the seven state-owned banks, namely Bank Bumi Daya, Bank Dagang Negara, Bank Pembangunan Indonesia and Bank Ekspor Impor Indonesia, were merged into Bank Mandiri in 1999. The Bank Bali corruption scandal, however, impeded the progress of bank re-capitalisation and reforms of the banking sector.

In an effort to lift the ailing banking sector, a new government regulation in 2001 requires banks to hold a capital adequacy ratio of at least 8%, in line with the standards of the Bank for International Settlements based in Basel. The capital adequacy ratio of banks improved slightly during the first half of 2007, but declined again, to 19.3%, at end-2007 compared with 20.5% at end-2006.

While banks have gained importance as financial intermediaries in the course of economic development, the Jakarta Stock Exchange (JSX) only became active when financial reforms were implemented in October 1988. From a low of 83 in early 1988, the JSX index rose to a high of 682 in April 1990. However, this high JSX index was not sustainable and dropped by 63% within the following two years. With support from the Government, appropriate measures to tighten supervisory regulations and garner public confidence were implemented in 1992 to revive the stock market. By June 1997, the JSX peaked at 725. But, the unfortunate economic crisis in 1997–1998 adversely affected the stock market again. Although the 49% foreign ownership cap for initial public offerings of Indonesian companies was lifted in late 1997, the JSX index continued to decline. With changes also occurring in the political arena, it was not until the Megawati presidency that the stock market stabilised in August 2002.

The stock market started to recover only in 2002, but it has grown strongly since. Although government issues dominate the bond market, the corporate bond market has attracted strong investor interest since 2006. Brokerage firms and insurance companies have come to play important roles in their industries as well. In 2008, high commodity prices have buoyed the performance of the stock market; however, higher interest rates have depressed performance in the bond market.

Ten years after Indonesia's near financial collapse, the country's banks are well on the way to recovery in mid-2008, showing sustained credit growth and improved rates on non-performing loans (NPLs), return on assets, capital adequacy ratios and loan-to-deposit ratios. Since 2005 the central bank has severely restricted lending to business sectors with higher than average rates of NPLs, defined as loans with monthly repayments overdue more than 101 days. It has postponed indefinitely its July 2007 deadline for banks to comply fully with its "uniform collectability classification" standard on syndicated loans due to a substantial increase in NPLs by state banks. Banks are under pressure to improve financial performance in a bid to be rated as an "anchor" bank ahead of the planned 2010 industry consolidation. The central bank or Bank of Indonesia (BI)'s 2004 Indonesian Banking Architecture plan laid out the future direction, outline and structure of the Indonesian banking system. It required anchor banks to have a minimum capitalisation of 80 billion rupiah by end-2007 and 100 billion rupiah by end-2010. In January 2008, BI affirmed that all 128 commercial banks in the country fulfilled the minimum capitalisation requirement.

Under the government's restructuring and divestment programme, most of the heavily indebted banks that were nationalised during the 1997–98 financial crisis have been sold back to the private sector. Majority stakes in nationalized banks were sold to foreign investors, and minority interests in state banks were sold to the public via the stock market. The government's stake in nine domestic private banks has been divested and sold to foreign investors as controlling shareholders since 2002, leaving the government with holdings in only five of the country's total of 128 banks. As of April 2008, the government owns both Bank Mandiri and Bank Negara Indonesia, the country's two largest lenders by assets. It also has a controlling stake in Bank Rakyat Indonesia, Bank Ekspor Indonesia (a trade-financing entity) and Bank Tabungan Negara.

Malaysia

Malaysian banking development began with the opening of a branch of the Chartered Bank in 1875 in Penang. Banking soon expanded to Malacca and Kuala Lumpur. Those days, commercial banks were known as exchange banks, since they mainly dealt with foreign exchange transactions relating to external trade. The first locally incorporated bank was established in 1913.

The central bank, Bank Negara Malaysia (BNM) was established in 1959 under the Central Bank of Malaysia Ordinance. BNM made use of reserve and liquidity ratios, interest rate variation, selective credit controls and moral suasion to regulate money and credit. The commercial banks are the most important group of financial intermediaries. The assets of commercial banks made up 61% of those held by the banking institutions as a whole. By October 2007, there were 33 commercial banks in Malaysia.

In line with the trend of interest rate liberalisation, Malaysian banks were allowed to fix their own interest rates on loans and deposits from October 1978. This "free market" approach led to a general increase in the interest rates. Since then, commercial banks would charge interest rates on loans based on cost of funds plus a margin that depended on borrower's credit standing. The only exception was rates quoted to some priority sectors.

In Malaysia, commercial banks have to adhere to certain lending guidelines stipulated by the central bank on the Bumiputera community, low-cost housing and small- and medium-scale enterprises. For instance, they are expected to lend 30% of total loans to the Bumiputera community. Furthermore, the banks are required to extend new loans approved and disbursed 500,000 ringgit and below to small- and medium-scale enterprises. In addition, one-half of the allocated quotas have to be extended to Bumiputera borrowers. Nevertheless, the number of priority sectors eligible for preferential interest rates have declined over the years.

The fragility of the banking system was exposed after the country was hit by the Asian financial crisis. Before the crisis, credit expanded at an annual average of nearly 30%. However, a large proportion of the lending went into property development and stock market investment, which led to a surge in the number of non-performing loans (NPLs). In 1998, an asset management company, Pengurusan Danaharta National, was given the task of buying NPLs from banks and rehabilitating them. A sister agency, Danamodal National was also set up to re-capitalise ailing financial institutions.

The outbreak of the financial crisis also led to the imposition of currency and capital controls by the Government in September 1998. Besides pegging 3.8 ringgit to 1 US dollar, BNM also required all export and import settlements to be made in foreign currencies. Furthermore, travellers are not allowed to carry with them more than 1,000 ringgit when entering or leaving the country. The travellers are also not allowed to take out more foreign currencies than they brought in. Lastly, investors have to maintain their invested funds in ringgit for a year. In February 1999, the Government replaced the 12-month holding period with exit taxes. A 30% capital gains tax would be levied for profits repatriated within 12 months, while a 10% capital gains tax would be levied for profits withdrawn after 12 months. The two-tier capital gains tax was subsequently replaced by a flat 10% tax in September 1999. However, the levy has since been lifted in May 2001.

The merger programme instituted by the Government to restructure the financial sector to enhance global competitiveness was completed in 2000. 58 commercial banks, merchant banks and financed companies, all locally owned were re-organised into 10 banking groups. In 2001, Bank Negara Malaysia mapped out a ten-year Financial Sector Masterplan (FSMP) to further sharpen the banking sector's competitive edge. The current task involves building up the domestic capacity and pegs local bank performance against international standards. Islamic banking, which has been growing rapidly in recent years, has also been included in the masterplan.

The equity market in Malaysia has been an important avenue for direct financing especially when the economy is buoyant and share prices are high. Before the 1997–1998 financial crisis, the Government had plans to liberalise the capital market. When the economic crisis erupted, market capitalisation fell drastically within a year from 807 billion ringgit in 1996 to 376 billion ringgit in late 1997. As the region recovered from the crisis, the Kuala Lumpur Stock Exchange (KLSE) too strengthened. In tandem with the development of the financial sector, the Malaysian Government introduced a ten-year Capital Market Masterplan (CMM) in early 2001 to position and steer the Malaysian capital market towards global prominence by making fund-raising more attractive to both investors and borrowers. The focus, however, is on the corporate bond and venture capital markets. A number of other initiatives were undertaken. Foreign majority ownership of unit trust companies is allowed from 2003. Innovative financial products such as bond futures will be introduced with the launch of the Malaysian Derivatives Exchange (MDE) in June 2001. The rights of minority share-holders have also been strengthened. The KLSE is now also empowered to act against errant directors of listed companies.

In keeping with the FSMP, the government has been trying to boost areas of Islamic finance like insurance and securities. In September 2006, the government launched the *Malaysia International Islamic Financial Centre* (MIFC) initiative under which financial institutions can conduct Islamic financial business in international currencies. To boost the MIFC initiative, Bank Negara signed a memoranda of understanding with both the Qatar Financial Centre Regulatory Authority and the Dubai Financial Services Authority in March 2007 to jointly develop international Islamic finance. Other incentives were later announced to expand the MIFC initiative — Islamic fund-management companies can be wholly owned by foreigners; these companies may invest all their assets abroad; fund-management companies will be given income-tax exemption on all fees received in respect of Islamic fund-management activities until year of assessment 2016; and a RM$7 billion fund will be set up by the Employees Provident Fund to be managed by Islamic fund-management companies.

Instead of charging interest, which is proscribed by the Koran, Islamic banks offer alternatives to conventional banking instruments. These include profit sharing, leasing and capital-market instruments, such as zero coupon bonds that are sold at a discount to their face value. Bahrain and Dubai have also emerged as important centres for Islamic banking and financial services. BNM regulates the Islamic banks under the Islamic Banking Act of 1983. At end-June 2007, Islamic-banking assets in Malaysia reached RM$143.7 billion at end-June 2007, up 8% from the start of the year and representing 12.1% of total financial-institution assets at that time, according to the Ministry of Finance. The FSMP has set a goal of increasing this market share to 20% by 2010.

Philippines

The first formal bank in the Philippines was established in 1851. Since then, banking has evolved in line with the growth of the economy. The Philippines' banking sector comprises the central bank, the commercial banks, thrift banks, rural banks, two special government banks and offshore banking units. The Central Bank of Philippines (CBP) was established in 1949. With CBP in place, a managed currency system was adopted. The activities of the central bank include the sale and purchase of gold and foreign currencies, determination of foreign exchange rates and regulation of the nation's money and credit. To regulate the volume of credit creation by financial institutions, CBP used a number of well-known instruments such as reserve ratio requirement, liquidity ratio, interest rates ceilings and selective credit controls.

Since the economic crisis in the early 1980s, CBP had to follow a tight monetary policy partly in compliance with the conditions associated with the IMF stand-by credits granted to the Philippines from time to time. Thus, as a complementary measure to the external adjustment programme and to contain inflation, monetary and credit policy instruments were relied upon to restrain the growth rates in reserve money, domestic liquidity and net domestic assets. Among the instruments used were the open market operations with the issuance, for the first time, of high-yielding Treasury bills and Central Bank bills. In 1993, a new Central Bank Act was promulgated to establish the present central bank — Bangko Sentral ng Pilipinas (BSP).

The BSP has greater independence and more effective powers in the management of monetary policy. The BSP is mandated mainly to ensure a stable price environment conductive for economic growth.

Foreign exchange liberalisation was undertaken by the Philippine central bank in the 1990s. Exporters of goods and services were given full autonomy to dispose of their foreign exchange receipts as they deemed fit. Restrictions on payment modes other than through letters of credit were liberalised for export and import transactions. In addition, all prior requirements relating to central bank approval on export transactions were lifted, as were quantitative restrictions on the amount of foreign exchange that may be purchased from banks on service payments. In order to encourage inward investment, full and immediate repatriation of foreign investment, including profit remittances, were allowed. Further, any type of inward investment could be made without prior central bank approval.

The commercial banks experienced rapid growth in the post-war period. Since the mid-1960s, however, growth decelerated because of the appearance of deposit-substitutes in the money market that earned interest rates well above the rate fixed by the central bank. The financial reforms of 1976–1977 and the lifting of interest rate ceilings in 1980–1981 boosted the growth of savings and time deposits. To promote long-term credit and inter-bank competition, changes made in 1980–1981 reduced the legislated specialisation among the financial institutions. A modified form of universal banking was legislated. "Expanded commercial banks" were distinguished from "commercial banks". The former required a capital of 500 million pesos and could cover domestic and international banking as well as enjoy the powers of an investment house (underwriting, securities dealership and equity investment).

In 1995, the Philippine banking sector saw the entry of ten more foreign banks. Although activities of these foreign banks were limited to wholesale banking, their entry acted as a catalyst to encourage additional mergers among the domestic banks. The consolidation process was further sped up due to the Asian financial crisis.

The securities market in the Philippines is relatively small in comparison to that of Singapore and Malaysia. Market capitalisation as a percentage of GDP in the Philippines is 58, while that of Singapore and Malaysia is 209 and 156 respectively (see Table 10.4). The capital market in the Philippines can be characterized as follows. Firstly, the equity primary market is relatively underdeveloped given that the Philippine Stock Exchange (PSE) lists only some 200 companies and that less than 100 of the country's top 1,000 largest corporations have a listing. This is attributed to the nature of the Philippine industrial organization, that is, the Philippine companies are tightly held and generate most of their capital requirements from captive banking institutions. These companies are generally cautious in releasing information and have very little pressures from their shareholders. Secondly, the Philippines has a relatively more developed bond market than some other ASEAN countries as it has offered diverse financial instruments and long-term debt instruments. It has a significant public bond market because of the need to fund chronic fiscal deficits. Since mid-1998, the government bond market has been regulated by the Bureau of Treasury rather than by its central bank. Currently, the market is almost all short term (mostly three-month bills) and hence generates a liquid secondary market supported by a scripless settlement system. On the other hand, the Philippine corporate bond market is very much smaller than the public bond market. The corporate bond market is regulated by the Securities Exchange Commission (Daquila, 2005).

As elsewhere in ASEAN, the PSE index is easily influenced by trends in the global financial markets as well as changes in domestic economic and political conditions. Similarly, like other stock markets in the region, the PSE index was not spared of the effects from the economic crisis. The PSE index plunged from 3,448 in early 1997 to a seven-year low of 1,082 in 1998. Subsequent uncertainties in the domestic political conditions as well as terrorist threats have resulted in the sluggish recovery of the stock market and the PSE index continued to hover around 1,100 in 2001. To promote transparency and improve corporate governance, the present Government, lead by President Arroyo, has implemented various regulatory measures to boost investors' confidence.

Singapore

The first bank that was established in Singapore was an office of the Union Bank of Culcutta in 1840. Soon, British, Dutch, French and American banks also started setting up their offices. The first local bank began operations in 1903, but had to be liquidated in 1913. The other local banks, however, survived and thrived. Notable among them was the Four Seas Communications Bank established in 1906. Local banks that set up during 1912–1919 later joined together in 1932 and formed the present Overseas Chinese Banking Corporation (OCBC). When Singapore was part of the Federation of Malaysia, banks operations were under the control of the Malaysian Central Bank. The Monetary Authority of Singapore (MAS) was established in 1970 to act as the central monetary institution. The MAS performs most of the functions of a central bank. The only exception is the non-issuance of currency. However in 2002, the responsibility of the Board of Commissioners of Currency was transferred to MAS, and since then the Currency Board ceased to exist.

A study of Singapore's monetary policy noted the following empirical facts: (i) domestic interest rates were determined by external factors and the most dominant factors were the foreign exchange rates; (ii) real investments were not significantly affected by domestic monetary variables and hence the Keynesian multiplier effect on GDP via monetary policy may not be a realisable proposition; and (iii) domestic consumer prices were most significantly determined by import prices (and unit labour costs) and not directly by monetary variables. As prices go up, due to world market price increases, domestic nominal incomes go up and the MAS supplies more money as an adaptive response. Singapore often uses exchange rate changes as an anti-inflationary policy. For that purpose, it sells or buys foreign currency. In this case, level of money supply is a by-product. If monetary variables have no links with prices, interest rates and investment, then there is little that monetary policy can do to raise income and employment in a recession or control inflation and excess demand in a boom. (Lim *et al.*, 1988).

In its 1984 report, the MAS noted that there were persistent pressures on the Singapore dollar to appreciate due to a number of factors, notably Central Provident Fund contributions and budget surpluses that drain liquidity from the domestic banking system. MAS subsequently bought US dollars and sold Singapore dollars. This injection of liquidity expanded the monetary base or the basis of which the banking system created credit. The *modus operandi* holds good up to this day.

Although MAS also used cash ratio adjustment, its effectiveness in reducing any existing inflation is limited, given that inflation in Singapore is almost always "imported". Similarly, changes in the discount rate can also influence the money supply. But the MAS re-iterated that "the MAS position is that the rediscount rate merely accommodates existing market rates and is not a policy instrument." (Lim *et al.*, 1988). In regard to the use of other monetary policy instruments, namely moral suasion and selective controls, these were used on occasions. For instance, selective credit controls were imposed in 1974 to curb inflation. In March 1974, the MAS requested banks to channel 70% of the additional lending for productive activities. This measure lasted for a while and was dropped in 1975.

From 1975, commercial banks in Singapore were free to set their own interest rates on deposits and loans, subject to market forces. Previously, interest rates were determined by a banking cartel. Exchange controls were also removed completely for all intents and purposes in Singapore in 1978. Although, Singapore was only mildly affected by the Asian financial crisis, the pace of financial liberalisation was hastened. Local banks were encouraged to merge with or acquire other local banks so as to emerge stronger and thus have the capability to face more intense competition. The acquisition of Post Office Savings Bank by the Development Bank of Singapore (DBS) and the merger between Keppel Bank and Tat Lee Bank both took effect in 1998. Three years later, in 2001, the Overseas Chinese Banking Corporation acquired Keppel Capital. This is followed in the later half of 2001, by the amalgamation of Overseas Union Bank with United Overseas Bank.

To establish a regional presence, Singapore banks also acquired banks in other ASEAN countries. In 1999, the United Overseas Bank paid 15 billion baht and S$312 million to acquire a significant stake in Thailand's Radanasin Bank and the Philippine Westmont Bank respectively. DBS had also bought in several banks since 1998. Besides holding a 52% stake in the Thai Danu Bank, DBS is also a substantial shareholder of Bank Philippines and PT Bank Buana of Indonesia.

To allow more competition in the domestic banking industry, the MAS eased rules on foreign banks by handling out three different categories of banking licences to foreign banks, namely Qualifying Full Banks (QFB), Restricted Banks (RB) and Qualifying Offshore Banks (QOB). Banks with QFB status are allowed to have up to ten locations of which five may be branches and the remainder off-site ATMs. They are also authorised to operate a shared ATM network.

Efforts have been made to further develop the capital markets, notably the bond market. The Government initiated an Approved Bond Intermediary (ABI) scheme where selected funds will enjoy tax exemptions on interest. Furthermore, statutory boards and Government-linked companies (GLCs) have been encouraged to issue bonds, a step taken to precipitate the growth of the debt market. Consolidation in the equity market was seen when the Singapore Exchange (SGX) was established in December 1999, a result of the merger of the Stock Exchange of Singapore and the Singapore International Monetary Exchange. SGX became a publicly listed company in November 2000. In December 2007, the SGX made radical changes to its junior board — Sesdaq (Stock Exchange of Singapore Dealing and Automated Quotation) — by renaming it Catalist.

In January 2008, the Basel 2 regulatory framework was adopted in Singapore. Minimum Tier 1 and Total Capital Adequacy ratios have been maintained at 6% and 10% respectively. In 2001, major amendments were made to the Banking Act, the main legislation governing the industry, through the Banking (Amendment) Bill in order to strengthen prudential safeguards and corporate governance as well as providing banks with greater operational flexibility. The Banking Act was amended again in January 2007 to enhance the MAS' powers for dealing with distressed or insolvent banks.

Local banks have, over the past few years, ventured overseas to tap the regional market, establishing branches and representative offices in Hong Kong, China, India and South-east Asia. DBS, for example, in January 2006 acquired a 37.5% equity stake in Cholamandalam Investments and Finance Company, a major Indian consumer-finance house. The new company, renamed Cholamandalam DBS Finance, had about 200 outlets in India as of end-2007. UOB has also been active in building up its regional presence. In June 2004, it acquired a 23% equity stake in Bank Buana Indonesia, and in October 2005 it completed the purchase of an additional 30% stake. In April 2004, OCBC acquired a 22.5% equity stake in Indonesia's Bank NISP.

Singapore banks are also trying to expand into mainland China, given the liberalisation of the financial sector that followed China's accession to the World Trade Organisation. In January 2006 OCBC bought a 12.2% stake in Ningbo Commercial Bank for S$120m; its stake was diluted to 10% when Ningbo went public in 2007. In October 2007, DBS launched a range of renminbi deposit services, mortgage loans and general insurance products for Shanghai residents. In the same year, DBS Asset Management bought a 33% stake in Changsheng Fund Management Company. As of July 2008, DBS had branches in Beijing, Shanghai, Guangzhou, Shenzhen and Suzhou, and representative offices in Tianjin, Hangzhou, Fuzhou and Dongguan. In December 2007, UOB incorporated locally in China, allowing it to expand its local currency business there. In June 2008 UOB acquired a 15.38% stake in Evergrowing Bank (China).

Thailand

In 1888, the first banking office was set up by the Hong Kong and Shanghai Bank. The branches of foreign banks dominated the Thai banking industry up to 1941. During 1942–1945, the banking industry changed hands from foreign to local owners. Five new local commercial banks were opened during the period to replace the branches of the foreign banks. At the end of Second World War, foreign banks re-appeared. Seven new local banks were also founded during the 1945–1962 period. The enactment of the Commercial Banking Act of 1962 heralded a new growth phase in Thai banking.

In 1942, the Bank of Thailand (BOT) was established as the central bank. BOT performs all the functions of a central bank. It manages the public debt, administers foreign exchange controls and supervises the financial system. In order to ensure a sound financial system, BOT prescribes the ratios of cash reserves to total deposits, capital funds to total assets and interest rates. Furthermore, it gives advice and direction to the financial system in line with government economic policies, and the country's development objectives. In 1985, to promote priority economic sectors and to give greater stability and flexibility to the financial system, the Government pursued a less restrictive monetary policy. This policy emphasised changes in the loan policies of financial institutions and adapting the interest rate structure to economic circumstances. A government review after the Asian financial crisis found that BOT was performing too many functions. Thus, it is expected that the central bank will be shedding many of its supervisory functions so that it can concentrate on its policy responsibilities, in particular price stability.

In 1989, the central bank removed interest rate ceilings on commercial bank time deposits with maturities longer than one year. Interest rate ceilings for the other types of deposits were also eliminated in 1992. To enhance competition and protect small borrowers, the central bank also required commercial banks to announce their minimum retail rate, based on the cost of funds as a benchmark rate for small but good quality borrowers.

Thailand also removed its foreign exchange controls to encourage the freer mobility of capital. Three rounds of foreign exchange liberalisation had been implemented. The first round, instituted in 1990, allowed commercial banks to authorise foreign exchange transactions in trade related activities without prior approval from the central bank. In 1991, exchange controls were further loosened. Controls related to capital account transactions were lifted. However, outward direct investment above a certain limit and the acquisition of foreign real estate or securities by Thai residents still required approval from the central bank. Exporters were also allowed to accept baht payments from non-resident baht accounts without prior approval from the central bank and to use their export proceeds to service external obligations. The third round of foreign exchange liberalisation saw the limit on outward transfer of direct investment by residents raised. The limit on bank notes taken to neighbouring countries was also increased.

Like in most Southeast Asian countries, Thailand provides financial assistance to priority economic sectors. Financial assistance included (i) increased credit allocations to those sectors; (ii) financial assistance to export manufacturers; (iii) assistance for rice exporters; (iv) special assistance to exporters affected by the baht exchange rate adjustment; (v) changing the regulations governing the rediscounting of promissory notes arising from exports, small industrial undertakings and animal husbandry.

In 1992, the Thai Government established the Bangkok International Banking Facilities (BIBF). The BIBF was created to boost the role of Bangkok as the regional financial centre for the Indo-Chinese region and Myanmar. BIBF operations included taking deposits or borrowing in foreign currencies from abroad and lending foreign currencies except for retail banking. In order to encourage the further development, the BIBF offered participating institutions various incentives such as lower corporate income taxes, exemption from any withholding taxes, stamp duties and special business taxes.

Thailand was one of the more severely affected countries during the Asian financial crisis. In return for seeking financial assistance from the

IMF, the country had to fulfil several conditions set out by the IMF. The central bank had to raise foreign ownership of banks to help re-capitalise the local banks. Five of Thailand's seven independent commercial banks now have a significant foreign investor presence. They include the Thai Farmers Bank, the Bangkok Bank and the Siam Commercial Bank. Similarly, two of the five nationalised banks, namely Radanasin Bank and Nakornthon Bank had been sold off to foreign investors.

A number of new institutions were set up to restructure the financial sector and restore confidence. The Financial Institutions Development Fund (FIDF) was established to prevent bank runs and systemic risk. The main responsibility was to guarantee the deposits and liabilities of financial institutions. This guarantee, however, is to be later phased into a self-financed and limited-deposit insurance scheme. The Thai Government established two more institutions. A Financial Sector Restructuring Authority (FRA) was formed with the objective of auctioning off the assets of closed financial companies, and the Thai Asset Management Corporation (TAMC) was created to manage non-performing loans of the banking sector.

The Bank of Thailand (BOT), Thailand's central bank, had planned to shut down the FIDF in 2007 but postponed that date to 2012. This was because during the Asian financial crisis, the FIDF played a controversial role in extending funds to many of the shuttered finance companies and commercial banks. It ran up huge losses and as of end-2007, FIDF debt amounted to 1.1 billion baht, or just over one-third of Thailand's total public debt. The government decided that it no longer wanted to shoulder the burden of the standing guarantee on all public deposits that the BOT has provided to depositors and creditors since 1997 through the FIDF. A new Deposit Protection Agency (DPA) will be established and membership of the agency is compulsory for commercial domestic and foreign banks in Thailand.

Other ASEAN Countries

Unlike other developed countries, Brunei, a high-income country, does not seem to have a need for a central bank. All functions of the central bank, including the issue of currency, are being undertaken by the Ministry of Finance. With nine banks operating in Brunei, there are plans to expand

Islamic banking and efforts have been made to attract investors into the Brunei International Financial Centre established in mid-2000.

The developing economies of Cambodia, Laos and Myanmar and Vietnam are characterised by weak banking sectors. While expansion of banking services is evident in the early to mid-1990s, the 1997–1998 regional crisis has suppressed further growth of the banking sectors in these economies. The proportion of non-performing loans increased after 1997 and resulted in restructuring of the domestic banks in both Laos and Myanmar. Equity markets in these countries are virtually non-existent. The growth and eventual maturation of the banking sector usually precede the development of other more sophisticated financial instruments found in the bond and equity markets.

Due to historical reasons, Cambodians generally do not trust the banking system. Huge withdrawals of deposits often occur during adverse economic and political conditions, as witnessed during the 1997–1998 period. This has largely contributed to the development of informal credit markets to finance small businesses and farming activities. An absence of a formal banking network in the rural areas has also contributed to the rise of this informal market. In Myanmar, private money lenders are common and provide funds even in the urban areas. The costs of funds acquired using such means can be exorbitant and interest rates which are many times the official rates can be as high as 20% per month. This informal allocation of funds points to the existing gap for banks and other financial intermediaries to perform a more prominent role in the developmental process.

The banking sector in Vietnam, on the other hand, has advanced relatively more rapidly with a comparatively diversified system consisting of state-owned, joint-stock, joint venture and foreign banks. While non-performing loans made by state-owned commercial banks are a major concern, the Government is committed to re-capitalise these loans by 2004 with assistance from the World Bank and the IMF. Progressive efforts in Vietnam's banking sector have led to an upgrade of debt ratings by Moody's and Standard and Poor's. In fact, an improved rating of its five-year bonds by Standard and Poor's has encouraged Vietnam in 2002 to consider offering a US dollar bond.

In view of the current credit crisis ravaging global financial markets, countries like Vietnam, Cambodia, Laos and Myanmar will experience less impact due to their lack of integration with the global financial market, lower exposure to problem investments and institutions, as well as lower leverage ratios. The banking systems in these countries are at the initial stage of development and thus the fallout from the current financial turmoil will be limited. In fact, most Southeast Asian banks, having cleaned up their balance sheets after the Asian Financial Crisis, are entering the present credit crisis with relatively strong capital bases to weather the financial turbulence. To instil confidence in their banking systems, the ASEAN-4 economies of Indonesia, Singapore, Malaysia and Thailand have all taken steps to guarantee banks' deposits. In the Philippines, although the central bank has said that the banks' combined exposure to subprime securities was less than one percent of the assets of the country's banking system, it is planning to quadruple its bank deposit insurance in order to boost confidence in the banking system amid the global credit crisis.

2008 Banking Crisis

The subprime crisis broke out in the United States around August 2007. It happened when houses started to fall in value and many mortgagees could not repay the mortgage instalments, resulting in foreclosures. Housing loans, also known in the United States as *Ninja* (no income, no jobs, no assets) loans, had been given out very freely and indiscriminately, fuelling the housing boom. When the housing bubble burst, the panic spread. In addition, the lenders of the loans had packaged the mortgages and sold them all over the world, with the insolvency problem being thus also spread all over the world, particularly in Western Europe.

In Southeast Asia, the stock markets plunged. They have a free-fall as in other stock markets all over the world. The investment banks and some insurance companies in the US got into trouble over the toxic mortgages. A run on the banks happened in some parts of the world. But before this happened in Southeast Asia, the Southeast Asian governments, one after the other, declared that they guarantee all bank deposits in both local and foreign banks. That saves the situation from turning ugly.

In Iceland, the government first guaranteed only deposits of Irish banks, resulting in panic in the foreign banks in Ireland. This had to be quickly corrected. In Australia, some financial institutions were not placed under the guarantee, resulting in a run on these institutions. Customers started to queue up to withdraw money from them to transfer them to institutions that had the government guarantee.

In Singapore, a few banks sold to customers bonds that become problematic because the parent bodies, such as Lehman Brothers, in the United States, have become bankrupt. The sharing of responsibility between the customers and the banks is still being worked out. Since the three local banks in Singapore are cash-rich with very high capital adequacy ratios and high cash ratios, and with the Singapore government guaranteeing all bank deposits, a potential banking crisis in Singapore was averted. The banking system remains very stable and sound. This stability and confidence in the banking system is particularly important to Singapore, as she also functions as a financial hub in the region.

In short, in our view, the Federal Reserve Bank has failed to (1) serve as an effective regulator by allowing the subprime ninja loans to grow and spread its toxicity and (2) by not serving as a lender of last resort when it allowed the Lehman Brothers to go bankrupt when it sought its help and help was not given.

The US subprime crisis has had tremendous adverse impact on the stock markets of Southeast Asia, but thus far the unemployment rate and the exchange rate have still exhibited much stability, though fear of deterioration has occasionally reared its ugly head on these three fronts. If the unemployment rate increases drastically and the exchange rate depreciates too much, then the stock market crisis in Southeast Asia will become a full-blown economic crisis even if the banking system remains intact.

Highlights of Sound Financial Practices

The development of a sound and strong banking system requires, amongst many factors, an effective regulatory and supervisory framework and a competent governing authority, namely the Central Bank, that also acts with integrity. Financial regulations in both Malaysia and Singapore have been managed with prudence. Regulations formulated by the Bank for International Settlements using the Basle Standards have been adopted and effectively implemented to allow financial institutions to develop into strong and well-capitalised companies of international standing. In 2007, the

Financial Times ranked Development Bank of Singapore and Singapore's United Overseas Bank among the top 500 global companies, an affirmation of a favourable framework within the financial sector.

Of paramount importance in sound financial management is the system of checks and balances, requiring accountability of all financial institutions. Both on-site and off-site examination of banks' internal controls and accounting procedures should be regularly conducted to ensure that appropriate measures are consistently applied and the best practices followed. From time to time, these regulatory procedures should be reviewed and adapted to the changing global environment. Currently, with the global financial crisis triggered by the US subprime mortgage market problems, there is a pressing need to strengthen and intensify the financial system surveillance and supervision of financial institutions. Governments will have to rethink how they should regulate and supervise the financial sector in order to both safeguard public funds and prevent a recurrence of the current financial turmoil. In the developed countries, the regulators should require commercial and investment banks and insurers to hold more capital and liquidity while policy-makers in emerging economies will have to relook the pace of liberalisation and how much trust to place in the ability of financial markets to regulate themselves. While financial supervision and reforms are vital to prevent a recurrence of a future crisis, over-regulation could stifle the healthy development of the financial sector. This is because securitisation is an important innovation to preserve even if it had contributed to the subprime crisis. Financial regulators could delay needed liberalisation and risk hindering innovation if they over regulate the financial sectors in the wake of the ongoing market turmoil.

Key Points

1. When money is used as a medium of exchange, cost of transactions is lowered. Furthermore, there is no need for 'double coincidence of wants' to occur in order to exchange. The existence of financial intermediaries allows the efficient transfer of scarce financial resources from savers to investors.
2. The ASEAN-5, particularly Malaysia and Singapore, have been able to manage their domestic inflation rates at a fairly low level.

3. Southeast Asian countries are in various stages of financial development. Singapore and Malaysia have deep financial sectors. On the other hand, transitional economies such as Cambodia, Laos and Vietnam have low levels of monetisation. This could be attributed to the large rural sector where barter trade is more prevalent.
4. Automation, technology and internet are changing the banking industry tremendously. Productivity as a result increases. The use of internet also makes banking a borderless business.
5. Financial sector reforms were observed in Southeast Asia as early as the 1970s. The areas of liberalisation include interest rates, credit controls, capital accounts and exchange rates. Banks in most of Southeast Asian countries were allowed to determine their own deposit and lending rates. Foreign exchange controls were also removed to encourage freer movement of capital. However, credit to priority sectors exists in some countries.
6. When the Asian financial crisis struck the region, financial reforms were cited as one of the factors. Nevertheless, Singapore, in its attempt to upgrade its financial centre status, has continued liberalising its financial sector. More competition has been increasingly allowed into the industry. Mergers and acquisitions both locally and overseas were also encouraged. The Malaysian Government also encouraged the local banks to merge at the height of the 1997/98 crisis. It had to introduce capital controls to stabilise its exchange rate of 3.8 ringgit to 1 US dollar. Debt restructuring agencies were set up to rehabilitate the banking systems in Indonesia, Malaysia and Thailand. Indonesia and Thailand sought IMF help to handle the exchange rate crisis.

Suggested Discussion Topics

10.1 Discuss the link between money supply and the rate of inflation in Southeast Asian countries.
10.2 Discuss, with reference to Southeast Asia, the close link between the development of the financial and banking sector and the development of the economy.
10.3 Can the commercial banks create money? If so, are there limits in this creation? Discuss.

References

Economic Intelligence Unit, 2008, *Country Finance*, various issues, http://www.eiu.com.

DAQUILA, Teofilo. C., 2005, *The Economies of Southeast Asia: Indonesia, Malaysia, Philippines, Singapore and Thailand*, New York: Nova Science Publishers.

DJIWANDONO, J. Soedradjad, 2005, *Bank Indonesia and the Crisis: An Insider's View*, Singapore: Institute of Southeast Asian Studies.

LIM, Chong Yah (ed.), 1996, *Economic Policy Management in Singapore*, Singapore: Addison-Wesley.

MASUYAMA, Seiichi, Donna VANDENBRINK and Siow Yue CHIA (eds.), 1999, *East Asia's Financial Systems: Evolution and Crisis*, Japan, Tokyo: Nomura Research Institute and Singapore: Institute of Southeast Asian Studies.

NG, Beoy Kui, 1985, *Some Aspects of the Informal Sector in the SEACEN Asian Countries*, Staff Papers No. 10, Kuala Lumpur: SEACEN Research and Training Centre.

NG, Beoy Kui, 1995, *Financial Reforms in the ASEAN Countries: Approach, Focus and Assessment*, Nanyang Technology University, School of Accountancy and Business Working Paper 10–95.

Further Readings

AZIZAH, Talib (ed.), 1993, *Monetary Policy in the SEACEN Countries: An Update*, Kuala Lumpur: SEACEN Centre.

BROOKS, D. H. and M. QUEISSER, 1999, *Financial Liberalisation in Asia: Analysis and Prospects*, Paris: Development Centre of the OECD and Asian Development Bank.

COLE, David C. and B. F. SLADE, 1996, *Building a Modern Financial System: The Indonesian Experience*, New York: Cambridge University Press.

LEE, Sheng Yi, 1990, *The Monetary and Banking Development of Singapore and Malaysia*, Singapore: Singapore University Press.

LIM, Chong Yah, 1967, *Economic Development of Modern Malaya*, Kuala Lumpur: Oxford University Press, Chapter 8: Currency and Banking.

LIM, Chong Yah *et al.*, 1985, "Banking and money", *Economic Structure and Organization*. Singapore: Oxford University Press.

LIM, Chong Yah *et al.*, 1985, "Finance", *Economic Structure and Organization*. Singapore: Oxford University Press.

LIM, Chong Yah, 2007. "The IMF and exchange rate crisis management", *Singapore Economic Review*, 52(3).

LIM, Chong Yah, "The Asian financial crisis and the subprime mortgage crisis: A dissenting view", book chapter in *Singapore and Asia in a Globalised World: Contemporary Economic Issues and Policies*, CHIA, W. M. & SNG H. Y. (eds.). Singapore: World Scientific, 2008.

World Bank, 2006, East Asian Finance: the road to robust markets, Washington, D.C: The World Bank.

ZAHID, Shahid N. (ed.), 1995, *Financial Sector Development in Asia*, Hong Kong; New York: Oxford University Press.

Chapter 11

Population Explosion and Characteristics

From the point of view of mere numbers, ants are many hundred times as successful as men. I have seen in Australia vast regions empty of human beings, but populated by innumerable hordes of termites, but we do not, on that account, consider termites superior to ourselves.

Bertrand Russell, *Has Man a Future?*

Objectives

✓ Survey some theories of population and fertility.
✓ Show that Southeast Asia's population is growing faster than the world average.
✓ Explain the faster than average population growth rate.
✓ Examine the implications of a faster population growth rate.
✓ Discuss the issues of internal migration.
✓ Highlight the population policies implemented by two Southeast Asian countries.

Introduction

The population issue has received much attention in recent years for two main reasons. Firstly, there is the rapid growth of the world population in many developing countries. It took the world 150 years (1750–1900) to double its population from 728 million to 1.6 billion. In sharp contrast, within 37 years (that is from 1950 to 1987) the world population doubled from 2.5 billion to 5 billion. The rate was even faster for Southeast Asia, the region took only 30 years to double its population from 184 million in 1950 to 360 million in 1980. In 2006, the world population stood at 6.5 billion. The United Nations and the World Bank have projected that by 2050, world population will reach 8.9 billion. Of this total, it is estimated that over 80% will be living in the developing countries. The impact of this enormous population size on the economies of the developing countries and the quality of life of people is thus a crucial issue. There is also the related problem of population distribution within countries. How the population is distributed within a country, between different ethnic and religious groups, between different industries and occupations and between urban and rural areas, often becomes of great significance to the growth and development of a country.

The relationship between population size and economic development, however, is not unidirectional. A country's population size and growth affect and are affected by its economic development. The danger of population explosion on the difficulty to uplift the quality of life in developing countries has to be constantly borne in mind.

Population and Fertility Theories

Malthusianism and Neo-Malthusianism

In 1798, Reverend Thomas R. Malthus (1766–1834) published his pessimistic theory entitled "An Essay on the Principle of Population". The main tenet of his population theory was that population growth was a vicious cycle and in a way, a self-regulating process. Human beings would not suppress procreation deliberately. Thus, as long as favourable conditions prevailed, they would give birth to more children. But it would reach a point in time when the rise in population would result in an oversupply of labour. With other factors of production remained fixed, diminishing returns set in and this caused wages to fall back to subsistence level. Malthus also postulated that with food supplies growing at an arithmetic progression and population at a geometric progression, in the long run, there would be famines. Together with other "positive checks" such as wars and epidemics, the growth in world population would be controlled.

Malthus in his later editions suggested a few other measures, which he called "moral restraint". Some of the highly controversial measures he advocated included the abolition of welfare laws. According to Malthus, such laws would make the country poorer, since the poor had the tendency to have more offspring when conditions improved. Malthus also advocated that couples should delay starting a family until they had the economic capability to do so. Implicitly, this also means marriage at a later age. Contraception, however, was not recommended because of Malthus' religious background.

Fortunately, Malthus' pessimistic predictions did not materialise. There are three main flaws in his argument. Firstly, population need not grow in geometric progression. With family planning, rapid population growth can come under control. Besides, with the emancipation of women and higher standards of living, depopulation can take place, as the opportunity costs of bringing up children increases. These limits to population growth, however, do not apply to countries that are poor and that do not practice family planning. Secondly, Malthus assumed that countries practised autarky and ignored the benefits of specialisation and trade. As pointed out by some observers, the occurrences of food shortages were mainly due to poor distribution and not inefficient slow rate of food production. Another flaw in Malthus' theory of population is his failure to take into consideration the benefits of science and technology in food production. With advancement in agricultural science such as the Green Revolution, food output is growing at a rate much faster than that predicted by Malthus. The result is that in Europe and in many other parts of the world, human beings live well above subsistence level. Real wages have gone up because of productivity increase, despite increase in population growth.

The revival of Malthusian belief is known as neo-Malthusianism. Like their predecessor, neo-Malthusians believed that population would grow at an unsustainable rate, if left unchecked. The increase in population would exert undue strain on natural resources; not only on food, but also on other basic necessities such as land, water, energy and clean air and lead to a lower standard of living. A common warning issued by some neo-Malthusians was that the oil wells would run dry in about 25 years. Take Brunei, for instance, some experts predicted that the reserves would dry up some time after 2018. Thus, to avoid misery, population growth might have to be contained, and this could be achieved primarily through a reduction in fertility and having smaller families. Unlike Malthus, neo-Malthusians were not against the use of contraception. In addition, they supported family planning programmes, voluntary sterilisation, if not also abortion.

Neo-Malthusianism has its fair share of criticisms too. Their views again failed to reflect that higher food output could be obtained through better seeds, better cultivation methods and technology. However, conclusions on the limited supply of non-replaceable natural resources such as crude oil are not so obvious. Oil prices undergo large and precipitous fluctuations depending on the prevailing economic and political conditions. With alternative sources of energy that have yet to be fully developed, the threat of energy crises erupting again is real. On the other hand, one may argue that with a slower population growth, the depletion of oil reserves could only be slowed down but not reversed. Similarly, with the demand for clean water expected to increase due to a growing world population and the supply being constricted by pollution, some observers warned that conflicts over water could easily occur in coming decades. These views are supported by the World Resources Institute. On food output they wrote, "The increase in food production in developing countries is remarkable. It is also contrary to the Malthusian vision that prevailed in 1960s." They further commented that "the world's agricultural production of food and other commodities has increased during past decades and outpaced population growth... data (however) show that this increase did not occur everywhere." They also cautioned on the supply of freshwater. "Although essentially a renewable resource on global scale, freshwater is being extracted from some river basins at rates approaching those at which the supply is renewed and from some underground aquifers at rates exceeding natural replacement.... Attention to wastewater recovery and treatment methods and to the potential for changing industrial processes to produce less wastewater and fewer effluents is needed." (World Resources Institute, 1990).

Of importance to note is that population growth rates differ from country to country. Even in the same country, they may differ over time. Singapore, for example, in the 1960s and early 1970s when employment opportunities were limited and economic prospect very uncertain, advocated and pursued an active anti-natal policy with "Two is Enough" as a slogan. By the 1990s, when fertility rates sharply declined, and there was a fear of population decline, the anti-natal policy was changed to a pro-natal policy. In the People's Republic of China, the change was much more drastic, from a pro-natal population policy after the establishment of the PRC in 1949 to a one-child policy after 1979.

Neo-Malthusianism thus has no universal applicability. In countries with growing population pressures and declining standards of living, the advocacy for small family size and a higher quality of life appeals to economic and social rationality. For poor countries, it is argued that high rates of population growth can trap a nation in a vicious cycle of poverty, as shown in Diagram 11.1.

Theories of Fertility

One question modern theories of fertility seeks to explain is the anomalous relationship between fertility and income, that is, why the rich tend to have fewer children than the poor. According to Becker (1981), children can be viewed as consumer durable goods. Thus, in a decision making process, a couple's objective is to maximise their utility derived from a basket of "goods" comprising, *inter alia*, the number of children. On the other hand, the couple is constrained by time and costs.

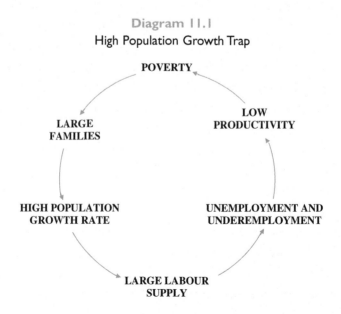

Diagram 11.1
High Population Growth Trap

Diagram 11.2 shows the effect of a rise in income on fertility. With a budget constraint depicted by the line T_0T_0, a couple will attain the highest level of satisfaction by having C_0 children and by consuming G_0 units of goods and services. When income rises, the budget line shifts outward (T_1T_1). The couple can now afford to have more children (C_1) and at the same time consume more units of goods and services (G_1). However, an increase in income will also raise the parents' opportunity cost of time. The relative price of children to other goods will increase and this causes the slope of the budget line to rotate inward (T_2T_2). The couple will now consume more goods and services (G_2) but will have fewer children $(C_2,$ where $C_2 < C_0)$. The emphasis on child quality further limits the number of children a couple desires.

Some researchers disagreed with Becker (1981) that explicit and opportunity costs are the only determinants of family size. Easterlin (1983) approached the issue from a different perspective. He argued that there were two reasons why people control fertility, namely the demand for children and natural fertility. According to Easterlin (1983), demand for children was a matter of taste. On the other hand, natural fertility, defined as the number of children born when procreation was not suppressed deliberately, was determined by biology and culture. Easterlin (1983) also believed that the cost of controlling fertility played a part in limiting births. The cost included

Diagram 11.2
The Effect of Income on Fertility

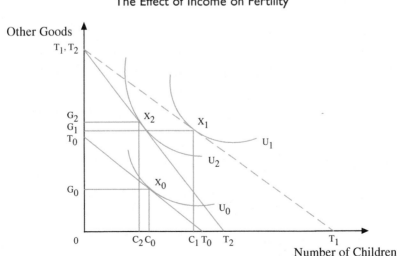

not only the explicit cost of contraceptives but also the stigma associated with practising contraception.

Kuznets (1974) in a seminal study observed that "the less developed nations are prolific because under their economic and social conditions, large proportions of the population see their economic and social interest in more children as a supply of family labour, as a pool for a genetic lottery and as a matter of economic and social security in well-organised but non-protecting society".

Faster Population Growth — Causes

In 1975, the population in Southeast Asia constituted 7.9% of the world population. This figure rose to 8.5% in 2006 (see Table 11.1). As against this, the region makes up only 3.4% of the total surface area of the world. Southeast Asia, thus, is a quite a densely populated region.

There is also considerable cross-country diversity in population size. As can be seen from the same table, the 10 Southeast Asian countries can

Table 11.1

Population Size, 1975 and 2006

	1975		2006	
	Million	% of World	Million	% of World
Indonesia	132.6	3.267	223	3.410
Vietnam	48.0	1.183	84	1.284
Philippines	42.0	1.035	86	1.315
Thailand	41.4	1.019	63	0.963
Myanmar	30.2	0.743	48	0.734
Malaysia	12.3	0.302	26	0.397
Cambodia	7.1	0.175	14	0.214
Laos	3.0	0.075	6	0.091
Singapore	2.3	0.056	4	0.061
Brunei	0.1	0.004	0.4	0.006
Southeast Asia	329	7.859	554	8.479
World	4,058	100	6,538	100

Source: World Bank, *WDI Online*, 13 Nov. 2008, http://publications.worldbank. org/WDI/.

be classified into 3 broad groups: small, medium and big. Indonesia is by far the biggest country in Southeast Asia, making up 40% of the region's population. With a population of 223 million, Indonesia is also the 4th most populous country in the world. As the third largest country in Southeast Asia, Vietnam has 15.2% of the region's population; we may classify the country under medium size in the region. There are five other medium-sized countries, namely, the Philippines (16%), Thailand (11.3%), Myanmar (8.6%), Malaysia (4.7%) and Cambodia (2.5%). The three least populous countries are Laos (1.0%), Singapore (0.7%) and Brunei (0.07%). We have used 10 to 80 million as medium-sized countries. Countries below 10 million are classified as small size and countries above 80 million as large size.

The view that Southeast Asia's population is growing at a faster rate than the world average is supported by figures in Table 11.2. When comparison is made for the period 1960–2006, all the countries in Southeast Asia

Table 11.2
Average Annual Population Growth Rates, 1960–2006

	1960–1969	1970–1979	1980–1989	1990–2006	1960–2006
Myanmar	2.2	2.3	1.8	1.1	1.6
Indonesia	2.2	2.3	1.8	1.2	1.6
Cambodia	2.4	–0.2	2.9	2.4	1.2
Vietnam	2.1	2.3	2.1	1.4	1.7
Thailand	3.0	2.7	1.7	1.0	1.8
Singapore	2.3	1.5	2.3	2.5	1.9
Laos	2.2	1.7	2.5	2.4	1.9
Malaysia	2.9	2.4	2.8	2.5	2.3
Philippines	3.0	2.7	2.4	2.0	2.2
Brunei	4.6	4.0	2.9	2.4	3.0
Australia	2.0	1.6	1.5	1.0	1.3
US	1.3	1.0	0.9	1.0	0.9
Japan	1.0	1.1	0.6	0	0.6
UK	0.6	0.1	0.2	0.2	0.2
World	2.0	1.9	1.7	1.2	1.5

Source: World Bank, *WDI Online*, 13 Nov. 2008, http://publications.worldbank.org/WDI/.

(except Cambodia) have higher average annual growth rates compared to that of the world.

Notwithstanding the higher growth rates, nearly all Southeast Asian countries show a slowing down of these growth rates. This is consistent with the global trend. There are, however, exceptions. The picking up of average annual growth rates in Cambodia and Laos can be attributed to the gradual restoration of a peaceful environment that is conducive to population growth. In the case of Cambodia, the period with negative growth rate coincided with the period of genocide where nearly three million Cambodians perished under the Khmer Rouge Government during 1975–1979.

On the other hand, the acceleration of growth rates seen in Singapore has to be explained differently. In 1970s, the family planning programme implemented by the Singapore Government was so successful that population growth rate plunged from 2.3% to 1.5%. However, by the late 1980s, it was realised that any further fall in population growth rates could have inimical effects on the quality of life and economic growth. To address the problem of rapidly declining population growth rate, the Singapore Government on the one hand, implemented pro-family policies and on the other, loosened immigration requirements.

The simplest and most commonly used measures of fertility and mortality are the crude birth rate and the crude death rate respectively. As can be seen from Table 11.3, in recent decades, there was a marked decline in both birth and death rates in all Southeast Asian countries. Another phenomenon is that, in most of the countries, the death rate declined faster than the birth rate. The decline in birth rates, however, was not uniform. The biggest fall was experienced by Vietnam where between 1980 and 2006, the crude birth rate fell by 53%. Philippines had the smallest corresponding decline of only 28%. The Southeast Asian birth rates of 20–27 per 1,000 persons are typical of those of developing countries.

The rapid decline in the crude death rates can be attributed to the advances made in the fields of medicine, nutrition, and public health. In terms of crude death rates, many countries in Southeast Asia, including Malaysia, the Philippines, Thailand and Vietnam, have reached the rates displayed by the developed countries. For instance, in 2006, the crude death rate in the Philippines is 5 per thousand of population. This compares well with those of Australia and the US, with crude death rates of 6 and 8 respectively.

Table 11.3

Crude Birth and Death Rates (Per 1,000 Persons), 1980 and 2006

	Crude Birth Rate		Crude Death Rate	
	1980	2006	1980	2006
Singapore	17.1	10	5.2	4
Thailand	27.7	15	7.5	8
Vietnam	36.1	17	8.4	5
Brunei	30.6	22	4.6	3
Indonesia	33.5	20	12.1	7
Malaysia	31.4	21	6.5	4
Myanmar	35.7	18	15.0	10
Philippines	36.4	26	8.6	5
Cambodia	39.5	27	26.6	9
Laos	45.1	27	19.5	7
Japan	13.5	9	6.1	9
UK	13.4	12	11.7	10
Australia	15.3	13	7.3	6
US	15.9	14	8.8	8
World	27.2	20	10.4	8

Source: World Bank, *WDI Online*, 13 Nov. 2008, http://publications.worldbank. org/WDI/.

The difference between the crude birth rate and crude death rate yields the rate of natural increase. It is not surprising that Singapore has the lowest rate of natural increase, while transitional economies such as Cambodia and Laos have the highest natural growth rates.

The decline in crude death rate is also reflected in the fall in infant mortality rates and longer life expectancy (see Tables 11.4 and 11.5). Immunisation programmes against deadly diseases such as measles, poliomyelitis, diphtheria and tetanus have largely contributed to the lowering of the infant mortality rates. All the Southeast Asian countries except Myanmar saw a drop in infant mortality rate, with Singapore and Thailand experiencing the biggest decline of more than 70%. Cambodia had the lowest decline of only 25%. Further, Southeast Asians are also living longer. Life expectancy

Table 11.4

Infant Mortality Rate (Per 1,000 Live Births), 1980 and 2006

	1980	2006
Singapore	12	3
Thailand	45	8
Brunei	18	9
Malaysia	31	12
Vietnam	50	17
Philippines	65	32
Indonesia	79	34
Laos	135	75
Cambodia	110	82
Myanmar	94	104
Japan	8	4
Australia	11	6
UK	12	6
US	13	8
World	78	73

Source: World Bank, *WDI Online*, 13 Nov. 2008,
http://publications.worldbank.org/WDI/.

in 2006, ranged from a high of 82 years for Singapore females to a low of 57 for Cambodian males.

Nevertheless it should be pointed out that compared to the industrialised countries, there is still scope for further decline in the infant mortality rate in most Southeast Asian countries, especially in Laos, Cambodia and Myanmar. Similarly, the convergence is not as close when the expectation of life at birth figures is compared. For instance, the expectation of life at birth for women in Cambodia is 61, whereas that of the corresponding figure for Singapore is 82 and for Japan 86.

On the whole, it can be said that infant mortality decreases and life expectancy increases with per capita income. However, it should also be stressed that the relationship between health and economic development is not simple and straightforward. Other factors such as environmental

Table 11.5

Life Expectancy at Birth (Number of Years), 1980 and 2006

	Male		Female	
	1980	2006	1980	2006
Cambodia	38	57	41	61
Laos	44	63	46	65
Myanmar	49	59	54	65
Indonesia	53	66	56	70
Vietnam	58	68	62	73
Thailand	61	66	66	75
Philippines	59	69	63	74
Malaysia	65	72	69	76
Brunei	69	75	73	80
Singapore	69	78	74	82
UK	71	81	77	81
US	70	81	78	81
Australia	71	83	78	83
Japan	74	83	79	86
World	61	70	65	70

Source: World Bank, *WDI Online*, 13 Nov. 2008, http://publications.worldbank.
org/WDI/.

sanitation, availability of health facilities, levels of education and to some extent climate, also affect life expectancy and health. Life expectancy and infant mortality depend critically on nutritional adequacy and the degree of development of health facilities. In spite of the improvement in the provision of basic healthcare, the ratio of physician to people is still rather low in most Southeast Asian countries. The average figures, of course, hide serious nutritional problems among poor regions and poor households. Families of landless labourers, smallholding farmers, small-scale fishermen, urban unemployed and the slum dwellers are particularly susceptible to malnutrition.

One of the most striking examples of lopsided health-related infrastructure development is to be found in the percentage of population with access to safe water and sanitation. In all the Southeast Asian countries except

Singapore, the urban population enjoys a greater access to safe water compared to their rural counterparts. Another example of this lopsided situation is found in the distribution of physicians between the rural and urban areas. In Thailand, there are three times as many physicians in Bangkok as in the rest of the country. While unequal distribution of physicians will remain, another related and growing problem is that of "brain-drain". Increasingly, doctors from the ASEAN region especially Malaysia, Thailand and the Philippines have been and still are emigrating abroad in search of better opportunities and a more fulfilling life. In Malaysia, the most-highly discriminated groups, for whatever reasons, are non-ethnic Malays and that encouraged the emigration of such skilled professionals.

Faster Population Growth — Implications

As mentioned in the introduction, the relationship between population growth and economic development is bi-directional. But, in this discussion, we will only concentrate on how population size and growth affect economic development. The positive economic implications of a longer life span include the additional years of participation in the country's labour force, greater incentive on the part of parents to invest in their children's education and an increase in productivity per worker as a result of better health and vitality.

On the other hand, too rapid a population growth without an economic growth of at least equivalent magnitude leads to a lower standard of living. Although all the Southeast Asian countries enjoy higher standards of living over the years, the rate of improvement differs. With the low per capita growth rates, countries may suffer from the vicious cycle of poverty and the low-level equilibrium trap (Lim, 1997). When per capita income is low, the savings rate is low and this leads to a low investment rate. With a low investment rate, the rate of economic growth continues to be low.

The rapid growth in population size will also act as a pressure on the other factors of production. In the case of land, the larger the population size, the higher the population density. As a consequence, problems such as overcrowding, severe traffic congestion and pollution will emerge, particularly in the bigger urban areas. All these result in a lower quality of life for the people.

The employment rate will be also affected by the country's population explosion in several ways. First, the need for labour services will fall with insufficient investment. Second, the amount of training available per worker will decrease. Although this does not have an immediate impact on the workers, the effect will be felt in the longer term. The productivity of workers will stagnate. There is also the possibility that advancement in technology will render some skills obsolete, resulting in structural unemployment. Similarly, each country's citizen will enjoy a lower amount of educational and health-care services. This indirectly affects the quality of the labour force.

Population Density

With such a small land area, it is no wonder that Singapore has a very high population density of 6,269 people per square kilometre in 2006. Among the other Southeast Asian countries, the Philippines and Vietnam have relatively high densities too. Laos has the lowest population density within Southeast Asia. The overall national density, however, tends to mask the uneven regional distribution of population. The population density in Indonesia is a case in point. Java, which is the most populous island in Indonesia, has a density of over 600 people per square kilometre, while the large islands of Sulawesi and Kalimantan have densities of only 74 and 17 respectively.

As for population pressure relative to arable land, the density ratios are as follows: Brunei, 5,800 people per square kilometre; Cambodia, 375; Indonesia, 1,136; Laos, 672; Malaysia, 1,336; Myanmar, 475; Philippines, 1,551; Thailand, 455 and Vietnam, 1,275. It can be seen from these figures that Brunei has the highest density ratio. However, it has the highest GNI per capita in the region largely because of its production and export of one natural resource, namely, petroleum. While this shows the limitation of density as an indicator of overall population pressure, in some countries (e.g., Indonesia and Vietnam) it does signal the increasing pressure on agricultural resources and in public services.

Dependency Ratio

The proportion of men and women on the one hand, and of children, youth, and the aged, on the other, within a country's population have an impact on the composition of the labour force in the present and future, on their ability to contribute to economic activities and on their ability to reproduce which, in turn, will affect the fertility and the mortality rates. At least one-fifth of the Southeast Asian population is concentrated in the younger age group i.e. below the age of 15 years. The inter-country variations are quite significant. In Cambodia and Laos, the proportion of population under 15 years of age in 2006 was 37 and 39% respectively. In Brunei, Indonesia, Malaysia, Myanmar, the Philippines and Vietnam, the range was 27 to 36%, while in Singapore, and Thailand, the proportion of population was below 30%.

The Singapore case (19%) is comparable to the industrialised countries. In the European Union the proportion was 16% and in the United States it was 21% in 2006. The preponderance of a young population in Southeast Asia has certain economic and social implications. Firstly, the youngest within the young population require childcare and related health services. In the relatively poor societies, a high proportion of children are undernourished, and some suffer from vitamin and protein deficiencies. Evidently those who survive the malnourished childhood will make up part of the future labour force and the malnutrition suffered during the early years can have adverse consequences on the physical and mental development of the young people. This in turn affects their productivity and earnings. Another implication of a large proportion of young people is that greater investment will have to be made in primary schools and similar facilities. This may mean the diversion of scarce funds away from more immediate needs for development in agriculture and industry. Finally, the large proportion of young population in Southeast Asia also means that the dependency ratio is high, which implies that every person at working age has to support, on average, relatively more people.

Another prominent feature is the very small percentage of persons aged 65 years and over. On average, less than 7% of the population in Southeast Asia (except for Singapore) was aged 65 years and above in 2006 compared to a proportion of 18% for the European Union and 12% for the United States. However, the proportion of older people in Southeast Asia is expected to increase because of the twin effects of an increasing life expectancy and lower birth rates. Such an increase will definitely raise many issues relating to the well-being and the caring of the aged.

It should be pointed out that a high dependency ratio need not necessarily imply that only a small proportion of the population is economically active. This is especially true in most of the agricultural countries, where it is usual for young children between the ages of 7–10 years old to participate in economic activities. Indeed, in subsistence farming where the family is the productive unit, both children and old people provide significant labour inputs. There is no retiring age in most rural societies and hence old people continue to work as long as they are physically able and in most cases well beyond the age of 65 years. This does not imply that the labour of children and old people are essential and vital for rural and agricultural development. Often, modernisation of agriculture goes hand in hand with rural children going to school and the elderly moving out of active economic activity.

Another interesting demographic indicator is the sex ratio (males per 100 females). In much of Southeast Asia, the figures in 2007 range from 95 in Thailand to 99 in Philippines. Brunei has the highest sex ratio of 107 males to 100 females. This can be attributed to the relatively high immigration of skilled workers and professionals. The lowest sex ratio is seen in Cambodia with 87 males per 100 females. A plausible explanation is that many young males lost their lives during the politically unstable years of the past.

Employment

It is said that severe unemployment is already one of the most serious problems facing the developing countries and is a main feature of the economic landscape of most countries of Southeast Asia. While the causes of unemployment and underemployment are varied, we will limit the scope of the discussion to the impact of population trends and policies on the labour market. The most serious form of unemployment is "Ricardian unemployment", which is caused by an excessive supply of labour in relation to other complementary factors of production (Lim, 1981). The unemployment rates in the large agricultural countries in Southeast Asia such as Indonesia and Thailand are often misleading, because those figures do not take into account the existence of underemployment, disguised unemployment, and seasonal unemployment, which are all widespread in the rural areas. At the same time, because of poverty and the limited social welfare facilities, most people in the developing countries must find employment even if it means being paid an income well below subsistence level. If these factors are taken into consideration, it is highly likely that the unemployment rates in the Southeast Asian countries would be much higher than the recorded rates.[1]

The modern sectors of the economy (industry and services) will undoubtedly have to play a greater role in absorbing the ever-increasing labour force, since agriculture can hardly provide any new jobs. The implication of this is that unemployment tends to be concentrated among the new and young entrants to the labour market. Inactive and unemployed youths are a cause of concern since they represent a waste of precious human resource and may directly or indirectly lead to social and political instability.

On the other hand, while the growing labour force may exceed the ability of the country to generate sufficient employment, there exists at the same time, skilled labour shortages in certain sectors and regions within many Southeast Asian countries. For example, in Malaysia, the plantation sector had suffered from chronic labour shortages, while Singapore experienced labour shortages in the construction sector. In the case of Brunei, it is said that there is a general unwillingness on the part of the local labour (meaning ethnic Malay Bruneians) to take up employment in the private sector, as there are plenty of jobs in the public sector which are made very attractive by the extensive and generous fringe benefits. However, in the 1990s, the easy availability of jobs in the public sector has begun to shrink. This is because the low oil price has placed a brake on the expanding public expenditure. The Government's desire for the private sector to play a bigger role in the economy also unintentionally contributed to the decline. Brunei is now facing rising youth unemployment, since many are prepared to wait for public sector jobs rather than work in the private sector.

The declining fertility in future will also affect the labour force participation rates. While this impact is currently non-existent in most of the Southeast Asian countries, the problem is already being discussed in Singapore. With the rate of new entrants to the labour market slowing down and an ageing population, this has important implications on productivity and the quality of work. In 1997, at the National Day Rally, the Government announced

---

[1]According to Oshima (1978), if underemployment were to be taken into account this could mean unemployment rates of 10% or more. See Oshima, Harry T., "Structure and Development in Southeast Asian Countries", *Proceedings of Japan Economic Research Centre Conference*, Tokyo, September 1978.

further liberalisation on policies relating to foreign workers, allowing more foreign professionals to work in Singapore. The move was to allow expertise that was not available locally to fill the gaps. The large importation of 'foreign talent' at the apex in the private and some public sectors has, however, created some controversy and much anxiety in Singapore.

So, in Southeast Asia, some countries face labour shortages and most labour surpluses, and within the same economy, some sectors have draught in labour supply, others have floods. The same population policy thus cannot be applied to all countries alike in Southeast Asia. However, the case for family planning is applicable to all, particularly if it is viewed from individuals' point of view and the quality of life of members of the family.

Education

Until the early 1960s, most economic development literature emphasised the role of accumulation of physical capital such as machinery, factories, and physical infrastructure in the development process. Since then, attention has been focused on increasing the productivity of human capital. It is now well recognised that the levels of education, skills, health and nutrition are important for economic growth and development.

Since the 1950s, there has been a substantial growth in the education system in the Southeast Asia region especially among the original ASEAN countries. Though the quality of education differs, nearly all the countries in Southeast Asia have come close to universal primary education. At the secondary level, there are marked quantitative differences, and there is still considerable scope for improvement, quantitatively and qualitatively. Among the Southeast Asian countries, the Philippines, Singapore and Malaysia have the highest enrolment ratios in secondary schools. However, these ratios are still relatively low compared to the developed countries. The enrolment ratios for higher education are again comparatively low in Southeast Asia. In 2005, Singapore has a tertiary enrolment ratio of 26%. This is to be contrasted against the developed countries with an average enrolment ratio of 69%. However, one must also bear in mind that both Singapore and Malaysia have sent a large number of their students overseas for their university education. This could partially explain the relatively low tertiary enrolment ratios. Besides, except Singapore, the quality of tertiary education in Southeast Asia is generally non-comparable with most of those in developed countries, particularly in the humanities and so-called soft sciences. Most Southeast Asian universities do not fall within the best 1,000 universities in the world. Most are just universities in name but not in standard.

Urbanisation and Internal Migration

Over 60% of the Southeast Asian population reside in rural areas. The rapid growth of the cities in Southeast Asia (see Table 11.6) caused by a continual flow of rural dwellers to urban areas and the natural increase of urban population have brought about considerable problems such as overcrowding, pollution and traffic congestion, if not serious unemployment and rising crime rates.

Although the percentage of urban population has increased considerably over the years, the proportion, by global standard, remains low in most countries, notably in the transitional economies (see Table 11.7). With the exception of Singapore and Brunei, the percentage of urban population in

Table 11.6

Average Annual Growth Rate of Urban Population, 1960–2006

	1960–1969	1970–1979	1980–1989	1990–2006
Thailand	3.7	5.1	2.9	1.9
Singapore	2.6	1.5	2.1	2.5
Myanmar	3.9	3.0	2.1	2.6
Vietnam	4.2	2.9	2.4	3.3
Brunei	8.3	4.1	3.7	3.3
Malaysia	5.3	4.7	4.5	4.4
Philippines	3.9	4.0	4.9	3.8
Indonesia	3.8	4.9	5.0	4.4
Cambodia	3.6	0.3	3.3	5.2
Laos	4.0	5.0	5.5	4.1
World	2.9	2.7	2.7	2.1

Source: Derived from World Bank, *WDI Online*, 13 Nov. 2008, http://publications. worldbank.org/WDI/.

Table 11.7

Percentage of Urban to Total Population, 1980 and 2006

	1980	2006
Cambodia	12	20
Vietnam	19	27
Laos	12	21
Myanmar	24	31
Thailand	17	33
Indonesia	22	49
Malaysia	42	68
Philippines	37	63
Brunei	60	74
Singapore	100	100
World	39	49

Source: World Bank, *WDI Online*, 13 Nov. 2008,
    http://publications.worldbank.org/WDI/.

Southeast Asia ranged from 20% in Cambodia to 63% in the Philippines, compared with the global average of 49%. That of Indonesia, the biggest country in the region, is 49% urbanised.

Internal migration takes two forms, namely rural-rural migration where people move from one rural area to another. This type of migration is normally part of Government's deliberate effort to release pressure in densely populated regions. Rural-rural migration can be found in Indonesia and to a lesser extent, Malaysia. To attract new settlers, land and cash are offered.

The other form of migration, which is more common, is where people move from rural areas to towns and cities. The motivations behind the shift are mainly economic. The harshness due to poor harvest or unemployment and underemployment coupled with the lure of higher expected income move many people from rural to urban areas. Other factors include the pursuit of education, the search for a better social environment and the setting up of a new household. The last factor is a major cause of mobility among females in the rural areas of the ASEAN countries. A rough measure of how prevalent rural-urban migration is in a country will be the ratio of urban population growth to total population growth. Most Southeast Asian countries have a figure greater than one indicating the presence of rural-urban migration, with the highest seen in Indonesia (3.3 times). Singapore has ratio close to unitary, because it is a city-state.

In Indonesia, apart from people moving from villages to nearby cities on a daily basis, the long-term migration pattern is mainly urban bound and inter-island, that is, migration from one island to another. Furthermore, the pattern is also increasingly becoming "multi-polar". This means that there has been an increase in the number of urban areas attracting migrants. On a provincial basis, areas such as Lampung, East Kalimantan, Central Sulawesi, Maluku and Irian Jaya showed substantial increases in lifetime migrants in the 1990 census compared to the 1970 census. Part of this movement was intra-rural, from Java especially, and was due to the Government's trans-migration programme.

In Malaysia, the volume of internal migration has also increased. However, unlike Indonesia's multi-polar pattern, Malaysia's migration pattern is bi-polar, with three main foci. They are Selangor together with the Federal Territory, and Penang on the north-west acting as the urban-industrial, commercial and administrative points for the migrants while Pahang serves as the agricultural focus. Another feature of Malaysia's migration pattern entails short-distance moves and is largely intra-rural in nature. Indeed, intra-rural movement accounts for 45% of total internal migration in the country. This can be attributed to the rural development and land resettlement schemes implemented by the Malaysian Government. The other major development is the completion of the North-South Highway that stretches from Johor Bahru at the southern most tip of the peninsular to Kangar in the northern state of Perlis. This major highway link has reduced road travelling time and has enabled the manufacturing industries particularly in Penang and Kedah to tap a larger pool of manpower from the once rural areas of the states of Kedah, Perlis and Perak.

In Thailand the rural-urban migration pattern tends to be unidirectional, that is, there is a tendency for migrants to move towards the Bangkok Metropolis. This has also been identified as circular migration in that most of the migrants return to their villages from temporary jobs in the towns and cities. This type of migration has grown so large in scale that it has created what might be considered a new class of people who are neither urban nor rural in either their role in the production process or outlook (Fuller *et al.*, 1983). Generally, most of these migrant workers are from the rural agricultural sector possessing minimal skills and experience that are relevant to the urban sector. Fluctuating world prices of agricultural products and the decline in agricultural outputs because of growing exhaustion of the soil have forced many farmers to look for a steadier source of income to feed their families thus bringing them to the cities. This circular migration phenomenon can also be found, but a lesser extent, in other primate cities of Southeast Asia, such as Kuala Lumpur and Jakarta.

In the Philippines, the migration pattern also tends to gravitate towards one city — Manila. However, a contrasting feature of the migration pattern in this country is that unlike the migrants in the other ASEAN countries, women (especially between the ages of 15–29 years) are predominantly among the urban bound migrants. In most of the Southeast Asian region the migrants are usually young, single, well-educated and usually male. This phenomenon of female dominance in the rural-urban migration pattern in the Philippines may reflect the greater emancipation of women in the Philippines and the proliferation of service industries in the Metro Manila area.

Although the number of large cities has not increased substantially, one consequence of increasing urbanisation (increase in percentage of urban to total population) that is of concern is the rapid growth of a few large cities in Southeast Asia. In 2006, two cities, namely Jakarta and Manila support a population of more than 10 million each.

It can be seen that in Southeast Asia, the primate cities (that is, the largest city of the country) are the capitals of their respective countries. As shown in Table 11.8, of the nine cities, Phnom Penh has the highest city to urban population percentage (49.5%), while Kuala Lumpur has the lowest percentage (8.1%). This could be attributed to the availability of destinations that people from rural areas can migrate in Malaysia.

The emergence of large cities has certain economic and social implications. Their inhabitants can exert political and economic pressure on the Governments.[2] They can also exert pressure on the system supplying the

---

[2]In this edition, currently circa November 2008, there is an open stalemate confrontation between the Bangkok-based opposition and the rural-based elected Thai government.

Table 11.8

Population in Primate Cities as a Percentage of Urban Population, 2005

Country	Primate City	Population ('000)	As a Percentage of Urban Population
Malaysia	Kuala Lumpur	1,405	8.1
Indonesia	Jakarta	8,843	11.9
Vietnam	Ho Chi Minh	5,072	22.6
Philippines	Manila	10,761	20.3
Myanmar	Yangon	3,928	26.7
Thailand	Bangkok	6,706	32.3
Cambodia	Phnom Penh	1,465	49.5
Brunei	Bandar Seri Bagawan	22	n.a.
Laos	Vientiane	746	n.a.

Source: United Nations Population Information Network, *World Urbanisation Prospects: The 2007 Revision* (http://www.un.org/popin/functional/population.html).

necessary social amenities that often prove to be inadequate. These social amenities include water, electricity, sanitation and waste disposal, housing, transport, health and education. At the same time the existence of poverty and the twin problems of unemployment and underemployment loom large in most cities in the less developed countries, bringing about urban slums and the various social problems associated with them. Singapore, being a city-state, has no rural-urban migration problems and also no migration problem to the primate city, easing the pressure to clear slumps and under-employment and unemployment considerably.

Conversely, a concentration of population in the primate cities could serve as an area in which income generated flows from one region to another region. With an increasing and large population size, economies of scale can be reaped. When the size of the population grows substantially large, the mega city enjoys economies of concentration. Within pockets of the population, various occupations and trades emerge and thrive. Benefits of close proximity allow for efficient communication and transportation. The wealth thus generated will flow to other regions of the country. This is addressed in the circular cumulative causation theory which is explained in greater detail in Chapter 13: Trinity Development Model and Southeast

Asian Development. The advantages are associated with a concentration of population that develops into a mega city and such advantages will be further accentuated with an adequate infrastructure. The mega city, if well-grown and well managed, will serve as a focal point of economic concentration thereby enriching other regions of the country.

In Southeast Asia, the performance of the housing sector varies across countries. On the one hand, Singapore, which has no rural population inflow to start off with, has a very successful public housing scheme, whereby 84% of its population is housed in government-built Housing Development Board (HDB) flats and about 91% own their homes. In Malaysia, the Government has embarked on an ongoing programme to construct low-cost housing. For example, over 343,800 low-cost houses under the Sixth Malaysia Plan (1990–1995) were planned for construction but only 76% of the target was achieved. Indeed, in Malaysia the housing problem has always been acute. In Kuala Lumpur itself, the demand for low-cost houses has always exceeded the supply because of the continuing inflow of migrants into the city in search of jobs. This trend, if left unchecked, will cause a proliferation of squatters and eventually increase the proportion of the urban poor. Similar observations, perhaps in a more severe form, can also be made about Bangkok, Manila, and Jakarta where slum dwellers are to be found in the cities proper and along the fringes.

The growth of Kuala Lumpur, Manila, Bangkok and Jakarta has also meant that there is an increased need for urban transport. Urban transport is vital to the development of any modern city because it enables the movement and access of people and goods between various locations. The urban transport system can also affect other urban public services such as access to hospitals, schools, police and fire services. In most countries the urban transport system is also a large scale employer. The increased demand for urban transport has meant, in most cases, a rise in traffic congestion and its attendant problems of air and noise pollution in cities.

In the light of problems created by rapid urbanisation, the Governments in Southeast Asia have undertaken several types of policies to overcome them. In order to relieve pressure arising from urbanisation, some Governments have implemented policies to make small and medium-sized towns more attractive so as to act as alternatives to the larger cities. This policy of decentralising population away from cities is particularly relevant to Thailand and the Philippines where the bulk of their urban population is found in their respective primate cities. For example, in Thailand the Government has been promoting five other cities to bring about a better distribution of its population. The five cities are Chiang Mai, Khon Koen, Nakornatchsima, Chonburi and Songkla/Hatyai. In addition, under the Fifth Five-Year Plan (1981–1986) the Government had also supported a policy to encourage the growth of industries outside the Bangkok metropolis. This effort has been continued under the Seventh Five-Year Plan to include the vicinity towns around the Bangkok Metropolis, the Eastern Seaboard and some regional urban areas around the Kingdom.

On another level, policy-makers also try to control the rate and direction of rural-urban migration. At times, both the Manila and Jakarta Governments have implemented close-door policies on immigrants. Such policies proved difficult to enforce and gave rise to inefficiency and corruption. Also they failed to stem urban growth significantly. Another method used by the Indonesian Government was the implementation of the transmigration programme aimed at easing the population pressures in Java. In Malaysia, although the land settlement schemes under the Federal Land Development Authority (FELDA) have been successful in slowing rural-urban migration, the costs of re-settlement have been high.

It has also been suggested that a rural development strategy be implemented to reduce the concentration of population in urban areas. Such a strategy includes raising incomes of rural dwellers, providing infrastructure and services, promoting a range of agricultural and rural development programmes by expanding employment opportunities in the form of off-farm jobs for agricultural workers. Rural development, paradoxically enough, is needed for urban development, that is, to allow cities to grow without the problems of excessive population in slums.

The rate of urbanisation, which is expected to rise, will undoubtedly have an impact on the employment situation. As pointed out earlier, the rate of unemployment is usually higher in the urban areas than in the rural sector. This is because in most cases urbanisation in Southeast Asia has not been accompanied by an increase in employment opportunities through industrialisation as experienced in the developed countries in the past. While it is argued that migrants from rural areas add to the pressure on the urban labour market, it must also be pointed out that they may be assets to the urban economy. This is because these migrants are mainly young (between the ages of 15 and 29), better educated and motivated. Another impact of urbanisation is related to the female labour force participation rate. In most cases, urbanisation tends to result in an increase in female participation in the labour market. It is true that both rural urban migration and the increasing female labour force participation exert pressure on the availability of jobs. However, in most countries, steady economic transformation is possible through policies that free up the markets and allow for optimal utilisation of human resources.

Population Policies

In Southeast Asian countries, the formulation of population policies at the national level could be traced back to the 1950s and 1960s. The emphasis during that period was on fertility control. This was achieved mainly through family planning programmes, where Governments undertook propaganda activities to encourage people to use one of the several forms of contraception that were made widely or cheaply available. The successfulness of the programmes, however, depends on several factors. Couples that are relatively more well off, or with higher level of education, or already have the desire to have smaller families are more willing to practice contraception. However, in some countries such as the Philippines, contraception is not as commonly practised due to its religious background. Thus, it is no surprise that the Philippines has relatively low contraceptive prevalence rates in Southeast Asia. Sterilisation and abortion were also used to control the number of children a couple has.

Another common approach that is used by Governments to influence the level of fertility is to alter the incentives of having children. This can be done in two ways, namely monetary and non-monetary. The former method involves the use of taxes and subsides. For example, to limit the number of children born to a couple, the Government can either remove subsidies or impose taxes on the couple when the number of children they have exceeds that stipulated by the Government. The use of non-monetary method includes increased education for girls and increased employment opportunities for women outside the household. Unlike family planning programmes which reduce fertility, the use of incentives or disincentives can either reduce or encourage fertility.

A mix of the two methods is often utilised by the Government to effectively achieve its objective of population control. Other country-specific tools of population policies include population redistribution and management of international movements of people. In this section, the population policies of Indonesia and Singapore are described. Indonesia, the largest country in Southeast Asia, has been trying for the past few decades to bring down its population size and growth. The low growth rates shown earlier indicated that the country is quite successful in the implementation of its population policies. On the other hand, Singapore, which successfully brought down the population growth rates to developed country levels in the 1970s and early 1980s, is now faced with the task of persuading its people to have bigger families.

Indonesia

Population management has always been an issue in Indonesia's modern history. During 1945 to 1966, when Sukarno was Indonesia's President, overpopulation was not seen as a problem. The former President even pursued a pro-natal population policy. To Sukarno, it was the uneven distribution of population that posed a threat to the country's development. Therefore, since the 1950s, transmigration programmes have been drawn up to move the people to the not-so-crowded islands. Even after Suharto took over as Indonesia's President in 1965, transmigration was still commonly used to redistribute the country's population. By 1993, it was reported that 4.5 million people had been resettled from the more densely populated Java, Bali, Madura and Lombok regions to the less densely-populated eastern part of Indonesia. To encourage people to move, the Government gave 2.5 hectares of land to non-farming resettlers. On the other hand, farming resettlers were given only 2 hectares of land. Notwithstanding the unequal enticement, statistics showed that transmigration was not as successful as the Government had projected. For example, while Java's population was growing by 2.5 million annually, the Government had only managed to resettle 250,000 people every year from the island. The unsuccessful movement of people could be attributed to the increasing employment opportunities, which keep on attracting people to move to these more densely populated areas. To keep the resettlers from going back to where they came from, the Indonesian Government announced that it would bridge the economic gap between the more developed western Indonesia and the less-developed eastern regions. At the same time, the Government also encouraged the establishment of new industrial centres by providing more public facilities in eastern Indonesia. In 1996, to further encourage people to transmigrate, cash incentives were offered by the Government.

Although the first Government was pro-natal, the concept of birth control began to spread in the 1950s through the Indonesian Planned Parenthood Association. In 1967, the Suharto Government agreed to the association's suggestion of making family planning nation-wide. One year later, the National Institute for family planning was established. In January 1970, the Institute was replaced by the Badan Koordinasi Keluarga Berencana Nasional (National Family Planning Co-ordinating Body) or BKKBN. The objective of BKKBN is to promote small families through the use of contraceptives.

Two major functions are performed by BKKBN. It involves in the distribution of contraceptives. The organisation is also in charge of training healthcare professionals in the provision of contraceptive services and educating the general public in contraception practices. However, it is a Herculean task to conduct its activities in Indonesia simultaneously, given the country massive physical size. Thus, BKKBN began its family planning programme first in the densely populated islands of Java and Bali. In the mid-1970s, it expanded the activities to the other more developed provinces and by 1980, BKKBN's programmes covered all of the remaining provinces. BKKBN not only distributes contraceptives through the Ministry of Health clinic system but also enlists the help of community organisations and local volunteers. To further enhance its effectiveness, BKKBN set up offices in all the provinces. Besides organising programme activities and the physical distribution of contraceptives, these autonomous provincial offices also negotiate with the central office targets for contraceptive prevalence and guidelines for programme activities.

To entice more families to participate in its family planning programmes, BKKBN initiated a community welfare project. Under this scheme, villages that were able to increase the number of participants would be eligible for a health and nutrition programme, which included a weighing programme for children under five, nutrition education and subsidised food supplements, rudimentary maternal and child health services and other programmes designed to improve community health, education, employment, and the status of women.

In view of Indonesia's large rural population, it is indeed surprising that the country was able to achieve significant success in its family planning programmes. Total fertility rate fell more than half from 5.6 in 1970 to 2.5 in 2006. The proportion of women using contraceptives also increased from 27% in 1980 to 61% in 2006. However, the Government's ability to fund its family planning programmes was weakened by the recent Asian financial crisis and the Government has the intention to privatise some of the services. The impact of the Government's decision on privatisation on the country's population growth can only be seen in the future.

Singapore

In late 1965, the Singapore Family Planning and Population Board (SFPPB) was established with the objective of implementing the family planning policy of the Government. Its main objective then was to reduce the crude birth rate from about 32 per thousand in 1964 to 20 per thousand by 1970. Throughout the 1960s and 1970s the 'Stop-at-Two' slogan was the family planning catchword.

With the benefit of hindsight it is easy to see why the Government pursued an anti-natal policy during the 1960s and 1970s. During the period, crude birth rate was around 30 per thousand and population was growing at an average rate of 2.5% per year. The Kandang Kerbau Hospital in Singapore was even labelled as the "biggest human factory on earth". Coupled with a period characterised by high unemployment, low savings rates, housing shortage and inadequate educational and health facilities, it was against this background that it became vital for the Government to reduce the population growth rate in order to plan for social and economic development of the country. To this end, the Government introduced a host of incentives and disincentives. These included the legislation of induced abortion, promotion of voluntary sterilisation, lower priority in choice and admission to primary schools for the third, fourth and subsequent children; income-tax relief was limited to only three children; and paid maternity leave was limited to only two confinements. All these measures, aided by increasing number of women going to work, had an almost immediate effect on the total fertility rate which fell from 4.7 in 1965 to the replacement level of 2.1 in 1975. And since then it has continued to drop and at 1986, the figure stood at 1.4, well below the replacement level.

The prospect of a declining population in the not too distant future had led the Government to institute a new population policy in early 1987. The 'Stop-at-Two' slogan was replaced by 'have three or more (children) if you can afford'. Mr. Goh Chok Tong, then First Deputy Prime Minister also announced a string of monetary and non-monetary incentives. The monetary incentives were given to buffer the high cost of child rearing in Singapore and included the following: (1) An income tax rebate of up to S\$20,000 for couples with a new-born third child. The rebate can be used to offset against either or both the husbands and wives income tax liabilities. (2) A higher third child relief of S\$750. (3) An enhanced child relief for the fourth child with an amount equivalent to S\$750 plus 15% of the mothers' earned income, subject to a maximum of S\$10,000. (4) A further tax rebate of 15% of earned income for working mothers, and (5) Subsidies and rebates for child-care and maid levy respectively.

The non-monetary incentives included (1) Children from three-child families would have the same priority in school registration as those from one- and two-child families. Furthermore, priority would be given to children from three-child families when there is competition for admission and (2) Families who wanted to upgrade their flats to larger units would, on the birth of their third child, be given priority in housing allocation. Besides these non-monetary incentives, women would be given compulsory counselling before and after abortions. This was to discourage abortions of convenience. Similarly, women who had less than three children would be counselled before going for sterilisation. This is a sharp contrast against what happened during the 1970s and early 1980s, where induced abortions were legalised and sterilisation encouraged.

Were these incentives effective in addressing the rapid decline in birth rates? A preliminary study revealed that the effect was short-lived (Yap, 1995). Although the new population policy succeeded in encouraging couples to have more babies, especially third and fourth order births, the growth of third order births lost its momentum in 1990. The targeted replacement level of 2.1 was still not achieved.

The decline in the birth rates remains a major concern to the Government. In the National Day Rally 2000, Prime Minister Goh Chok Tong announced further incentives, widely known as the "Baby Bonus" Scheme, to encourage couples to have more babies. Under the scheme, a Children Development Account will be opened for a family once a couple has a second or third child. For the second child, the Government will contribute S$500 per year into the account and up to another S$1,000 per year to match dollar-for-dollar contributions from the parents. The quantum is even larger for the third child, with contributions of S$1,000 and S$2,000 respectively. However, the Baby Bonus will stop once the child is six years old. Working mothers will also get eight weeks of paid maternity leave for their third child, instead of just for the first two children as provided under the Employment Act. Whether these enticements will effectively reverse the declining fertility trends in the long run is yet to be seen.

Since the announcement of the "Baby Bonus" Scheme in August 2000 and the effective implementation in April 2001, the fertility rate in 2007 stood at 1.29, a decrease of 9.3% from 1.41 in 2001. While many have applauded the Government's bold move towards a pro-natal stance, the 2007 figure has not been encouraging. Besides monetary incentives, other factors should require serious consideration in formulating suitably admissible pro-natal policies to reverse the trend of falling fertility rate. This may include, amongst others, the ample provision of childcare facilities and support, sufficient flexibility in employed work arrangement for women and even public education on the intangible benefits of children. Nonetheless, it is only through a longer passage of time that the resultant outcome of the population policy would emerge and it may be too early to form any perceptive conclusion.

Key Points

1. Notwithstanding the slowing down of population growth rates in Southeast Asian countries, the rate of growth in the region is faster than the world average. Possible explanations include a lower crude death

rate due to longer life expectancy and better healthcare facilities. Another reason is the declining of infant mortality rates.

2. A rapid population growth without an equivalent growth in national income leads to a lower standard of living. Furthermore, countries experiencing population explosion may suffer from the vicious cycle of the low-level equilibrium trap. When per capita income is low, the savings rate will be low. This leads to a low investment rate. With a low investment rate, the rate of growth will thus be low.

3. Another implication of rapid population growth is on unemployment. The most serious form of unemployment is Ricardian unemployment, which occurs when labour supply is too excessive in relation to other complementary factors of production. However, declining fertility rates can also cause problems, as in the case of Singapore, it affects future labour participation rates.

4. Besides having optimum population size and growth, a country should also invest in the development of human resources. Through education, the productive capacity of the labour force will improve. Although universal primary education is achieved in most Southeast Asian countries, there are still great differences in the secondary and tertiary education among countries in the region. Nearly all the countries have standards well below those of the developed countries, either in quantity or in quality or both.

5. A common phenomenon in countries with a dualistic economy is internal migration, i.e. people move from rural to urban areas. The main reason is to seek employment. However, uncontrolled rural-urban migration causes problems such as overcrowding, traffic congestion, pollution and insufficient sanitation amenities. All these affect the quality of urban life.

6. The capital cities are particularly prone to population explosion in Southeast Asia, and attempts, mostly not too successful, are being carried out to lessen the very rapid population growth rates in the primate cities.

7. The main objective of population policies in most Southeast Asian countries is to control fertility achieved mainly through family planning programmes. Another approach is to alter the incentives, both monetary and non-monetary, of having children. To obtain optimal results, a mix

of the two approaches is often used. Country-specific policies are also employed. For example, in order to release population pressure on some islands, the Indonesian Government implemented transmigration programmes to move its people to less crowded islands.

Suggested Discussion Topics

11.1 With special reference to Southeast Asian countries, discuss the claim that the relationship between population growth and economic development is bi-directional.

11.2 Why has there been such a rapid rise in the urban population of nearly all Southeast Asian countries in, say, the last forty years and particularly in the primate cities? Can this 'Great Trek' be checked? Is it desirable to limit or check this movement?

11.3 Is it possible to have a developed country with an under-developed people? Why don't the Southeast Asian countries invest more on human capital, including adult education and the training and re-training of workers? Is the problem too difficult to manage? Discuss.

References

BECKER, Gary, 1981, *A Treatise on the Family*, Cambridge, Massachusetts: Harvard University Press.

EASTERLIN, Richard, 1983, "Modernisation and fertility: A critical essay", *Determinants of Fertility in Developing Countries*, Vol. 2, R. BULATAO and R. LEE (eds.), New York: Academic Press.

FULLER, Theodore D. *et al.*, 1983, *Migration and Development in Thailand*, Modern Social Science Association of Thailand.

KUZNETS, Simon, 1974, *Fertility Differentials between Less Developed and Developed Regions: Components and Implications*, Discussion paper no. 217, Yale University.

LIM, Chong Yah, 1997, "The low-income trap: Theory and evidence", *Accounting and Business Review*, 4(1), 1–19.

LIM, Chong Yah, 1981, *Economic Development in Southeast Asia*, Singapore: Federal Publications.

OSHIMA, Harry T., 1978, "Structure and development in Southeast Asia countries", *Proceedings of Japan Economic Research Centre Conference*, Tokyo.

World Resources Institute, 1990, *World Resources 1990–91*, New York, Oxford: Oxford University Press.

YAP, Mui Teng, 1995, "Singapore's three or more' policy: The first five years", *Asia-Pacific Population Journal*, 10(4), 39–52.

Further Readings

HAUSER, Philip M. *et al.*, 1985, *Urbanisation and Migration in ASEAN Development*, National Institute for Research Advancement, Tokyo.

MARAVIGLIA, N., 1990, *Indonesia, Family Planning Perspectives in the 1990s*, World Bank, A World Bank Country Study, Washington, D.C.

MYINT, Hla, 1972, *Southeast Asia's Economy: Development Policies in the 1970s*, New York: Praeger Publishers.

SHANTAKUMAR, G., 1994, *The Aged Population of Singapore*, Singapore: Singapore National Printers.

SHANTAKUMAR, G., 2002, "Aging populations and income security: A framework for analysis and action", book chapter in *Public Policy in Asia: Implications for Business and Government*, edited by Mukul G. Asher, David Newman, and Thomas P. Snyder, Westport, CT: Quorum Books.

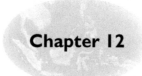

Chapter 12

The Asian Financial Crisis

Lenin was right. There is no subtler, no surer means of overturning the existing basis of society than to debauch the currency.

John Maynard Keynes, *The Economic Consequences of Peace*

Objectives

✓ Trace the course of the crisis and its subsequent recovery.
✓ Provide explanation for the crisis.
✓ Highlight the counter-measures undertaken by the various crisis-hit countries.
✓ Summarise the lessons learnt from the crisis.

Introduction

It has been some years since the eruption of the infamous Asian financial crisis (1997–1998). The crisis took many people by surprise. From the 1960s, many countries in East Asia had been enjoying double-digit growth, a rate that was unmatched by other countries or regions, including those of all the developed countries. The remarkable economic performances were termed as the "East Asian Miracle" by the World Bank (1993). However, dreams turned into nightmares when the Asian economic tsunami started in Thailand in mid-1997 and spread quickly to the other countries in the region through a process called negative circular cumulative causation.

Stock markets tumbled to their all-time lows. Exchange rates were a mere fraction of their pre-crisis values, and banks were overloaded with non-performing loans. Surprisingly, the recovery of the East Asian economies was equally speedy. By the second half of 1999, nearly all the crisis-hit countries had exhibited positive GDP growth rates. We may thus consider this phenomenon as a V-shaped recovery process. However, Table 12.6 shows that in US dollar terms, the per capita income of capital-control economies in Southeast Asia fared much better when 1996 was compared with 2004.

Several interesting developments of the Asian financial crisis were observed. Numerous explanations had been put forward to account for the crisis. What caused the crisis? Did the crisis spell the end of the "East Asian Miracle"? Would the financial crisis recur? These were but three of the many frequently asked questions. Some important observers went as far as saying that the East Asian economic miracle was nothing but a mirage (Krugman, 1993 and 1997). Also of interest to note is how countries reacted to the crisis. Some countries, namely Thailand, Indonesia and South Korea turned to the IMF for assistance. In return, these countries had to implement structural reforms to resuscitate their economies. The issue of how helpful these IMF policies were in resuscitating the countries' economies has remained a bone of contention.

One of the most fervent dissenters of IMF's restructuring policies was Dr Mahathir Mohamad, then the Prime Minister of Malaysia. Instead of going to the IMF, he introduced selective capital controls for Malaysia. His decision to close the external capital account was criticised by the IMF, the World Bank and leaders of some industrialised countries. Ironically, the IMF contended subsequently that it might have been too harsh in the administration of its policies on the three countries and that Malaysia's capital controls might be a viable option. Besides capital controls, Dr. Mahathir also advocated regulating international currency trading. Despite strong economic fundamentals, Singapore was also affected by the regional crisis. To overcome the crisis, the country implemented drastic cost-cutting measures. Poor sentiments due to weak economic conditions also gave rise to political and social unrest in some countries, notably Indonesia, and to a much lesser extent, Malaysia and Thailand.

Crisis: Recession and Recovery

The devaluation of the Thai baht on 2nd July 1997 set off a massive melt-down of the foreign currency markets in the region. Table 12.1 shows the severity of the fall in the exchange rates of the eight East Asian countries. Within about half a year, only half the value of the Korean won or Thai baht was left. For Indonesia, the exchange rate depreciated even more, by as much as 83% by July 1998. By January 1998, the Malaysian ringgit fell by 42%. The Asian economic crisis and the recession started with the exchange rate collapse of these countries.

By 1998, most of the East Asian countries were in recession. Among the eight crisis countries, Thailand was the most severely affected, experiencing six consecutive quarters of negative growth lasting from the 3rd quarter of 1997 to the last quarter of 1998. The other crisis countries in East Asia — Indonesia, South Korea, the Philippines, Malaysia, Singapore, Hong Kong, and Japan — also experienced recession with varying degrees of severity. Table 12.2 shows the number of quarters each country was in recession. But these are ex-post data, affected by the measures each country had taken to end the crisis.

In sharp contrast, China and Taiwan were spared from the economic downturn. The GDP figures of China continued to show robust growth, with

Table 12.1

Depreciation of Exchange Rates (Per US$)

	June 1997	Lowest Rate	Lowest Month	Depreciation
Indonesian rupiah	2,427.9	13,995.9	July 1998	−83%
Thai baht	24.318	52.551	January 1998	−53%
South Korean won	887.03	1,693.65	January 1998	−47%
Malaysian ringgit	2.5157	4.1941	January 1998	−42%
Philippine peso	26.355	43.657	September 1998	−40%
Japanese yen	114.32	144.59	August 1998	−21%
New Taiwan dollar	27.882	34.699	August 1998	−20%
Singapore dollar	1.4264	1.7566	August 1998	−19%

Source: LIM, Chong Yah, 2000, *A Post-Mortem on the East Asian Exchange Rate Crisis*, Keynote address at the 7th Conference of the East Asian Economic Association held in Singapore.

Table 12.2
Number of Quarters in Recession

Thailand	6
Japan	6
Hong Kong	5
Indonesia	5
Malaysia	5
South Korea	4
Philippines	3
Singapore	2

Source: LIM, Chong Yah, 2000, 'From Recession to Recovery in East Asia: A Non-IMF and Non-World Bank Explanation', *Accounting and Business Review*, Vol. 7, No. 2, 145–162.

real growth rates of 8.8%, 7.8% and 7.2% in 1997, 1998 and 1999 respectively. Similarly, real quarterly growth rates for Taiwan were all positive for the period 1997–1999. Both had and still have capital control before, during and after the crisis.

The exchange rate crisis also led to the collapse of the stock market and the property market and these in turn escalated the volume of the non-performing loans (NPLs) of the commercial banks. East Asian countries witnessed the collapse of their stock markets almost all at the same time, as illustrated in Table 12.3. Stock markets in Bangkok, Jakarta, Kuala Lumpur, Manila and Singapore saw their lowest points in September 1998. The collapse in Kuala Lumpur was the most serious; only 21% of the pre-crisis highest value was left. This explained the drastic move by the Malaysian Government led by its charismatic Prime Minister Dr Mahathir Mohamed to have capital controls starting from that month.

Dissatisfaction caused by poor economic conditions spilt over to the political arena. On 13–15 May 1998, Indonesia experienced one of the worst riots in its modern history. The riots in Jakarta were reported to be started due to the shooting of four Trisakti University students. The students had been demonstrating peacefully for weeks demanding the resignation of ageing President Suharto.

Table 12.3

Collapse of Stock Markets

	Highest Pre-crisis Date	Lowest Date	Amount Depreciated
Kuala Lumpur Composite	25 February 1997	1 September 1998	−79%
Bangkok SET	22 January 1997	4 September 1998	−76%
Philippines SE Composite	3 February 1997	11 September 1998	−67%
Jakarta SE Composite	8 July 1997	21 September 1998	−65%
Korea SE Composite (KOSPI)	17 June 1997	16 June 1998	−65%
Straits Times Index	17 February 1997	4 September 1998	−62%
Hang Seng	7 August 1997	13 August 1998	−60%
Taiwan SE Weighted	26 August 1997	5 February 1999	−46%
Nikkei Average	16 June 1997	9 October 1998	−38%

Source: LIM, Chong Yah, 2000, *A Post-Mortem on the East Asian Exchange Rate Crisis*, Keynote address at the 7th Conference of the East Asian Economic Association held in Singapore.

Shocking findings revealed that most of the rioters were not students, but the young urban poor. These people were using the demonstrations to advance their agenda and to vent their dissatisfaction against the Suharto Government. This subsequently turned into riots against the minority ethnic Indonesian Chinese. The riots also spread to the other parts of Indonesia such as Surabaya. Rioters looted and set fire on houses, shops and super-markets. Death toll was put at 1,188 in Jakarta and Tanggerang. During the riots, it was also reported that more than 4,940 buildings were damaged, of which 4,240 were shops, shopping malls, restaurants, automobile workshops and more than 500 were bank offices. On 21 May 1998, Suharto resigned as the President of Indonesia, after 32 years in absolute power. He was succeeded by Bacharuddin Jusuf Habibie, his Vice President. On 20 October 1999, Abdurrahman Wahid became Indonesia's President, after winning the country's first contested presidential election.

The financial crisis did not confine itself to the East Asian region. Russia and Brazil were also hit by the crisis. Beginning from the middle of 1998, there were already signs that Russia's fragile banking system was in an emergency state. To make things worse, the Russian Government was facing one of its greatest political crises since the disintegration of the former

Soviet Union. Internal strife was breaking down the Coalition Government, greatly impeding the much-needed radical economic reforms. At the same time, there was also growing discontent among the common folks, as general prices escalated and food shortages became acute. On 17 August 1998, unable to defend its currency any longer, Russia devalued the rouble. At the same time, the country defaulted on its domestic Government debts and declared a 90-day debt moratorium. On 2 September 1998, Russia floated the rouble.

The cause and effect process was, as expected, a (regional) circular cumulative one. The exchange rate crisis, the stock market crisis, the property market crisis, the debt crisis, and the banking crisis led to a full-blown economic crisis. In some countries, due to inappropriate management, social and political problems also arose. A schematic representation of the crisis is illustrated in Diagram 12.1. A chronology of the Asian financial crisis is also given in the Appendix at the end of the chapter.

As all the original five ASEAN members were in trouble, regional self-help effort, such as the currency swap arrangement then in existence, was not effective. Moreover, Japan, the world's second largest economy, had been in the doldrums since the bursting of its asset bubbles in 1990.

Diagram 12.1

East Asian Crisis: Origin and Spread

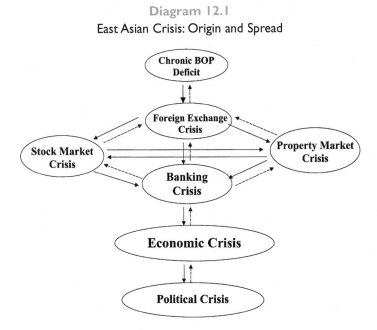

As stated earlier in the circumstances, Thailand, Indonesia and South Korea thus sought the help of the IMF. Malaysia introduced selective capital controls. Singapore opted for drastic domestic cost-cutting measures. The writer himself played a pivotal role in this Cesarean operation (Lim C. Y., 1998). Hong Kong propped up the stock market with government surplus fund. Thus, each country found its own way to survive and to overcome the crisis.

Of the eight crisis-ridden economies in East Asia, four countries, namely Indonesia, Hong Kong, Malaysia and Japan, still showed negative growth rates in the first quarter of 1999. The remaining four crisis-hit countries, namely Thailand, South Korea, the Philippines and Singapore had already achieved positive growth rates. Nevertheless, nearly all the eight Asian crisis economies showed positive growth rates in the 2nd, 3rd and 4th quarters of 1999, and also positive growth rates in 2000. Therefore, the crisis in terms of negative GDP growth rate was only in 1998. The recovery in 1999 was led by South Korea, Malaysia and Singapore with real growth rates of 10.7%, 5.6% and 5.4% respectively. The quarterly GDP growth rates of the East Asian economies are given in Table 12.4. However, in terms of real GDP per capita (local currency), only Singapore and South Korea had recovered from the recession in 1999. Nevertheless, most East Asian stock markets had rebounded and reached record levels in the second half of 1999 or early 2000.

The quick recovery of the economies can be attributed to several factors. Basically, the crisis countries had become more competitive after their exchange rates had been considerably devalued. Furthermore, the productive capacity of the countries, with the exception of Indonesia, remained more or less intact. Finally, favourable external conditions also helped in the speedy recovery of these economies. Diagram 12.2 shows the V-shape recovery of the East Asian economies.

Causes

External Imbalance Theory

All the eight East Asian market-oriented recession countries shared one important common characteristic — free substitutability of their domestic

Table 12.4

Quarterly Growth Rates of Both Crisis and Non-Crisis Economies, 1Q 1997–2Q 2000

Economy \ Year	1Q 97	2Q 97	3Q 97	4Q 97	1Q 98	2Q 98	3Q 98	4Q 98	1Q 99	2Q 99	3Q 99	4Q 99	1Q 00	2Q 00
Crisis														
Indonesia	7.0	6.0	2.5	1.4	-6.2	-14.6	-16.1	-17.7	-9.4	1.8	0.5	4.3	3.2	4.1
Thailand	3.8	5.1	-3.2	-7.5	-13.4	-12.8	-9.5	-3.7	0.9	3.5	3.6	6.5	5.2	6.6
South Korea	4.9	6.2	5.5	3.6	-3.6	-7.2	-7.1	-3.7	4.6	9.8	12.3	13.0	12.8	9.6
Philippines	5.0	5.7	4.9	4.8	1.7	-0.8	-0.7	-5.3	1.2	3.6	3.1	4.6	3.4	4.5
Malaysia	8.5	8.4	7.4	6.9	-0.2	-5.2	-10.9	-2.0	-1.3	4.1	8.1	10.6	11.9	8.8
Hong Kong	5.4	6.4	5.8	2.5	-2.6	-3.1	-6.9	-5.6	-3.2	0.7	4.5	8.7	14.3	10.8
Japan	3.8	1.2	1.8	-0.5	-2.9	-1.1	-3.2	-3.1	-0.4	0.7	1.0	-0.2	0.7	0.8
Singapore	4.2	8.6	11.1	7.9	6.2	1.6	-0.6	-0.8	0.6	6.7	6.9	7.1	9.8	8.6
Non-Crisis														
China,	11.6	11.4	12.9	6.8	8.3	1.8	9.6	6.3	8.3	7.1	7.0	7.6	8.1	8.3
Taiwan	6.6	6.2	6.9	7.0	5.7	5.2	4.2	3.4	4.2	6.6	5.1	6.1	7.9	5.4

Source: LIM, Chong Yah, 2000, *A Post-Mortem on the East Asian Exchange Rate Crisis*, keynote address at the 7th Convention of the East Asian Economic Association, in Singapore.

Diagram 12.2
V-Shape Recovery of GDP Growth Rates, 1997–1999

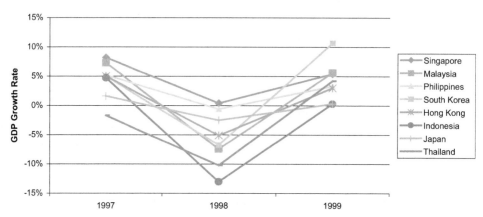

Source: LIM, Chong Yah, 2000, *A Post-Mortem on the East Asian Exchange Rate Crisis*, Keynote
address at the 7th Conference of the East Asian Economic Association held in Singapore.

currency to the US dollar, and *vice versa*. They had no capital control, not
even against speculative short-term capital flows. This free substitutability arrangement existed in balance of payments surplus countries of Japan,
Singapore and Hong Kong as well as in the balance of payments deficit
countries of Indonesia, Thailand, South Korea, the Philippines and Malaysia.
Indeed, the latter five crisis countries had suffered from, to use the original IMF terminology, *serious fundamental disequilibrium* in the balance
of payments before the outbreak of the crisis. This balance of payments
disequilibrium arose from the countries' biased investment mix, which was
in favour of non-tradables. Besides being used for land speculation, foreign
currency denominated short term loans were taken to fund projects such as
the construction of deluxe houses, luxurious golf courses and prestigious
mega-projects that cannot be exported and thus limiting the ability to earn
foreign exchange for the country.

This serious fundamental disequilibrium in the balance of payments of
the five crisis countries is reflected in their chronic current account deficits
(see Table 12.5). In the case of Indonesia and Thailand, their balance of
payments deficits lasted for more than 13 years. In other words, for transaction purpose alone, the supply of domestic currency exceeded the demand
for it every year for at least 13 years. The seriousness of the chronic current

Table 12.5
Current Account Balance as a Percentage of GDP, 1985–2007

Economy / Year	1985	1986	1987	1988	1989	1990	1991	1992	1993	1994	1995	1996	1997	1998	1999	2000
Crisis																
Indonesia	-2.1	-4.8	-2.7	-1.6	-1.1	-2.6	-3.3	-2.0	-1.3	-1.6	-3.2	-3.4	-2.3	4.1	4.1	4.8
Korea, Rep. of	-0.8	4.4	7.4	8.0	2.4	-0.8	-2.8	-1.3	0.3	-1.0	-1.7	-4.4	-1.7	12.6	6.4	2.4
Malaysia	-1.9	-0.4	8.0	5.3	0.8	-2.0	-8.5	-3.7	-4.5	-6.1	-9.5	-4.6	-4.8	13.5	16.0	9.4
Philippines	-2.4	0.9	-1.3	-1.0	-3.4	-6.1	-2.3	-1.9	-5.5	-4.6	-2.7	-4.8	-5.3	2.4	10.3	8.4
Thailand	-6.0	-1.1	-0.7	-2.7	-3.5	-8.5	-7.7	-5.7	-5.0	-5.6	-8.2	-8.1	-2.0	12.5	8.9	7.6
Hong Kong	9.4	8.5	9.9	8.8	11.5	8.5	6.6	5.3	7.0	1.2	-4.3	-1.4	-3.6	1.8	5.8	4.3
Singapore	-0.0	1.8	-0.5	7.7	9.9	8.5	11.4	12.0	7.3	16.4	17.3	15.9	15.9	21.3	30.1	14.3
Japan	n.a.	n.a.	n.a.	n.a.	2.2	1.5	2.0	3.0	3.1	2.8	2.2	1.4	2.2	3.2	2.4	2.5
Non-Crisis																
China	n.a.	n.a.	0.1	-0.9	-1.0	3.1	3.3	1.3	-1.9	1.3	0.2	0.9	4.1	3.3	1.6	1.9
Taiwan	14.8	21.6	17.5	8.1	7.6	6.8	6.9	4.0	3.1	2.7	2.1	3.9	2.4	1.3	2.0	2.9

(Continued)

Table 12.5 (Continued)

	Economy \ Year	2001	2002	2003	2004	2005	2006	2007
Crisis	Indonesia	4.2	3.8	3.2	2.6	0.2	2.9	2.5
	South Korea	1.7	1.0	2.0	4.0	1.9	0.6	0.6
	Malaysia	8.3	8.4	12.9	12.5	14.6	16.3	15.9
	Philippines	1.9	5.7	1.8	2.4	2.0	4.5	4.4
	Thailand	5.4	5.5	5.6	4.5	-4.3	1.3	6.1
	Hong Kong	6.1	7.9	10.8	9.7	11.4	12.1	13.3
	Singapore	16.8	17.7	29.2	26.1	18.6	21.8	24.3
	Japan	2.1	2.8	3.2	3.7	3.6	3.9	4.5
Non-Crisis	China	1.5	2.8	3.2	3.3	7.2	9.4	8.6
	Taiwan	6.5	9.1	10.2	6.2	4.5	6.7	8.3

Source: Lim Chong Yah, "Southeast Asia: The Long Road Ahead", May 2001,
Chapter 12: The Asian Financial Crisis, pp. 313.

Note: 2000–2007 data extracted from ADB, Asian Development Outlook 2008.
Japan's data is from IMF.

account deficit problem is also depicted in Diagrams 12.3 and 12.4. From 1990 to 1997, all the seriously hit crisis countries were in current account deficits. Thailand's cumulative current account deficit from 1990–1997, for example, was nearly 43% of its GDP in 1997. Therefore, under such circumstances, the exchange rate was bound to fall. If the exchange rate is fixed, foreign exchange reserves would fall or foreign debts would accumulate

Diagram 12.3

Current Account Balance as a Percentage of GDP, 1990–2000

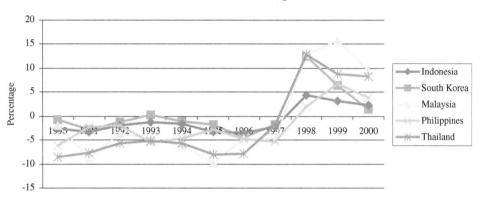

Source: LIM, Chong Yah, 'From Recession to Recovery in East Asia: A Non-IMF and Non-World Bank Explanation', *op. cit.*

Diagram 12.4

Cumulative Current Account Balance (as a percentage of 1997 GDP), 1990–1997

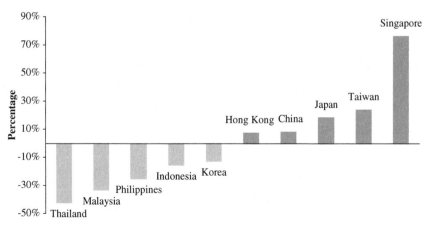

Source: LIM, Chong Yah, 'From Recession to Recovery in East Asia: A Non-IMF and Non-World Bank Explanation', *op. cit.*

or both. As the five seriously hit countries also had free substitutability of their domestic currencies vis-à-vis the US dollar, they all suffered from serious speculative attacks on their exchange rates. Their serious balance of payments problem was masked by their impressive economic growth rates. Incidentally, this masking can happen to other countries and other regions as well, with the US not excluded from it.

Professor Lawrence Summers, who was around that time Secretary to the US Treasury, aptly remarked that any country with a balance of payments deficit on current account exceeding 5% of GDP was in danger of an exchange rate collapse. Some of the East Asian economies had a deficit exceeding this 5% benchmark for many years and yet the exchange rate did not collapse until mid-1997 and 1998. This was because their exchange rates were propped up by the inflow of long-term foreign direct investment (FDI) and short-term speculative capital inflow, often to take advantage of the fixed exchange rate system and the interest rate differentials. Larry Summers' benchmark may not be as applicable to the US dollar, being used globally as an international store of value and an international medium of exchange. It applies, however, to all other countries, including Japan, China, Singapore, Australia and New Zealand.

With free substitutability, the age-old Gresham's Law, developed under the gold standard system, also operates: bad money chases out good money. The US dollar, then under pressure to appreciate, disappeared in the domestic market with more and softer currencies such as the Thai baht and the Indonesian rupiah being used to meet all obligations, particularly foreign exchange commitments.

The velocity of circulation of these soft currencies galloped at increasing speed. Liberal financial markets allowing free and complete capital mobility added to the surfeit of *hot money* around. Statistics show that private capital inflow into Indonesia peaked at initial 6.5% of GDP in 1996 but declined to 2.6% in 1997. The flow then took on a serious reverse turn. Notwithstanding IMF intervention and financial assistance, private capital outflow reached a record high of –8.4% of GDP in 1998, –7.6% in 1999 and even in 2000, –7.0%.

The balance of payments crisis soon developed into an exchange rate crisis. With the supply of the domestic currency increasingly exceeded the foreign demand for it, the exchange rate would fall or the good money would disappear under a fixed exchange rate system. *The excessive transaction demand and the speculative demand in combination brought down the exchange rate.* The Thai Central Bank was reported to have spent US$23 billion to defend the fixed exchange rate but to no avail, as the deficit was too serious, and the speculative demand too great. Thailand later borrowed from the IMF only US$16 billion as a rescue package; a sum much smaller than it had just spent unsuccessfully to defend the baht. In early 2003, Thailand did not hesitate to repay the IMF loan in full, much to the credit of Thailand.

In short, the collapse of the exchange rate had at its source (1) the *fundamental disequilibrium* in the balance of payments and (2) the *free substitutability* of their domestic currency. These are the two basic inter-related sources or causes of the crisis.

Japan and Singapore had no balance of payments problem. Their exchange rates, however, also declined although not to the same extent as the deficit economies of Indonesia, Thailand, South Korea or Malaysia. Japan and Singapore, nonetheless, also suffered from the *regional circular cumulative causation effect*, or what is usually also called, the *regional contagion effect*, or the *tom yam effect*.

By way of contrast, neither Taiwan nor China nor Vietnam had this exchange rate problem, simply because they had capital controls. For example, foreign companies in Taiwan must obtain approval from the Central Bank and the Ministry of Economic Affairs before they can borrow from overseas. A cap of US$3 billion for conversion of overseas funds into New Taiwan dollars is enforced by the Central Bank and except for remittances related to exports and imports, companies that need to remit more than US$50 million must seek relevant approval. The offshore market in New Taiwan dollars was closed previously but has since been allowed to expand its operation in loan provision. Nonetheless, measures are in placed to regulate the activities of these offshore banking units. For example, the total loan amount cannot exceed 25% of the foreign bank's total net worth. China and Taiwan also had balance of payments surpluses, besides formidable foreign exchange reserves.

Singapore's effort of not internationalising the Singapore dollar also played a part in insulating the economy from the financial crisis. Banks were not allowed to extend Singapore dollar denominated credit facilities exceeding S$5 million to non-bank non-residents. This restriction was lifted only in March 2002. However, non-resident financial institutions continue to be subjected to this S$5 million ceiling.

The chronic balance of payments deficit problem can also be viewed from the perspective of overvalued exchange rates. It was believed that the over-valued currencies, which were conducive to investment and consumption, were one of the culprits for the large current account deficits experienced by most of the regional economies. To some extent, one could argue that the high exchange rates were a consequence of the type of exchange rate regimes generally found in East Asia. Although Hong Kong is the only economy that officially maintains a currency board system, the others actually pegged their exchange rates to a basket of currencies. But in most cases, the relative weightage of the US dollar in the basket was often so high that it became an implicit peg to the US dollar. Moreover, the stable exchange rates also prompted huge capital inflows to take advantage of favourable interest rate differentials, which further temporarily strengthened regional currencies.

When the economies were still booming, not many people paid atten-tion to this aspect of overvalued currencies, as everyone was comfortable and euphoric with high growth rates. With a fixed exchange rate system, domestic financial intermediaries could borrow at low rates from interna-tional markets without much exchange rate risks; local producers could pur-chase imported machinery and equipment at relatively low costs and locals were grabbing foreign luxury goods under the fallacy that this "East Asian Miracle" would go on *ad infinitum*.

In fact, as early as the mid 1990s, there were already signs that the strong currencies of Asian economies were biting into the international competi-tiveness of their exports. Since the spring of 1995, when the US dollar started to appreciate against the yen and European currencies, the exchange rates of the Asian currencies effectively strengthened against the yen and European currencies. This translated into a loss in price competitiveness and slower export growth, which contributed to the widening trade and current account deficits. For instance, Thailand experienced a slowdown in export growth of -1.3% in 1996, a far cry from an annualised average of 23.1% over the preceding decade (Iijima, 1997).

In short, the complete liberalisation of exchange rates can expose a coun-try to an exchange rate crisis, especially if there is also chronic fundamental disequilibrium in the balance of payments coupled with non-performing loans within a rigid fixed exchange rate system. Domestic liberalisation and de-regulation, such as liberalising government-licensed import and export monopolies should precede exchange rate liberalisation, not vice versa.

Alternative Theories

Many other theories were put forward to explain the causes of the Asian financial crisis. These theories include Panic Theory, Speculative Theory, Contagion Theory, Excess Capacity Theory, Incompetence Theory and Conspiracy Theory.

A common flaw in the first three postulations, that is Panic Theory, Speculative Theory and Contagion Theory, was that they did not identify the root causes of the financial crisis. The Panic Theory and Speculative Theory highlighted the uncertainty and some consequences of the crisis. Before the speculative cultures are there, there must be causes. For speculation to happen there must be some foundation for the speculators to act. Some root causes have to trigger off the panic. The same logic can be extended to the Contagion Theory, which is just an extension of the Panic Theory but with wider geographical implications. Though, it is not incorrect to say that both panic and speculation aggravated the effects of the Asian financial crisis, they themselves were not the root causes of the crisis. Nonetheless, they might have set off the crisis.

The Excess Capacity Theory is nothing new, similar to the hog cycle theory and cobweb theorem. In the case of the hog cycle theory, hog prices in ancient days collapsed when there was an obvious oversupply of hogs. In the case of the East Asian exchange rate crisis, the external dimension had to be added. There was an oversupply of the domestic currency relative to the demand. This led to the collapse of the exchange rate. An overvalued exchange rate led to the excess capacity, to the inability to sell in external markets, thus aggravating the adverse balance of payments problem.

Proponents of the Incompetence Theory argued that the East Asian's success was due to an increase in the utilisation of factors of production and not due to an increase in the Total Factor Productivity (TFP). A few questions have to be answered. First, which sector is incompetent, the public sector, the private sector or the financial institutions? Second and more importantly, does a lower level of competence necessarily lead to a financial crisis? Specifically, the lack of transparency, inadequacies in the regulation and supervision of financial institutions, poor corporate governance and lax internal controls were commonly cited as the causes of the financial crisis. The problem began, however, when the East Asian Governments started liberalising their financial sectors.

Indonesia began to open up its financial sector in 1988, which amongst others, allowed wealthy domestic investors to set up new private banks. At the same time, they allowed foreign investors opportunities to hold joint ventures with existing domestic Indonesian banks to establish new financial institutions. Thailand, in 1992, set up the Bangkok International Banking Facilities (BIBF) that enabled domestic institutions to raise and lend foreign currencies offshore and onshore. In 1995, Malaysia set up the Labuan International Offshore Centre and handed out ample incentives to attract heavy weight financial institutions.

Under the euphoria of the liberalisation process, financial institutions did not practice prudent lending and borrowing. They followed a sub-prime lending policy. Furthermore, regulations and rules were not strictly enforced. There were rampant inter-party lending and the amounts often exceeded that allowed by the authorities. Lastly, it is not uncommon in certain countries for bigger conglomerates to own a bank in order to extend loans to companies within the group on a preferential basis. Like earlier theories, the Incompetence Theory in general or financial system weaknesses in particular, is, in our view, at best an aggravating factor. Otherwise, how does one explain the absence of a crisis in China, Vietnam or Taiwan? The banking system and corporate governance in China and Vietnam were definitely not superior to those in the East Asian crisis economies. Furthermore, reports such as the World Competitive Year Book and that published by the World Economic Forum showed that China and Vietnam were in the same, if not worse off position in terms of competence and competitiveness than nearly all the crisis countries. The Corruption Perception Index of China in 1997 was much more serious than that of Malaysia, South Korea and Thailand.

The Conspiracy Theory assumed a Machiavellian or malevolent US Treasury, the IMF and the World Bank. Their intention, it was claimed, was to show that East Asian economies were "paper tigers". When the economies collapsed, East Asian corporations, particularly their financial institutions, would be sold at fire sale prices. The external perpetrators of the crisis would then come forward to buy up these corporations, an ingenious way of neo-colonising these places. However, the fallacy of the argument is that it fails to explain why the first and severely hit nations were Thailand, South Korea and Indonesia, all long-time friends of the USA, and not China and Vietnam, which were communist nations or at best nominally communist nations.

Counter-Measures: A Study of Selective Countries

Thailand, Indonesia and South Korea

Thailand was the first to turn to the IMF for financial support. Besides having to reduce its current account deficit to 3% of GDP, the Thai Government had to cap its inflation at 5%. This was achieved by setting a higher rate of interest. The value-added tax was also increased from 7% to 10% to ensure a small budget surplus for the country. Further, the Thai authority had to step up its regulation and supervision of the financial sector. Commercial banks and finance companies were required to strengthen their capital base. Banks were also encouraged to seek foreign participation. To facilitate this requirement, limits on foreign ownership for troubled banks and finance companies were relinquished.

Similar to Thailand, Indonesia had to commit itself to liberalising the economy, undertaking structural reforms, slashing tariffs on key products and revamping its banking sector according to IMF's recommendations. Besides, IMF required Indonesia to reduce the current account deficit to less than 3% of GDP and to cap inflation at 5%. In addition, Indonesia was also expected to phase out a number of monopoly controls on key commodity imports including wheat and soybeans. On 1 November 1997, Indonesia closed 16 banks on IMF's order, a day after the IMF announced its financial assistance package to Indonesia.

South Korea also approached the IMF for help. The Korean Government agreed to cut its current account deficit to less than 1% of GDP and limit its inflation to less than 5%. The Government also had to balance its budget by 1998 through higher taxes and lower spending. Insolvent banks and ailing financial institutions would be merged or acquired by foreign banks.

To allow more foreign competition and participation, foreign sharehold-ing was raised to 55%. More foreign banks and brokerage houses were allowed to establish their subsidiaries in the country. The *chaebols,* Korean conglomerates, were also on the restructuring list of the IMF. They were encouraged to borrow more from the financial markets, instead of from the banks. The Government was also not allowed to rescue troubled groups through subsidies and tax breaks. The IMF was very strict about the moral hazard principle.

A controversial point is whether policies administered by the IMF were useful in stabilising the economies, particularly the exchange rates, of the three countries. Sachs (1997) pointed out that the Asian financial crisis pre-sented a completely different set of problems that the IMF is familiar with. He was of the view that the IMF one-size-fits-all policy was not going to work on Southeast Asian countries. The usual IMF prescriptions of cut-ting budget deficit and raising interest rates to stem inflation can only be applied to a Government that runs big budget deficits. This was not the case in Southeast Asia. Before the crisis, Thailand, Indonesia, Malaysia and the Philippines were having budget surpluses. Inflation rates in these countries were also low. Moreover, the closing down of insolvent banks would only create more panic and bank runs. Therefore, not only would these policies fail to restore investors' confidence in the affected countries, they might even aggravate the already fragile situation. Sachs suggested that the coun-tries should adopt fiscal and monetary policies that were slightly expansion-ary to offset the decline in foreign loans. He was also in favour of merging the weaker banks with stronger ones so as to help in the recapitalisation of weaker banks.

Another criticism came from Stiglitz (1999, 2002). He lamented the IMF (and the World Bank) for imposing conditions on countries seeking finan-cial assistance and argued that such practices were "counter-productive". We have produced Diagram 12.5 that charts the path of the exchange rates of Thailand, Korea and Indonesia. Using the exchange rates at the time the countries approached IMF for help as a reference point, the graph shows that the exchange rates did not stabilise. Instead they deteriorated. This is especially true in the case of the Indonesian rupiah, which by June 1998 was only 26% of the value left after seeking IMF help. Also of significant interest is that although the Philippines has been receiving financial assistance from

Diagram 12.5
Exchange Rate Movements, August 1997–June 1998

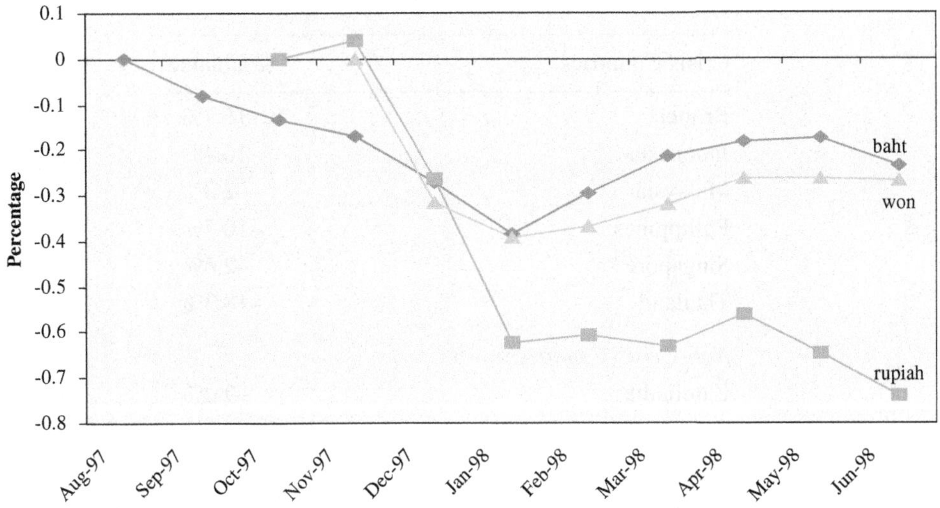

Source: Datastream.

the IMF even before the eruption of the Asian financial crisis, the exchange rate and the economy were not insulated from the crisis. By September 1998, the peso had shed 40% of its June 1997 value. Furthermore, it should be reminded that these crisis countries have to make provisions to repay their loans from the IMF. The IMF loans are not free grants. The loans were extended with stipulated conditions from the IMF.

Stiglitz (2002) is of the view that the policies imposed by the international organisations, namely the IMF, the World Bank and the U.S Treasury (a major influence in the decisions made by the IMF) collectively termed the "Washington Consensus" further aggravated the Asian crisis. While the intention of these organisations were to help the economies in crisis, more often than not, the Washington Consensus represented "a curious blend of ideology and bad economics, dogma that sometimes seemed to be thinly veiling special interest" (Stiglitz, 2002). The stark reality in economic policy prescription centers on the institutional beliefs and the past experiences that shaped the thoughts of policy makers. An economic policy that has worked well in one country at a specific period in time may not be suitable for another economy. The doctrine of the Washington Consensus, based on free markets and minimal government involvement, advocated rapid capital

Table 12.6

Per Capita Income Changes of Crisis and Non-Crisis
ASEAN Countries, 1996 and 2004

Crisis Countries	% Change
Brunei	−16.7%
Indonesia	−10.4%
Malaysia	−2.0%
Philippines	−10.7%
Singapore	−2.6%
Thailand	−18.3%
Non-Crisis Countries	
Cambodia	+9.0%
Laos	+56.3%
Myanmar	+17.4%
Vietnam	+66.0%

Source: Lim Chong Yah (2007), "The International Monetary Fund and Exchange Rate Crisis Management", *Singapore Economic Review*, Vol. 52, No. 3, pp. 285–294.

market liberalisation during the Asian financial crisis, further aggravating capital outflow. Despite the huge bailouts from IMF, Indonesia, Thailand and South Korea continue to experience declining private capital inflow in 1998 and 1999 (see Table 12.6). This is in contrast to Malaysia who managed to reverse the fall in private capital inflow in 1998 without IMF's help. The recommendations of the Washington Consensus were indeed imposed without careful consideration of their dire consequences: the adverse impact on the weak financial system, the business community and the eventual economy wide domino effects that resulted in political unrest and an impoverished nation.

It is now obvious that countries that did not follow IMF recommendations recovered much faster than those that did. In particular, Malaysia contained the crisis by imposing capital controls to the vehement criticism of the IMF. That was in 1998. However, in December 2002, IMF officially acknowledged the effectiveness of the capital controls which the Malaysian Government has since gradually reduced. In the past, IMF was ideologically anathema to any form of capital control, including any restriction on very short-term speculative capital movements, including by hedge funds. In the author's view, the IMF has deprived itself of a very useful and powerful instrument of exchange rate stabilization and orderly exchange adjustment.

Of course, capital control *per se* was, and never is, the magic wand for economic and social development. Nor is it *per se* the most desirable option or target to pursue. It was just a means to an end. At the early stage of economic growth, when speculative attacks on currencies can be frequent and disastrous, capital control could contribute to the stability of the exchange rate. It could also allow for orderly exchange rate adjustments and the ordering shifting of gears. Hopefully, this phase could and should usher in the liberalization of the domestic economy, particularly the strengthening of the financial infrastructure and the liberalization of trade, both foreign and domestic trade. The sequence should not be the opposite: exchange rate liberalization before domestic economic liberalization (Lim Chong Yah, 2007).

Malaysia

On 2nd September 1998, Malaysia introduced selective capital controls to ward off further speculative attacks on its currency and at the same time to inoculate its economy from the global financial instability. Some of the measures are highlighted in text box below. IMF, one of the greatest critics of Malaysia's selective capital controls, said that Malaysia "had taken a step backward". Not only would the controls weaken investors' confidence, they would also cut off the much-needed foreign capital to resuscitate the economy. The implementation of capital controls would also delay the necessary structural reforms. Paradoxically, in September 1999, one year after Malaysia had implemented its controversial capital controls, the IMF commended Malaysia for using the very same capital controls that IMF had condemned earlier to give the country the opportunities for reforms. Nevertheless, a concern regarding the pegged ringgit remains. If the US dollar rises too much, Malaysian exports can become uncompetitive. If the US dollar falls too much, the Malaysian imports would be very expensive. The US currency was meant for the USA, not Malaysia. What was sauce for the goose might not be sauce for the gander. However, the pegging to the US dollar only at a fixed rate worked in Malaysia. There are doubts, however, whether it would work well in the long run. There are also doubts about excessive exchange controls.

HIGHLIGHTS OF MALAYSIA'S CURRENCY CONTROLS

- Fixed exchange rate at RM3.80 to US1.
- RM500 and RM1,000 notes would be taken out of circulation.
- All export and import settlements must be done in foreign currencies.
- Malaysians will need approval to invest more than RM 10,000 abroad.
- Maintain proceeds in ringgit for a year if they own the security for less than one year. This was subsequently replaced with a flat 10% capital gain tax in September 1999 and then removed in May 2001.
- Travellers into and out of Malaysia may not carry more than RM 1,000. Visitors will not be allowed to take out more foreign currencies than they brought in.

However, the use of exchange controls in Malaysia is not new. In 1994, when Malaysia experienced a surge of short-term capital inflow, the country introduced selective exchange controls such as barring residents from selling short-term monetary instruments to non-residents and imposing external liability ceilings on banks. The controls were removed after six months. When Malaysia was a part of the Sterling area under British rule, exchange controls were also introduced to help to protect the British Pound Sterling. Malaysia thus did not have to introduce a special law to institute exchange controls.

Singapore

As Singapore has a small domestic demand, any attempts to prime pump the economy in the Keynesian style through a budget deficit and a cheap money policy will have a very limited domestic impact. The foreign leakage

Diagram 12.6

Route to Recovery

Decrease in Price

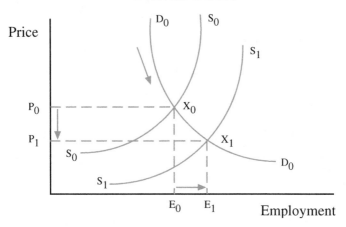

Source: LIM, Chong Yah, 1994, "Economic Theory and Economic Reality", *Accounting and Business Review*, Vol. 1, No. 1, 73–84.

is simply too large. Singapore thus had to cut domestic costs and prices to increase external demand (Lim, 1994). Diagram 12.6 illustrates this strategy graphically. The fall in export price and cost of production stimulate the quantity demanded from abroad and this increases the employment level from E_0 to E_1.

As labour cost make up a significant portion of the costs of doing business in Singapore, a cut in wages together with other costs is thus necessary to nurse the economy back to health. In Western industrial countries, employment flexibility is endured. This policy means massive unemployment during recession. The situation is accentuated by minimum wage legislation in these countries. When there is wage flexibility, as practised in Singapore, employment can remain at or near the original level when aggregate demand falls. This is shown in Diagram 12.7. During a recession, the demand curve shifts from D_0 to D_1. When wages are allowed to fall in tandem, i.e. from W_0 to W_1, employment can be maintained at or near the pre-crisis level.

Thus, during the Asian financial crisis, when the economy took a downturn and registered lower growth in the second quarter of 1998, the

Diagram 12.7
Wage Flexibility and Employment Level

Flexible Wage Structure

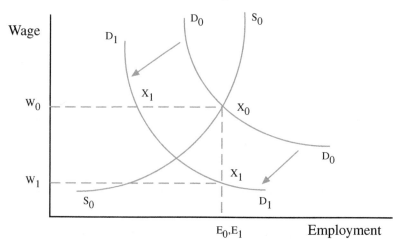

Source: LIM, Chong Yah, 1994, "Economic Theory and Economic Reality",
Accounting and Business Review, Vol. 1, No. 1, 73–84.

Government decided to implement off-budget measures. A S$2 billion cost-cutting and spending measures package was adopted by the Government to counter the crisis in June 1998.

In November 1998, the Government and the National Wages Council saw the need to have a more comprehensive cost-cutting package. The largest share of the S$10.5 billion package was devoted to the reduction of labour cost, which accounted for 72% of the package. This took the form of a cut in the compulsory CPF contribution by employers from 20% point to 10% point and a further National Wages Council recommendation of a cut in the variable wage component by 5 to 8% of total wages. All in all, the S$10.5 billion worked out to about 7.5% of Singapore's GDP for 1998. The NWC also suggested the introduction and implementation of a Monthly Variable Component of wages. This is to increase the flexibility of adjusting wage costs. To reduce the costs of doing business in Singapore, part of the cost-cutting package included a cut in non-wage costs such as rentals, telecommunications and utility charges, transport costs and government fees. Besides cost-cutting measures involving wage and non-wage costs, the Singapore Government also allowed some fall in the exchange rate with a view to maintain the competitiveness of Singapore's exports. This fall in the nominal exchange rate by some 18% of the pre-crisis level took place soon after the collapse of the regional exchange rates. These measures, particularly the cost-cutting measures, must have contributed importantly to the speedy economic recovery of Singapore.

Lessons Learned

There are several important lessons that can be learnt from the Asian financial crisis.

Firstly, GDP growth rates are necessary but insufficient measures of the economic well-being of a nation. The severity and trend in the balance of payments deficit should not be overlooked, particularly its long run position. Gresham's Law can also operate with exchange rates, if they are freely and fully convertible. Once the balance of payments position is considered important, then it follows that the investment mix in favour of export tradables also becomes important, if a serious balance of payments crisis is to be avoided.

Secondly, in addition to an appropriate investment mix, the investment climate must be conducive to investment, particularly of the type that will bring in foreign exchange. Corruption, nepotism and cronyism are likely to be inimical to the growth of an export-oriented investment mix, in favour of the protected domestic sectors, particularly domestic import and export monopolies.

Thirdly, an inefficient banking system, particularly the central banking system, can certainly contribute to a speculative attack on the domestic currency, particularly the exchange rate. The run on the bank has to be extended to include a preparedness for an unanticipated exchange rate depreciation.

Fourthly, another important lesson is that the internal health and internal balance in the economy should take precedence over the fixed exchange rate system. This implies the adoption of a trade-weighted managed float exchange rate system, under which the exchange rate adjustment automatically will equilibrate between transaction demand and transaction supply of the domestic currency. A fixed rate with full and free exchange rate convertibility is more prone to speculative demand and can easily give rise to drastic depletion of the foreign exchange reserves and the collapse of the exchange rate. The danger comes when the US dollar appreciates excessively.

Fifthly, the East Asian countries should also give much more priority in reforming, upgrading, liberalising and deregulating their domestic economies with a view to make them more internationally competitive than prematurely *"laissez-fairing"* their exchange rate or the external value of the currency, on the same principle that the internal value of money too should not be put on a *laissez-faire* basis. Some built-in discretionary control over capital accounts can help to lessen speculative demand for non-balance of payments reasons.

Sixthly, not all countries in East Asia suffered from the same economic malaise during the crisis. Domestic demand was stagnated in Japan. There was, however, falling export demand in Singapore. In Indonesia, the fear was of falling domestic supply. A domestic response suitable for one country need not thus be suitable for another.

Seventhly, the roles of supranational organisations must be re-examined. The IMF is neither an ideal nor a good multi-national institution for an exchange rate rescue operation. This is because the IMF firstly, goes beyond the short-term stabilisation of the exchange rate as an immediate objective. Secondly, the IMF is ideologically emasculated by ruling out altogether exchange control on hot money or speculative demand for foreign exchange as a possible rescue operation, or even as a precautionary measure. Thirdly, the IMF's *modus operandi* of raising interest rate and creating budget surplus in a recession could lead the economy to an even more serious recession, unemployment and political instability, as had come to pass in Indonesia and to a lesser extent, Thailand.

Eighthly, each nation in Southeast Asia must be prepared for an unanticipated crisis, such as the exchange rate crisis of 1997–1998. In good years, it will have to build up, *inter alia*, foreign exchange reserves and budget surpluses to meet unforeseen contingencies. In the Asian financial crisis, it is instructive to know that Singapore had to use up to about 7.5% of the GDP to bring about a sure and quick recovery.

Ninthly, the World Bank and the IMF should not overlap excessively in their functions. The World Bank should concentrate on long-term economic development and poverty alleviation and poverty eradication particularly the promotion of a stable, effective bureaucracy. The IMF should concentrate on the very important subject of short-term stability in exchange rates and orderly balance of payments' adjustments. This indeed is the basic function of the IMF as perceived by Keynes, the founder. The IMF should not take on a Don Quixote role.

Finally, a World Central Bank should be set up specially to help in the smooth functioning of the global central banking and commercial banking systems. Reforms in the banking, particularly central banking and monetary system, the deficiencies of which contributed heavily to the crisis, should fall within the purview of the new World Central Bank.

Position in 2004

As a postscript, the writer pointed out in a conference paper in 2005 that all the capital-control economies in Southeast Asia displayed faster positive growth rates between 1996 and 2004. On the other hand, as Table 12.6 shows, all the other non-capital control economies in Southeast Asia, including Singapore, displayed negative growth rates.

Crisis Recurrence

While the current account affects changes in a country's exchange rate, it is not a complete explanation of such changes. The capital account must be considered too. Capital accounts have long-term foreign direct investments (FDIs) and short-term capital flows. The short-term capital flows are affected by, *inter alia*, the relative interest rates. Statistics by the Bank for International Settlements in April 2007 reported that as much as US$1.7 trillion of foreign exchange was traded globally per day. Timely data on short-term capital flows, however, are not readily available. The situation becomes more complicated when different exchange rate regimes are considered. Between free-floating rates and fixed exchange rates lies a host of hybrid exchange rate regimes. To name a few, this range from the adjustable peg to the crawling peg and the managed float. Given the current global monetary and financial environment, sound management of a country's exchange rate becomes more of an art than science.

Will the East Asian financial crisis recur? There is a strong probability for the crisis to recur, if the countries continue to follow the past practice of ignoring chronic deficits in their balance of payments, particularly on their current accounts. If countries continue to have a fixed exchange rate regime, particularly in the face of long-term fundamental disequilibrium in the balance of payments and with full exchange rate convertibility, they are likely to have another financial crisis. The old road is unsure and unsafe and should be avoided. However, Table 12.5 and Diagram 12.3 show that all the affected economies displayed respectable balance of payments surpluses since 1998. Although full exchange rate convertibility encourages optimal trade and optimal capital flow, it also gives full scope to currency speculators given the present global monetary and exchange rate environment. The general solution formula for developing countries, including those in Southeast Asia, appears thus:

(a) Have full convertibility of the exchange rates on current accounts,
(b) Have full convertibility on long-term capital account,
(c) Have some discreet control over short-term speculative capital account, and
(d) Have a free-floating or managed float exchange rate system against a basket of currencies.

A gradual decline in the exchange rate is a preferable option to a precipitous fall, as had happened during the 1997–1998 crisis. A very market friendly exchange rate policy, which we advocate, must be distinguished from a market only exchange rate policy. According to the Triple C Theory (see Chapter 13: Trinity Development Model and Southeast Asian Development) which is also a stage and sequential theory, policy choices and options that operate well for developed economies need not necessarily operate equally well for developing economies. One size and one practice may not suit all economies at different stages of development.

Subprime Crisis

The current (2008) subprime mortgage crisis in the United States has already wreaked havoc on the global financial landscape and increased uncertainty about the outlook for the world economy. The Southeast Asian countries are not immune to the credit crisis as volatility has markedly increased in Asian equity markets and the stock markets have sold off across the region.

Nonetheless, Southeast Asian economies have not been seriously impacted unlike Western Europe due to their lack of exposure to U.S. mortgage securities and availability of liquidity in domestic markets. One reason is that macroeconomic fundamentals are much healthier than they were a decade ago; Asian countries have reduced their fiscal deficits and are now running current account surpluses and have sufficient foreign exchange reserves to act as a buffer against future crisis. In addition, domestic spending on non-tradeable investment projects is no longer excessive, unlike in the past. Central banks in Southeast Asia have also improved their management of capital flows, thus mitigating the risk of exchange rate overvaluation, credit booms and asset bubbles. Furthermore, corporate balance sheets in the Southeast Asian countries have improved as debt-to-equity ratios have been reduced sharply and foreign currency borrowing is no longer a large component of the corporate sources of funding.

Southeast Asia's relative resilience to the subprime crisis has highlighted the progress it has made in reforming its banking systems. The limited exposures of Asian banks to subprime, coupled with well-capitalized balance sheets, have allowed Asian interbank markets to remain calm while the interbank markets in the United States and Europe have been in chaos. Thus far, Asian economies have coped well with the financial turmoil. However, as the subprime crisis is prolonged, Southeast Asia would be adversely affected by the severe downturn in the U.S. economy. Although there is no telling how long the turmoil will last, Southeast Asian economies can learn several lessons from the subprime crisis. First, they should be aware of the dangers of abundant liquidity, rapid credit growth, and sustained asset price inflation. Second, Southeast Asia governments must be careful in striking the right balance between financial liberalization and prudent regulation. While the countries should continue to develop their capital markets and encourage the growth of their financial institutions as part of its broader economic and financial development, the subprime crisis has shown that financial innovations — whether new products, new structures, or new market players — do not come without risks. In short, policymakers and regulators should ensure that sufficient resources are devoted to financial surveillance, supervision, and risk management in order to mitigate the risks engendered by innovations and developments in financial markets (Khor and Kee, 2008)

A third lesson is that economic fundamentals are essential for any nation to weather any economic crisis. Weak economic fundamentals, such as highly leveraged corporate balance sheets and large current account deficits, led to a loss of confidence in 1997, resulting in the Asian financial crisis. Presently, the strong macroeconomic fundamentals of the Southeast Asian nations have enabled them to remain relatively resilient in the current turmoil. The challenge is to ensure that Southeast Asia learns from the past and current credit crisis so as to be able to ride the next wave of economic boom that comes along.

Key Points

1. The Asian financial crisis saw the massive devaluation of the exchange rates, share and property prices and an escalation of banks' non-performing loans. With the exception of Taiwan and China, the other East Asian countries suffered from the regional circular cumulative causation effect of the crisis that first appeared in Thailand.
2. The crisis had its roots in the chronic current account balance deficit and the free substitutability of currencies. This came about because of bias in the investment of non-tradables against the backdrop of free exchange convertibility.
3. East Asian countries responded to the crisis differently. Thailand, Indonesia and South Korea approached the IMF for financial assistance. Malaysia implemented selective capital controls. Singapore overcame the crisis by deflating domestic costs.
4. Exchange rates of countries that had gone to the IMF for help did not improve. Their exchange rates continued to deteriorate after the IMF was called in for help.
5. A World Central Bank should be set up to help in the smooth functioning of the global banking system, particularly in the light of mismanagement of the US-generated sub-prime crisis.

Suggested Discussion Topics

12.1 What causes the East Asian financial crisis (1997–1998), did the crisis spell the end of the "East Asian Miracle" and will the financial crisis recur? Discuss with special reference to the Southeast Asian countries of Thailand, Malaysia, Singapore and Indonesia.

12.2 Was the East Asian economic miracle a mirage? Discuss with reference to the S curve hypothesis.

12.3 Do you agree that "a very market friendly exchange rate policy must be distinguished from a market only exchange rate policy"? Discuss this statement in the light of the experiences of the East Asian financial crisis (1997–1998).

12.4 What does the "Washington Consensus" mean? Is it the cause or the cure for the East Asian exchange rate crisis? Why is Stiglitz so upset about the Washington Consensus approach?

References

IIJIMA, Ken, 1997, "Background and impact of the Asian currency crisis", *Pacific Business and Industries*, 4(38).

KHOR, Hoe Ee and KEE Rui Xiong, "Asia: A perspective on the subprime crisis", IMF issue on *Finance and Development*, 45(2), June 2008.

KRUGMAN, Paul, 1994, "The myth of Asia's miracle", *Foreign Affairs*, Nov/Dec issue, 73(6).

KRUGMAN, Paul, 1997, "Asia's miracle is alive and well? Wrong, It never existed", *Time Magazine*, 150(13).

LIM, Chong Yah, 1994, "Economic theory and economic reality", *Accounting and Business Review*, 1(1), 73–84. Also appeared in HOOI, Den Huan and KOH, Ai Tee (eds.), 2001, *Economic Essays by Lim Chong Yah*, Singapore: World Scientific, 99–110.

LIM, Chong Yah, 1998, "National wages council: Memoranda to the Prime Minister, 1972–1998", NWC Secretariat.

LIM, Chong Yah, 2007, "The IMF and exchange rate crisis management", *Singapore Economic Review*, 52, No. 3.

SACHS, Jeffrey D., 1997, "The wrong medicine for Asia", *The New York Times*.

STIGLITZ, Joseph E., 1999, "The world bank and the millennium", *The Economic Journal*, 109(459), 577–597.

STIGLITZ, Joseph E., 2002, *Globalisation and its Discontents*, New York: Norton.

World Bank, 1993, *The East Asian Miracle: Economic Growth and Public Policy*, Washington, D.C: The World Bank.

Further Readings

ARIFF, Mohamed and Ahmad M. KHALID, 2000, *Liberalisation, Growth and the Asian Financial Crisis: Lessons for Developing and Transitional Economies in Asia*, Cheltenham: Edward Elgar Publishing.

ARNDT, H. W. and Hal HILL (eds.), 1999, *Southeast Asia's Economic Crisis: Origins, Lessons And The Way Forward*, Singapore: Institute of Southeast Asian Studies.

BOMHOFF, Eduard J., 1999, "Lessons from the asian financial crisis", *Accounting and Business Review*, 6(1), 1–16.

CORDEN, Max, 1999, *The Asian Crisis: Is There A Way Out?*, Singapore: Institute of Southeast Asian Studies.

LIM, Chong Yah, 1998, "The solution to the Asian currency crisis", keynote address at the International Conference on *The New Role of Government in a Market Economy* organised by Osaka University and the Nanyang Technology University in Singapore. Available on www.stern,nyu.edu/~nroubini/asia/AsiaHomepage.html.

LIM, Chong Yah, 2000, "Postmortem on the East Asian exchange rate crisis", keynote address at the *7th Convention of the East Asian Economic Association* held in Singapore.

LIM, Chong Yah, 2000, "From recession to recovery in East Asia: A Non-IMF and Non-World Bank Explanation", *Accounting and Business Review*, 7(2), 145–162. Also appeared in HOOI, Den Huan and KOH, Ai Tee (eds.), 2001, *Economic Essays by Lim Chong Yah*, Singapore: World Scientific, 224–240.

LIM, Chong Yah, 2008, "The Asian financial crisis and the subprime mortgage crisis: A dissenting view", book chapter in *Singapore and Asia in a Globalised World: Contemporary Economic Issues and Policies*. CHIA, W. M. & SNG H. Y. (eds.), Singapore. World Scientific.

ZHANG, Peter (ed.), 1998, *IMF and Asian Financial Crisis*, Singapore: World Scientific.

Appendix

Chronology of the Asian Financial Crisis

1997

14–15 May	Speculators attacked the Thai baht. Thailand and Singapore jointly defended the currency.
19 June	Dr. Amnuay Viravan resigned as Thai Finance Minister.
27 June	Bank of Thailand suspended 16 finance companies.
2 July	Thailand floated the baht and called on IMF for 'technical assistance'.
	Bangko Sentral ng Pilipinas defended the peso aggressively.
8 July	Bank Negara defended the ringgit aggressively.
	Bank Indonesia widened its rupiah trading band.
11 July	Bangko Sentral ng Pilipinas allowed the peso to float within a wider band against the US dollar.
14 July	IMF offered an additional financial support to the Philippines.
	Bank Negara abandoned the defence of the ringgit.
17 July	Monetary Authority of Singapore allowed the Singapore dollar to depreciate.
24 July	Currencies of Indonesia, Thailand, Malaysian and the Philippines plunged.
11 August	The IMF announced Thailand's rescue package.
14 August	Bank Indonesia floated the rupiah. The rupiah sank further.
20 August	IMF approved a $3.9 billion standby credit for Thailand.

16 September	Indonesia postponed projects to reduce budget deficit.
20 September	Dr. Mahathir said international currency trading should be regulated.
8 October	Indonesia announced that it would turn to IMF for help.
14 October	Thailand established the Financial Restructuring Agency and Asset Management Company.
17 October	Malaysia announced belt-tightening budget.
20–23 October	Hong Kong stock market lost nearly 25% of its value.
27 October	Asian jitters spilt over to world stock markets. The Dow Jones Industrial Average Index saw its biggest one-day fall.
31 October	IMF unveiled Indonesia's $40 billion aid package.
1 November	Singapore and Japan each pledged to extend a US$5 billion loan to Indonesia.
	Indonesia closed 16 banks.
7 November	Stocks in Asia tumbled as currency uncertainties shook South Korea and high interest rates and falling property prices plagued Hong Kong.
	Panic spread to Latin America.
17 November	Bank of Korea floated the won.
19 November	Korean Finance Minister Kang Kyong-shik resigned.
21 November	South Korea indicated that it would seek financial assistance from IMF.
30 November	Zhu Rongji indicated that the yuan would not be devalued.
4 December	IMF agreed to provide $57 billion of financial support to South Korea.

18 December	Dissenter Kim Dae-jung was elected President.
31 December	Indonesia announced a reform package through merger of 7 existing banks into 3 entities by July 1998.

1998

5 January	Thailand announced decision to ask IMF to ease its bailout terms.
6 January	Indonesia unveiled its 98/99 budget. The rupiah plunged further.
12 January	Peregrine, one of Asia largest independent investment banks, collapsed.
22 January	The rupiah collapsed. Intervention by Indonesia drove the currency back to close at 11,800 to US dollar.
10 February	Indonesia announced its plan of having a currency board.
17 February	Indonesian Central Bank Governor Sudradjad Djiwandono was sacked.
23 March	Indonesia nearly doubled interest rates to boost its currency and control inflation.
13–15 May	Massive racial riots occurred in Jakarta and other major cities.
21 May	Dr. B J Habibie succeeded Suharto as Indonesia's President.
5 June	A deal was reached to reschedule the Indonesia's massive corporate debts.
24 June	Dr. Mahathir named Daim as Special Function Minister.
29 June	South Korea shut down five ailing banks.
	Dr. Richard Hu delivered a statement on Singapore's off-budget measures.

14 August	Hong Kong Monetary Authority intervened in the Hong Kong stock market.
17 August	Russia devalued its rouble and introduced a 90-day debt moratorium.
25 August	Rouble suffered its worst one-day fall.
28 August	Rouble trade was suspended.
	Malaysian Central Bank Governor Ahmad Mohamed Don and Deputy Fong Weng Pak resigned.
31 August	Wall Street suffered its second largest point loss and triggered another round of stock market routs in Asia.
2 September	Malaysia fixed the ringgit at RM3.8 to US$1.
	Anwar Ibrahim was sacked as Deputy Prime Minister and Finance Minister.
	Russian central bank abandoned support for the rouble.
20 September	Anwar Ibrahim was arrested.
29 September	US Federal Reserve cut interest rate by 25 basis point to inoculate the US economy from the Asian financial crisis.
	Anwar Ibrahim arrived in court with a black eye.
24 October	2,000 Anwar's supporters clashed with police in Kuala Lumpur.
28 October	Brazil unveiled austerity plans to shore up its economy.
2 November	Anwar's corruption trial began.
12 November	Singapore's National Wages Council recommended, *inter alia,* wage cuts.

1999

3 January	Unrest in Aceh killing at least 25 people.
13 January	Brazil devalued its currency.
4 February	Malaysia replaced its restriction on funds repatriation with an exit tax.
13 March	Indonesian Government closed 38 insolvent banks.
4 April	Anwar's wife formed political party.
14 April	Anwar was sentenced to six years of jail for corruption.
28 April	The IMF provided further financial assistance to Russia.
7 June	Anwar's sodomy trial began.
12 July	Kuala Lumpur Composite Index hit 22-month high.
29 July	Malaysia unveiled plan to merge 58 financial institutions into 6 core groups.
6 August	IMF suspended loans to Indonesia because of irregularities in loan-recovery deal involving PT Bank Bali.
30 August	East Timor voted for Independence from Indonesia.
1 September	Malaysia's one-year restriction on repatriation of foreign investor's money came to an end.
20 October	Abdurrahman Wahid and Megawati Sukarnoputri were elected Indonesia's President and Vice-President respectively.
29 November	Dr. Mahathir won the General Election but lost some seats to Parti Islam SeMalaysia.

2000

26 March	Dr. Mahathir was re-elected President of UMNO.
1 April	Singapore employers' CPF contribution was restored by 2%.

29 May	NWC recommended pay increments and bonus payments.
8 August	Anwar was sentenced to nine years of jail for sodomy.
15 September	IMF approved disbursement of US$399 million to Indonesia for banking reforms, corporate restructuring and governance.
20 October	68 banks in Indonesia have been closed since the onset of the crisis in 1997.

2001

9 February	Thaksin Shinawatra was elected Thailand's Prime Minister.
May	10% capital gain tax imposed by Malaysia in September 1999 to control capital flows was removed.
23 July	Megawati Sukarnoputri became Indonesia's President following the impeachment of Abdurrahman Wahid.
October	The Thai Asset Management Corporation was formed to manage the existing non-performing loans of the banking sector.

2002

December	IMF officially acknowledged the effectiveness of Malaysia's imposition of capital controls in stabilising the economy.

Source: Reuters Business Briefing, Stern School of Business web page
(http://www.stern.nyu.edu/~nroubini/asia/asiahomepage.html)
LIM, Phyllis, Sabrina SIA and Yien Ling TANG, The Asian Economic Crisis — Singapore's Option, Final Year Project, 1999/2000. Economic Intelligence Unit (EIU) Country Reports, various issues.

Chapter 13

Trinity Development Model and Southeast Asian Development

There is no reason why Third World leaders cannot succeed in achieving growth and development if they can maintain social order, educate their people, maintain peace with their neighbours and gain the confidence of investors by upholding the rule of law.

Lee Kuan Yew

Objectives

✓ Describe the Trinity Development Model.
✓ Analyse the development of Southeast Asian countries against the Theory.
✓ A short comparison between the Spence Report and the Trinity Growth Theory.
✓ Provide general solutions to end abject poverty.

Introduction

In spite of impressive and unprecedented economic progress, the world is still characterised by a dichotomy, that of the extreme haves and the extreme have-nots. Three questions on global economic growth and development and underdevelopment have persistently challenged the minds of growth and development economists. First, why are there still so many very poor countries? Second, why are some countries able to break away from the extreme poverty circles and enjoy superlative economic growth rates? Third, why do economic growth rates of affluent and matured nations become much slower? The Trinity Development Model, which has three parts: the EGOIN Theory, the Triple C Theory and the S Curve, is used here to explain these three very interesting, intriguing and important phenomena. The Trinity Development Model is also used here to describe, prescribe and predict the growth and development process of countries in Southeast Asia.

The EGOIN Theory

According to the EGOIN Theory, the level of economic development of a country is a direct function of its EGOIN; the higher and better is its EGOIN, the higher will be the economic achievements of the country. Conversely, the lower is the level of EGOIN, the lower will be the level of economic development. In other words, the lower is the level of EGOIN, the higher will be the level of economic backwardness.

What then is EGOIN? It is a joint-acronym for Entrepreneurship (E), Government (G), Ordinary Labour (O), Investment (I), and Natural Resources (N). In terms of capital, EGO is human capital, I is physical capital and N is natural capital. The EGOIN Theory emphasises on the strategic and dynamic role of EGO, the human capital, which is the active agent of development. This is contrasted against IN which are important but inactive agents. The centre of EGO is G, the Government or political leadership. On G's right is O, and on its left is E. In a command economy, there is no E. This explains its inability to develop economically. The command economy depends only on GO, an incomplete duo, not a complete trinity. Likewise, in a purely laissez faire capitalist economy based only on the survival of the fittest, without a high quality O, the country will not be able to have sustainable growth and development or achieve a high level of economic advance. The development of O means investment in human capital, which includes the training and re-training of urban workers and of rural farmers. Workers here are broadly defined to include professionals and managers.

EGO is just like the Chinese character man (人). At the top or commanding height is G, supported by E on the left and O on the right. This structure

Diagram 13.1
Ego and Man

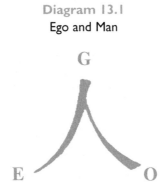

is depicted in Diagram 13.1. If G is removed, the man will have no head.
If both E and O are removed, the man will lose both his legs. Similarly, if
either E or O is removed, the man has to depend only on his other leg to
move around. An analogy between physiology and economics can thus be
drawn. Without a head (G), a country's economy is bound to falter. On the
other hand, the economic progress of a country without a quality E or O or
both will proceed at a much slower pace.

G, the critical factor, includes the quality of the bureaucracy: its effectiveness, integrity and development orientation. The bureaucracy is the hand-
maiden of the Government, or as the Malay language beautifully puts it,
"Kaki tangan pemerentah" (literally, the legs and hands of the Government).
However, it is not the amount of power the Government has over the population that is important; it is its aptitude and attitude or its skills and orientation that are vital. If the orientation is not the upliftment of the quality of
life of the people, but that of the rulers, the achievements will be like the
pyramids of Egypt or the equally impressive imperial tombs of China, or
in the modern world, the mounting financial indebtedness of the country.
It is instructive when considering G to remember what Lao-Tze had said,
"Govern a great nation as you would cook a small fish. Don't overdo it".

Also included in G is the ability of the Government to help in the growth
and development of the economy. This includes fiscal and monetary management. The lack of ability in the management of foreign exchange that had
resulted in the upheavals in many of the Southeast Asian countries during the
1997–1998 Asian financial crisis underlines the critical role of G. Laos's G is
not as growth and development-oriented as Singapore's, largely explaining the
difference in the per capita income of these two Southeast Asian countries.

Entrepreneurs (E) play an important role of being the innovators in an economy. They may or may not be inventors or capitalists. Entrepreneurial functions include the introduction and spread of new and better methods of production and distribution, the finding of new markets, the discovery of new sources of material supply and new methods of mobilisation of resources, and the introduction and spread of new products and services. For example, the first person or organisation to introduce mobile phone or palm pilot services to a country is an entrepreneur in our context. The country would benefit from the act of the entrepreneur through enhanced productivity and greater convenience. In addition, the first person to introduce the skill of removing cataract to a country or a village, thereby saving hundreds and thousands of people from going blind, is also considered to be an entrepreneur. One point needs to be emphasised here is that entrepreneurship has to be guided by market forces. It is very difficult to develop entrepreneurship in the absence of market forces, as producers may end up producing goods and services not needed by the market. Contrasting with a command economy, there are two important aspects of a market-oriented economy. Firstly, the production of goods and services in a market-oriented economy is oriented towards what the domestic and international markets want; the production process is not decided by one person or an oligarchy. The consumers are sovereigns in a market-oriented system. Secondly, the utilisation of factor inputs, such as capital, labour, land and technology, is in accordance with market prices. In other words, the marginal product per dollar spent on all the factor inputs should be the same, at least in theory.

For E to function properly, the G must take on an enabling, supporting and facilitating function, not an inhibiting, subjugating, or supplanting role. Similarly, if and when G owns a commercial organisation, steps will have to be taken to ensure that they are run meritocratically, commercially and competitively. Thus, the interrelationship of EGO or even EGOIN is equally important, if all are to play a strategic joint role in the development process.

EGO has another aspect: the motivating force. Nations and individuals do things to satisfy their pride and self-esteem. This pride or EGO may be good or may be bad. It may be excessive or difficult to satisfy. But the pride is there: it motivates action to satisfy the urge, which may be dignity, honour or just greed. When EGO is the motivation there is still, however, the need to have the capability to carry out the motivational drive. In EGO as a whole, the ability is called social capability. But social capability itself is not enough to carry out economic development. One must add IN to EGO to get EGOIN, to transform social capability to economic capability: the delivery mechanism or the productive capacity.

For a more detailed analysis of the EGOIN Theory, please refer to my book on *Development and Underdevelopment* (Lim, 1991), in which the historical development of Japan, Taiwan and Singapore is separately analysed against the Theory. Similar analysis of Malaysian economic development from the Bangkok Engagement in 1874 can be found in another book of mine, entitled *Economic Development of Modern Malaya* (Lim, 1967), written before the EGOIN Theory was formally formulated (Lim, 1991). For an application of the Trinity Growth Theory to more recent economic development, see "The Trinity Growth Theory: The Ascendancy of Asia and the Decline of the West", in Hooi and Koh (eds.), *Economic Essays by Lim Chong Yah* (Lim, 1996).

Although IN are passive development agents, the importance of their roles should not be underestimated. When Robinson Crusoe was shipwrecked on a South Sea island, he had with him a knife, a gun and some gunpowder, some food, some seeds, some clothes, etc. Without these passive agents, he could not have survived. Today, the productive capacity of an economy is impaired without the support of the economic infrastructure (I): the roads, the ports, the bridges, the dams, the irrigation canals, the reservoirs, the factories, the offices, the hospitals, the TV stations, the telecommunication system, etc. All these have to be built up, often over the years. When Karl Marx said that a capitalist system's development is based on "accumulate, accumulate and accumulate" he had in mind mainly savings, but I think he must have in mind past savings as well. Past savings, when invested, to Karl Marx means accumulated physical capital formation.

Without enough domestic savings, physical capital formation cannot be developed. As John Hicks, Evsey Domar and Roy Harrod pointed out, the rate of growth of an economy is the direct function of the rate of savings. The higher is the savings rate, the higher will be the rate of growth. In an open economy, strictly, we should include net investment inflow to augment domestic investment from domestic savings.

$$\frac{\Delta Y}{Y} = \frac{S}{Y} \cdot \frac{\Delta Y}{I}$$

where

$\Delta Y/Y$ is the rate of growth

S/Y is the savings function

$\Delta Y/I$ is inverse of the incremental capital output ratio (ICOR).

As for N, in the Third World, it is often un-utilised, under-utilised or mis-utilised, explaining its underdevelopment. When N is utilised, it lifts up the development process. Some countries depend so much on N (oil is an example) for its development. But one still needs the human factor, the active agent, to utilise the natural resource. Brunei's dependence on oil export for its very high per capita income is well known. Singapore's dependence on its strategic location (N) too should not be forgotten.

IN are thus important integral parts in the development process, for EGO needs tools to work with to be effective. N includes location, but location has meaning only when it is built up or can be built up, be it a seaport, an airport, a plantation, a factory or a house. Thus, EGO without IN are emasculated factors of development. The EGOIN model, depending on five joint variables, is thus a multi-determinant, organic theory, not a single-causal theory.

The Triple C Theory

Although not clearly stated, the EGOIN Theory does not highlight the international dimension in the development process. The Triple C Theory, as a part of the Trinity Growth Theory, brings forth the regional and global dimensions to the centre stage. Growth, according to the Triple C Theory, is propelled by three engines: the domestic engine, the regional engine and the global engine. No nation in the modern world is an island unto itself. Even the biggest nation in the world, China, (by population size) has to trade with the outside world and would like to benefit from the discoveries, inventions, innovations, technologies, and investments from the outside world. Indeed, in the spectacular 2008 Beijing Olympic Games opening ceremony, of the only two Chinese proverbs quoted and displayed on the wide TV screen was "三人行, 必有我师也", meaning men, groups and nations can all benefit by and through learning from one another in work and in play.

(Incidentally, this proverb was also quoted by me in the at times considered seminal work on the Singapore economy in Lim Chong Yah *et al.*, *Policy Options for the Singapore Economy*, published in 1988.)

The cumulative causation theory, which forms the basis of the Triple C Theory, postulates that wealth tends to create wealth and poverty tends to accentuate poverty. The three engines are the three Cs, or Triple C. The causation is circular, because investment creates income, the extent of which depends on the marginal propensity to consume, but the rise of income and expenditure itself will generate more investment. In other words, the multiplier and accelerator interact on each other in the development process, and this process can be upward or downward. The process is not uni-directional, and the cause and effect are mutually interactive.

Besides, as pointed out earlier, the cumulative causation theory has its regional and global aspects. Wealth in a centre can spread to other growth centres within a country. The spread can also be across borders. When demand from Japan or the US increases, the exporters to these countries enjoy the spill of wealth from these developed importing countries. Similarly, recession can spread from country to country and from region to region. An illustration of circular cumulative causation is that the economic ascendancy of China has clearly benefited Southeast Asia in one way or the other. As pointed out in Chapter 4, China's share of global consumption of natural rubber, which is an important export of the region, has increased significantly from 6% in 1960 to 26% in 2006. Similarly, the development of Cambodia and Laos may be given a boost by the rapidly growing Vietnam and Thailand through economic linkages. When there are barriers to trade, to the flow of information and knowledge and when there are barriers to the flow of investment (or capital), wealth from one centre cannot flow to another centre. In other words, a purely autarkic country is also immune to the spread of recession as well as affluence. This explains the economic backwardness of North Korea, despite the affluence of South Korea. The 38th parallel is not just a demarcation line, but also an impenetrable barrier for factor flow and the flow of goods and services.

The regional and global engines are very important sources of growth. Studies have shown that the openness of an economy is closely correlated with the per capita income of the country. A simple analysis in Chapter 7 shows that there is a perfect ranking relationship between per capita income and export orientation among the ASEAN-5 (see Table 7.4). A study by the

World Bank (Collier and Dollar, 2002) also shows that the 24 developing countries that increased their integration into the world economy over the two decades achieved higher growth in incomes. On the other hand, poverty has risen for countries that have been unable to increase their integration with the world economy. In East Asia, the most "cut-off" economies include North Korea, and they are also the poorest in per capita income. In Southeast Asia, the most open economies are Singapore, Brunei and Malaysia, and they have the highest per capita income.

Diagram 13.2 illustrates the working of the Triple C Theory. Of the three engines of growth, the domestic engine is the most important. If the domestic engine dysfunctions, the country remains poor, as wealth or affluence cannot be spread from the region or the world, and the domestic engine is a function of its EGOIN. The importance of the domestic engine is captured succinctly by a Chinese proverb that says, "人必自辱而后人辱之, 国必自灭而后国灭之". Literally translated, it says, "a man must first have disgraced himself, then others will disgrace him; a country must first have defeated itself, then others will defeat it". In other words, to have rapid growth and development, one must not only have the will for growth and development, but must also first put one's house in order for growth and development to take place. One cannot depend solely and mainly on external forces, including external aid, to initiate and sustain the growth and development process. Trading an economy out of poverty is by no means without merit as an advocacy, especially when trade is defined to include trade in services, such as international tourism.

Diagram 13.2
Triple C Theory

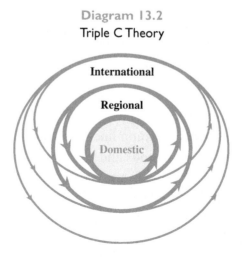

In 1979, Deng Xiaoping, stood at the narrow Shenzhen River separately Hong Kong and Shenzhen, asked, "How can a small river be a deciding line between poverty in Shenzhen and affluence in Hong Kong?" Today, this divide is widely known there in Chinese as "一河之別", the difference of a river. Shenzhen was then a small fishing village and a vegetable farmland supplying fish and vegetables to neighbouring Hong Kong. With the "open door" policy that followed and with Shenzhen attracting and welcoming investment and skills from Hong Kong, in less than three decades, Shenzhen has become a modern booming industrial and commercial township of 10 million people, with lots of factories from Hong Kong relocating there. It shows that wealth can flow from an established growth center to a peripheral location, if barriers are removed: the quintessence of the Triple C Theory.

Recently, Malaysia declared that Southern Johor be made a special growth centre with a view to attract the re-location of investments primarily from Singapore. Probably Malaysia has in mind the Hong Kong to Shenzhen experience. However, important dissimilarities in the comparison should be borne in mind.

The S Curve

The S Curve, as shown in Diagram 13.3, classifies the world's economies into three broad groups: one, the low-income with low growth rate group, also known as turtle economies; two, the middle income with high growth

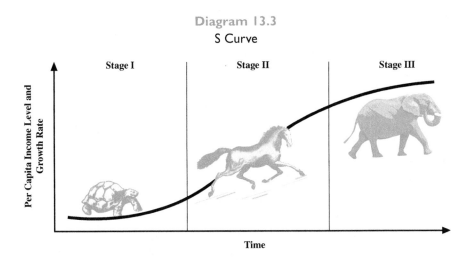

Diagram 13.3
S Curve

rate group, known as the horse economies; and three, the high income but low growth rate group, known as the elephant economies. The main criterion of classification is growth rate. The growth rate must be secular, long term in nature not over a month, a quarter, a year or two, but at least over a quinquennium, or better still, at least over a decade. The three stages of growth and development roughly, adequately, but not perfectly, correspond to pre-industrial, industrialising and post-industrial economies or societies. Tables 13.1 and 13.2 categorises selected economies in the world into the three broad groups. Table 13.1 shows the growth level while Table 13.2 shows the 10-year average growth rate before and after Asian Financial Crisis of these economies.

Strictly, the vertical axis in the above diagram should be EGOIN per capita. Per capita income used is just a convenient proxy. It should not imply cause and effect relationship between the two axes to the extent as in the EGOIN per capita analysis.

Table 13.1

Differing GNI Per Capita, 2007

	GNI Per Capita (2007)	
	Atlas Method (Current US$)	PPP (current International $)
Turtles		
Bangladesh	470	1,340
Burundi	110	330
Congo, Dem. Rep.	140	290
Haiti	560	1,310
Madagascar	320	920
Malawi	250	750
Mongolia	1,290	3,160
Papua New Guinea	850	2,060
Philippines	*1,620*	*3,730*
Rwanda	320	860
Sierra Leone	260	660
Zambia	800	1,220
Zimbabwe	340	n.a.

(Continued)

Table 13.1 (*Continued*)

	GNI Per Capita (2007)	
	Atlas Method (Current US$)	PPP (current International $)
Horses		
Cambodia	540	1,690
China	2,360	5,370
India	950	2,740
Indonesia	1,650	3,580
Korea, Rep.	19,690	24,750
Lao PDR	580	1,940
Malaysia	6,540	13,570
Myanmar	n.a.	580 (2000)
Thailand	3,400	7,880
Vietnam	790	2,550
Elephants		
Australia	35,960	33,340
Brunei Darussalam	26,930	49,900
Canada	39,420	35,310
Denmark	54,910	36,300
France	38,500	33,600
Germany	38,860	33,530
Hong Kong, China	31,610	44,050
Japan	37,670	34,600
New Zealand	28,780	26,340
Singapore	32,470	48,520
Sweden	46,060	36,590
United Kingdom	42,740	33,800
United States	46,040	45,850

Source: World Bank, WDI Online, 22 Sep. 2008, http://publications.worldbank.org/WDI/.
Note: Number in parentheses refers to the year.

The turtle economies display low growth rates. They are like the elephant economies. However, the turtle economies suffer from low-level equilibrium trap, whereas the elephant economies suffer from high-level equilibrium trap. Their basic difference lies in their per capita EGOIN or its resultant

Table 13.2
Differing GDP Per Capita Growth Rates, 1988–2007

	GDP Per Capita Average Annual Growth Rate		
	1988–2007	1988–1997	1998–2007
Turtles			
Bangladesh	**2.8**	2.0	3.7
Burundi	**–1.9**	–3.1	–0.6
Congo, Dem. Rep.	**–4.4**	–8.0	–0.8
Haiti	**–2.1**	–3.4	–0.9
Madagascar	**–0.3**	–1.4	0.9
Malawi	**0.7**	1.2	0.1
Mongolia	**1.5**	–1.6	4.6
Papua New Guinea	**0.4**	2.0	–1.2
Peru	**1.1**	–0.7	2.8
Philippines	*1.9*	*1.5*	*2.3*
Rwanda	**1.8**	1.2	2.4
Sierra Leone	**–0.4**	–5.1	4.3
Zambia	**0.1**	–1.8	1.9
Zimbabwe	**–1.5 (88–05)**	1.4	–5.3 (98–05)
Horses			
Cambodia	**6.3 (94–07)**	3.7 (94–97)	7.3
China	**8.7**	8.6	8.8
India	**4.7**	3.8	5.5
Indonesia	**3.7**	5.9	1.5
Korea, Rep.	**5.2**	6.7	3.8
Lao PDR	**4.0**	3.6	4.5
Malaysia	**4.2**	6.4	2.0
Myanmar	**4.7 (88–05)**	2.1	7.9 (98–05)
Thailand	**4.9**	7.2	2.6
Vietnam	**5.7**	5.5	5.9
Elephants			
Australia	**2.1**	1.9	2.3
Brunei	**–0.5 (88–06)**	–0.9	0.0 (98–06)
Canada	**1.7**	1.0	2.3
Denmark	**1.7**	1.7	1.7
France	**1.7**	1.6	1.7

(Continued)

Table 13.2 (*Continued*)

	GDP Per Capita Average Annual Growth Rate		
	1988–2007	1988–1997	1998–2007
Germany	**1.8**	2.1	1.5
Hong Kong*	**3.3**	3.5	3.2
Japan	**1.8**	2.6	1.0
New Zealand	**1.3**	0.8	1.9
Singapore*	**4.6**	5.8	3.4
Sweden	**1.8**	0.8	2.8
United Kingdom	**2.1**	1.9	2.4
United States	**1.9**	1.8	1.9

Source: World Bank, WDI Online, 22 Sep. 2008,
     http://publications.worldbank.org/WDI/.
Note: Number in parenthesis refers to the period. *New or incipient elephants.

income. Their similarity lies in their low rates of per capita income growth (Table 13.2). Turtle economies are numerous in the world, particularly in Africa. Examples are Malawi and Rwanda in Africa, North Korea and the Philippines in Asia, and Peru and Nicaragua in Latin America. Examples of elephant economies are Japan in Asia and Great Britain in Europe. The horse economies gallop like horses. East Asia has many such economies, such as South Korea and China in Northeast Asia and Singapore and Vietnam in Southeast Asia.

As the speed of growth of the horse economies is much faster, in terms of per capita income, they tend to converge with the elephant economies. They will, however, diverge from the turtle economies. Elephant economies normally grow, in terms of real per capita income, at less than 3–4% per annum, whereas horses at more than 4%, at times much more than 4% per annum. Turtles, like elephants, at best in general will grow at 3–4% per annum. At worst, the growth rates are negative, such as in the Democratic Republic of Congo, Haiti, Burundi and Zimbabwe. There is no retrogressive growth developing economy in Southeast Asia. Actually, turtle economies appear to be a dying breed in Southeast Asia; this is so as more and more Southeast Asian economies are joining the horses club. Of note is that we have classified Brunei and Singapore as elephant economies, mainly because of their very high per capita income but also because of the slow rate of growth for Brunei, indeed negative growth rate for the period 1988–2007 (see Tables 13.1 and 13.2). As Table 13.3 shows, Singapore's Gross Fixed Capital Formation slowed down for the period 1998–2007 from the preceding period 1988–1997, in line with the corresponding decline in per capita income. Singapore, of course, is an incipient elephant, a very new elephant, looking at in 2008, but this is not reflected from the average growth statistics from the past period 1988–2007.

Why is it that turtle economies have such low growth rates? Firstly, their EGOIN is poor. They are poor nations to start off with. They have thus not much to spare to invest in economic infrastructure (ΔI), or in social infrastructure (ΔEGO). Neither have they achieved and accumulated much in capital stock (I) and human capital (O) to being with. More often than not, they also do not have good, able and development-oriented Government (G). And if they also do not pursue a market-oriented economy (poor E),

Table 13.3

Differing Gross Fixed Capital Formation as a Percentage of GDP, 1988–2007 (Annual Average)

	1988–1997	1988–1997	1998–2007
Turtles			
Bangladesh	21	18	23
Burundi[a]	10	11	9
Congo, Dem. Rep.[b]	9	10	7
Haiti[a]	20	14	27
Madagascar	16	12	20
Malawi[c]	17	17	17
Mongolia[a]	30	31	29
Papua New Guinea[a]	20	21	18
Peru	20	21	19
Philippines	20	22	17
Rwanda	17	14	19
Sierra Leone	9	8	11
Zambia	15	11	20
Zimbabwe[d]	18	20	15

(Continued)

Table 13.3 (*Continued*)

	1988–1997	1988–1997	1998–2007
Horses			
Cambodia[a]	14	11	17
China[a]	35	32	37
India	25	23	27
Indonesia	25	27	22
Korea, Rep.	33	36	30
Lao PDR[e]	27	14	29
Malaysia	30	37	23
Myanmar[f]	12	12	n.a.
Thailand	32	38	25
Vietnam[g]	28	23	31
Elephants			
Australia[a]	24	24	24
Brunei[h]	23	28	17
Canada[d]	20	20	20
Denmark[a]	19	19	20
France[a]	19	20	19
Germany[a]	21	22	19
Hong Kong	26	28	24
Japan[d]	27	30	24
New Zealand[d]	21	20	22
Singapore	31	35	27
Sweden[a]	18	19	17
United Kingdom[a]	17	18	17
United States[d]	18	17	19

Source: World Bank, WDI Online, 22 Sep. 2008,
http://publications.worldbank.org/WDI/.
Notes:
　　a: Data refer to the period 1988–2006.
　　b: Data refer to the period 1988–2004.
　　c: Data for 2002 are not available.
　　d: Data refer to the period 1988–2005.
　　e: Data available for 1988, 2000–2006.
　　f: Data refer to the period 1988–1997.
　　g: Data available for 1989, 1994–2007.
　　h: Data refer to the period 1989–2006.

Diagram 13.4

Differing Average Annual GDP Per Capita Growth Rates (%), 1988–2007

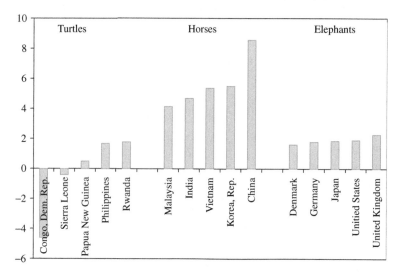

Source: Table 13.2.

and do not utilise their natural resources or have no natural resources (N), they continue to be poor economically. The odds are very much against them. Some of them may succeed in having a higher per capita income growth rate but when they do not practise family planning, the only tangible success they have will be higher population growth rate and more people. The quality of life of the people remains low. The low-level equilibrium trap process is shown in Diagram 13.5.

The horse economies have high savings and high investment rates, often supplemented by more investment from abroad. They are also most likely to practice family planning. China, for example, goes as far as to implement a one-child family system for the majority Han Chinese. This reflects the high priority they place on economic welfare and economic well-being. China is prepared to discard or drastically modify their command economy for a market-oriented, forward-looking economy. E in China was not there under the erstwhile communist dictatorship. Entrepreneurship (E) has, however, since 1979, emerged and is still emerging after the Chinese Government adopted a "perestroika" open door policy. When they have a market-oriented policy, they are also likely to develop a high degree of international trade orientation, and the transfer of knowledge and technology from the developed

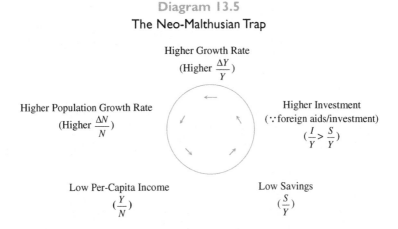

Diagram 13.5

The Neo-Malthusian Trap

Higher Growth Rate
(Higher $\frac{\Delta Y}{Y}$)

Higher Population Growth Rate
(Higher $\frac{\Delta N}{N}$)

Higher Investment
($\because$ foreign aids/investment)
($\frac{I}{Y} > \frac{S}{Y}$)

Low Per-Capita Income
($\frac{Y}{N}$)

Low Savings
($\frac{S}{Y}$)

countries. Vietnam too has emerged on this growth and development path since the opening up of the country in 1986. The Vietnamese calls their perestroika "Doi Moi".

Why has the elephant group displayed a slow growth phenomenon? Being elephants, they consume a lot. Their savings rates are low. Their investment rates are low (see Table 13.3). They have an increasing proportion of their people belonging to the old-age groups. If their investment rate is low, their growth rate is expected to be low. In the elephant economies, birth rates are low, because the opportunity costs of raising a family become much higher. Family formation is thus less emphasised than the quality of life of the present generation. Earlier, in Chapter 9 on "Fiscal Policy", we have noted in Table 9.4 and Diagram 9.1 that in the elephant economies, their government development expenditure is also very low in relation to their GDP. This, in a way, reflects the already higher state of capital formation and infrastructure development in the elephant economies. With their physical infrastructure already built up and capital stock accumulated, the developed economies would find it more difficult to achieve further impressive physical capital development. Diminishing returns can set in easily. Another airport in a city may be redundant. Another MRT network in the same city may also be redundant. In addition, the rising labour cost and land cost in the elephant economies also work in favour of the flow of investment to the developing countries that are capable of absorbing the investment inflow.

The horse economies, having a lower per capita income, can benefit enormously from the transfer of technology, organisations and the production processes from the developed economies. The transfer is a quantum leap. The scope for such quantum-leap transfers is much less among elephant economies. However, elephant economies do not stagnate or decline as prognosticated by Adam Smith, Karl Marx, Joseph Schumpeter and John Maynard Keynes. Because of new technological inventions and institutional development, our investigation shows that they only display slower, not zero, growth. The one-time widely-held stagnation thesis does not hold water. The dismal science is not that dismal after all. Whether in the very long-run there will be growth in the present elephants depends very much on their future EGOIN and the inter-connectivity factor, particularly in the rate of advance in technological knowledge in the world and in their will for more economic affluence. The distant horizons appear unlimited. The spread of prosperity too appears unlimited, and in Southeast Asia in recent decades, certainly accelerated.

Southeast Asia

Unlike in the First Edition (2001) of this book, in this Third Edition we have classified all the ten, except three, Southeast Asian economies as horses, no longer turtles. The Philippines ironically and most unexpectedly is the only turtle economy left in Southeast Asia. As real income per capita growth rates for the last two decades (1988–2007) shown in Table 13.2, the Philippines is the only developing economy in Southeast Asia that had a low growth rate of 1.9%, far below the expected growth rate of at least 4% to be horses.

The other non-horse economies are Brunei and Singapore. Both are very special categories of elephants. Brunei is an elephant by growth rate (−0.5%) and by per capita income (very high). Brunei is an oil-rich country with a small population. Oil export is the main, if not the only substantial export. But if one calculates oil production by volume (real GDP) over the two decades which is what the social accountants have done, Brunei has had a slightly average negative growth rate. But when it comes to per capita income, prices of oil are factored in. The very high price of fuel oil (above US$100) today as against US$1.9, say, in 1972, immediately jacks up very much Brunei's standards of living and her per capita income in US dollar terms. But because of her very high per capita income, very high growth rates become difficult to achieve (the S Curve).

Singapore appears to be the only incipient elephant economy in Southeast Asia in terms of per capita income, a developed infrastructure (I), a developed O and a high level of public service competence (G). However, her investment rates are very high, more like those of the horse economies, though they show signs of secular decline. Family formation has declined more like that of the developed countries. However, to ensure that Singapore continues to develop like horses, the Government has continued to give top priority to the continuation of good governance and good bureaucracy, and the importation of foreign talents and foreign labour to augment the limited local supply. Singapore appears to fear the plateauing of her economy, and thus has taken active steps to invigorate it; to pre-empt it from becoming like a true full-blooded elephant, with high consumption, low savings rate, low investment rate and low growth rate, if not a backward sloping supply curve of labour as well. Without sizeable import of foreign labour, Singapore's economy would and would have slowed down more perceptibly. For a foreign-labour dependent small economy like Singapore, GDP, the usual measure used, can be deceptively much higher than the per capita measure or the productivity per capita measure.

Nearly all the other seven Southeast Asian economies galloped past the 4% benchmark with ease. Thailand and Vietnam led the way with 4.9% and 5.7% growth rates respectively. Even Myanmar showed 4.7% and Cambodia, 6.3%. Obviously for the seven horses, their EGOIN rates were such that in the last two decades, taking the pluses and the minuses, they showed that they could achieve in terms of growth rates in real per capita income. The Philippines appears to be the odd man out, because of the inadequacy of investment (I), both domestic and foreign, and this is closely associated with the poor investment climate, which in turn is a function of the far below-par public administration (G). The weak I and G greatly outweigh the reasonably high levels of education of the Filipinos (O) and the quality of their entrepreneurship (E). Neither the Spence Study nor the earlier World Bank Report on Asian miracles included the Philippines on their lists.

For the countries badly affected by the 1997–98 Asian Financial Crisis, the latest decade per capita income figures were disappointing. The riders appeared to have difficulties in managing the horses. Indonesia, the worst hit of the lot, displayed only 1.5% average growth rate and Thailand 2.6%.

But for capital-control Southeast Asian countries, their overall performances have been brilliant: Vietnam at 5.9%, Myanmar 7.9% and Laos 4.5%.

The Spence global study shows that the selected 13 economies that have galloped at high speed displayed the following five features (Spence, 2008). The 13 countries include 3 from Southeast Asia. The countries are, in alphabetical order, Malaysia, Thailand and Singapore. But all three, in varying degrees, suffered badly in the Asian Crisis, explaining their deceleration in growth rates during 1998–2007 when compared with 1988–1997. Our prognosis that they are horse economies is based not only on their overall performance for the past two decades, 1988–2007, but also on an optimistic forecast of continued high growth rates, after the political houses are put in order. Thailand and Malaysia have temporary serious leadership selection problems. And Indonesia too will have a General Election in July 2009, the outcome of which remains uncertain. But they all have a plentiful supply of literate labour (O), natural resources (N), reasonable standards of infrastructure development (I) and a commitment to a market-based outward-looking economy (G), including the welcoming of foreign investment. In other words, these countries are resource rich and labour abundant, and the infrastructure is reasonably well-developed with a fairly respectable connectivity factor. Horses, however, do gallop at different speeds. One should not, however, expect all the Southeast Asian horses to gallop at the same speed as their northern neighbours, such as China, or as India in South Asia.

The Spence's five ingredients for superlative growth rates (horses in our lingo) are:

(1) To fully exploit the world economy (our Triple C Theory)
(2) To maintain macroeconomic stability (our G)
(3) To muster high rates of saving and investment (our I)
(4) To let markets allocate resources (our I)
(5) To have committed, credible, and capable governments (our G)

The seven economies of Southeast Asia appear to have satisfied most of these conditions for rapid growth. In the EGOIN Theory, O and N are included. O refers to the investment in human capital and N in natural capital.

When we include O as underutilized human capital increasingly becoming properly utilised coupled with increasing export capability (Triple C Theory), then the explanation for rapid growth becomes more convincing. Indeed, one should include N particularly for Myanmar. For recent years, productions of gas and gems have gone up immensely for Myanmar and they are exported to neighbouring Thailand, China and India. This adds another fillip to economic growth. This is in the face of US embargo of trade with Myanmar because of the former's outrage of the political situation there.

Also, all these seven Southeast Asian countries have a low starting base, a good-potential S factor. Accelerating of growth is possible and probable with the acceleration of domestic and foreign investment combined. The course they take is industrialisation, tourism and the exportation of their natural resources.

The Philippine outlier case has to be explained in terms of poor quality G, particularly general public governance, especially law and order, adversely affecting the investment climate. The consequence is very low foreign investment, low tourist arrivals and also low domestic investment. High population growth rate also brings down the growth rate in per capita income growth. However, if public governance can be improved, there is no reason why the acceleration of growth in the Philippines will not follow, but like the rest of Southeast Asia that have high fertility rates, the income acceleration process in the Philippines would, however, have to be bigger and more self-sustaining.

The Southeast Asian economies show that elephant economies like Singapore can escape the high-level equilibrium trap and horse economies like Thailand and Indonesia can take a temporary U turn. The S Curve is a tendency, not an iron law. They also show that prosperous neighbours can contribute to affluence if the connectivity factor (the C factor) is enhanced. Whilst all economies will face uncertain future, the S Curve analysis in particular does throw some light into their future in terms of the probability of high or low growth rates, especially if their ΔEGOIN can be guessed at or prognosticated. Without doubt too the volatile G factor plays a much more important role in the growth dynamics of developing countries, including all the countries in Southeast Asia. The Spence study is a refreshing change in terms of diagnosis, prescription and prognostication, in part because it almost runs parallel to the EGOIN Theory and the Triple C Theory, except that the EGOIN Theory first made its appearance in 1984 (Lim, 1984) and the Spence Report was published only in mid-2008.

Solutions to Poverty

Alfred Lord Tennyson said, "The shell must break before the bird can fly." How to ensure that the shell of low-level equilibrium trap be broken, so that the economy can take off and be transformed from a turtle to a horse economy?

Each country and each economy has specific and special problems of its own, and often the solutions will have to be country-specific and economy-specific. But generally, for turtle economies to metamorphose into horse economies, the following steps appear necessary.

(1) A sustained and sustainable good savings and investment system (I and E)
(2) A sustained outward-looking, market-oriented economic policy and practice (Triple C and E)
(3) A sustained good knowledge transfer system (O)
(4) The proper and fuller utilisation of natural resources (N)
(5) Sustained and sustainable family planning system (O)
(6) A good development-oriented Government and bureaucracy (G)

In other words, the EGOIN has to be elevated to a higher level to ensure and sustain the transformation process. The six factors form an organic whole.

And of the six conditions, the sixth factor, a clean, capable, development-oriented Government and bureaucracy, is the most difficult to attain. The other five conditions are very much a function of the last determinant. As stated elsewhere, "The Jews could not move out of slavery from Egypt without Moses" (Lim, 1997). Here, slavery refers to modern 21st century economic slavery, as manifested in very low income, very low productivity, very high unemployment and under-employment, low expectation of life, and very low general quality of life for the majority of the population.

Nearly all Southeast Asian countries, for various reasons, have become horse economies, but most of them are very new or incipient horse economies. It will take three to six decades of sustained superlative growth before absolute poverty can be totally eradicated in these countries. The road ahead is still a long one for Southeast Asia.

Key Points

1. The Trinity Development Model comprises three interrelated parts, namely the EGOIN Theory, the Triple C Theory and the S Curve.
2. EGOIN is the acronym for Entrepreneurship (E), Government (G), Ordinary Labour (O), Investment (I) and Natural Resources (N). The first three components are active agents of development, while the latter two are passive agents.
3. The Triple C Theory postulates that economic growth is propelled by three engines: the domestic engine, the regional engine, and the global engine. According to the Theory, economic growth as well as misfortune can spread not just internally but also across national borders.
4. The S Curve categorises countries into turtle economies, horse economies and elephant economies. Turtle economies are characterised by low income with low growth rates; horse economies are characterised by middle income with high growth rates and elephant economies are characterised by high income with low growth rates.
5. Most countries in Southeast Asia are considered as horse economies, although classification in some cases is not that clear-cut. The Philippines is the only turtle economy left in Southeast Asia. Singapore and Brunei, for various reasons, are classified as elephant economies; Singapore as the emerging or incipient elephant economy.
6. Solutions to eradicate poverty must be country- and economy-specific. But generally, they should include a sustained and sustainable good savings and investment system, an outward-looking, market-oriented economic policy and practice, a good knowledge transfer system, proper and fuller utilisation of natural resources, family planning and a good and able development-oriented Government and bureaucracy.
7. The World Bank Spence Report has a lot of similarities in common with the Trinity Growth Theory in explaining why countries could have superlative growth rates.

Suggested Discussion Topics

13.1 Explain the Trinity Development Model and use it to explain the different levels and rates of development in Southeast Asia.

13.2 Appraise the conditions for the elimination of poverty and economic backwardness in Southeast Asia.

13.3 What are the similarities in the explanation of the superlative economic growth rates between the Trinity Growth Theory and the Spence Report? Discuss this in the context of Southeast Asian Development.

References

COLLIER, Paul and David DOLLAR, 2002, *Globalisation, Growth, and Poverty: Building an Inclusive World Economy (World Bank Policy Research Report)*, Washington, D.C.: The World Bank, New York: Oxford University Press.

LIM, Chong Yah, 1967, *Economic Development of Modern Malaya*, Kuala Lumpur: Oxford University Press.

LIM, Chong Yah, 1984, "The causes of development", *Singapore Economic Review*, 29(2), 63–82.

LIM, Chong Yah, 1991, *Development and Underdevelopment*, Singapore: Longman.

LIM, Chong Yah, 1996, "The trinity growth theory: The ascendancy of Asia and the decline of the West", *Accounting and Business Review*, 3(2), 175–199. Also appeared in HOOI, Den Huan and KOH Ai Tee (eds.), 2001, *Economic Essays by Lim Chong Yah*, Singapore: World Scientific, 125–146.

LIM, Chong Yah, 1997, "The low-income trap: Theory and evidence", *Accounting and Business Review*, 4(1), 1–19. Also appeared in HOOI and KOH (eds.), *op. cit.*, 147–166.

SPENCE, Michael (Ch.), 2008, *The Growth Report: Strategies for Sustained Growth and Inclusive Development*, by Commission on growth and development, Washington, D.C: The World Bank.

Further Readings

BAUER, Peter T., 1971, *Dissent on Development: Studies and Debates in Development Economics*, London: Oxford University Press.

HICKS, J. Richard, 1959, *Essays in World Economics*, Oxford: Clarendon Press.

ICHIMURA, Shinichi, 1998, *Political Economy of Japanese and Asian Development*, Tokyo: Springer.

KRUMM, Kathie and Homi KHARAS (eds.), 2003, *East Asia Integrates: A Trade Policy for Shared Growth*, Washington, D.C: The World Bank.

LEWIS, Arthur W., 1970, *Tropical Development 1880–1913*, London: Allen and Unwin.

LEWIS, Arthur W., 1984, "The state of development theory", *American Economic Review*, 74(1), 1–10.

LIM, Chong Yah, 1994, "Economic theory and the economic reality", *Accounting and Business Review*, 1(1), 73–84. Also appeared in HOOI and KOH (eds.), *op. cit.*, 99–110.

LIM, Chong Yah, 1994, "Which nations will dominate the world? A review article on Lester Thurow's head to head", *Accounting and Business Review*, 1(2), 261–273. Also appeared in HOOI and KOH (eds.), *op. cit.*, 111–124.

LINDER, Staffan Burenstam, 1986, *The Pacific Century: Economic and Political Consequences of Asian-Pacific Dynamism*, Stanford: Stanford University Press.

MYRDAL, Gunnar, 1957, *Economic Theory and Underdeveloped Regions*, London: G. Duckworth.

MYRDAL, Gunnar, 1970, *The Challenge of World Poverty*, New York: Pantheon Books.

SHINOHARA, Miyohei, 1999, *Economic Dynamism in East Asia and Japan: Collected Economic Articles*, Tokyo: Institute of Statistical Research.

SNG, Hui Ying, 2007, *Economic Growth and Transition: Econometric Analysis of Lim's S-Curve Hypothesis*, unpublished PhD thesis, Singapore: Nanyang Technological University.

World Bank, 1993, *The East Asian Miracle: Economic Growth and Public Policy*, Washington, D.C.: The World Bank.

World Bank, 1997, *World Development Report 1997: The State in a Changing World*, New York: Oxford University Press.

Name Index

A

Abdul Rahman, Tunku   xlix, 11
Abdul Razak, Tun   xlix, 11
Abdullah Ahmad Badawi   l
Abdurrahman Wahid   27, 154, 342, 375, 376
Abhisit Vejjajiva   lxii, lxiv
Acharya, Amitav   35
Ahmad Mohamed Don   374
Ahmad, Jaleel   174, 205
Ahtisaari, Martti   28
Akrasanee, Narongchai   151, 168, 232, 237
Amjad, Rashid   149, 168
Anand Punyarachun   lxiii
Anwar Ibrahim   374, 375, 376
Aquino, Benigno   lvi
Aquino, Corazon   30
Ariff, Mohamed   174, 193, 195, 205, 370
Arndt, H. W.   370
Arroyo, Gloria Macapagal   lvii
Asher, Mukul G.   261, 267
Athukorala, P. C.   222, 237
Aung San   liii
Aung San Suu Kyi   liii, liv, 11
Azizah, Talib   302

B

Bacchetta, Marc   199, 206
Balassa, Bela   155, 160, 168, 169, 174, 206
Banharn Silapa-Archa   lxiii

Barlow, Colin   92, 112
Basiron, Yusof   112
Bauer, P. T.   112, 400
Becker, Gary   308, 309, 336
Behrman, Jere R.   238
Belassa, B.   59, 61
Bhagwati, Jagdish   123
Bomhoff, Eduard J.   370
Booth, Anne   268
Bora, Bijit   199, 206
Bouasone Bouphavanh   xlvii
Bradford, Colin I.   195, 206
Brooks, D. H.   302

C

Cairncross, Alec   206
Chatichai Choonhavan   lxiii
Chavalit Yongchaiyudh   lxiii
Chen, Shaohua   15, 34
Chenery, Hollis B.   57, 61
Chia, Siow Yue   150, 169, 170, 238, 274, 302
Chng, M. K.   213, 237
Choummaly Sayasone   xlvii
Chowdhury, Anis   169
Chuan Leekpai   lxiii
Clark, Colin   48, 61
Cline, William R.   195, 206
Cody, John   149, 169
Cole, David C.   302
Collier, Paul   384, 400
Cordon, Max   370

Subject Index

Reviews of the First Edition

"This is an important and up-to-date (including a chapter on the Asian financial crisis and recovery) book by a most pre-eminent economist, who does not only have a distinguished academic career but also actual policy involvement at a high level. The book mixes accurate description with interesting theoretical analysis (notably the author's theories of EGOIN, Triple C, and the S Curve) and sensible policy recommendations."

Professor Yew-Kwang NG
Professor of Economics, Department of Economics
Monash University, Melbourne, Australia

"Southeast Asia has gone a long way to what it has become today. It has yet to travel another long road ahead to becoming an economically developed region. The author has successfully described the region's milestones and obstacles, both in looking back and in looking into the future. It also offers a useful theoretical construct to prescribe and predict Southeast Asia's development process. The book is to date the most comprehensive treatment of Southeast Asia as an economic region. It is even more valuable as it is written by an insider to the region and its development problems. This is the textbook the region has been waiting for. In fact, it is a book for every interested person to read."

Dr Hadi SOESASTRO
Executive Director, Centre for Strategic and International Studies (CSIS)
Jakarta, Indonesia

"There are very few economists in Southeast Asia today who can write authoritatively about Southeast Asian economies, and Professor Lim is prominently one among these few. The book leads the readers through more than 40 years of postwar development to the present day where many of these Southeast Asian nations are recovering from the recent devastating economic crisis. Professor Lim's insights into the economic history and development of countries in Southeast Asia make the readers feel comfortable to go through the book quickly. After finishing it, most of us should feel confident that Southeast Asia is still a unique region, and despite the current economic crisis, there is still great economic future for Southeast Asians."

Dr Medhi KRONGKAEW
Professor of Economics and Director, Institute of East Asian Studies
Thammasat University, Bangkok, Thailand

"This is an important study of the economies of South-East Asia. Professor Lim draws upon many years of research and experience to make comparisons between countries and to track changes over time. His title reflects his optimism but also his caution. Much has been done. Much remains to be done. There is a long road ahead before the countries of South-East Asian can look back on their achievements and say that they are fully developed at last."

Professor David REISMAN
Visiting Professor of Economics
Nanyang Technological University
Singapore

"This book provides a comprehensive analysis of Southeast Asia's economic progress and prospects. Written by one of the region's most distinguished development economists, the book will be welcomed by graduate students and researchers and by policy makers in the region, all of whom will learn much from this authoritative and insightful volume."

Professor Colin KIRKPATRICK
Professor of Economics and Director
Institute for Development Policy and Management (IDPM)
The University of Manchester, Manchester, UK

Reviews of the Second Edition

"Professor Lim has drawn on his vast experience as teacher and high-level policy adviser in Singapore to offer us an extremely lively and informative volume. He comprehensively surveys the historical record and future prospects of a group of countries whose remarkable growth record offers many lessons for the theory and practice of development economics. Equally, he offers valuable insights into the reasons why this group has recently faltered, but also why there are solid signs of recovery for some of them. An added bonus are Professor Lim's engaging style of writing and his helpful 'discussion guides' to each chapter. This is going to be a great book for me in my new MSc course on 'China and the Pacific Rim'."

Professor Roger SANDILANDS
Professor of Economics
University of Strathclyde, Glasgow, UK

"Students, scholars, and policymakers involved with Southeast Asia's economic development owe a large debt of gratitude to Professor Lim Chong Yah for sharing his life-long scholarship and many insights on economic and public policies in this comprehensive and accessible textbook. It is arguably the best introduction available in the market today concerning Southeast Asia economies and directions they may consider in addressing the challenges of the 21st century."

Professor Mukul ASHER
Professor of Economics
Lee Kuan Yen School of Public Policy, National University of Singapore

"This certainly is a remarkable book on a region of considerable strategic importance. What makes this volume so remarkable is the width of coverage and depth of insights that can only come with years of relentless pursuit in the name of empirical enquiry."

Professor Mohamed ARIFF
Executive Director
Malaysian Institute of Economic Research (MIER)

"From his base in Singapore, Lim Chong Yah has been a leading international figure in the Economics profession of Southeast Asia for several decades. This book shows why.

Professor Lim writes on a broad canvas, but with great attention to detail and much insight. He combines clarity of expression with an authoritative style and deep country knowledge. Scholars, students, government officials and business people — indeed, anybody with an interest in this fascinating part of the world — will want to have this book on their shelves. It will certainly be required reading for my class."

Professor Hal HILL
H.W. Arndt Professor of Southeast Asian Economies
Australian National University

"Professor Lim has written a superb volume, one that is a 'capstone' to his extraordinary career as a scholar and public person. My students at the University of Hawaii enjoyed the first edition of the book immensely. They found it to be readable, content-laden and extremely useful particularly because they were fairly new readers of scholarship on Southeast Asia. However, Professor Lim's volume clearly is aimed at a broad readership including advanced scholars from economics and related disciplines. His choice of topics and the manner by which he treats them elevates his book to the 'must read' list of scholars and policy makers whose intellectual interests include Southeast Asia's future."

Professor Robert L. CURRY, Jr
Emeritus Professor of Economics, California State University Sacramento and
Visiting Lecturer, University of Hawaii at Manoa

"This is the best and ideal textbook on Southeast Asian (or ASEAN) Economies. To learn or teach about ASEAN economies is very important to the understanding of East Asia, which is an essential pillar in the trilateral leading groups of nations in the world, along with EU and NAFTA. ASEAN is crucial to the East Asian grouping. This is an up-to-date book, covering current and topical economic issues like regionalism as well as the 1997/98 financial crisis. All ten countries of ASEAN are covered, from the basic fundamentals of each country to the complicated problems of international competition and complementarity in East Asia including Japan and China. The book is recommendable to students, businessmen and intellectuals living or working in Southeast Asia."

Professor Shinichi ICHIMURA
Former President and Founder, East Asian Economic Association &
Emeritus Professor of Economics, Kyoto University

CPSIA information can be obtained at www.ICGtesting.com
Printed in the USA
BVOW11s2233040915

416732BV00008B/15/P